Trans Activism in Canada

Trans Activism in Canada
A Reader

Edited by Dan Irving and Rupert Raj

Canadian Scholars' Press Inc.
Toronto

Trans Activism in Canada: A Reader
Edited by Dan Irving and Rupert Raj

First published in 2014 by
Canadian Scholars' Press Inc.
425 Adelaide Street West, Suite 200
Toronto, Ontario
M5V 3C1

www.cspi.org

Canadian Scholars' Press Inc. gratefully acknowledges financial support for our publishing activities from the Government of Canada through the Canada Book Fund (CBF).

Library and Archives Canada Cataloguing in Publication

Trans activism in Canada : a reader / edited by Dan Irving and Rupert Raj.

Includes bibliographical references and index. Issued in print and electronic formats.
ISBN 978-1-55130-537-0 (pbk.).--ISBN 978-1-55130-538-7 (pdf).-- ISBN 978-1-55130-539-4 (epub)

1. Transgender people--Political activity--Canada. 2. Transgender people--Canada--Social conditions.
I. Irving, Dan, 1974-, editor of compilation II. Raj, Rupert, 1952-, editor of compilation

HQ77.95.C3T73 2014 323.3'270971 C2014-900322-6 C2014-900323-4

Cover design by Em Dash Design

Printed and bound in Canada by Webcom.

Canada

Dedication

For Jordan Roberts, Amala Ghosh, and Dr. H. (Royal Ottawa Hospital).

For our Canadian activist friend, Kyle Scanlon (1971–2012), and all activists so far who have struggled for a better future for trans people—and for those who are still finding the courage to do so.

Contents

Part IIIB: Transformations in Health

Acknowledgements

Dan Irving:
There are many people whose inspiration, love, friendship, and mentorship have made this book possible. When I began to search for trans social justice communities in Toronto, I was told repeatedly, "You have to meet Rupert Raj!" It is an honour to have worked with Rupert on this project. It took a while for the opportunity to present itself, but I am certainly glad it did.

Gratitude must be expressed to the two peer reviewers for their detailed and thoughtful comments on the manuscript. They were invaluable to us in further strengthening the solid contributions to the book. Cameron Duder worked to provide us with a nuanced index that does justice to trans scholarship and activism; we thank you. Special acknowledgement needs to be extended to Daniella Balabuk, our editor at Canadian Scholars' Press. Her enthusiasm, encouragement, guidance, and work on the volume are much appreciated, and the book is stronger for it.

I am indebted to trans activists Mirha-Soleil Ross, Viviane Namaste, Trish Salah, and Jamie Lee Hamilton, who work relentlessly to integrate multiple social issues into trans organizing. Their provocations for action were not sugar-coated to be palatable to middle-class professionals and academic audiences. For them, activism is a matter of life or death, not a popularity contest.

Transitioning during grad school is challenging, yet I was able to witness the importance of developing strong intellectual and political friendships. My "femme daddy" and supervisor extraordinaire, Dr. Shannon Bell, kept things both interesting and focused. Her pushing me hard when I needed it most demonstrates her commitment to cultivating critical trans scholarship. The close friendship of Tammy Findlay and Sabine Hikel made all the difference as we struggled for spaces within masculinist leftist environs to pursue our work. reese simpkins and I carved out space to navigate the performance of trans masculinities through encouraging the good while containing the bad and the ugly—just where post-op shirtless football in the park fits into the equation is a matter of perspective.

Many contributors to this volume are professionals whose work within their fields and institutions is crucial to trans people's well-being. Being in the care of both Carol Baker, a therapist in the LGBT program at the Sherbourne Health Centre, and Dr. Norman Barwin was certainly invaluable to mine.

As leading steering committee members of the "Sexin' Change: Reclaiming Our Genders and Bodies" conference, jd Bowles and Nicola Brown made evident time and again just how important grassroots organizing, accessibility, and mutual support are for evoking transformative change. Leanne Gillard was more than a member of the steering committee and my ally. I was blessed to share four years of my life with her, and for that, I will always be grateful.

Many people in Ottawa contributed to making the six-year period that this book took to come to fruition a lot easier. My colleague and friend Margaret Denike, former coordinator of Human Rights at Carleton University, encouraged the development of a course on transgender human rights and supported critical approaches to human rights. I am grateful to Jodie Medd for her critical trans activist praxis and her support of my work, but most importantly, for her invitations to dinner and living room dancing with Nick and Amelia to remind me of life outside of it. Jennifer Evans also lent much encouragement toward the project and other trans activist endeavours through co-authoring an op-ed piece supporting Bill C-389 and bringing trans scholars to speak at Carleton. Jen may not be dancing with the (trans) stars, but she certainly can swim with them!

To the guys in the two-spirit group—Mike, Andre, and Alex—thanks for the pleasurable distractions that demonstrated the need for trans activism to be fun. And to Alicia Furness Baker and Ignacio Santander Alfonso, thanks for the intellectual conversation and vegan suppers, and for helping me catch Fergus, our once-feral cat.

I could not have done this without my chosen family. A warm acknowledgement to the fabulous Ms. Krystal Caring for all the Sunday dinners and constant reminders to just "put one foot in front of the other and keep going!"; to my adopted brother, Sharpe Doppler, for all the teachings, listening, and laughs; to Leo R. Kengis, my sunny boy, whose courage, gentle spirit, and fortitude is truly inspiring; and to my dearest friend, Judy Piers-Kavanaugh, for more than words can express. Fear may have had a place at the table, but judgment never has. Thank you.

Acknowledgement is also due to my parents, Irma and David Irving, for their unconditional love and support; and, finally, to my partner, Melissa Autumn White. Thank you for the editorial assistance and hours of conversation about the project, but, moreover, for just being you. Your brilliant mind, steely fighting spirit, and relentless pursuit of justice in the midst of uphill battles and a cruel world are remarkable. It certainly hasn't been easy.

Rupert Raj:
To three people who unconditionally validate(d) me, not only as a person, but also as a male (trans boy/man): Amala Ghosh, my dear sister, who was there for me from the very start—when no one else was—and who remains my best "fan" and best friend to this day; the clinical psychologist at the Royal Ottawa Hospital, who was there for me at the vulnerable ages of 17 and 18, just shortly after my parents had tragically died in 1968. She did not pathologize me for presenting as androgynous, but rather acknowledged me as "possibly transsexual" and facilitated my gender journey by telling me about a book that mentioned Dr. John Money of the Johns Hopkins University Gender Identity Clinic in Baltimore and Dr. Harry Benjamin in New York City (whose associate gave me my first testosterone shot); and Jordan Roberts, my cherished female partner, whom I have known since 1981 and with whom I reconnected in 2012. Jordan is "the love of my life" and my raison d'être.

Foreword

Aaron H. Devor

This is a book that needed to be written. This is a book that needs to be read—by a lot of people, not just Canadians and not just trans people. We Canadians are characteristically modest about our accomplishments. We tend to quiet understatement, and we tend to demure attention for our achievements. Living, as we do, within the media sphere of the United States, we often know more about, and think more highly of, what happens there. We have a tendency to think of ourselves as a bit slow and awkward by comparison. When it comes to trans activism, this book provides a welcome antidote.

The voices represented in this volume speak loudly and clearly about a very particularly Canadian, quiet, kind, caring, perseverant dedication to broad social justice. Time and again, the authors in this book tell about how they saw a need, and shouldered the responsibility to do what they could to bring about change for the better. They knew that there would be no quick wins, no easy victories. They knew, too, that there would be very little glory. They didn't do their work in order to garner recognition for themselves. The activists who did the work described in these pages did it because it needed to be done, and someone had to do it. They were there. They saw the need. They did it.

It took an especially hardy type of bravery to be active in the early days of trans activism in the 1970s, 1980s, and 1990s, when Marie-Marcelle Godbout, Michelle De Ville, Jamie Lee Hamilton, Rupert Raj, Raven James, Sandy Leo Laframboise, and others, such as Stephanie Castle and Gayle Roberts of the Zenith Foundation in Vancouver, were making waves. We all owe a deep debt of gratitude to those folks who were willing to be publicly identified as trans advocates when the public was so abysmally ignorant about, and generally overtly hostile toward, anything to do with trans. I vividly remember the ways that even the most sympathetic cis people unabashedly stared at trans people, like they were watching some kind of a freak show. And those were the people who were *trying* to understand. It only got worse from there, too often ending in death by abuse or suicide. The courage that those who are now our elders exhibited back then was breathtaking in the face of such gale-force exclusion, rejection, and hatred, often compounded by racism, sexism, colonialism, ableism, poverty, and other pernicious multipliers. Having known many of our pioneers, I am most pleased to see them being recognized and appreciated in this way, and I hope that others who were there, working shoulder to shoulder with them, will also have a chance to tell their stories one day soon.

The bulk of *Trans Activism in Canada* is concerned with trans activism in the second millennium. As I read through the many stories of bold initiatives to place more control of trans lives in the hands of trans people, I was once again struck by the vast difference that the development of strong communities has made in terms of quality of life for trans people. Even those in remote and rural areas now know that they are not the only ones. The way we do things may be different away from the big cities, but the story is similar. We need each other. We have each other. We can, and will, be there for each other. Yes, life is still very, very difficult for many, many trans people. We are still losing far too many trans people to the effects of isolation and despair. Yet, what comes through, especially in "Part II: 'Changing the Way We Change': Critical Reflections on Doing Trans Activism" and "Part III: Transforming Institutions from the Inside," is that we have momentum now. We are finding our strength. We are finding our allies. No one is doing it for us. We are doing it for ourselves. And we are changing the way we see ourselves, and the way the world sees us.

In these sections, we hear from the people who are driving this change. We hear about how they are doing it, through thoughtful introspection and active interventions. They are changing the world one person at a time and in groups, and they are taking on institutional bureaucracies. We hear about small towns and big cities. We hear about reaching out to individuals with a sensitive respect for where they are, and about reaching inside of big organizations, learning their ways, and bringing them to better places. These are huge tasks, and we hear from the trans activists in this book about how to do these things with respect for others, and for self. Perhaps most importantly, one of the main themes that runs through these accounts is that we can do this. These are stories of confidence and hopefulness born of success. Although we are far from done with the work of trans activism in Canada, these chapters are inspirational. Kudos to Dan Irving and Rupert Raj for teaming up to bring all of this together, allowing us to know something about all of the fine, brave people who have done, and continue to do, the work of trans activism in Canada.

Introduction

Dan Irving and Rupert Raj

MAKING WAVES

Trans Activism in Canada brings together the work of an entire community of trans activists and their allies to address poverty, isolation, violence, education, health care, and best practices for developing trans programming and services in existing organizations and creating new initiatives to meet the needs of this diverse population. Drawing on feminist, anti-racist, de-colonial, and queer approaches to politics, this assemblage ranges from radical in their attempts to achieve justice for trans people to a more cautious and incremental approach. Taken together, this collection represents a vibrant, passionate, and disparate group whose conversations and knowledge emerge to form an understanding of the foundation of trans activism in Canada, an indication of the breadth of trans politics, and an appreciation of the different pathways toward change.

DOING TRANS ACTIVISM: AN HISTORICAL OVERVIEW

Trans Activists as Knowledge Producers

The construction of knowledge concerning trans identities and the material lives of trans people is a political engagement. *Trans Activism in Canada* centres the voices and experiences of trans-identified people from various socio-economic, political, and cultural backgrounds as the experts on their own lives and as active agents of change.

University-educated, professionally trained, or graduates of the school of hard knocks (as one contributor puts it), trans and two-spirit people are fully capable of articulating the layered complexity of their everyday lives and experiences navigating the systemic power relations that order Canadian society. As demonstrated throughout this text, they have struggled with a lack of social services, the absence of social and informational networks for trans people, the exclusion of trans women from women's shelters, and the psychological and medical gatekeeping of the health professions.

Storming the Gates of the Ivory Tower: The Emergence of Transgender Studies

The rich tapestry of early trans activism in the 1970s and 1980s saw the development of relationships that produced immense wisdom. Communities of individuals were forged based on an understanding of the plurality of sexed embodiment, gender identities, and the issues impacting the material lives of their members. This turn in the tide offered vital lessons in the best ways to navigate formal and informal networks to improve the quality of life for marginalized subjects.

The activism that has taken place over the last four decades has very clearly contributed to current debates concerning sex and gender oppression, as well as put forward concrete strategies to resist the subordination of marginalized communities. Nevertheless, these voices and struggles are habitually under-represented within academic research on sex and gender variance. Sadly, when trans identities are acknowledged within social and behavioural science research, they are often presented as objectified and fetishized versions of trans embodiments and identities.

Seeking to confront the absence of trans voices within academic knowledge production and to combat the invisibility of trans people's actual lives, trans scholars (such as Sandy Stone, Susan Stryker, Aaron Devor, and Viviane Namaste) added layers of complexity to debates concerning gender and sexuality throughout the 1990s and early 2000s.[1] These movements toward inclusion saw trans allies within universities provide classroom and conference space to trans individuals, community organizers, and students. In so doing, trans and two-spirit people worked to fill this newly created space and expand knowledge of the ways that normative expectations of embodied sex and gender identity are mediated by multiple forms of power and sites of governance—from state and institutional levels of governance to the most intimate and personal aspects of life. Gradually, albeit in a very limited capacity, trans subjects began to be addressed in earnest within the realms of critical scholarship.

The ever-burgeoning and dynamic interdisciplinary field of Transgender Studies resulted from these pioneering efforts. As a field of critical scholastic inquiry, researchers within Transgender Studies seek to enrich knowledge of trans subjectivities and oppression by uncovering the multiple power relations that shape trans people's conceptions of themselves, and to produce alternative knowledge to buttress resistance efforts. Critical in nature, this field not only seeks different understandings of sex and gender but also aims to transgress such governing technologies.

Trans Activism in Canada features chapters written by transsexual and two-spirit activists engaging in these early political endeavours. Their contributions enrich the debates concerning historical and contemporary elements of trans, feminist, anti-poverty, and de-colonial struggles.

Contributing to (Re)New(ed) Directions in Transgender Studies

While identity-based research is invaluable in rendering trans people intelligible within society, it is crucial to comprehend that trans oppression and activist efforts do not occur in a vacuum. Problematizing trans subjectivities in terms of various technologies of governance that symbolically and literally extend life to some while denying it to others is a key priority for current work in Transgender Studies.[2] It is important to note that trans scholars demonstrate how nationalism,[3] race,[4] post-9/11 security regimes,[5] and capitalism[6] mediate the production and performance of embodied sex and gender expressions. This intellectual shift reflects the challenges trans activists face beyond the university that have strengthened such academic disciplines as Women's, Gender, Sexuality,[7] and Human Rights Studies,[8] as well as Nursing, Social Work, Psychology, Epidemiology, and Law. *Trans Activism in Canada* contributes to this turn toward more nuanced understandings of power relations in Canadian society and the different ways that trans people in various parts of the country are affected.

MEET THE EDITORS

The framework and composition of this book represents an amalgamation of our strengths and the commitment we share to materialist analysis, social justice, and anti-racist politics. Rupert Raj, a trans man who transitioned in the early 1970s, brings over four decades of experience engaging in various forms of trans activism. Raj currently works as a psychotherapist in the LGBT program at the Sherbourne Health Centre, where he applies his trans therapeutic model to assist in the self-empowerment of sex- and gender-variant clients; he also works with gay, lesbian, bisexual, and pansexual people and their families. Additionally, he operates RR Consulting, a private practice through which he engages with service providers and organizations to offer space and resources for education and training on sexuality and gender diversity.

Dan Irving also identifies as a trans man. He began transitioning in 1998 and has been teaching in the field of Transgender Studies for over a decade. Irving received his doctorate from York University in 2005 and holds a position as an assistant professor in the Sexuality Studies and Human Rights programs in the Institute of Interdisciplinary Studies at Carleton University. Critical political economy provides the framework for his scholarship, which emphasizes the ways in which neoliberal rationalities infuse trans subject formations and approaches to politics. This materialist approach to trans theory and activism problematizes human rights politics and other reformist interventions. His doctoral research critiqued trans activist efforts to forge alliances with LGB organizations, feminist organizations, and the labour movement based primarily on conceptualizing transsexual and transgender in terms of narrowly defined sex and gender categories.

WE CANNOT BE "FIXED"!

Trans Activists Engaging in "Trans-" Activism

Engaging in trans activism requires an understanding of the historical and contemporary lives of people who identify as trans. Part of this knowledge includes examining how struggles to distinguish our "true selves" in the wake of social unintelligibility perpetuates tensions between trans networks and branches of the state, various institutions within health care and education sectors, and non-profit organizations. Narrow classification schemes based on binary sex and gender, limited service and/or political mandates, ignorance of gender variance, and the multiplicity of sexed embodiments, as well as the anger, anxiety, and fear that can erupt from such ignorance, are at odds with both the desire and the concrete need to belong.[9] We need to feel like we belong within our communities and broader society. A sense of belonging is especially important to those who have endured the consequences of what Christopher Shelley refers to as "repudiation" or what Viviane Namaste identifies as the "systemic erasure" of trans populations and networks throughout local, provincial, and national contexts.

Trans identities and experiences are not limited to sex and gender categories, nor can they be reduced to sex and gender variance. We are parents, students, national subjects, temporary migrants, labourers, employees, and workers. Some of us are homeless, incarcerated, residents of mental health facilities, or living in assisted housing. The issues that frame trans activist terrain reach far beyond merely establishing the meaning of trans and two-spirit identities.

So what do we mean by "trans-"[10] activism? "Trans-" works on two registers: first, as an identity category—defining who we are is a significant factor that influences the strategic decisions concerning what can be done to improve the life chances[11] of those whose lives challenge the narrowly defined sex/gender binary system. *Trans Activism in Canada* is poised to confront misunderstandings of trans subjectivities circulating throughout progressive leftist, feminist, queer, and environmentalist spaces. But "trans-" also denotes movement—nothing is fixed. The socio-economic, political, and ecological conditions of being are constantly in flux. Trans individuals demonstrate the ways that sex and gender shifts and changes over the course of a lifetime. In no chapter in this collection is "trans" reduced to a singular or fixed meaning. Furthermore, the very meaning of trans activism and the issues to be politicized are not static.

Critical trans scholars and activists are wary of the consequences of privileging singular and homogenizing categories such as "trans," "transsexual," "two-spirit" persons, "man," and "woman." As you the reader make your way through the three sections of the text, it is instructive to ask yourself: Whose subjectivities and experiences are subordinated when "trans" oppression is discussed solely in terms of gendered violence? How do bordered categories perpetuating an insider–outsider dichotomy serve to govern the self and others? And, finally, how does an ontological focus undermine both solidarity between marginalized groups and our political imaginations to envision other ways to resist oppression?[12]

The second register on which "trans-" works is in informing our approach to activism. Situating identities and subjugation amidst colonialism, nationalism, hetero/homonormativity, and neoliberalism influences our approach to trans- activism. Trans oppression is a social phenomenon that is inseparable from whiteness and racism, misogyny, and classism. As Vek Lewis (2011) explains, "We need tools and analysis that can comprehend how such marginalization is produced in relations in specific sites and at specific junctures" (p. 190).

FROM OBJECTS TO OBJECTIVES

This is the first book devoted entirely to discussing trans activism in Canada. We produced the book with three major objectives in mind: (1) to acknowledge some of the trans activist endeavours in Canada beginning in the 1970s that "paved the way" for current activist interventions; (2) to offer space to examine different activist approaches; and (3) to offer practical advice to those struggling to improve contemporary environs while extending hope to future activists fighting for a just and democratic tomorrow. Another important objective, however, is to emphasize the importance of self-care for trans activists.

"What Is Missing from Our Communities Is Self-Love"

The various forms of systemic violence to which trans people are subject do not exist beyond the individual, or "out there" in wider social, familial, institutional, and governmental contexts. The constant struggles, atomization, misrecognition, and misrepresentation, as well as harassment, register what Judith Butler (1997) calls a "psychic life of power" that affects our minds and bodies. This causes many trans people to turn the rage, desperation, and/or shame they experience against themselves. As many of the authors express with raw candour, this can manifest through self-mutilating behaviours, drug and alcohol use, self-isolation, and suicide. Self-care, celebrating one's accomplishments and tenacity, and developing a sense of pride in oneself and in one's cultures and communities is a vital component of resistance. The empowerment of such self-love renders trans individuals more capable of assisting other marginalized subjects.

Who Heals the Healer?

Personal and collective regimens of care are crucial for the preservation and protection of trans activists. Mental, physical, and spiritual exhaustion are job hazards for "professional transsexuals" and "gender workers." It is therefore vital for trans activist endeavours to make space to address the injurious aspects of this work through debriefing and sharing experiences with other members of activist collectives, creative and artistic pursuits, or through organizing celebratory events.

Exhaustion also impacts trans allies. Co-workers, collaborators, family members, health care practitioners, and educators often fight alongside trans individuals or alone as advocates within exclusionary spaces. The work that allies do in everyday life situations—such as offering a steely glare to someone staring at a trans person on the bus—can create compassion fatigue[13] and/or vicarious traumatization.[14]

It is our desire that this book will function to ease the fatigue that trans activists may experience as they constantly face multiple forms and gradations of violence. We hope that this text will signal to students new to this particular arena of politics (or to any person who may reach for this book) the importance of finding common ground. You are not alone, nor are the struggles you face insurmountable.

Infighting, Backbiting, and Other Low-Intensity Forms of Lateral Violence

Addressing lateral violence is another important consideration when advocating for self-care. Lateral violence refers to various forms of aggression that oppressed populations take out on each other. Within trans milieus, such violence can occur through reinforcing gender, racial, ableist, and other forms of hierarchy. Such violence is often unintentional; nevertheless, its impact is serious. The politics of "passing"—concerning an individual's ability to be read in society as *authentically* female or male—illustrates this. So does the unreflective use of medicalized terms such as "primary" and "secondary" to credit and legitimize transsexual individuals who pursue medical transition and live according to their gender identity earlier in life than individuals who transition later and may not necessarily seek to embody their gender identities. Another form of lateral violence is using words (e.g., "tranny") without acknowledging the misogynist, racist, class-based, and moralistic elements of a term's history.

THEORETICAL APPROACHES

Social Justice

Social justice as a critical approach to political praxis frames this book. While contributors may differ in social location and activist milieu, they share a commitment to achieving the three tenets of social justice—equity, democracy, and a just redistribution of resources—and are keenly attuned to the socio-economic, cultural, and political power relations ordering Canadian society. Working within social justice frameworks, these contributors seek to uncover colonialism, patriarchy, heteronormativity, and capitalism to challenge the insidious nature of these ruling regimes—especially in the lives of the most marginalized trans populations. Social justice approaches posit that gender, sexual, racial, and economic discrimination are not private, individually contained acts; instead, such violences are consistent with systemic technologies of governance.

Contributors focus their discussion on ways to improve the quality of life for trans people, operating on the premise that trans-identified individuals are severely compromised by forms of self-degradation and epistemic, state, social, and interpersonal violence. The differences among contributors strengthens this collective effort to open spaces for discussion concerning how "trans-" activism can work to achieve social change.

Anti-Racism and De-Colonial Trans-Politics

Many contributors to the book call attention to the ways in which whiteness serves to legitimize some trans subjects while denigrating others. Highlighting whiteness in terms of whose identities, experiences, and issues merit attention within Canadian society is crucial. Whiteness denotes a particular moralistic and prescriptive code of behaviour that frames the Canadian national imaginary. As many contributors point out, this normative code must be subject to constant scrutiny, and those with white privilege must be accountable to the ways that this plays out in their everyday lives. What does it mean when "we" don't recognize the murdered and missing women working as prostitutes and/or living on the streets as a trans political issue? What message is articulated when achieving symbolic recognition for trans people through enshrining "gender identity" in the Canadian Human Rights Act (i.e., Bill C-279) takes priority over lobbying the government for more resources for social housing and increased funding for programs that offer skills training or health care? Anti-racist theoretical approaches to the study of trans activism render embodied sex and gender performance as inseparable from processes of racialization. As contributors to this text demonstrate, such awareness impacts the ways that trans oppression is framed and resistance strategies are created.

Trans Activism in Canada also reflects a de-colonial approach to "trans-" politics. As the lived experiences of some contributors can attest, the binary sex/gender system and the subsequent subjugation of sex- and gender-variant subjects is the legacy of settler colonialism, which is currently manifested by genocidal efforts to eradicate indigenous knowledge of plurality, mutability, and flexibility when it comes to sex and gender. As two-spirit commentators point out, their derogating self-understandings of their sex/gender difference reflected Western knowledge that was produced in residential schools, through organized religion, and in colonial government policy and administration. The belief that they were freaks and outcasts had to be unlearned so that they could relearn about their two-spirit and transsexual identities from indigenous knowledges that honour such difference.

Social Change through (R)evolution

Life would be easier if we could simply smash the gender binary and achieve complete transformations of oppressive power structures; however, as the contributors demonstrate, social change occurs gradually. What sets social justice activists, including trans activists, apart from more liberal reformers is the fact that incremental changes to improve the lives of marginalized subjects are understood as means to greater ends. Every chapter in this book demonstrates that the majority of trans and two-spirit subjects cannot afford to wait for major progressive shifts. Meeting their needs for housing, health care, employment, education, and community is often a life-or-death matter requiring immediate attention. The perspectives and experiences detailed throughout this volume reveal the arduousness of having to navigate the current conditions within multiple sites throughout Canadian society without the privilege of being able to take significant time for reflection and analysis.

METHODS

As *Trans Activism in Canada* brings together the diverse voices of a community of trans activists and their allies, so the tone and presentation of each contribution in this collection is varied. Some are academic and offer analyses of research while others are conversational and extremely personal. Rather than impose uniformity in terms of style, structure, and format, we have chosen to let the papers remain in their original form, respecting and preserving the contributors' experiences, feelings, opinions, and voices. In doing so, we hope to present the variations that exist in terms of experience and approaches to change, and to encourage an appreciation of these differences.

Personal Narrative

Contributors use various methods to address the material lives of trans people and "trans-" activist struggles for social change. Many chapters present personal narratives and a reflective approach in sharing the authors' experiences. Whether in essay format, an interview, a round table discussion, or a poem, this method of inquiry offers readers multiple insights by presenting knowledge to demystify trans identities and experiences, as well as to introduce complex ideas and conditions in accessible forms, thereby grounding activism as an everyday activity conducted by ordinary people.

Archival, Qualitative, and Case-Based Research

Many of the chapters authored by scholars and professionals are based on more "traditional" scholastic methods. These methods include drawing upon the personal archives of historical activists to ascertain how strategies have been used to gain recognition for trans subjects as legitimate members of society and reflect the political climate framing that period. Other contributors base their pieces on the qualitative research projects that have been conducted with specific trans demographics and social service providers. Their information and analysis is derived from interview and survey data that engaged research participants in guided discussions concerning particular issues that will enable activists to develop a more in-depth knowledge of trans subjectivities and institutional logics, as well as barriers to trans positivity and inclusion. Case-based research refers to an in-depth focus on specific trans individuals and their experiences. Couched within a social justice framework, case files are analyzed with the intent of comprehending how social structures and systemic logics influence individual ways of being in the world.

Community-Based Research

Unlike the majority of academic research, in which scholars develop their own research agenda and then extract information from communities, investigators employing community-based research (CBR) study topics that have been identified by marginalized communities as the most pressing. HIV/AIDS education and health care are examples derived from this book. The research teams working on these projects consist of trans people who deal with the issues directly. Their input and direction in all phases of the research ensures that the most pertinent questions are being asked and that the analysis reflects the realities of everyday life. CBR also includes steering committees and advisory boards comprising professionals, policy-makers, municipal or provincial government officials, and managers of non-profits to ensure that realistic recommendations for change are made and that the products of such studies can be implemented concretely. The commitment of CBR researchers to equity, democracy, and resource redistribution is made evident by their projects functioning as empowering and capacity-building endeavours; that is, those that belong to community members.

STRUCTURE OF THE BOOK

Trans Activism in Canada is presented in three parts, with each part further divided into two subsections. When read in sequential order, these sections reflect efforts to achieve substantial social change from the ground up. "Part I: Transforming Experiences of Oppression into Opportunities for Social Change" offers a glimpse into the material lives of trans-identified individuals in historical and contemporary contexts, highlighting the harsh repercussions that befell the authors due to their sex/gender, racial, and economic alterity. This sets the stage for a deeper understanding of the realities of trans people and the challenges they face. This section serves to orient the reader toward discussion concerning which issues, strategies, and voices ought to form the landscape of trans resistance and politics rooted in social justice.

Drawing on their experiences of struggling for social change, contributors to "Part II: 'Changing the Way We Change': Critical Reflections on Doing Trans Activism" offer critical reflections on trans politics and provide insight into the affective dimensions of "trans-" oppression, as well as its impact on trans activism. Trans subjects are governed by the colonialist, capitalist, imperialist, and hetero-patriarchal relations that frame Canadian society, despite a significant number of trans people being excluded from the Canadian nation as an "imagined community."[15] Whereas Part I demonstrates the ways that trans individuals are affected by structural, institutional, and interpersonal violence, this section emphasizes the impact that such violence can have on trans activist networks. The chapters included here also offer practical solutions regarding how to address this violence individually and as a community, as well as techniques to cultivate more vibrant, equitable, and socially just cultures of resistance.

"Part III: Transforming Institutions from the Inside" addresses ways that trans activists work with, and within, various organizations to improve the quality of life for trans subjects. The pieces included in this section discuss the challenges of evoking change in institutional cultures and health care organizations. In addition, contributors offer practical tips and best practices for navigating bureaucracies based on their own successes and current struggles.

THE FUTURE IS NOW AND IT BEGINS WITH YOU

We hope that this book will strengthen existing trans activism across Canada. Furthermore, we hope that the critical questions, discussions, and emotional responses that *Trans Activism in Canada* provokes will inspire new projects and new directions that will shape the future of "trans-" activism.

NOTES

1 For more information about the ways that hyper-feminine gender performance was produced through transsexual women's interactions with gender identity clinics, see Sandy Stone's chapter, "The Empire Strikes Back: A Postranssexual Manifesto," in *Body Guards: The Cultural Politics of Gender Ambiguity* (1991). Susan Stryker discusses the monstrosity of transsexuality and the ways that such embodied narratives reveal the artificiality of sex and gender taken for granted as natural in society in her 1994 article

"My Words to Victor Frankenstein above the Village of Chamounix: Performing Transgender Rage." Aaron Devor's book *FTM: Female-to-Male Transsexuals in Society* (1997) offers an in-depth account of the ways that trans men negotiate their masculine gender identities from an early age, their transitioning processes, and their lives as men. For an exploration of the ways that transsexual and transgendered people were rendered non-existent through bureaucratic and governmental policy and practice, see Viviane Namaste's *Invisible Lives: The Erasure of Transsexual and Transgendered People* (2000).

2 This shift toward "trans-" scholarship seeks to investigate the impact of various governing technologies on embodied sex and gender. For example, Lane R. Mandlis's "Whose Crazy Investment in Sex?" (2011) emphasizes the efforts that psychiatric, medical, and legal professionals expend to ensure a particular understanding of normative sex and gender that privileges non-trans embodied performances while exiling transsexuals from the category of "human." Lucas Cassidy Crawford's article, "Transgender Without Organs? Mobilizing a Geo-affective Theory of Gender Modification" (2008), critiques the ways that transition narratives privilege urban spaces to the detriment of rural or small town environments that for many trans people are home. The ways that difference is negotiated within rural spaces may assist us in thinking through issues of visible sex and gender alterity.

3 See Aren Aizura's "Of Borders and Homes: The Imaginary Community of Transsexual Citizenship" (2006) and "The Romance of the Amazing Scalpel: 'Race,' Labour and Affect in Thai Gender Reassignment Clinics" (2011) for a discussion of the ways that nationalism mediates transsexual embodiments of the "proper" citizen subjects.

4 For an exploration of race and the insidious power of whiteness, see Bobby Noble's article "Sons of the Movement: Feminism, Female Masculinity and Female-to-Male (FTM) Transsexual Men" (2004), and Sarah Lamble's "Retelling Racialized Violence, Remaking White Innocence: The Politics of Interlocking Oppression in Transgender Day of Remembrance" (2008).

5 Toby Beauchamp's "Artful Concealment and Strategic Visibility: Transgender Bodies and U.S. State Surveillance After 9/11" (2009) discusses the ways that normative embodiment of sex and gender is produced through national security regimes and practices. Individuals determined to be "gender deviants" will simultaneously be targeted as threats to the nation.

6 See Dan Irving's "Elusive Subjects: Notes on the Relationship between Critical Political Economy and Trans Studies" (2012); "The Self-Made Trans Man as Risky Business: A Critical Examination of Gaining Recognition for Trans Rights through Economic Discourse" (2009); and "Normalized Transgressions: Legitimizing the Transsexual Body as Productive" (2008) for an exploration of the ways that capitalist productive logics influence trans individuals' representation of themselves. Dean Spade discusses intersections between neoliberal economic rationalities and trans subjectivities in "Compliance Is Gendered: Struggling for Gender Self-Determination in a Hostile Economy" (2006).

7 For Canadian examples of the emergence of trans feminist scholarship, please see Krista Scott-Dixon, *Trans/forming Feminisms: Trans Feminist Voices Speak Out* (2006), and Bobby Noble's *Sons of the Movement* (2006).

8 For an article concerning teaching "trans-" human rights, please see Dan Irving's "Against the Grain: Teaching Transgender Human Rights" (2013).

9 Mildred L. Brown and Chloe Ann Rounsley discuss transsexuality and address questions that arise concerning this specific gender identity and its embodiment in *True Selves: Understanding Transsexualism—For Families, Friends, Coworkers and Helping Professionals* (1996).

10 See Susan Stryker, Paisley Currah, and Lisa Jean Moore's article, "Trans-, Trans or Transgender?" (2008) for an exploration of the turn Transgender Studies is taking toward more expansive possibilities of the

notion of "trans-." They explain that the prefix "trans" means movement. Transgender Studies scholars have concentrated mainly on horizontal movement across binary sex/gender categories. The hyphen following trans signifies opening the field to new areas of study to examine the ways that sexed and gendered bodies and performances are intrinsic to other assemblages of power relations.

11 Critical scholars, such as Dean Spade in his book *Normal Life: Administrative Violence, Critical Trans Politics, and the Limits of the Law* (2011), use the term "life chances" to challenge liberal democratic notions of equality, success, and humanity. Critical scholars draw attention to the ways that racialized, sexualized, colonized, and sex- and gender-variant bodies are increasingly being denied access to various forms of recognition, status, social services, education, income, housing, and so forth that form the basis of a livable life. Moreover, an increasing number of people are being denied their humanity altogether as they are cast from the social and become members of surplus populations.

12 Wendy Brown, in her book *States of Injury: Power and Freedom in Late Modernity* (1995), argues that our understandings of oppression tend to focus on what we lack as individuals in relation to the symbolic ideal structuring Western liberal democratic societies (i.e., the citizen as a white male heterosexual property owner). In the chapter "Wounded Attachments," Brown argues that identity is formed significantly through this lack, and members of marginalized communities define themselves according to the terms of their subordination. The possibility of sustaining the strength of political movements, as well as cultivating shared desires for equitable futures in solidarity with others, is arrested by the bond that individuals form with their own injury.

13 "Compassion fatigue" refers to a defensive hardening or shutting down of allies after bearing witness repeatedly to the serious repercussions of oppression.

14 "Vicarious traumatization" refers to the ways that bodies, minds, and spirits are porous. The traumatic effects of physical, sexual, and emotional violence, as well as various other forms of abjection including impoverishment, homelessness, and illness, are not limited to the individual experiencing them directly; rather, this violence has significant impact on others.

15 See Benedict Anderson's *Imagined Communities: Reflections on the Origin and Spread of Nationalism* (1991) for a discussion of the way the nation is a constructed phenomenon based on the production of similarity amongst those recognized as its members. The sense of belonging to a national community emerges through the exclusion of others and the continual governing of those considered to be within national boundaries. The basis for belonging to the "Canadian nation" is rooted in whiteness, Anglo-chauvinism, heterosexuality, normative embodiment of sex and gender, and a middle-class or working-class social location.

REFERENCES

Aizura, A. (2006). Of borders and homes: The imaginary community of (trans)sexual citizenship. *Inter-Asia Cultural Studies, 7*(2), 289–309.

Aizura, A. (2011). The romance of the amazing scalpel: "Race," labour and affect in Thai gender reassignment clinics. In P.A. Jackson (Ed.), *Queer Bangkok* (pp. 143–162). Hong Kong: Hong Kong University Press.

Anderson, B. (1991). *Imagined communities: Reflections on the origin and spread of nationalism*. London: Verso Books.

Beauchamp, T. (2009). Artful concealment and strategic visibility: Transgender bodies and U.S. state surveillance after 9/11. *Surveillance and Society, 6*(4), 356–366.

Brown, M.L., & Rounsley, C.A. (1996). *True selves: Understanding transsexualism—For families, friends, coworkers and helping professionals.* San Francisco: Jossey-Boss.

Brown, W. (1995). *States of injury: Power and freedom in late modernity.* New Jersey: Princeton University Press.

Butler, J. (1997). *Psychic life of power: Theories of subjection.* Stanford: Stanford University Press.

Crawford, L.C. (2008). Transgender without organs? Mobilizing a geo-affective theory of gender modification. *WSQ, 36*(3-4), 127–143.

Devor, A. (1997). *FTM: Female-to-male transsexuals in society.* Bloomington: Indiana University Press.

Irving, D. (2008). Normalized transgressions: Legitimizing the transsexual body as productive. *Radical History Review, 100*, 38–59.

Irving, D. (2009). The self-made trans man as risky business: A critical examination of gaining recognition for trans rights through economic discourse. *Temple Political and Civil Rights Law Review, 18*(2), 375–395.

Irving, D. (2012). Elusive subjects: Notes on the relationship between critical political economy and trans studies. In A. Enke (Ed.), *Transfeminist perspectives: In and beyond transgender and gender studies* (pp. 153–169). Philadelphia: Temple University Press.

Irving, D. (2013). Against the grain: Teaching transgender human rights. *Sexualities, 16*(3-4), 319–335.

Lamble, S. (2008). Retelling racialized violence, remaking white innocence: The politics of interlocking oppression in Transgender Day of Remembrance. *Sexuality Research and Social Policy, 5*(1), 24–42.

Lewis, V. (2011). Critical research and trans activism in Latin America: An interview with Vek Lewis. In V. Namaste, *Sex change, social change: Reflections on identity, institutions, and imperialism* (2nd ed., pp. 181–203). Toronto: Women's Press.

Mandlis, L.R. (2011). Whose crazy investment in sex? *Journal of Homosexuality, 58*(2), 219–236.

Namaste, V. (2000). *Invisible lives: The erasure of transsexual and transgendered people.* Chicago: University of Chicago Press.

Noble, J.B. (2004). Sons of the movement: Feminism, female masculinity and female-to-male (FTM) transsexual men. *Atlantis, 29*(1), 21–28.

Noble, J.B. (2006). *Sons of the movement: FtMs risking incoherence on a post-queer cultural landscape.* Toronto: Women's Press.

Scott-Dixon, K. (2006). *Trans/forming feminisms: Trans feminist voices speak out.* Toronto: Women's Press.

Shelley, C. (2008). *Transpeople: Repudiation, trauma, healing.* Toronto: University of Toronto Press.

Spade, D. (2006). Compliance is gendered: Struggling for gender self-determination in a hostile economy. In P. Currah, R.M. Juang, & S.P. Minter (Eds.), *Transgender rights* (pp. 217–241). Minnesota: University of Minnesota Press.

Spade, D. (2011). *Normal life: Administrative violence, critical trans politics, and the limit of the law.* Cambridge: South End Press.

Stone, S. (1991). The empire strikes back: A postranssexual manifesto. In K. Straub & J. Epstein (Eds.), *Body guards: The cultural politics of gender ambiguity* (pp. 280–304). New York: Routledge.

Stryker, S. (1994). My words to Victor Frankenstein above the village of Chamounix: Performing transgender rage. *GLQ: A Journal of Gay and Lesbian Studies, 1*(3), 227–254.

Stryker, S., Paisley, C., & Moore, L.J. (2008). Trans-, trans or transgender? *WSQ: Women's Studies Quarterly, 36*(3-4), 11–22.

Part I Transforming Experiences of Oppression into Opportunities for Social Change

Part I is dedicated to enriching readers' understanding of trans identified people's everyday lives in historical and contemporary Canadian contexts. Readers will be able to discern the similarities and differences amongst various trans and two-spirit identities, as well as the ways that both time and location influence trans people's lives. This section makes it evident that the material lives of trans people cannot be reduced to their transgressing normative sex and gender categories; rather, one's ability, race, class, and gender are key factors determining quality of life. The socio-economic and political repercussions that befall the authors due to their marginalized status in relation to these multiple governing categories orient readers towards broader conversations about which issues, strategies, and voices ought to be placed at the forefront of trans social justice politics.

In this section, Jamie Lee Hamilton (Chapter 2), Elizabeth "Raven" James (Chapter 4), Sandy Leo Laframboise (Chapter 5), and Michelle Boyce (with her daughter, Jessica) (Chapter 7) offer raw personal narratives of their sex/gender identities and experiences, and explore how various forms of oppression hinder the "life chances" of members of marginalized communities. The authors and individuals who are the subject of historical inquiry and interviews featured in this section illustrate the ways that "trans-" politics emerged organically from the will to survive within the most adverse conditions and the desire to create change that will improve the lives of those rendered abject in Canadian society.

Three key themes emerge when the texts in Part I are placed in conversation. The first relates to the need to recognize the way that other governing relations mediate trans oppression. All contributors and subjects of inquiry (i.e., Rupert Raj, as examined by Nick Matte in Chapter 3, and Viviane Namaste's interview with Michelle De Ville in Chapter 1) identify as transsexual and/or two-spirit; however, they refuse to contain their life experiences within sex and gender categories. Their social location vis-à-vis colonialism, nationalism, Anglo-chauvinism, citizenship status, capitalism, hetero-patriarchy, and ableism shapes their material realities.

The second theme relates to the need to complicate notions of dispossession. The authors featured here are not atypical. Loss and degradation are par for the course for an alarming number of trans people. Racialized, feminine, dis/abled, and visibly variant people who are marginalized from the legal labour market, denied access to essential social services, and barred from social spaces (e.g., gay bars) are put in a disadvantaged position. The consequences of such abjection—impoverishment, malnutrition, alcohol and substance abuse, abuse and trauma, police brutality and incarceration, severely compromised physical and mental health, and suicidal ideation—as well as the isolation presented here, are typical for many trans people. Nonetheless, trans and two-spirit individuals are not powerless. No one in this section presents as a victim or clings to what Wendy Brown refers to as "wounded attachments." As Susan Gapka's poems, "My Name Is Susan" and "Pause and Reflect," stress, we will not—and cannot—give our power over our lives away. Trans and two-spirit individuals' steadfast commitment to the cultivation of their inner strength and their innovative capacities to create the change they long to see can work to raise the suspicions of those who may highlight their vulnerability and precarity to legitimize efforts to "save" or "protect" them. As all the varied works included in this section attest, trans people's agency, or power to act on behalf of themselves and others, exists within the here and now.

Elements relating to the politics of representation serve as the third major theme of this section. Closely related to agency, contributors demonstrate that trans and/or two-spirit individuals are the experts when it comes to their own identities and experiences. In addition to content, trans people's expertise concerning their own lives is demonstrated through method. Jessica Boyce, now a high school student, writes the concluding portion of her mother, Michelle Boyce's, essay on parental alienation syndrome and the challenges of parenting through personal and relationship transition. Jessica's perspective and her ability to come to grips with difference enable readers to challenge dominant discourses that deem transition as having negative impacts on children. Other examples of addressing the politics of representation through method include Michelle De Ville's discussion, in an interview conducted by Viviane Namaste, of circumstances for francophone transsexuals and cross-dressers living and working in the East Side of Montreal. Like Namaste, Nick Matte employed his institutional location within the university to document Rupert Raj's work as a transsexual activist. Trans activists must be subjects, not objects, of scholastic and non-academic inquiry. Moreover, the most marginalized members of trans demographics must play central roles in organizing to improve their well-being. After all, who better to decide what changes need to be made, or programs implemented, to enrich the lives of racialized, sex- and gender-variant, queer, poor, dis/abled subjects than those whose daily lives are ordered by such experiences?

When contributors speak of prostitution and other criminalized acts, alcohol and substance use, street activity, gender illusionism and drag performances, obtaining hormones from underground markets, or incarceration in prisons and mental health facilities, they risk being exoticized and sensationalized. We chose to begin the book with these voices because they (and so many others like them) were—and continue to be—the people doing the bulk of the work within various trans activist milieus. Just as women's, LGB(T)Q, and indigenous movements often showcase normative notions of success to demonstrate value, deservedness, and respectability, sex workers, impoverished and homeless individuals, racialized subjects, dis/abled people, and substance users are not often represented as the face and voice of trans activism, despite having to endure intense hardship and sacrifice to "pave the way" (De Ville) for future generations of trans activists. Obscuring such vital contributions to the history of trans activism in Canada and silencing these voices serves as a form of lateral violence. The most subjugated layers of trans demographics are not powerless nor are they voiceless. This confronts readers with a challenging question: Who is listening?

Chapter 1 "We Paved the Way for Whatever Tolerance They Have in Their Lives": An Interview with Michelle De Ville, "The First Door Bitch in Montreal"

Viviane Namaste

Michelle De Ville has been involved in Montreal's trans communities for over 30 years. She brings a perspective not always heard in academic studies on trans people, specifically the lives and work of trans people in bars. Rendering these experiences and forms of labour visible is a central theme in Viviane Namaste's contributions to Transgender Studies.

Viviane Namaste (VN): Tell me a bit about your entry into the trans milieu here in Montreal.

Michelle De Ville (MD): Well, first of all, I think it was [through] a meeting with two people who were already starting a transgendered route; [they] were taking hormones. They were from the Ottawa region … they were in gay bars. That would be 1977. I was 19. That was my first contact with people who were living that reality.

VN: You met them in a bar?

MD: Yes, I met them at Le Jardin, which was on Stanley Street in the old gay village. It was a men-only club. But they were so outstanding and different and everything, and they would dress as men but with visible breasts showing and women's boots. But no makeup. And that's where I met them and many [other] friends who would later on become transgendered themselves.

VN: At that time in Montreal there was also PJ's. Is that correct? Tell me a bit about the PJ's scene.

MD: Yes PJ's was there. That was the place to be for what was then called "les grandes de l'ouest" [laughs]. Transsexuals and transvestites who [were] living and going out in the West End…

VN: Were there shows?

MD: Yes, there were drag shows seven days a week. That [club] was high-end compared to low-end Cléopâtre. Cléopâtre was really the armpit of drag bars at the time. So when you were in the West End you were at PJ's. If you were from the East End, basically the poor area, you were going to Cléopâtre.

VN: And did the same girls go to both?

MD: Some of them were travelling, going back and forth, but it was very unusual.

VN: Was there a language split because the west historically has been more English in Montreal?

MD: There was, yes. I would say that most of the girls I met at PJ's were anglophones, and at Cléopâtre, the few times that I'd been there, [they] were mostly francophone. So there was a language barrier.

VN: Interesting. You mentioned Le Jardin and that it was a men-only club, even though there were some visibly trans women there. One of the first interviews that I read that you had done was in a magazine called *Fuzzbox* way back in 1990. You talked about the contradictions of the gay male community, particularly in the 1980s in Montreal. Gay male bars that were men-only and wouldn't allow ladies in or would have a ladies' night once a year, but which even on the ladies' nights were not always friendly to trans women. Talk to me about that.

MD: Things have changed a lot. My first recollections of the concept of ladies' night would be at Studio One—not even two blocks away from PJ's, between Mansfield and Metcalf on Ste-Catherine. Studio One was a gay men-only club that I remember frequenting back in '76. By approximately '78, '79, they decided to have ladies' nights—it was a money thing. They wanted to fill up the club on slow nights, just on Mondays and Tuesdays. It's a very small club; I remember the capacity was 212. Typically the girls there were mostly what we call "lipstick lesbians" or simply a girl roommate of a gay man or a girl working in the hair salon of [some guy]. So there were girls that were mostly … I don't like the term, but "fag hags." It was a big success.

VN: So that was Studio One … and then around '99, when you did the *Fuzzbox* interview, you were talking about KOX.[1]

MD: Yeah I was talking about KOX specifically…

VN: Black Eagle and stuff.[2] So what was the situation?

MD: Well, then it was—my God!—it was anti-effeminate men or feminine men. It was mostly about that and looking a bit too femme was a problem.

VN: Would they bar entry if someone looked too femme?

MD: I know they did, yes. And that was the same logic back at Buds on Stanley but back in '76, '77, they were doing that. When we were there with high-heeled boots or dyed hair, they would chase us out. So basically try to look as masculine as possible. It was the same thing 15 years later at the first KOX. I remember one instance when I had a ponytail and they chased me around the place—they told me to remove the elastic in my hair. They were quite rough about it, without touching me, but very unpleasant. And I said fine, I removed it. And then I found a guy who had an elastic in his hair, and I pointed him out to the doorman, and he said, "Yeah, but he doesn't look like you do," pointing the finger at my look. That's the way it was, so basically men who were too feminine or whatever were not accepted there, not even tolerated.

VN: Before we turned on the tape recorder, you were telling me about 1980 and the New Wave scene in Montreal. Tell me about your experiences and impressions of that scene.

MD: I was very interested in the disco era and I had my first experiences in bars like the Limelight, which was *the* place to be. It was a very tolerant place for everybody—men, women, transgendered, transvestites—everybody was very accepted. And that's back in '75, '76. So that was a very cool place to be, but suddenly, in '79, there was a "disco sucks" revolution where everybody was burning disco records. Overnight it became *out* and New Wave arrived. There was some effort from Limelight to continue with a new style of music, but it was too late. And a lot of the clientele went to a club called The Glace on Stanley Street. It was a really tiny place, interestingly enough in the same building where the events that created our Stonewall, Truxx, took place. The Truxx, where 146 people were arrested, was on the main floor. Under it was The Glace, which played rockabilly and New Wave music. The crowd was—mostly an aesthetic look—all about rockabilly and Elvis Presley for the boys, Brigitte Bardot for the girls. And for some reason, I was the only transgendered person there, and I was accepted exactly as I was. I never had harsh words said to me, they accepted me as Michelle, referred to me as she, and were very welcoming and weren't patronizing at all. It was a lovely time that was very nice.

VN: Throughout the eighties did you stay in New Wave milieu?

MD: Yes. Actually, that opened up all kinds of possibilities for me. I started a short-lived modelling career and a movie career. That's all linked to the rapport I had at that club. And then The Glace closed because of the competition that The Beat created, and that's back in '82. I was invited by The Beat's owner, Pierre Viens, who later bought Cabaret Mado, Sky, Unity, and all kinds of places like that. His first club was The Beat, and I started working there in April '83.

VN: What did you do?

MD: I was a waitress, and the year after, in '84, I was the first door bitch in Montreal. I was the one deciding who would be getting in, and not getting in, to the club.

So, yes, it was very beneficial for me, not only on a personal level but also on a professional level. I was still doing shows at PJ's, Cléopâtre's, and other places since starting in '81. I was separating my career, meaning that there were "drag shows," but as a tran[s]gendered person I thought it was not really beneficial for me to do that. But I needed the money, so I did shows like that.

VN: Who did you do?

MD: I started off with Brigitte Bardot. It was a sentimental because I used the first record I'd ever owned, from when I was nine years old, "Harley Davidson"—that followed me for quite a while. Through PJ's and the drag connection and Armand Monroe, I was able to get some movie contracts—small, nothing big.

VN: Tell me the movies you're in.

MD: I did two. It was a Concordia student who did them; there was no dialogue or anything like that. I made one in '80, '81, with the neoïst movement, that's Monty Cantsin. I did one film with them along Lachine canal. I don't think the film was completed; I never saw the final result. I only know that I almost fell in the canal in February—I remember that. And then in '82, through my friend Claire Nadon, who was making my leather clothes, I met Bashar Shbib. He was her boyfriend at the time and a film student at Concordia. I made a short film with him called *Or dur* as in "solid gold," not garbage. And in '83 I did *Amour impossible* with

Bashar. I was able to introduce this film at the gay film festival in Montreal, Winnipeg, New York, and Toronto. And then in '84 I got myself involved with Elite Productions. I did a couple of films: *Blind Rage* with Shannon Tweed and Michael Ironside, one in the Hitchhiker series, and when I came back from France in '86, I did a film with Bashar called *Eviction*.

VN: Okay, I'm going to shift gears and ask you about a list that you made of all of the women in the trans milieu—the transvestites and transsexuelles—who died. You listed their names, their ages, and their cause of death. Why did you do that list? And what does it represent to you?

MD: In 1989, I started a group specifically geared toward transgendered and transsexuals in the HIV crisis. I was working at Comité Sida Aide Montréal, CSAM, on Hôtel de Ville, and I saw a need because there were groups of mostly gay men. And I had heard that transsexuals, transvestites, and transgendered people [were] going to these groups and being called "he" or "him." And I thought that's dreadful that these girls, who are dying—because in those days AIDS was a death sentence—couldn't even get some kind of respect from their own community. In my book, the trans community should be within the gay community, we should be a whole, that's what we say about LGBT rights. We're supposed to stick together, but the reality is totally different. So I thought there was a need to create a group that would be just for us, the transgendered community. I was not HIV-positive, and I'm still not, but I've lost so many people to AIDS. That list you referenced was a kind of research I was doing, to see the scope of the disaster and how important it was to have a group that would be just for us—so I created that group.

VN: How long did it run for?

MD: It stopped about May or June 1990.

VN: You ran a group at Spect(r)e de Rue as well. Tell me about that.

MD: In 1994, I created another group. It didn't last very long because during the day it was also a drop-in centre. That was difficult for me to handle because not only did I have the HIV thing to face, but also it was a drug-needle centre—that was a bit too difficult. I used to think that the only thing you had to do was convince somebody to go to rehab and they would be okay. I stopped working there when somebody told me that only 1 out of 10 people who went to [...] rehab will never use drugs again. And I think the next day I didn't show up, [and] I never showed up again. I said this is too big for me and I can't fight it by myself.

VN: Fair enough. Was the drop-in for everyone who used drugs or was [it] just for the girls?

MD: My group that I created was just for transgendered people, and I remember that other people were invited but they had to be trans-friendly and basically keep a low profile. And we had very few people. It was not as successful as CSAM had been, four years previous.

VN: Tell me about the fashion show you organized, in memory of Oogie, in the late nineties.

MD: It would be '99. First of all, I had organized one back in '85, for Claire Nadon, who had a boutique that I was managing. I had decided to mount a fashion show at The Beat, so I had a little bit of experience, but not much. But then I realized that I could pitch the idea of a fashion show to the owner of Cléopâtre, and since I had always supported the work of Stella,[3] it was a way that I could help out in an original setting with all the people that I knew in the trans community. You mention Oogie, but the first one in the spring of '99 was for Dany Solari. It was not a good choice.

VN: Who was she?

MD: When I started in fashion and the more trendy circles of Montreal, the only person I looked up to was Dany Solari. She claimed that she was Brazilian, but I think she was actually from Uruguay. And she was a cat [meow]. She was very Amanda Lear in her look and was doing very well at the 1234 on Mountain—which was a bit of an equivalent to Studio 54 in New York—with, what is called, theatrical fashion shows and later on with other shows. I thought it was appropriate that she would be the first one; however, she was not a very popular person so it was not a big success.

But the Oogie show was a huge success. By coincidence, it fell on the day of my birthday, July 30, 1999, or maybe 2000. And what's interesting is that the owners told me (this is in the middle of summer) that the show had to start at 8 p.m., while it was still light outside, and it had to end before people started to come in for the club. So I was basically supposed to greet people when the doors opened at 8 p.m., start the show at 9 p.m. [at] the latest, and everything had to be over by 10 p.m. These were the rules, and I had to abide by them. So for the Oogie show I had 18 people, 18 people who [agreed] to work for free for the cause of Stella, [and] I was emceeing the show in both French and English, and doing a number as well—I did all of that in an hour. I can't believe how I did it but I did it, and the club was filled, you were there. It was filled to capacity, so that was a big success.

VN: Nice. She's known as a costume designer in the scene?

MD: In those days, if you were a female impersonator, or a transgendered person doing shows, it meant that you were making your own costumes because the salaries were usually so low that there was no way you could have purchased costumes or had them made for you. So if you were a performer, you were also a seamstress.

VN: I just have a couple of other questions. You may not want to answer this one, so I remind you to feel free not to, but you deposited a complaint with the police ethics commission. Do you want to talk about that?

MD: Sure. I don't have a problem with that. It was a situation that happened back in 1994; I was leaving Cléopâtre's, to [go to] my car parked on St-Dominique a block away. I was going to get my car to go to another club, and suddenly there's a police car that stops and asks where I'm going. And before I could reply, they had the huge spotlight on, blinding me; I couldn't see who was talking to me. I told them that I was going to my car. And their response was, "Oh, because dressed like that, we thought you were going to the Douglas," meaning the Douglas psychiatric ward, and they drove away. It was not going to be the end of it for me. I got in my car and pursued them from St-Dominique all the way to Amherst, and blocked their way with my car, an LTD '76. They could not get any further; I walked over and said "What are your names?" They had removed their badges and said the number on the car would be sufficient if I had anything to complain about. So I took their word for it. I took the number down, and I made a complaint to the police. From the moment I made the complaint I was hassled, for six days in a row, by the police, including once when I was driving with my lawyer. We stopped for him to get some cigarettes. The police told him to go get a cigarette, that they had to speak to me alone. And my lawyer said, "No, if you have anything to say to her, you'll say it in front of me. And by the way I'm a lawyer." And from then on they never bothered me again. The case took a year to appear in court, and they had found two look-alikes, two policemen who looked like the ones who had called me those names. When I told them the number of the patrol car, they told me that there was no way to track down a car, to know whose it was, and that basically policemen were grabbing just any car that was in front of the station. They had no idea who had taken which car. Which to me was just amazing. Basically that's it ... that was the end of that, and they never bothered me after again. I never got anything for that except a lot of exposure in the newspaper article.

VN: This is a broad question, so answer it any way you'd like, but looking back—this is for an anthology that wants to look at the history of trans communities, trans people, trans lives in Canada—what's the single most important change you've seen for the situation in Montreal in the time that you've been involved?

MD: Of course, anyone who has seen both situations—back in the late seventies and today—would say "Wow, what progress!" But I don't think it is; there's a certain progress, in the sense that you don't get shot at or arrested or beaten up on every street corner, but there are all kinds of new problems that are even more frightening than the ones that we had in the late seventies. For instance, we didn't have crack in '78; we didn't have AIDS in '78. And today, you're given the false idea that you are accepted and tolerated—more tolerated than accepted, first of all. The fact that doctors give hormones away freely, that it doesn't seem to be a problem, but they still don't offer you a job. We still pretty much have to work as sex workers. Now it just has a different face: instead of working on a street corner, they work out of apartments or really badly concealed bordellos or massage parlours. So it's basically, I don't want to be vulgar, but it's basically "same shit, different smell." I guess it bothers people less today because it's hidden away. You call that progress? I don't think so. And maybe there's less violence because it's in closed environments, so it's less dangerous. But it's pretty much the same.

VN: Last question. What can people—especially people who weren't there, who are reading this interview and learning about the history of trans lives and communities in Montreal—what can they learn from that history?

MD: That we paved the way. I think we, and I'm talking about people who started in 1980, paved the way for whatever tolerance they have in their lives. With their open minds and the dialogues that they're able to have with health professionals or family members, we dedramatized what a transgendered life was all about. And I think that we should be heard for what we went through. Well, I guess I wasn't listening to many people myself when I was in my twenties, but I think it's important, you learn from a community to grow and move forward. You need to see the present but you also have to live with the past and try to not repeat the same mistakes. That's what I believe.

NOTES

1 KOX was part of Station C, a complex of two gay bars and one lesbian bar in Montreal in the 1980s that would only accept women on select ladies' nights.

2 "Black Eagle" makes reference to a specific leather bar. Leather bars typically cater to a particular demographic within gay communities who engage in leather lifestyles: bondage, discipline, sado-masochoistic (BDSM), and/or fetish practices. Feminist, queer, and trans scholars and activists are critical of the misogynist attitudes and behaviours of many within these groups. Such misogyny is reflected in bar dress codes, which often state clearly that feminine attire is prohibited. De Ville raises points concerning the impact of such exclusion on trans women and feminine-identified subjects.

3 Stella is a community-based sex worker's organization founded by sex workers in 1995. Guided by the principle of empowerment, Stella includes women, transsexuals, and transvestites in all levels of the organization to address the needs of sex worker communities.

Chapter 2 The Golden Age of Prostitution: One Woman's Personal Account of an Outdoor Brothel in Vancouver, 1975–1984[1]

Jamie Lee Hamilton

As someone who's been an on-again, off-again sex trade worker for most of my life, let me say how fortunate I feel to be here sharing with you a glimpse of my life story and perspective on the Vancouver sex trade. Many other voices are unable to be here today because they are deceased or "missing." We honour them and pay tribute to their lives by coming together at a conference of this nature. While I offer my individual story as someone who works in the sex trade, it is necessary that activists focus their efforts beyond prostitution in and of itself and toward the wider social implications of providing this vital service within heteronormative, neoliberal, and moralistic Canadian society.

I believe that my recollections of the "golden age of prostitution" in the West Side of Vancouver can inform contemporary strategies to gain social justice for sex workers. I speak to the ways that prostitutes played valuable roles in each other's lives, as well as to the ways that we contributed to the vitality of our neighbourhoods and communities. I also emphasize the need to gain widespread critical attention to how the criminalization of sex work contributes to class-based, racist, colonial, misogynist, transphobic, and sexualized violence.

From a very early age, society placed me in harm's way. I do not say this to place blame, but, rather, simply to state a fact. I had no choice regarding the poverty and the victimization that I faced throughout my young life; however, I did make a choice to escape the pain, suffering, humiliation, and hopelessness that often accompanies living in poverty. Uncertain about what life had in store for me, I chose to be involved in the sex trade as a young teenager. My involvement in this industry from then onward taught me significant lessons concerning how cruel society can be.

In the eyes of many, whether they be middle-class professionals and neighbourhood residents, radical feminist organizers or some trans individuals themselves, my choosing the sex trade as a means of escape was, and remains, questionable. I wish to premise my remarks by saying I don't wish to have my comments construed as mean-spirited, and I hope my thoughts will be taken as a direct, truthful, accurate, and enlightening account of my life as a sex trade worker over the past 38 years. Did I make the right choice? I believe that the fact that I'm alive and well and speaking to you today speaks directly to that question.

It cannot be denied that being involved in sex work at an early age was probably really disastrous for me. Nevertheless, being involved in prostitution should not, and does not, make me a bad person. Certainly being a sex worker should not make me a criminal. Even though sex workers engage in prostitution for many reasons—including, for some, survival—we *are not* agreeing to place ourselves in harm's way. In fact, let's be clear here: fear and injury come with being a sex worker, and yet, contrary to popular discourse, such harm does not usually come at the hands of a bad customer. Sadly, it comes at the hands of our own legal and justice systems, which I was brought up to believe were there to protect me and uphold my rights. It is old, tired, and outdated laws that have done the most damage to prostitutes.

My first encounter with the legal system and its failure to protect me happened when I was 17. As I was walking home alone one night after being out on the hustler track on Granville Street, a police officer drove alongside me and motioned me over. He had a dog barking in the back of his car. I was fearful, similar to what one feels when they may have a bad trick. He asked for my identification, which I provided. From my ID, he obviously knew I was 17, and he said I shouldn't really be out late at night. I relaxed, assuming he was there as a protector. Then he asked me get in the car, and I asked him why. He had some unusual reason, like he wanted to check my ID with the communication system they were using. He said he knew I was prostituting and that he was going to drive me to my home in the West End, a few blocks away. I said, offering no explanation, that I could walk home. He refused to accept this and insisted I get in the car. I ended up in Stanley Park with this vicious police dog in the back seat barking wildly. I realized I was in a locked car. I also knew officers carried deadly guns. Imagine how fearful I was as a teenager. I tried to shake that terror off but couldn't. He forced me to provide oral sex.

As I recovered from that traumatic experience, I became immersed in "whore-ganizing," as we called it then. The working stroll of the West End during the seventies and early eighties was a heady, glorious time that I refer to as "the golden age of prostitution" in Vancouver. The West End working stroll was not littered with the condoms or needles that the "not in my backyard" (NIMBY) types complain about today. The streets were lined instead with beautiful ho's and hustlers who brought a spirited way of life to the West End neighbourhood. The seniors loved us, and we would often carry their packages home for them after their shopping excursions. We were a strong, vibrant community back then. This is where we contributed to life through living, loving, working, and playing. This is where we were safe.

We built our community of sex workers and hustlers; call it a family clan. Even when we were not plying our trade, we walked the neighbourhood streets calling out greetings to others. We hung out together for protection, lived and shopped together, ate in the same restaurants, and, when we worked Davie Street, we took coffee breaks together at the Columbia Inn. The Columbia Inn is featured in the 1984 documentary *Hookers on Davie*,[2] a film that provides an accurate reflection of our lives at that time.

Our area of the West End could best be described as an outdoor brothel. This outdoor-brothel model provided us with safety in numbers and a healthy, humane, and respectful way to engage in prostitution. We often worked in pairs or in little groups, writing down licence plate numbers for our safety. We were always on the lookout for one another. If one of the girls didn't return quickly enough from a date, we knew exactly where she was. We would round up a couple of hustlers and trannies and venture off immediately to ensure one of our family members was safe.

We did not allow pimps on our West End streets. If they showed up with their girls, we booted them off. As Raigen D'Angelo, a former hooker on Davie, recalls: "Of course, no pimps would want a trans woman at that time. They weren't making any money off me.... So, no, I didn't see the fascination with pimping. I found it to be disgusting. If the pimps really wanted to make money off prostitution, [they could] put on a fucking dress and go out there and suck some cock!"

West End hotels, including the Tropicana, Greenbrier, Rembrandt, English Bay hotels, Beach Lodge, Robsonstrasse, Centennial Lodge, and others, were accommodating to us and warmly welcomed us; moreover, they provided us with safety and security. As one can imagine, hotels did a brisk business by welcoming our trade. We didn't need to turn dates in darkened cars or dangerous, unlit alleyways. In fact, such a thing was unheard of during this time.

Along with the employees of Saint Paul's Hospital, the sex-worker community was a strong economic driver for the West End. During the golden era, we had a significant presence in the community and many local businesses profited from this. It seemed like we were forever shopping and getting our hair or nails done, always spending significant sums of money on ourselves and our friends. We bought our favourite toys and books at Little Sister's Bookstore. A number of us rented penthouse apartments around the Davie commercial stroll, which doubled as our working apartments. We never went hungry, nor did we live homeless.

We held our money in accounts in the four national banks located in a four-block radius of Davie Street. The banks welcomed us. We were always exchanging American dollars, as many of our paying customers came from the US. We liked these customers because the exchange rate boosted our income. The Johns from the US were noted for their generosity. As Raigen states, "They would tip you beyond the price you agreed on. If you made them really happy, they showed their appreciation by tipping you well."

But soon, things would change. (Today there are no banks in this area of Davie Street. I find this fact interesting.) In a sign of things to come, just after my 21st birthday, sex workers suddenly began being targeted by the police. This was around the time of the Penthouse Nightclub closure. This became traumatizing. Police officers were driving our stroll, photographing us without our permission, following us, compiling information on where we lived, worked, what hotels we used. They even worked undercover in the bars and bathhouses where we and the hustlers hung out.

I had a distasteful experience on the night of Halloween. I was charged with soliciting and put in jail. I remember rogue police officers throwing firecrackers at me as they booked me. They thought it was funny, seeing me jump around, really frightened. Maybe they wanted to terrorize me, or perhaps they believed in their mixed-up minds that torturing me might set me on the right moral path. The police made me strip in front of them, they strip-searched me, and then they threw me in the male section of the jail. I got through that night because other working girls had also been targeted. We shared the cells and stayed up all night at "Motel Hell" sharing our stories. This was great, since being together provided us with some measure of comfort *and* a setting to politically organize. I bet the police and legislators never banked on us mobilizing forces in their dungy cells!

The next morning I had to appear before the judge. The night before I had called my mother, the one person in my life who I knew was always trying her best to protect me. As an Aboriginal woman, she was a victim of the residential school system and a strong fighter for justice. I remember the judge's stern words to this day: "We have to keep people like this off our streets." His words were a prophetic sign of things to come.

The end result of my night in the clinker was that I was restricted from being in a certain geographical area. I was not allowed to go home, since my home was located within the boundaries of this restricted area, which of course was the West End prostitution stroll. So much for having any rights. Having no choice, I was forced to relocate out of my community, just as other sex workers were. The law was being used selectively against us, an obvious abuse of power by the police and the state.

As a result, the West End became a political hotspot. During this period, two well-organized groups were agitating against us: Concerned Residents of the West End (CROWE) and Shame the Johns. CROWE was led by a very outspoken middle-class male, Gordon Price, who later became a right-wing politician. The group worked day and night to disrupt our business and our lives. They antagonized us beyond belief.

Unfortunately for us, the members of CROWE and the other group, Shame the Johns, had political friends. They lobbied the Attorney General, Brian Smith, to bring forward an injunction to prevent us from being in the West End. As Becki Ross[3] noted, the injunction was granted by one very moral judge, Chief Justice Allan McEachern, who bought the line that prostitutes were a nuisance to the "good citizens of the neighbourhood" and were disrupting their peace and quiet. It needs to be pointed out that, while these anti-sex-worker groups were quick to portray this section of the West End as residential, the neighbourhood also had a significant commercial identity. Sex workers plied their trade in the commercial part that had many 24-hour businesses operating seven days a week.

Although there were many feminist lawyers, none came forward to assist us during this turbulent time. Not even the BC Civil Liberties group took a stand for our rights. We were harshly and cruelly evicted from the West End. We fought back, but we were no match for the middle class, who believed our way of life to be offensive to their own morally righteous way. While we were making good money, our income was now going to pay the fees of lawyers whom we hired to take on our cases as the police went on a rampage, entrapping us and then charging us with solicitation. The resulting fines that were levied against us also took their toll. We needed to continue working to pay off those hefty fines that were leaving us cash-poor. During this time, in the early 1980s, I worked as a gender illusionist at BJ's show lounge.

We tried valiantly to fight back against the state. In those days, we didn't have financial advisors, but looking back now, perhaps the feminist movement could have assisted us with income advice, including ways to invest it. We organized protest marches and held our whore-ganizing meetings at the Columbia Inn with Sally DeQuadros and Marie Arrington. They mobilized us under the group Alliance for Safety of Prostitutes (ASP). We marched on Broadway in 1983 to fight the mayor's anti-soliciting bylaw and demonstrated in 1984 in the West End. We took to the street with signs calling then-mayor Mike Harcourt our pimp. The City was happy to collect the fines from our soliciting charges, but did not lift a finger to assist us in improving our lives. As we marched, we found it necessary to wear black masks to protect our identities to prevent even further charges.

After the West End evictions, I watched as the murder of sex workers first began. Prior to the injunction, no murders of sex workers had taken place. In 1990, Cheryl Ann Joe, a single Aboriginal woman with two young children, was brutally killed in the Downtown Eastside. I realized I couldn't stand by and allow anyone to be treated in the manner that Ms. Joe had been. I reignited the fire in my belly and began speaking out for the rights of drug-addicted Downtown Eastside sex trade workers.

Along with other sex workers, allies, and members of the queer community, we sought to bring public attention to the victimization and violence directed at the sex worker community. Our friends were disappearing, and we knew they were being killed. We were the first to charge that a serial murderer/predator was in our midst, while the police and the city were in complete denial. I remember us calling for a reward for his capture, and the mayor, Philip Owen, saying, "We will not fund a location service for hookers." This is what drove me, accompanied by a few brave friends, to dump the 67 pairs of stiletto shoes on the steps of City Hall as a symbolic plea to government officials and the media to address the fact that women were going "missing" from the city's Downtown Eastside. This act alone had the desired effect and brought us national and international attention.

After my civil disobedience at City Hall, I found a rather generous retired businessman and rented a space that was suitable for a drop-in centre. After the injunction, being a sex worker activist had its challenges. But thanks to wonderful brave women such as Dr. Becki Ross, whom I met through the queer community, and a few others, we started the Grandma's House drop-in, which operated under the legal name 9–5 Working Society. The 9–5 stood for the hours we were open—nine at night until five in the morning.

Our outspokenness for the rights of sex workers led to our group being targeted by the police and new CROWE-type vigilante groups such as OZ. OZ stood for "orange zone"; I guess they couldn't stand to use the word "red." This group, led by Cindy Chan-Piper, was just as bad as the CROWE and Shame the Johns groups had been a decade earlier.

In this sex worker battleground, politicians such as Lynne Kennedy, Dr. Hedy Fry, and Libby Davies stepped forward. Mayor Harcourt appeared beholden to his friends in CROWE and the West End Shame the Johns. Carole Walker, an influential leader of Shame the Johns, ran for municipal office under Mayor Harcourt's Civic Independent team and also ran with COPE in the 1988 municipal election alongside her colleague Libby Davies.

Like the 1980s, where we attempted to be heard and asked others to respect our place in society, the 1990s to the present has brought us another battle. This time we are in battle to prevent our deaths, to not allow our culture to be completely erased. I want to close by saying that the law cannot be used to target a segment of the population just because the righteous in society have moral concerns about how we live our lives. The sex worker movement is focused on ensuring that human respect and dignity remain intact in our society. It's a fight for equality, fairness, and justice, and *we are not going away.*

The outdoor-brothel concept, which we worked under in the West End, is an ideal model we should adopt. It produced no harm and allowed us to carry out our work in relatively respectful, safe, and harm-free conditions. History has shown us that there was little violence against sex workers during the golden era and before. Dr. John Lowman, a criminologist at Simon Fraser University, has conducted extensive research that shows little or no recorded violence against sex trade workers prior to 1978.[4]

Until victimization in our society has disappeared, until violence is stopped, until poverty has evaporated, and until sexual abuse has ended, we are always going to have prostitution. It is often the only option for survival. Using selective enforcement measures to address and decrease prostitution has not worked. Treating prostitution as a nuisance or a crime is *not* a solution.

As an activist, sex worker, researcher, advocate, and community leader, I say criminalizing sex workers only feeds the distorted minds of men who come down to our strolls perpetuating and inflicting further harm onto us. This approach of portraying prostitution as a nuisance ensures that the killing fields remain ripe and that sex workers become easy pickings.

Criminalizing sex workers leads directly to prostitution genocide. In fact, since the charges were laid against Willie Pickton, another 26 women have gone missing or been murdered in the course of carrying out their work, and I can assure you that Mr. Pickton didn't murder those 26 women.

Reducing and eliminating harm against sex trade workers has to be made a priority. We cannot allow class, social status, or extreme feminist ideologies to divide us or influence us into not making the necessary fundamental shifts needed to reduce harm to sex workers.

Moreover, we must not allow the misguided who have cloaked themselves as our modern-day helpers to distort the prostitution issue. Calling it "rape" or "sexual violence" as the Vancouver Rape Relief (VRR) organization does, and then claiming as they do that sex workers are acquiescing to rape and being silenced by the exchange of money, is mortifying. Actually this statement alone perpetuates hate against sex trade workers, and those who espouse this line should be charged with hate crimes.

I suggest that sex workers deserve far better in life than extreme ideology. I ask you all, especially for those who are no longer here with us, to consider allying with us to decriminalize prostitution. I ask you to join other progressive pragmatic women and men in rejecting the distorted thinking that leads local groups like VRR to propagate the abolishment of prostitution. VRR and other groups claim that welfare is a solution to prostitution, but is it? Everyone I have ever known who has had to rely on welfare, myself included, finds it demeaning and dehumanizing. All the women who wound up on the pig farm were economically disadvantaged *by* the system. Women on welfare couldn't survive in that system and found themselves out on the streets in order to survive.

All attempts to abolish prostitution, and there have been many, have failed miserably. In fact, this approach has led directly to our deaths. Let's raise that bar together, my friends. Let's say "No more violence against sex trade workers." I know we can do it.

NOTES

1 This chapter is based on a conference presentation I delivered at the EVA BC/FREDA Centre in Vancouver, BC, November 9, 2012.

2 *Working Davie Street* [original documentary title, *Hookers on Davie*]. (1984, April 5). Dir. Janis Cole and Holly Dale. Spectrum Films. Retrieved from www.imdb.com/title/tt0087423/

3 Dr. Becki Ross is an associate professor at the University of British Columbia. For a portion of her research on this subject, see Ross, B. (2010). Sex and (evacuation from) the city: The moral and legal regulation of sex workers in Vancouver's West End, 1975–1985. *Sexualities, 13*(2), 197–218.

4 Please see Lowman, J. (1986). Street prostitution in Vancouver: Notes on the genesis of a social problem. *Canadian Journal of Criminology, 28*(1), 1–16; and Lowman, J. (1990). Notions of formal equality before the law: The experience of street prostitutes and their customers. *Journal of Human Justice, 1*(2), 55–76.

Chapter 3 Rupert Raj and the Rise of Transsexual Consumer Activism in the 1980s

Nick Matte

Ever since transitioning in the early 1970s, Rupert Raj has devoted his life to developing transsexual communities, promoting transsexuals' interests, and making trans people more socially acceptable. Raj has lived and worked in Ottawa, Calgary, Vancouver, and Toronto. As a visible trans activist, he developed community and support through years of effort, publishing a widely circulating newsletter called *Metamorphosis* and providing uplifting mottos such as "Peer-Experienced is the best counsellor" and "It takes one to know one." He has made a lasting impact on Canadian and international trans organizing, working with activists and interested groups around the world.

A great deal of scholarship has discussed the emergence of a transgender social movement in North America and elsewhere during the second half of the twentieth century (Stryker, 2008; Hill, 2011; Smith, 2010; Meyerowitz, 2002). This chapter looks specifically at Raj's work during the 1980s and argues that one of the key strategies employed by trans activists like Raj during that decade was to conceptualize transsexuals as a medical/patient-consumer group (Stryker, 1999; Denny, 2013). By representing transsexuals as a consumer group, Raj was able to critique existing medical research and services, as well as act on behalf of trans people's interests (Raj, 1979).[1] In doing so, Raj and other activists contributed a more holistic sense of how trans people's issues extended beyond those defined by medical experts and other institutional figures. Raj also built community and community resources to combat the isolation facing many trans people. I therefore argue that consumer identity became an essential factor for creating trans community and for improving social situations to better suit the realities of being a transsexual in the 1980s.

One of the first times Raj appeared in a trans publication was in 1978, to advocate for another trans person, Inge Stephens. In an article detailing Stephens' social and legal battles, he told readers of the trans publication *Gender Review*, "I have personally come to know and admire Inge for the naturally feminine, physically attractive and feminine woman she is" (Raj, 1978a). Overt and numerous references to Stephens' femininity were particularly important because her gender expression was under public dispute; she had been fired from her teaching job after changing sex. Like many middle-class transsexuals at the time, Stephens was counting on having the cost of her medical services paid for through her health care insurance, but insurance companies were beginning to object to paying for such treatments. Raj, who went by the name Nicholas Ghosh, described Stephens, of Montreal, Quebec, as both the director of the Association of Transsexuals of Quebec (ATQ) and as a fellow board member of *Gender*

Review. He used her story to construct a narrative that linked transsexuals through shared struggles, a narrative that seemed to transcend national boundaries. The article highlighted similarities facing transsexuals in Canada and the US, particularly in relation to social prejudice and the lack of legal protections against discrimination, and the personal significance and impact of medical authorities' diagnoses and recommendations.

The *Gender Review* article relayed the tribulations Stephens had faced from the perspective of the trans person in question, and objected to the inability of medical professionals to reach consensus or accurately diagnose and treat gender dysphoria and transsexualism. It told readers that between 1972 and 1978 Stephens had been examined and assessed by 18 different professionals, with one half diagnosing her as transsexual and the other half stating that she was not. The article referred to her situation as "a diagnostic split that would certainly frustrate and depress any candidate for TS reassignment!" (Raj, 1978b, p. 18). Characterizing her experience as typical of transsexuals, the article went on to tell readers that

> the Stephens' case indicate[s] the currently existing diagnostic dilemma confronting those psychiatrists and psychologists who must assess their so-called TS patients as "truly transsexual," on the one hand—or—in diametric opposition, "delusively psychotic," or "cowardly homosexual" (closet/cop-out gay) on the other. Such a diagnostic diameter ... has been used extensively to measure the validity of Ms. Inge Stephen's ... repeated claim that she is a woman within a genetically male but (after castration) hormonally-female body. (p. 18)

In the context of a supportive trans community, *Gender Review* provided public validation of Stephens' gender expression, especially important as an oppositional response to a wider social context in which Stephens' status as a transsexual woman was being denied.

Raj's early experience working on *Gender Review* with other leaders in the emerging trans community, such as Inge Stephens and Susan Huxford, came at a time in his life when he was also emerging as a major Canadian trans activist. In the coming years, he would work with numerous subgroups of people, locally, regionally, nationally and internationally, especially transsexual prisoners and transsexual men.

In 1981, after several years of working in mixed trans groups, Raj began his own publication, *Metamorphosis*, to focus specifically on the needs and interests of transsexual men. As a transsexual man himself, he had personal experience with many of the problems and situations common to female-to-male transsexuals who sought diagnosis and medical transition. At that time, it was primarily specialist researchers at formal gender identity clinics, such as the Clarke Institute for Psychiatry in Toronto, who oversaw the transitions of transsexuals (Steiner, 1985; Namaste, 2000). To transition, it was necessary to undergo a complex series of medical evaluations, often including psychiatric hospitalizations, for the purpose of being observed by the clinical researchers who would determine whether or not to approve the patient for hormone therapy or sex reassignment surgeries. The Clarke served all of Ontario, as well as most of Canada. Long waiting lists made it difficult to even begin the process. Also, because clinical research on transsexualism had focused primarily on transsexual women and transvestites, transsexual men were often at a loss dealing with clinical inadequacies, though this sometimes worked to their advantage.

In the early 1980s, Raj focused his efforts on building up a reputation for *Metamorphosis* and expanding its readership so that both transsexual men and their health care providers would know about, benefit from, and contribute to it. At that time, the notion that transsexuals could and should play a role in their own health care was progressive and even somewhat radical. Raj worked to develop connections with supportive clinicians and researchers to establish legitimacy for trans men's experiences so that they would become more aware of the specific issues trans men were facing. Raj built on the work of Reed Erickson, another transsexual man working on behalf of trans people, who had established the Erickson Educational Foundation (EEF) almost 20 years earlier, in 1964. Since then, the EEF had funded numerous medical research and clinical projects, including providing the groundwork for many of the gender identity clinics. Erickson, however, did not represent himself as a transsexual, nor did he speak as, or on behalf of, transsexuals. Erickson was part of an earlier generation of transsexuals whose primary aim was to integrate invisibly into mainstream society. As a millionaire philanthropist, his primary contribution had been to provide funding and guidance to develop the field of transsexual research. Raj's contributions differed, not only in that he lacked Erickson's economic power, but also in that he proudly announced himself as a transsexual man and explicitly valued the process of establishing interpersonal connections with other trans people, thereby establishing and nurturing trans communities through his efforts.

In April of 1983 Raj sent Erickson a promotional and information package soliciting his support. One of the documents Raj sent Erickson was a form letter clearly written to other trans men, asking them to "help me to help you and your 'fellow brothers' work 'towards male integrity'" (the MMRF motto) by becoming members of his organization, the Metamorphosis Medical Research Foundation (MMRF). For $25 a year, members would receive the *Metamorphosis* newsletter, a 15-page information packet, and a Confidential Contacts Directory listing female-to-male members. He also promised members "immeasurable service: information, referrals, news, communication, peer-support, literature on passing, male sex hormones and female-to-male transsexualism, personal(ized) correspondence, bimonthly newsletter, bibliography, membership card and certificate." Like other trans groups during this period, MMRF offered the opportunity for social contact and peer support, but its specific focus on trans men was highly unique and therefore set it apart as an invaluable resource to this "minority within a minority."

From early on, Raj presented himself and his foundation as both personal and professional. In the package of materials he sent Erickson, for example, was a promotional pamphlet called "Introducing Rupert Raj," which described his accomplishments, personal background, and social and professional work. The pamphlet was double-sided, and had three columns. The front page featured a headshot of a very professional-looking, moustachioed Raj wearing a suit and tie and described him as "a gender-dysphoric man (a post-operative female-to-male transsexual) who "peer-counseled transsexuals and … educated professionals, students and the lay public on transsexualism and the 'gender dysphoria syndrome.'" The pamphlet introduced Raj as someone with a multicultural heritage who "entertains no racial, ethnic, social or sexual prejudice." Perhaps most importantly, he described himself as a "Professional Transsexual Researcher, Educator and Counselor." He listed numerous professional associations and accomplishments, including affiliation with the ACLU of Southern California TS Rights Committee, the Foundation for the Advancement of Canadian Transsexuals (FACT), the Gateway Gender Alliance (as a Professional Associate), the Harry Benjamin International

Gender Dysphoria Association (HBIGDA), and the Society for Scientific Study of Sexuality (SSSS). The pamphlet also listed a number of Raj's media appearances on television and radio programs in Ontario. Raj's position as a professional service provider and a transsexual exemplified the changing relationship between trans people and the medical/counselling sector, and he was at the forefront of a new generation of transsexuals who devoted themselves to professional development, education through media activism, and peer counselling.

In addition to his efforts to establish community, Raj also engaged in what was likely one of the first attempts at community-based research in the trans community. He designed and circulated a five-page "Confidential Research Questionnaire," hoping to acquire specific information about trans men that would be valuable to researchers and trans men alike. He told potential respondents that his two primary purposes in circulating the questionnaire were to gain "general research (information and statistics) on the female-to-male-transsexual population" and "specific research (background information and particular circumstances) on the individual (potential) member/subscriber—in order to better facilitate the servicing of his special needs." Some of the questions mirrored classic psychiatric or counselling questions, such as "At what age did you first identify with males? Begin cross-dressing? Realize you were transsexual? Begin your transsexual transition? Begin hormone therapy? Who were your male role-models in childhood? In adolescence? In adulthood?" The questionnaire also included a whole page of medical questions, such as whether or not the respondent had experienced any specific "negative reactions to the male hormones" such as acne, hot flashes, or cirrhosis. In addition to asking questions that medical practitioners might ask, however, Raj also asked about trans men's experiences accessing health care. If the respondent had been a patient at a gender clinic, for example, Raj wanted to know whether the clinic "met all of their needs and if not, which ones?"

Raj's questionnaire was clearly designed to achieve a well-balanced profile of trans men's personal and social lives, as many questions also asked respondents about their social and cultural associations and experiences. It asked about their religious affiliations and communities and whether they associated with other females-to-males, males-to-females, transvestites, lesbians, gay men, heterosexual men, heterosexual women, whether they frequented gay, lesbian, or "straight" clubs, or were members of transsexual, homosexual, lesbian, or heterosexual organizations, groups, or societies. It asked what their opinions or attitudes were toward various groups.

Finally, Raj used the questionnaire to solicit messages that would provide peer support. He asked them what they thought the organization's greatest contribution could be and asked, "Do you have a message re: transsexualism/sex reassignment for other transsexuals? For treating/researching professionals? For the lay public? For your family? For your friends?" Raj sought to take the pulse of a relatively invisible minority of which he himself was part.

By the mid-1980s, MMRF was doing more than producing a publication; it was also providing an important social space for trans men and their friends and supporters to gather and share information and experiences, a precursor to the large conferences that emerged in the late 1980s. Much like transvestite publications had done in the 1960s, he invited readers to report on their success. Raj regularly hosted Valentine's and birthday parties and other gatherings in his home. In 1986, he planned a convention to coincide with the annual general meeting of the MMRF. Raj told readers that the gathering, at the Bond Place Hotel in Toronto, would feature a cash bar and dinner on the Saturday evening and a tour of Toronto on the Sunday. He expected 20 to 30 people to attend, including four to seven couples from the US, and he had invited several leading trans activists to come and speak about their "organizational activities and support services." Raj not only built community, he also created social space for interpersonal support and for trans people to create consumer-style activism. His events demonstrate the significant overlap between socializing and organizing that was characteristic of trans communities and groups in the 1980s.

Networking remained consistently essential to Raj's work, and by the late 1980s, he was pushing for more formal networks that made better use of trans people's contributions and efforts. In an article he wrote for *Transsexual Voice*, a trans publication out of Georgia, Raj told readers that "there is a tremendous need to tighten up the TS-TV network and to link together—for, there are now more TSs, TVs, TGs and GDs who need help and support than there are resources available" (Raj, 1985a, p. 1). Recognizing the significant growth of trans groups in Canada, the US, the UK, and Australia, Raj wrote: "This need to formalize a co-operative network (comprising professional, para-professional, lay, TS, TG, TV and other persons) is quite obvious" (ibid.), telling a story that underscored gaps in existing resources. Raj told readers that recently, as a result of his networking, he had been able to make a trans support group in Wisconsin aware of a local trans positive therapist who was interested in working with and supporting trans people. Raj's point was that at that time there was no formal way for them to locate one another, other than through him. He called the gaps in professional networking glaring, and in closing, he wrote: "Come on peers and professionals, let's link together and network now!" (ibid., p. 10). His solution, to create closer relationships between trans people and service providers, reflected the growth of a co-operative consumer-style activism that sought to address the needs of trans people by working with the professionals who studied and treated them.

Raj also used *Metamorphosis* to develop space for consumer-style activism by publishing reviews of new books and identifying which experts seemed to be truly advancing trans people's interests. For example, in 1985 Raj published a review of the recently released book *Gender Dysphoria*, an academic text compiled by experts at the Clarke Institute of Psychiatry (Hudson, 1985). The reviewer wrote as a trans person, however, and critiqued the work for its failure to consider the lived complexity of trans people's experiences. The review told *Metamorphosis* readers that "throughout transsexuals are described as having a disorder, and the major concern is to classify such disorders and to determine their etiology.... [I]f the Clarkists were to leave their ivory tower, they might find out something" (ibid., p. 3). It nevertheless recommended that all transsexuals read the book because it summarized academic thought and it could "be usefully compared to the real-life research that most of us are doing" (ibid., p. 3). As such, the review validated and recognized many trans people's frustrations with the gender clinic research model as being out of touch with their realities, as well as their efforts to negotiate the world as trans people.

Raj also printed a series of reviews that emphasized the difference between two primary groups of researchers: those who had trans people's interests in mind and those whose own interests created additional problems for trans people. In 1985, when Leslie Lothstein published the first clinical research text focusing on trans men, a book called *Female-to-Male Transsexualism*, many trans people and experts recognized that Lothstein's psychoanalytic interpretation had extremely problematic implications (Raj, 1982, 1984). Lou Sullivan, a trans man activist in San Francisco, reviewed the text for *Metamorphosis* readers, pointing out its factual inaccuracies and the fact that Lothstein was convinced that female-to-male transsexuals were lesbians in denial. Sullivan called Lothstein's book "dangerous and regressive," and compared it to the "early psychological theories of 'what makes a boy homosexual,'" which he noted had been "tossed away years ago" (Sullivan, 1984, n.p.). Comparing Lothstein's current theories about transsexualism to discredited theories about homosexuality, Sullivan, like Raj, sought to politicize and mobilize trans people against such experts. Sullivan wrote that it was unfortunate, however, that "transsexuals do not have the strength in numbers to demand that this repression STOP now" (ibid., n.p.). Sullivan's review had its intended effect, and readers responded with outrage about the book in the following issue of *Metamorphosis.*

The emergence of trans consumer activism wasn't simply oppositional, however. Raj also reprinted reviews from professional journals by experts who were clearly working with trans people's interests in mind and were also critical of Lothstein's work. In a review originally published in *Contemporary Psychology*, for example, Vern Bullough wrote that readers should be aware of "Lothstein's bias," and chastised Lothstein's generalizing about the instability of female-to-male transsexuals based on a sample group clearly suffering from issues more broadly associated with people of lower socio-economic status (Bullough, 1985, p. 3). Similarly, Raj reprinted another review of Lothstein's work from the Harry Benjamin International Gender Dysphoria Association's newsletter, by its president, Paul Walker. Walker warned readers that this book was "potentially damaging if read by patients or their parents—as they have and will." He also objected to the fact that Lothstein called sex reassignment surgery "experimental" without defining that term, saying that it was irresponsible to do so since his claim had "serious legal, economic and ethical implications" (Walker, 1985, p. 4). By providing such reviews for *Metamorphosis* readers, Raj drew a clear distinction between professional allies in the medical field and those researchers who saw transsexuals as fundamentally pathological examples of a mental illness.

By providing specific information relevant to trans men and publicizing the ways in which their situation was unique at that time, Raj was beginning to address the well-recognized fact that trans men, or female-to-male transsexuals, were an under-studied and underserved population. Despite Bullough and Walker's criticisms, for example, they both recognized that Lothstein's text was still the most significant study on female-to-male transsexuals to date. Sullivan, by contrast, had been compiling and circulating his own book, called *Information for the Female-to-Male Cross-dresser and Transsexual*, designed specifically for trans men. It discussed hormones, clothing, "passing," and dealing with medical professionals, among other topics (Sullivan, 1986). *Metamorphosis*, with its specific focus on trans men, printed a review of Sullivan's book that highlighted insufficient medical study as a specifically gendered issue. The reviewer wrote that Sullivan was beginning to rectify the medical bias toward interpreting transsexualism as a male-to-female phenomenon. As an example "of the distance in knowledge that lies between women who want to become men and men who want to become women," the review cited "the attitudes of most surgeons," who essentially discounted the possibility of serving the needs of female-to-male transsexuals (Stuart, 1986).

Recognizing a lack of sufficient research or medical services to meet the needs of trans men, activists like Raj, Sullivan, and others had devoted themselves to an important type of transsexual consumer activism: compiling and distributing useful information. From early on, Raj simultaneously sought out resources specifically for trans men while expanding his network. It was often difficult for trans men to locate surgeons with the expertise or the willingness to work with them, even amongst those specializing in sex reassignment surgeries. He asked his professional advisors and correspondents to help him identify surgeons who would operate on female-to-male transsexuals. In a letter he circulated widely, Raj asked for the names and addresses of "plastic surgeons anywhere in the world performing mastectomy, hysterectomy and/or phalloplasty on female-to-male transsexuals" so that he could add their contact information to his current list of 16. The Erickson Educational Foundation had been compiling a similar resource since surgeons first began performing sex reassignment surgeries in the United States, but the EEF did not publish its list, nor did it create a list specifically for trans men (Devor & Matte, 2007). As a result, it was often difficult for trans men to locate surgeons with the experience, expertise, or willingness to work with them, even amongst those specializing in sex reassignment surgeries.

For the many trans men who could not obtain phalloplasty, Raj also collected and circulated information about "urinary assistive devices" (UADs). He asked readers to submit their comments on Sanifem, for example, a device designed to allow women to urinate while standing in situations where using a toilet was not feasible. The company that sold Sanifem was also open to niche markets, as Raj discovered when he wrote to the company on behalf of trans men. Neither Raj nor *Metamorphosis* readers, however, thought that the device met their needs, as they felt it was not discreet enough to use at a public urinal.

Holding out hope that trans men could function in the absence of access to phalloplasty, Raj also worked to develop a prosthetic device appropriate for trans men's genital needs. Raj told readers that he had contacted a man in Brooklyn, New York, whom he described as a manufacturer of "solid, silicone rubber dildoes—mostly used by lesbians—which can be held in the hand or used with a harness during sexual relations" (Raj, 1985b). When Raj inquired about producing a customized device for trans men that could be used both for sexual relations and urination (the two primary criteria of interest to most trans men), he was told that an experimental prototype model could be designed for him to critique. While Raj voiced some concern that Canada Customs might not allow the device to be shipped through the mail, he promised readers he would keep them apprised. He later reported that the device was, unfortunately, not sturdy enough to suit their purposes (ibid). The effort nevertheless indicates the extent to which Raj not only worked to try to address trans men's needs, but also considered trans men to be a consumer group both within and beyond the medical arena.

Although few surgeons were working on developing phalloplasty techniques, Raj made a point of ensuring that readers and local trans men in Toronto had the best information on the latest techniques. Upon learning of microsurgeon Dr. David A. Gilbert's work, Raj invited him to become a professional consultant to his organization and come to Toronto to share his slide show with members. Raj also hosted a gathering in his home for six trans men and their partners, at which Dr. Leonard Hughes, a surgical resident of a cancer clinic in Buffalo, New York, presented a slide show of penis reconstruction for men who required it after various genitourinary cancers (Raj, 1986). At that time, trans men hoped that plastic surgeons might be able to use similar phalloplastic techniques on trans men as they could on non-trans men (Raj, 1983). In fact, Raj initially announced that his group would represent both transsexual men and men with "other genital deficiencies," though such men never seemed to become involved and it became clear that they were really only theoretically included.

By the late 1980s, clinics and surgeons were shifting their approach, recognizing transsexuals as a significant consumer group and trans men as a marginalized subset of that group. The fact that doctors had begun attending organized gatherings where trans people investigated their services and considered becoming patients reflected a shift in the stance of medical professionals from that of patriarchal expert to one of specialized service provider. This shift complemented the rise of trans organizations that represented trans groups as consumers and consumer activists, reflecting the fact that individual transsexuals no longer thought of themselves as simply patients. In an article on their experience performing phalloplasty in Singapore, Professor Ratnam of the National University of Singapore explained in great detail to Raj and *Metamorphosis* readers how they performed the surgery, what challenges they had encountered, and how they hoped to resolve such issues (Ratnam, 1986). By the late 1980s, when Raj published detailed information about the sex reassignment services offered at various clinics around the world, the information came directly from the clinics' promotional materials, a far cry from the earlier days of patients having to fight waiting lists and restrictive criteria to access sex reassignment surgeries (Raj, 1987a).

While Raj used *Metamorphosis* to promote the work of surgeons who were in the process of trying to perfect phalloplasty, he carefully represented consumers' interests by warning of the serious implications and possible negative outcomes they could experience if they underwent such surgery. In an article called "Ten Years Later: A Transsexual Looks Back," a trans man using the pseudonym of "Victor" described his "phallo nightmare" as a "horror story" (Victor, 1986). Stories like Victor's provided *Metamorphosis* readers with first-hand accounts of the potential pitfalls associated with transitioning and many of the details that physicians would likely gloss over or fail to account for in their descriptions. As such, they provided a significant arena for trans men to develop a consumer perspective, a precursor to some of today's open, online surgical databases of trans people's experiences as patients.[2]

By the end of the 1980s, Raj had contributed a decade of service to trans people, working hard to build communities and resources, and to politicize the relationship between trans people and health professionals so that it could become more co-operative and health-oriented rather than paternalistic and pathology-oriented. In an article titled "Healing the Breach: GD Consumers, Professional Providers Working Together," which Raj circulated widely and which was printed in numerous trans publications, he outlined his desire to see more action, especially on the side of medical professionals. He outlined specific recommendations, such as reinstating the "consumer advocate" position on the HBIGDA Board of Directors to serve as a representative of trans people's interests. He also advocated "lobbying together to effect needed reform of legal and administrative policies that currently preclude equal rights and opportunities to transsexuals" (Raj, 1987b). Despite the fact that many professional allies involved with HBIGDA supported such efforts, Raj told readers that he had received no reply when he inquired about the consumer advocate position, which had originally been held by trans man activist and counsellor Jude Patton in the 1970s but later eliminated. Trans activists in the late 1980s reported a similar lack of interest on the part of professionals around North America, except when they were soliciting patients. For example, trans activist Stephen Parent noted that several members of the New England trans community were interested in working with their local gender identity clinic to host HBIGDA's ninth International Conference, but that the clinic had no interest in working with them. By contrast, Raj reported that several trans communities had successfully co-hosted significant events with gender clinics in London, Toronto, and Philadelphia, but noted that, "in each instance, it was the consumer group who took the initiative to approach the professional sector."

Raj devoted the last few years of the 1980s to honouring and publicizing the work of his fellow trans activists, many of whom were struggling, unappreciated, to continue their work. Raj compiled a series of "tribute articles" about Phoebe Smith, Joanna Clark, Jude Patton, Georgia Saunders, Lou Sullivan, Judy Cousins, and Susan Huxford, all trans people whom readers may not have realized had been working on their behalf (Raj, 1988a, 1988b, 1988c, 1988d). Raj also similarly praised medical allies, but it was trans people's devotion to what Raj called "the community cause" that was particularly striking. In part, Raj outlined the work of community activists because of a disturbing trend he was seeing, which he made explicit in an article called "Burn-Out: Unsung Heroes and Heroines in the Transgender World" (Raj, 1987c, 1988e). Raj expressed concern that, of the few individuals carrying the burden of working on behalf of trans people, too many were suffering personally. For himself, he wrote that he had "been serving the transgender community ... for the past 15 ½ years without any form of monetary remuneration whatsoever!" Furthermore, he said, his "pre-occupation with the welfare of the transgender community is the reason why today I am without a paying career or a steady source of income." He told readers that he wasn't yet ready to resign, but that it was "now up to you, dear Sisters and Brothers, to work together—to take up the torch and to keep the flame of faith burning bright ... in solidarity" (Raj, 1987b). Indeed, he had assigned as the motto for that issue a slogan reminiscent of the US civil rights movement: "Brothers and Sisters—working together, we shall overcome." In a response piece, Joanna Clark echoed his sentiments, and said, "I don't know how [you] do it" given that trans activists had "NEVER gained the financial support to make a real impact" (Clark, 1988).

Eventually, Raj announced that he had decided to curtail his efforts, telling readers that he wanted to continue publishing *Metamorphosis*, but he also wanted to stop devoting all his time, energy, and finances to providing free peer support to others. Thus, he made a formal, public proclamation: "My relationships to members of the TS community will henceforth be of a professional nature" (Raj, 1988e). It took an entire decade for Raj to re-emerge as a visible, public figure in the trans community. By the year 2000, he was in clinical practice and working on a master's degree in Clinical Psychology. Since then, he has been an outspoken proponent of trans people's interests and his contributions have been recognized and honoured with numerous community awards. Few people are aware, however, that during the 1980s he was one of the first major international trans activists to create and sustain local, national, and international trans communities. Promoting trans people's interests as a consumer group was one of his key strategies, alongside networking and institutional advocacy. This chapter has only briefly touched on the extent of his work, in the hopes that future research will continue to investigate and understand the emergence and roots of trans activism and communities in Canada, North America, and globally.

NOTES

1 See Judith A. Cook and Jessica A. Jonikas, "Self-Determination Among Mental Health Consumers/ Survivors" (2002) for another analysis that blends agency and consumerism.

2 Up until 2009, a website called Transster provided extensive online references to surgical options based on information uploaded by patients; currently, more general sites (such as http://www.onlinemedicalt-ourism.com) provide more limited information.

REFERENCES

Bullough, V. (1985). Surgery is not necessarily the answer: A review of Leslie Martin Lothstein's *Female-to-Male Transsexualism*. *Metamorphosis, 4*(1), 3.

Clark, J. (1988). Burn out and the gender worker. *Gender Serve Newsletter, 4*, 1, 4.

Cook, J.A., & Jonikas, J.A. (2002). Self-determination among mental health consumers/survivors. *Journal of Disability Policy Studies, 13*(2), 88–96.

Denny, D. (2013). *Current concepts in transgender identity*. New York: Routledge.

Devor, A., & Matte, N. (2007). Building a better world for transpeople: Reed Erickson and the Erickson Educational Foundation. *International Journal of Transgenderism, 10*(1), 47–68.

Hill, R.S. (2011). "We share a sacred secret": Gender, domesticity, and containment in transvestia's histories and letters from crossdressers and their wives. *Journal of Social History, 44*(3), 729–750.

Hudson, D. (1985). Gender dysphoria: Development, research, management. *Metamorphosis, 4*(4), 3–4.

Meyerowitz, J. (2002). *How sex changed: A history of transsexuality in the United States*. Cambridge: Harvard University Press.

Namaste, V. (2000). *Invisible lives: The erasure of transsexual and transgendered people*. Chicago: University of Chicago Press.

Raj, R. (1978a). Transsexual oppression (continued). *Gender Review, 2*(September).

Raj, R. (1978b). Diagnostic diameter: TS identity—Delusion or reality? *Gender Review, 3*(December).

Raj, R. (1979). Gender dysphoria: Opposing perspectives. *Gender Review, 5*, 6

Raj, R. (1982). First F-M textbook! *Metamorphosis, 1*(3), 1.

Raj, R. (1983). Two penile restorations. *Metamorphosis, 2*(1), 1, 10.

Raj, R. (1984). Female to male transsexualism. *Gender Review, 3*(1), 4–5.

Raj, R. (1985a). The need to network. *Metamorphosis, 3*(5), 1–10.

Raj, R. (1985b). Penile prosthesis. *Metamorphosis, 3*(5), 8.

Raj, R. (1986). Annual general meeting. *Metamorphosis, 5*(2), 3.

Raj, R. (1987a). Gender identity programs. *Metamorphosis, 6*(1–2), 21–24.

Raj, R. (1987b). Healing the breach: GD consumers, professional providers working together. *Metamorphosis, 6*(1–2), 9.

Raj, R. (1987c). Burn out: Unsung heroes and heroines in the transgender world. *The Transsexual Voice*, 13–14.

Raj, R. (1988a). Tribute to Sister Mary Elizabeth. *Metamorphosis, 7*(1), 6–7.

Raj, R. (1988b). The "Gender Worker Award." *Gender Networker, 1*(2), 2–3.

Raj, R. (1988c). Tribute to Judith V. Cousins. *Gender Networker, 1*(1), 4.

Raj, R. (1988d). Tribute to Louis Graydon Sullivan. *Gender Networker, 1*(1), 8–9.

Raj, R. (1988e). Burn out and the gender worker. *Gender Serve Newsletter, 4*, 1, 4.

Ratnam, S.S. (1986). F-M sex reassignment surgery in Singapore. *Metamorphosis, 5*(2), 6–7.

Smith, B.D. (2010). "Yours in liberation": Lou Sullivan and the construction of FTM identity. Unpublished doctoral dissertation. University of Wisconsin-Milwaukee.

Steiner, B. (Ed.). (1985). *Gender dysphoria: Development, research, management.* New York: Plenum Press.

Stryker, S. (1999). Portrait of a transfag drag hag as a young man: The activist career of Louis G. Sullivan. In K. More and S. Whittle (Eds.), *Reclaiming genders: Transsexual grammars at the fin de siècle* (pp. 62–82). London: Cassell.

Stryker, S. (2008). *Transgender history.* Berkeley, CA: Seal Press.

Stuart, K.E. (1986). Book review: *Information for the female-to-male cross-dresser and transsexual. Metamorphosis, 5*(1), 11.

Sullivan, L. (1984). Untitled. *Metamorphosis, 3*(6), n.p.

Sullivan, L. (1986). *Information for the female-to-male cross-dresser and transsexual.* San Francisco: Zamot Graphic Productions.

"Victor." (1986). Ten years later, a transsexual looks back. *Metamorphosis, 5*(1), 14–15.

Walker, P. (1985). Book review: *Female-to-male transsexualism. Metamorphosis, 4*(1).

Chapter 4 Gender Strike! It's an Offence

Elizabeth "Raven" James

I was born on Sunday, February 27, at 6 a.m., during the coldest and darkest time of the year in Toronto; there was no telling then that my life would be the hard struggle that it has turned out to be. When I entered the world, my parents were happy—it seemed that they had given birth to a healthy baby boy. For that is the first question that people ask when a child is born: Is it a boy or a girl?

When I was a teenager, I was asked to leave the family home after I came forward about being transsexual. Needless to say, my parents and I, to this day, are not close. Despite their shortcomings, my parents did teach me how to get by in life and survive through difficult times—for that, I thank them.

For centuries, Aboriginal peoples have orally passed down traditions and information for future generations. The cultural and spiritual destruction brought to Turtle Island by the Canadian residential school system had, and continues to have, a negative impact on First Nations people. Both of my parents were victims of a residential school system that was designed to strip them of their language, culture, and traditional teachings and "civilize" them with Christianity. One of the many consequences was the devaluing of gender-variant people in Aboriginal societies. This was a major factor in my biological parents' failure to raise me properly and likely a contributing factor in their substance abuse and "hands-on" parental style. I do not hold my parents responsible for my crimes, but neither do I forgive them for their bad parenting. There was a time when revenge was all I could think about. Hatred consumed my soul, and I inflicted my rage upon the wrong people. Of course, I paid the price for my actions, and I still do to this day. My life has been less than conventional, and I want to share parts of it in the hope that someone, somewhere, might get something out of this recounting.

Transsexualism can be a difficult thing to deal with. This is the story of how I eventually reached my metaphorical castle in the sky, which, for me, means a goal or a dream that motivates you but is not quite attainable. Growing up, I was the person least likely to do hard drugs. I had the best of intentions—I was going to live a normal life, go to college, get a good-paying job, raise a family, and live a good life. Other people did narcotics, not me! Unfortunately, in my struggle to deal with being transsexual and two-spirited, I got into cocaine and ended up addicted to heroin. After being kicked out of my home, I started hooking. Feeling down about being disowned, narcotics were a way for me to escape the emotional pain of being rejected by my family and of enduring transphobic discrimination and prejudice. I had always known that I was female. I remained silent for a long time about what was in my heart and soul. Looking back, it was very unwise of me to come forward about my transsexualism to my parents, but you have to leave home at some point—and it was no big loss since my parents were difficult to live with and incapable of empathy.

My involvement with narcotics began soon after I left home, when a fellow hooker friend saw that I was sad and gave me some cocaine to cheer me up. It made me feel better, temporarily. Journeying across the country, I discovered the unbreakable, seductive power of heroin. My enjoyment of narcotics got the best of me, and I knew that it had gotten out of control when I began robbing banks. Being on drugs while hooking was bad enough, but holding up banks to acquire more drugs was worse. Using drugs is simply a short-term gain in exchange for long-term pain—it had not yet dawned on me that my actions were not the way to solve my problems.

Money can often be a barrier to gender reassignment surgery, and, for this reason, there are some transsexuals who turn to prostitution. When I began my quest for womanhood, I did not realize that it would become an unattainable dream. I needed money, so prostitution made sense. But during only my second week as a lady of the night, I made a rookie mistake and got myself busted by the vice squad. It was my first trick that Friday night, and I was anxious to break. I got into what I should have known was an undercover police car. When this man reached for what I thought was his wallet, he instead produced a badge. The only thing I said was, "Jesus fucking Christ!" While he was writing out the summons, he placed his hand on my knee. He remarked, "You look great," whipped out a camera, said, "Look sultry," and snapped a picture. I did my best to look scrumptious—this was for posterity after all! I beat the charge when my duty counsel ended a brilliant defence with the words "Your Honour, she's hungry." The experience was a warning of things to come. In my arrogance, I failed to heed that warning and would pay dearly for it.

When one is addicted to hard drugs, things can get out of hand—having to feed an addiction makes you capable of doing almost anything. I never thought I would become a bank robber. While involved in prostitution, I was severely abused and became even more full of hatred. I expressed that hatred in the violence I used when committing bank robberies. In the winter of 1994, I was going through a difficult time. I was 22 years old and into hard drugs. While many people my age were finishing college or university, I was a high school dropout full of anger and rage. While most people would not even think about doing something as dangerous as robbing a bank, my family upbringing had not been the best in the world—my father served eight years in a federal prison for robbing a bank in the 1970s—and I didn't view this crime in a typical way. It could almost be said that there was "something in the water" where I was raised. The tap water in Toronto is hard, so maybe that had something to do with it; on second thought, maybe not. I cannot escape my responsibility through metaphor—drat!

Having just broken up with my boyfriend, I was sad, depressed, and angry at the world. So on March 4, 1994, I launched my attack. I acquired a weapon, a machete, and picked out a bank to knock over. The one I chose was very close to the headquarters of the Toronto police force, and after I robbed the bank I ran toward that building. I hid behind a bus shelter, dashed across the street, and caught the Bay Street bus to the subway. I made my way home, amazed that I had pulled it off, and spread out the proceeds of the heist. I didn't do too badly: $9,376 for my efforts, which I crammed under my bed. Then Magical Peter came to visit me. Peter was a guy I kind of liked. He was a sweetheart; he was one of those white guys who was into

Native culture. I did sort of want him to be my boyfriend, but that didn't happen. Peter was going through a hard time, and we simply slept together on top of the almost $10,000 stuffed under my mattress. It did actually turn out to be a special night.

I wish I could have stopped there and not continued to rob banks; however, that caper was not my last. Since I was addicted to hard drugs, I didn't care too much about anything. Still, a few days later, I thought the jig was up: I was walking along Sherbourne Street and noticed out of the corner of my eye that two motorcycle cops heading northbound had turned around and started back toward me—Lizbound. I made out like I was running for the Carlton streetcar. I was very lucky that day; somehow I managed to keep my cool and hold it together.

There were rare times when I channelled my energy toward positive purposes. In late 1994, before things had gotten out of hand, I attended a protest to abolish on-reserve taxation. The Native upgrading program I attended gave us the day off school, and together we went to City Hall in downtown Toronto where 3,200 Native people were already assembled and ready to march. They had set up a large traditional drum on a flatbed truck to lead the way. In attendance were the usual representatives of Native agencies, community elders, and leaders. After the political speeches, the march began, and we made our way though the canyons between the skyscrapers of the financial district. I will always remember the sound of the grand drum and the smaller drums echoing off the towers of capitalism. The bankers and stockbrokers were in total astonishment. The police had blocked the entrance to the Toronto Stock Exchange, but they failed to protect a Revenue Canada building and a sudden rush toward the front doors got us in. We ended up taking over that government building for a month, during which time I led the daily prayer and smudge, and each morning we resolved to stay another day. I could never have imagined then that things would turn out the way they did.

I continued to pull bank heists and proceeded to dig a deeper hole. I was destroying my future, but that's what happens when you just say "Fuck it." Looking back, I had to learn the hard way. I was severely limiting my future, and there are better ways to deal with life.

One of my most desperate acts was when I took a hostage during my robbery of the Toronto Dominion Bank at King and Bay, in the heart of Toronto's financial district. Though it is preferable to produce a note or flash a weapon so no one gets hurt, I needed drugs and was in no mood to fuck around. I had just enough reckless abandon mixed with brazen arrogance to be able to commit this crime. Somehow I wasn't affected by fear or afraid of breaking the law. While I am well aware that actions such as bank robbery and hostage-taking are wrong, furious force—and a lack of remorse—became my signature trademark during this phase of my life.

I allowed my goal of obtaining sexual reassignment surgery (SRS) to become an unattainable dream, forever out of reach. Cooling my heels in federal prison following the TD Bank heist, I was furthest from my goal—but the day I abandoned hope was November 27, 1998. That was the only time that I really gave up on life and on ever undergoing sexual reassignment surgery. I had just completed the assessment process for SRS approval and was on a waiting list when provincial funding for surgery was stopped and cut. Gender strikeout! I took the news rather hard, and after weeks of hoping that the situation would somehow work itself out and that I would be grandfathered in, or the funding for the program would somehow be restored and I would be able to complete the transitioning process, I gave up. (I would eventually get the funding, but not until a good many years later.) After a torturous and crushing emotional storm, I accepted that I had done my best and that SRS was just not going to happen for me. I had been as patient as I could be, and on that day in late November, I was ready to exit this world. It was time to die. I was finished; there was no more fight or hope left inside of me. Suicide was to be my way of ending the emotional pain that I was experiencing.

My plan to die was not exactly suicide, in the strictest sense of the word. Rather, it was to cause a police incident and force the officers to shoot me dead. I went into a Chapters bookstore armed with a machete and chose a hostage to draw a quick police response. I originally targeted a large man, but when he was able to break free and run away, I replaced him with a smaller male store clerk. All hell had broken loose by then. The peace and serenity in the bookstore had degenerated into a massive frenzy. The Emergency Task Force team arrived; I expected that it would only be a matter of time before they shot me. There was a bargaining police guy there who was telling me to release my hostage. At the time, this did not really affect me. Looking back, I remember the chaos and havoc I caused that rainy November night, but I did not feel anything then. I suppose I snapped—but it didn't feel like how you might think snapping and losing it would feel. I was calm and ready to die. I released the clerk, and he went down the escalator while I managed to make my way up to the top floor of the bookstore.

The police had me surrounded, and their negotiator kept ordering me to surrender. I stood my ground and eventually the SWAT team did shoot me, but with an Arwen gun, which is a non-lethal launcher that fires steel rods bonded in hard rubber. I remember watching the projectile spinning end over end. I managed to stop and block it, destroying my left hand. I did not panic; I dropped my machete and straightened out my broken hand. I remember the utter shock in the eyes of the cops closest to me when I stopped the Arwen round and calmly realigned my shattered hand—like it was something I did every day. As I was blocked by book displays, shelving, counters, and tables, I was not able to make a rush at the police officers with their rifles aimed right at me. They fired another Arwen round, and it was a direct hit. This time I went down, but managed to get back up; as I did, I was tackled football-style. Those tough bastards—oops, I mean the wonderful boys in blue of the Emergency Task Force—arrested me. That was not the result I had intended—I had wanted to be terminated at the hands of the police. I think that night I cashed in on one of my two spirits.

I was transported to hospital for treatment and put in my own room complete with my own armed guard. This was to be expected, but the doctors and nurses were a little on edge. I spent the night under observation, and pictures of the physical damage I had received were taken—I did my best to look good. The nurses gave me morphine for the pain that I had managed to put aside during the course of the standoff with the SWAT team. After I was released from the hospital, I was transported directly to the city jail—do not pass go, do not collect $200. I didn't really care too much at that point. I was fed up with life, and I was up on some very serious criminal charges. That was it—nothing left to do but face the music. I was sentenced to federal prison, and my goal of getting sex reassignment surgery was as distant as ever. Off I went for a long stay at the iron fortress lodge that awaited me.

Somehow I managed to get through my time in a men's maximum security federal penitentiary, with me being a dainty pre-op inmate. I needed the rest to gather my spiritual strength and try again—and I have my ruthless father to thank for his "teachings." He was a cruel man, a severe alcoholic, and a mean son of a bitch with a short temper. He would administer brutal beatings on a regular basis. In his own way, he prepared me for the world. As much as I hate the man, I have to thank him for toughening me up and making it possible for me to survive the most difficult place a pre-op transsexual could be.

I made it though my time in men's maximum security prison with flying colours—not a good thing, considering I only did what I had to do. I am no angel, and during my time in prison I had a lot of time for personal reflection. When I finally got out, I managed to turn my life around. I conquered my addictions. I got my life back on track by rediscovering my Native culture and learning that being a two-spirited woman is a great gift. I also discovered that being transsexual is not the curse that I thought it was. I made the decision to keep trying, to fight the good fight, and went into counselling and got approval for surgery. I was finally able to complete my lifelong goal of getting sexual reassignment surgery.

Today's lesson might be on what happens when you drop out of high school, become a hooker, get addicted to heroin and cocaine, start robbing banks, and go to prison. This is my story of the lessons I learned during my time at the school of hard knocks—it is a different type of education. When you start caring about life again, the road to what you want is twice as hard. I have started to work toward a degree in social work at the University of British Columbia—it will take me a while, but I will get my degree. I want to be able to use my strength, hope, and courage to help other transsexuals and two-spirited people. I have the street smarts from my direct experience; I just need the book smarts.

That is my story of how I reached my castle in the sky. Thanks to the creator for giving me a second chance.

Chapter 5 Finding My Place: The High Risk Project Society

Sandy Leo Laframboise

This chapter details my journey toward personal acceptance and how it led to the creation of the High Risk Project Society (HRPS), a unique space for trans folks in Vancouver during the mid-1990s. During the 1990s, there were a few agencies and organizations beginning to do informal research on transsexual populations in the Downtown Eastside. I will discuss how the HRPS emerged from these circumstances, and how we shaped our application for funding according to particular psychological categories governing sex/gender. These definitions contributed to a strict funding mandate, which enabled transsexual women to receive specific services from which they had been excluded; however, it created some obstacles for the integration of the HRPS into wider transgender communities and political initiatives in Vancouver. While this is a price those at the HRPS were willing to pay to recognize the value-added place of mainly racialized, street-entrenched transsexual women who often used substances and did sex work, we believe that fundamental social changes cannot arise until communities take a serious look at transforming sex/gender as a governing social system.

In 1972, I came out of the closet, telling my parents, the people at my high school, and my friends that I was gay. My family was poor, so I worked the streets in Ottawa, selling my body for $5 a blowjob to older men to buy groceries. I hid this from my parents until I couldn't lie anymore. When I came out, my father reacted strongly, claiming he could not have a gay son and that he was going to change me. I ran away and was returned home a week later by police. My family then sent me for aversion therapy.

I lived first as a young gay boy who hustled the streets, and then as a male prostitute. Later I was a drag queen. In this milieu, it was okay for me to be effeminate on stage and perhaps a bit beyond the shows, since I became a local star. Yet this flexibility still was not present within my family; in fact, chaos erupted once my dad saw that I was developing breasts from the black market hormones I was taking. Thus began my lifelong arduous struggle with my family and with broader society. Fighting to belong is difficult—even today I sometimes wonder.

The struggle to find my place took another 17 years while I partook of drugs, alcohol, and other things transsexuals often do to escape our realities. In June 1989, a voice inside of me said that there more to life. I didn't want to be on the streets accepting perceptions of myself as a third-place oddity or a novelty to try. My destiny was not to be a freak of nature whose only validation as a woman and as a human being in an intimate relationship came from male clients. I was not going to accept oppressive presumptions of my station in life. The party was over.

I didn't realize how hard it was going to be to cope with life without the assistance of chemicals or alcohol. In fact, more difficulties arose for me while living in a women's treatment centre run by the Salvation Army. In addition to the church-run centre, I began attending the Salvation Army church. I became a "holy roller" and believed I had found an accepting place, and it was, as long as they did not know my scary secret—that I was a male-to-female transsexual.

Treatment wasn't easy, and I had much to learn regarding social skills. I worked hard to get ahead. I faced my anger and learned that I was a spiritual person who loved to pray. I worked all of the steps in recovery and attended social events organized by recovery programs. The more I got sober and the more grounded I was in my love for God, the more I felt I was lying to everyone.

There is more to life than the status quo, and I wanted to make the world better for myself and others. To do so, I had to come out of the closet for a second time in my life—this time sober. Can you imagine all the torment in my mind and heart? I was going crazy struggling with my faith and believing that we are all created equal in the eyes of God. Yet what would God and the church think now that I was conscious of what I had done to my body? What a trip, when you come out and tell a whole church congregation, a student union at college, and the media that you are transsexual and insist that you belong in the circle.

I attended Douglas College in New Westminster, British Columbia. Attending college as an out transsexual adult was rewarding. Throughout my studies, we did presentations to learn how to facilitate therapeutic group activities. I focused my entire curriculum on gender and sexual diversity and incorporated my own life experiences and the various risks to which I was subject. When I graduated, I had earned a Psychiatric Nursing Associate Diploma, with a specialization in gender diversity/HIV-AIDS/drug and alcohol rehabilitation. Along the way, there were struggles, including having to lodge a sexual discrimination complaint against another student, which I won. It was during this time, however, that I learned how to be human and fight for what I believe in, to stand up to bullies, and how to be in love.

I set out to save the world because I know what is wrong and what is right after all. I had a college diploma and a degree of life from the streets. So here I come, a reformed prostitute who knows best—a regular Florence Nightingale.

BACKGROUND OF THE HIGH RISK PROJECT SOCIETY (HRPS)

While transsexual individuals have been living and contributing to downtown communities in Vancouver for decades, it was not until the early 1990s that our identities, experiences, and needs became subject to inquiry amongst non-profit organizations and service agencies. In 1992, the Vancouver Native Health Society called an inter-agency meeting to explore the dilemmas of the transsexual population. Superficial research consisting of a head count and anecdotal evidence in Vancouver's Downtown Eastside indicated that the transsexual population had increased to approximately 60 individuals. This growth was due partly to the development of areas such as Granville Street, which precipitated the displacement of transgender folks to the Eastside.

In December 1993, the Zenith Foundation recognized the need to support a unique but ostracized segment of the transsexual population, and the HRPS was founded. Transsexuals had been noted by other agencies of the time, such as the Downtown Eastside Youth Activities

Society (DEYAS), Vancouver Native Health, and Lookout Emergency Shelter, to be the most isolated and difficult group to service. These agencies and programs seemed relieved to have somewhere to send these most troublesome people.

I joined the Zenith Foundation in 1993 as I was finishing my college studies in Psychiatric Nursing. I wanted to give back to my trans community, as I am one of those primary transsexuals who had been on the streets for so long. At one of the Zenith Foundation meetings, I met April Valle, Barbara Hammond, and Deborah Brady.[1] All of us were involved in a once-a-week meal program at First United Church for street-entrenched transgendered folks, spearheaded by Jamie Lee Hamilton and partially funded by the Zenith Foundation.

It wasn't long after I joined that there was a disagreement between the Zenith Foundation and Jamie Lee Hamilton concerning the program's direction. Wanting to provide more than a weekly meal, I saw this disagreement as an opportunity to take on the task of shifting the HRPS to a full-time program. I solicited the help of Deborah Brady, along with other agency representatives. In January 1994, a consumer-run safe place was established by the HRPS on the premises of Vancouver Native Health Society in the Downtown Eastside. This was a full-fledged volunteer-run facility for street-entrenched trans folks who were drug addicted and/or sex trade workers, and most of them were living with HIV. Supplies were donated by local agencies.

ORGANIZING PARAMETERS: EXPANDING THE HRPS AND LESSONS LEARNED

Deborah Brady and I applied to the Health Ministry of BC for funding to provide drop-in services to primary transsexuals—mainly women—as part of efforts to research the nature and needs of trans populations in Vancouver and expand the reach of the HRPS detailed above. We would learn through many conflicts the fraught terrain that naming presents. Producing programs for primary transsexuals who identified as trans women had consequences.

During the early 1990s, knowledge of trans demographics was influenced mainly by discourse produced in gender identity clinics and other psychological and medical professionals. At the time, "transgender" as an umbrella term used by trans community organizers included all those who self-identified within the broad scope of "gender identity disorders" as defined in the DSM-III. The main feature of all such disorders is a feeling of incongruity between anatomic sex and gender identity. Primary and secondary transsexuals, as well as cross-dressers, constitute subgroups in this category.

In the early stages of conceptualizing the HRPS, we decided to adopt the DSM terms; however, we sought further inclusivity by both expanding the category of primary transsexuality (i.e., those who came out early, often during puberty, and sought medicalized transition) and working to meet the needs of those classified within it. Our motivation to do so was based on personal experience and the data we collected walking the streets at night.

Recognizing individuals who often failed the "Real-Life Test" (RLT) as primary transsexuals exemplifies how we broadened the category. The RLT (later renamed the Real-Life Experience) is administered by provincial government–sanctioned gender identity clinics as a requirement for achieving approval for publicly funded sexual reassignment surgeries. Individuals must demonstrate that they can successfully live full time (i.e., at home, work, school, while volunteering, and throughout their social networks) in a role congruent with their sex and gender identities. The individuals we acknowledged often failed the RLT because they were prostitutes, drug addicted, and/or resorted to change while in puberty or in early adulthood through taking black market hormones.

Primary transsexuals frequently end up on the streets and are still largely excluded from social services. These trans folks usually have a dual diagnosis and a history of sexual abuse. Disrupted patterns of development and barriers to obtaining an education often leave primary transsexuals unemployable and suffering from acute deficiencies in social skills. They are most likely to work in the sex trade, to develop chemical dependency, and to engage in sexual behaviours that put them at high risk for all sexually transmitted infections and HIV. Primary transsexuals who are visibly gender variant and/or racialized are the most discriminated against—even within their own communities! They are in dire need of refuge and specialized services. Before the HRPS, they had no safe haven except for a few piecemeal approaches by the Health Boards.

There are sex/gender differences amongst primary transsexuals. When applying for funding for the HRPS, we privileged transsexual women because they are the most degraded and marginalized amongst trans demographics. They desperately needed access to services and community. Pressures toward gender conformity regarding dress and presentation are more intense for trans women. There were few female-to-male transsexuals (FTMs) in the street sex-trade population in the 1990s. Most seemed socially connected to the gender-divided gay scene and were safely ensconced in protected workplaces. Additionally, cross-dressers, or secondary transsexuals, benefited from access to male privilege. They were often socially accepted, had families and community supports, and were able to access legal employment and maintain their jobs long-term.

The High Risk Project was founded on a peer-support model. Marginalization, discrimination, rejection, humiliation, and violence are common and, after many years of such treatment, the defence mechanisms become part of the self and the individual appears sociopathic. These individuals comprise our members, clients, target group, volunteers, and friends. Due to this intense alienation, the community is difficult to penetrate, and trust takes time to build. We believed that a peer-support model was the best way to build a cohesive therapeutic community.

The work we did together with the HRPS was not easy. Another obstacle that we faced as an organization was the vast amount of labour this undertaking turned out to require. Our political pursuits were a full-time job in and of themselves. There simply was not the budget to hire and pay staff. We were full-time volunteers putting in a minimum of 40 to 60 hours a week. Organizers need to reflect on the ways that such rigorous demands on an individual's time and energy will impact volunteers, programs, and the organizations themselves.

It was also necessary to confront different visions amongst organizers and volunteers. Deborah and I had many intense moments when we disagreed about a course of action and both of us argued vehemently to convince the other that our direction was best. My focus was on social health services, and hers was on human rights. In several key early determinations, I won those arguments, so it was entirely my leadership that gave High Risk a focus on Aboriginal teaching and culture, and it was my initiative that took us into the HIV/AIDS work. Both of those areas led the HRPS to good sources of ongoing yearly funding that helped us to achieve many goals, including continuing to assist community social health service organizations to develop transgender-inclusive policies that would increase transgendered people's access to services. In the end, of course, we had to compromise to move forward.

Funding success and the increasing vitality of the HRPS presented us with personal hardships that we had not expected. Our success would constrict our private lives as the spotlight began to shine on the HRPS. Additionally, we not prepared for the hardship of life as outcasts when we received our first funding grant from the government. At that point, every agency that was competing for government funding started using the word "transgender" in reference to the list of clients that they were servicing. Given the competition for resources amongst social service and non-profit organizations, we felt the effects of being rigorously monitored and scrutinized by others working in different agencies. Some of the negative aspects of such competition had underlying gender, class, moralistic, and racial elements—they couldn't believe the success of such low-track "trannies"!

We also encountered problems finding a place within broader trans communities and movements. This was due partially to confusion concerning our use of the umbrella term "transgender" in some of our materials while being constricted by a narrow funding mandate that limited our service offerings to street-entrenched primary transsexual women. Since many trans individuals are marginalized from essential social services and need resources to improve their quality of life, one can only imagine the trouble that ensued when we were unable to care for the needs of the broader trans community!

We also learned a lot from efforts to expand the reach of the HRPS into other arenas of social change. After establishing the HRPS, Deborah Brady wrote a proposal to the BC Law Foundation, and we received a grant to look at the issue of transgender individuals and the law.

Finding Our Place: Transgender Law Reform Project was written principally by legal counsel and barbara findlay, with community input from members of the Zenith Foundation, including community activist and transgender advocate Jamie Lee Hamilton, and representation from the Cornbury Society, a cross-dressers group.

This document was influential in the hearing held to amend the BC Human Rights Code in the 1990s. Mary Woo Sims, the then-Human Rights Commissioner, and some BC government officials came to the HRPS drop-in centre and held a hearing session with street-entrenched members. The efforts to include "gender identity" in human rights protections failed; nevertheless, the inclusion of HRPS members in the hearing was a pivotal moment for me and Deborah because it signified a degree of state and societal recognition of sex workers, street-active transsexual women who often use substances and alcohol, as well as those with HIV/AIDS. They were significant enough to be consulted. Issues surrounding human rights inclusion for transgendered people incited debates within trans milieus. Many transsexual activists eschewed the moniker of "transgender," given their lack of confidence that this label would lend itself to addressing the specificity of their experiences. Furthermore, efforts to include "gender identity" in rights legislation threatened some women's organizations, and they opposed this campaign.

The HRPS had more success fitting in with the AIDS funding community and Aboriginal groups, as approximately half of our members were of Aboriginal or Métis ancestry. Local and international elders helped us and were strikingly accepting compared with the mainstream non-indigenous society.

We also learned from another losing battle in which the HRPS partook as a way of expanding our political reach. Many transgendered folks wanted assured access to disability benefits in BC based on their transgenderism. We opposed such a characterization, given that we felt that gender identity per se is not a disability; instead, social discrimination is the real problem. Our lack of success in the workplace is more often due to our "odd" appearance and rampant discrimination and not because we are disabled—although our life can be debilitating in itself (i.e., an argument can be made that we are dis/abled). We argued against inclusion in the criterion for eligibility for disability and lost. This would create some tensions concerning cultivating relationships within and across trans communities.

Every day was a battle for recognition. Politically we had to defend ourselves and prove the worthiness of the HRPS having received public funding. While finding our place was not easy, maintaining our place was extremely hard. Eventually, we simply could not handle the public ridicule levelled at us by gay, feminist, and transsexual organizations, as well as from factions of Aboriginal communities. After a few battles, I negotiated a severance package and left the HRPS. It was not long after I left that I was called back to do some consulting work that concerned our funders. A financial audit was called and a program review was sponsored by the then Vancouver Richmond Health Board. At the concluding interview, the auditors and program reviewers informed us that our books were flawless aside from a few ethical issues; there were no illegal improprieties.

Despite the positive results of our review, we voted to close down the society rather than struggle on as exhausted volunteers. To this day, both Deborah and I remain convinced that long-term progress for trans people lies in the social deconstruction of gender. At the end of it all, I have found my place, a place in life, a place in the circle where I have a voice. I will no longer be silent and accept the substandard norm for myself as a human being.

To this day, recognition appears piecemeal and uncertain. None of us chose this path. We are placed on this path from birth, for reasons no one can fully explain. Trans individuals feel natural in our identities, and like non-trans people, we seek to modify ourselves so we can live the fullest life possible. It is the responsibility of every person to empower themselves and others so that they may be fed, clothed, able to learn, and contribute to life.

That was our mission at the HRPS. We set out to make a proper place for transgender men and women—my place, your place, and our place in society—out of a sense of duty to present communities, as well as future generations who will reside in Canada. We thought we had a model that would inspire and assist other groups. Our outsider status fuelled the creative juices to provide a place that was different and innovative in many respects, and that modelled a good nursing approach to homeless care. The High Risk Project Society created such a place.

NOTE

1 Deborah Brady was instrumental in the development of the HRPS. She came from a privileged, religious, and wealthy background that afforded her a private school education and an opportunity to partake in the family business. Deborah read about Christine Jorgensen in *Life* magazine and was transfixed. She knew immediately that she was trans. However, this was socially unacceptable to her family, and they ostracized her. Deborah was a secondary transsexual as she married, had a child, and led a privileged life. She had SRS surgery at the age of 45. While transitioning, she sought out trannies in the sex trade to help her dress—I discovered later in our friendship that she had been one of my tricks!

Chapter 6 Two Poems

Susan Gapka

This poem describes a series of personal experiences that occurred following my public transition in September 1999. The second stanza relates to my experience of answering the telephone while working during a student placement in a councillor's office at Toronto City Hall. The third and fourth stanzas depict a swarming experience I had on a Toronto Transit Commission (TTC) bus en route to my weekly electrolysis appointment. My complaint with the TTC was never resolved satisfactorily. The fifth stanza relates to my experience as a student leader at York University. On one occasion the president of our student union attempted to physically attack me, but was restrained by other students. He was warned by police at his parents' home on New Year's Day for calling me a "freak."

MY NAME IS SUSAN
I am an ordinary person,
Facing extraordinary challenges.
My name is Susan.

I spell my name on the telephone,
"S–U–S–A–N, S U S A N
Yes, that is my name. Can't you see?
Once you meet me, you'll agree."

Riding the transit bus one quiet day,
Rambunctious youth a jumpin'
Too many times upon my foot.
I demand—"Stop your stompin!"

Quickly they turn upon me,
Onto the floor I land.
I scamper to the front of the bus
With one of my shoes in hand.

I am a political person.
It is justice that I seek.
My opponents conspire against me,
And sometimes call me a freak.

I am an ordinary woman,
Facing extraordinary challenges.
My name is Susan.

The first Canadian Trans Day of Remembrance (TDoR) was organized in 2001 in Vancouver. By 2004, events were also being held in Edmonton, St. John's, Ottawa, Toronto, and at Brock University in St. Catherines. On November 18, 2004, we rallied at the University of Toronto, marched to Queen's Park, and petitioned the Minister of Health for funding in the Legislature. At The 519 Church Street Community Centre (The 519), Kyle Scanlon organized their first annual TDoR, Toronto's signature event.The original inspiration for this poem occurred during a moment of silence on November 11, Remembrance Day, as our group was planning a Harm Reduction Fair. The original poem on drug policy was revised and my first public reading occurred at the first TDoR event at The 519.

PAUSE AND REFLECT
Trans Day of Remembrance (November 20, 2003)

Let us pause and reflect for a moment,
For transphobia is a mark against humanity,
My humanity—Our humanity.

Let us pause and reflect for a moment,
For those of us not here today,
For those of us who couldn't come out.
Those of us who could not withstand the fear and hate.
For those who just had to be themselves—no matter what!

Let us pause and reflect for a moment
For people like Shawn Keegan, Deanna Wilkinson, Cassandra Do and Kyle Scanlon...

When we come together to remember, we celebrate their lives.
When our allies support us, we acquire more strength and determination.
Let us pause and reflect for a moment....

Postscript: In early July 2012, Kyle Scanlon, my colleague and peer, committed suicide. This version is dedicated to his memory.

Chapter 7 When Dad Becomes Mom: The Story of One Mother's Love for Her Children, Parent Alienation, and "Happily Ever After"

Michelle Boyce and Jessica Boyce

> Children's best interests are not served by the bullying tactic of implacable parental opposition by one parent to continuing contact with both parents. Divorce may be inevitable between parent and parent, but divorce need not be inevitable between parent and child.
>
> —*Dr. Richard Green*

INTRODUCTION

While writing this chapter, a Facebook status flashed across my screen: "My 20-year-old son, whom I have not seen in nearly 10 years, will be spending a few days in the area over Christmas. His mother hasn't allowed him to see me, but he is now financially independent, so the ball will be in his court. Complicating things, his mother has been badmouthing me for all the years she has had him away from me. None of it is true, but who knows what his take on things is?" Like so many other trans parents, the woman who posted this will spend Christmas wondering if she will see her son.

Transitioning is not a neutral event. There are major risk factors accompanying transition for both the transsexual individual, their partner, and children, including: (1) spousal opposition to the transition; (2) parental conflict regarding the transition; and (3) the impact of an abrupt separation from either parent on children. Custody and relations between extended kinship networks need to be prioritized amongst trans activists addressing youth and family-related issues, especially since recent estimates suggest that up to one in four trans people have children (Bauer et al., 2010; di Ceglie, 1998; Tully, 1992).

This chapter buttresses ongoing initiatives to provide education and support to trans parents and families. While there has been amazing work done to address trans reproduction processes and parenting rights, I discuss some of the difficulties trans parents face regarding custody issues, as well as in maintaining a healthy relationship with our children throughout legal proceedings and beyond. While I raise points regarding legal precedents in Canadian case law in favour of transsexual parents, and address how to work with institutions such as the Children's Aid Society, my major concern lies with the interpersonal dynamics that often occur in the midst of marital breakdown. We transsexual individuals have to prove ourselves to be "normal," "deserving," and "worthy" within the family court system because our gender identities and transitioning processes challenge essentialist notions of sex, gender, and sexuality; trans people are suspect within heteronormative sites such as the legal system. There is a widely held conviction that children's mental health and well-being within the home, at school, and in their social networks will be impacted negatively by their parent's trans identity. This conviction can influence judges' decisions regarding custody in favour of the non-trans parent (Green, 2006). It is therefore important for trans legal activists to continue to ensure that knowledge of existing court rulings to the contrary is widespread, and to continue to educate the courts and legal organizations about trans identities and experience. Nevertheless, this discourse concerning trans individuals and the risk they pose to children must reach beyond our legal systems. Left unaddressed, the belief that a parent's trans identity impacts children negatively can erode kinship bonds, severely damaging parent–child relations.

I have interwoven my own personal narrative throughout the text to demonstrate the ways that trans parents are often denigrated by those closest to us. I introduce the concept of "parental alienation syndrome" to ensure that trans activists and organizers focus on trans oppression within nuclear and extended families, kinship groups, and communities as social networks so that we can organize to address such denigration.

MY STORY

My story begins in 1969, when the world was afire with rebellion, dissent, and protest. My arrival was a monumental event for both of my parents' families and all of them were present. I was only a second into my journey when the doctor cast a profound judgment that would set the stage for my life: "It's a boy!" And I screamed!

My childhood was a time of much violence and pain as I struggled to understand and honour my gender and sexuality. My first friend, Michelle, moved away after we were caught trading clothing at 4 years of age. This was my first cross-dressing experience, and Michelle was the first person to accept me as I was. At the age of 10, I was raped by my best friend, who was just as shocked as I was by his attraction to me. We didn't speak after that, and I didn't tell a soul.

When I was 16, I was a passenger in a van going 100 kilometres an hour when it crashed into a truck. My best friend, Dave, died on top of me, and his mother died beside me. I spent the next several months recovering from my devastating injuries—25 percent of my hip and six inches of my leg bone were missing, and I had suffered a brain injury. The doctors told my parents that people rarely recover from brain damage and that they would have to get used to the "new me." The orthopedic specialists wanted to amputate my leg due to a massive life-threatening infection. I fought with them daily, and the experience taught me to stick up for myself against those bent on making me do what they wanted. I kept my leg, and deep down, the tenacious will to fight. In the end, it was that will, the gender incongruence, and my determination that saved me from "the new me," or the part of myself that sought to suffocate my desire to dress like a girl. Nothing was going to quiet the girl inside, and once she broke free from bondage, the rest of me flooded back into place as I recovered.

Amidst all the uncertainty in my life—regarding my sexuality, gender, and identity—I had a steadfast desire to have a family and to parent. Perhaps that doesn't seem all that strange these days, but in the 1970s, gay, lesbian, queer, and transsexual individuals were not allowed to have families. Adoption, third-party parenting agreements, and artificial insemination, examples of the ways by which we can currently create families, were not available to us. My wish became a reality when I met a woman and fell in love. We had no secrets. She knew I dressed as a girl and was attracted to both genders. Together we had a son, and three years later, a daughter. From the moment of their birth, I had every intention of being their dad and only dressing as a girl in private, at night, or when nobody was home. It seemed like the perfect arrangement. My wife and I had a his/hers/ours closet and shopped for clothes together. We gave my "girl side" a name, Michelle, in honour of my childhood friend.

In our mid-twenties, the marriage began to fall apart, leaving friendship where love had resided. Unable to silence my gender dysphoria, I transitioned into a woman in 2000. I met a man that loved me for who and not what I was, and we moved in together. I thought I had found my "happily ever after." My ex-wife and I were best friends, I had a man I loved, and my kids were a large part of my life.

In 2002, my wife filed for divorce, and by 2004, the custody battle had begun to shatter my illusion of "happily ever after." Losing my children was not a price I had imagined having to pay when I began transitioning. My first gender surgery had been arranged by my ex-wife; therefore, for her to demand sole custody on the grounds that I am transsexual seemed unfathomable. Unfortunately, this was not the only challenge I would face in our custody dispute. One morning, I received a call from the Children's Aid Society (CAS). My ex-wife had filed a complaint bearing some loaded and erroneous charges. The CAS questioned my children while they were at school. The caseworker did what she could to support me over the phone for the hour that it took my family supports to travel to my home.

In light of my experience, I strongly suggest that any parent going through a separation create a file that demonstrates your fitness as a parent. It is crucial when dealing with child protection service organizations. My file contained a report from the office of the children's lawyers regarding my parenting skills; my children's last report cards from when I had full custody; and testimonials from family friends who could attest to my parenting skills. It also contained a letter from a Board of Education psychologist, who suggested that raising issues concerning my transition *may* create problems for my children:

> If no problems were being exhibited by the children, it would be risky to intervene with the children with respect to gender dysphoria. I emphasized that, because the two children were reported to be quite happy and well adjusted at school, it did not make sense at that point to take the risk of jeopardizing the children's peace of mind by bringing up the issue of gender dysphoria. (letter on file with author)

I sent the file to the CAS caseworker, and she realized the vexatious nature of the complaint. Her supervisor, however, demanded she get letters from my doctors and surgeons to verify the contents of my file. I felt like I was a freak of nature. While the CAS is institutionally and legally obligated to investigate, I believe the prevalent stereotype of all trans people as pedophiles provided some of the motivation for a continued investigation.

I arrived at the CAS office the next morning. However, I did not get to see my children again until the following day. Guilty until proven innocent, I was denied the right to see them until the investigation had been concluded. After CAS wrapped up its investigation of my ex-wife's complaint, the caseworker provided me with a letter clearing me of all accusations. And in the family court proceedings, the caseworker testified on my behalf, stating, "It was a pleasure meeting with you and your children. It is evident that you are concerned for the needs of the family and are able to make appropriate accommodations to ensure their well-being."

Justice Marshman ruled that, while my plan for custody access might be in the children's best interests, the fact that I had "involved the children too much in my transition" warranted full custody being awarded to their mother. Once my ex-wife had gained full custody, she took my son to see a counsellor because she believed that any further relationship he had with me would harm his own development. Such beliefs often result from popular—and pathologizing—discourses espousing that children of transsexual parents are likely to experience confusion concerning their own gender identity (see Freedman, Tasker, & di Ceglie, 2002; Green, 1978, 1998b for evidence to the contrary). Furthermore, her behaviour mirrored parental alienation. I was labelled as dishonest, and it may have been suggested that my children's possessions were not safe at my house. I struggled daily with missing my children and with the pain I felt when they were not with me. I was mourning for how our lives had been and grappling with how I desired my life to be. Letting go is not something a mom is good at, but eventually I found a way to survive.

The most profound day for me during this period was when I conducted an anti-homophobia/transphobia workshop at a youth shelter for kids who had been removed from their violent homes. When I began telling my story, they interrupted me with questions about my children. When asked if I ever saw them, I responded that I saw my kids only occasionally and it wasn't enough. The audience refused to accept my answer. They did not believe that seeing my kids 20 percent of the time was bad. For them, it wasn't *how much* time I had with my kids, it was about the *quality* of time and our experiences. They reminded me that children see the world and experience time differently; they tend to understand time through experiences. When kids are having a good time and experiencing good things, they remember that time as being valuable and long. This explains why my kids would often say "We are *always* with you"—a comment that used to enrage me. When children, however, are bored, that time is not remembered or valued and is forgotten. Negative experiences are remembered but not valued, so it doesn't fit into their model of time.

I finally understood thanks to the amazing youth at that shelter, and I grasped tightly to this new perspective. As much as it hurt me that I only saw my children for a short while each week, I concentrated on giving them the best experiences I could when I did see them!

SETTING PRECEDENTS: CASE LAW AS A BATTLEGROUND FOR CUSTODIAL RIGHTS

Many relationships involving gender transition end in separation or divorce. Recognition of parental rights for transgender persons has been a slow, ongoing process due to governing heteronormative discourses that signify transsexuals as dangerous. The visibility we give to the mutability of sex, and the way that sex/gender are posited as non-essentialist and self-determined facets of life, posits us as threatening to impressionable children:

> [P]arental divorce, developmental theories and widespread assumptions surrounding transsexual parenting have been used to argue that continued contact with a transsexual parent may have detrimental effects on the child's psychosexual development. Furthermore, it has been argued that the child's mental health will be affected by difficulties in comprehending the transsexual parent's transition, the disruption to their relationship with their transsexual parent, and conflicts in the relationship between their parents. It has also been argued that the quality of the child's peer relation-

ships may be adversely affected through the stigma attached to the transsexual parent; however, these arguments have not been empirically supported. (Green, 1998b)

Trans individuals and activists have challenged such erroneous assumptions in the legal system and achieved some positive outcomes. In 1995, Justice Williamson granted a transsexual woman joint custody of both her children, stating, "One cannot fail to see … the many positive qualities [she] offers as a parent. [She] is significantly involved with the children in their schooling and in their play. [She] includes [her] children in [her] interest in old cars and mechanics. [She] provides well for them in terms of food and clothing. [She] has developed positive relationships with other families in the area. [She] positively reinforces their self esteem" (*Ghidoni v. Ghidoni*, 1995 CanLII 1018 (BC SC)).

In 2000, Justice Theo Wolder of the Ontario Court of Justice in Brampton ruled in the *Forrester v. Saliba* case, stating that "the applicant's transsexuality, in itself, without further evidence, would not constitute a material change in circumstances, nor would it be considered a negative factor in custody determination." He continued: "Frankly, it is remarkable how little impact all this storm swirling about the parties has had upon this little girl. It appears from the evidence that [she] is a very well-adjusted, happy, healthy little girl, who in her own way has been able to accept the changes in her father and continues to enjoy a healthy relationship with her father, now a woman psychologically." Ms. Radbord, Forrester's lawyer, explained that "[w]e live in a transphobic culture … but it's clear that the test for custody and access is always the best interests of the child." She offered encouragement by stating that "the decision could inspire other transsexuals, who often give up fighting for custody because they assume the justice system will be biased against them" (Owens, 2001).

While the cases above are evidence of courts recognizing that gender identity is not relevant to determining one's fitness as a parent, the legal system remains entrenched in heteronormative logics. Fighting gender stereotypes of nurturing birth mothers and unattached fathers is pertinent to gaining rights as trans parents. Male-to-female transsexual individuals, for example, risk losing their children because many courts still prefer to award child custody to mothers. For fathers to be awarded sole custody, gross negligence or incompetence on the mother's part must be demonstrated.

COURT OF PUBLIC OPINION: POPULAR DISCOURSE AS OBSTACLE TO CUSTODY

While the legal system plays an important role in trans parents' lives, as well as those of their children and families, struggles to achieve justice for trans parents cannot be contained to formal institutional settings. Knowledge of transsexual people is gained and judgments concerning our ability to parent are made in many places through everyday interactions.

Misinformation concerning transsexuality and parenting is due in part to the lasting imprint that gender identity clinics (GICs) have had on the lives of trans individuals. In the past, GICs rendered transsexuals invisible by demanding a "clean" history. Participants in GIC programs were required to estrange themselves from any connection to their past, including their marital and parental roles. Transsexuals risked not being approved for sexual reassignment procedures if they did not abandon their families; the psychologist with whom they worked would consider it a failure to transition if they were to do otherwise. Parents who sought to embody their sex and gender identity had no choice but to divorce their spouse and recreate their life history so it would be congruent with their self-determined gender. Such changes to ensure that transsexuals could live true to themselves were institutional requirements; however, understandings of transsexuality as anathema to the nurturing, generous, and selfless qualities ascribed to parents spilled over into wider societal knowledge.

Trans parents are continuously asked, "How can you do this to your child(ren)? Don't you know other kids can be mean?" Yet children of trans parents do not exhibit any more difficulties in peer relationships (Freedman et al., 2002) than do children from other differing socio-cultural or socio-economic backgrounds. Research shows that the more accepting the children are of their transitioning parent, the less bullying and social suffering they face at school (Sales, 1995; White & Ettner, 2007). Children of transsexual parents do not have major psychosocial problems; they show heightened social sensitivity and report harassment, victimization, or persecution by peers (Freedman et al., 2002).

PARENTAL ALIENATION SYNDROME (PAS)

Those engaging in trans politics understand the necessity of comprehending how the subjugation of sex- and gender-variant subjects is exercised through the everyday interactions that frame our material lives. Parental alienation syndrome (PAS) serves to exemplify the ways in which interpersonal relations govern our lives. It is estimated that PAS occurs in as much as 20 percent of custody cases. Coined by Richard A. Gardner, "parental alienation syndrome" results from a combination of the "programming" or indoctrination of the child by one parent with the child's own contribution to the vilification of the other parent. This produces a binary of the loved/hated parent. Hatred or disdain for one parent occurs despite an absence of any form of abuse (Gardner, 1998). In addition to J.M. Bone and M.R. Walsh's (1999) four criteria for PAS—(1) access and contact blocking, (2) unfounded abuse allegations, (3) deterioration in relationship since separation, and (4) intense fear reaction by children—other signs include children calling their parent by their first name, and being cruel when speaking to, or of, their parent. Alienating parents believe that they have truth and justice on their side, and that the target parent is bad for the children. Such beliefs prevent alienating parents from understanding how injurious it is to deny their children the opportunity for a healthy relationship with their other parent. As Toronto-based family lawyer Brian Ludmer (2011) explains, "We know all these things, but changes in the court system, evaluators and mental health are not moving fast enough to help these families and reduce the long term effects of PAS on children."

During transition, children need support in accepting the new role the trans parent plays. When that support is not given, children are alienated from their trans parent. In custody disputes, it is often claimed that blocking access to a trans parent protects the child(ren) from the social issues arising from this difference; however, PAS practices *create* these issues. The grief, confusion, and anger that often arise in children when a parent transitions is manipulated by their non-trans parent, extended family members, or close family friends to create distance and bad feelings between them and their transitioning parent. In my case, the signs of PAS were obvious: access to my children was made extremely difficult, there was an unfounded abuse allegation, and my children started telling me that I was a liar and couldn't be trusted.

STRATEGIES FOR CHANGE

While our attention needs to be redirected to take into consideration PAS and other aspects of personal dynamics that impact relations between trans parents and our children, there are legal strategies that can lead to reforms. Brian Ludmer, quoted above, a Toronto-based lawyer with 25 years of experience in difficult custody cases, offers a few points to assist us in the struggle against PAS. He believes that the enforcement of court orders along with stiff financial penalties for contempt of court orders, and having a consistent judge working with a file will reduce opportunities for PAS. These interventions are necessary, and transsexual activists and allies must be prepared to work to demonstrate the character of the transsexual parent, and how they have consistently proven their ability to provide a loving environment for their children, because "Canadians might not know it but parenting is *not a right* in Canada like it is in the United States" (Ludmer, 2011).

Individuals related to transsexual parents, friends, and other individuals play a crucial role as allies within the ongoing dynamics that constitute everyday life. The constant bombardment of negative messages our children receive as a part of PAS is very difficult to counter when you are an "access parent." Others can assist the immediate family by making efforts to (1) foster close ties between the transitioning parent and their children, (2) foster a close relationship between the child and the non-transitioning parent, (3) assist parents in establishing co-operative approaches to child-rearing, (4) ensure extended family support of both parents, and (5) ensure ongoing contact with both parents (White & Ettner, 2004, 2007). Many people don't want to involve themselves in a custody dispute and actively remove themselves from the process. However, if one witnesses a parent practising alienation, they need to step in—the child(ren)'s mental health and well-being depend on it. Trans parents who can maintain contact with their children throughout their transition experience an improvement in their relationships around the six-year mark. This tends to be the case even when they have an extremely adversarial other parent (White & Ettner, 2007).

Children too can learn how to advocate for themselves and their families. They can be involved in some decisions surrounding transition that involve them directly, such as what name to use for the parent post-transition. One-third of children continue to use the pre-transition gender-specific identifier (i.e., "mom" for a female-to-male transsexual) while others adopt either their parent's first name, a neutral nickname, or a post-transition gender-congruent title (White & Ettner, 2007).

Changes within institutions can occur over time through greater insight into the fact that our trans or gender identification does not signify anything concerning our character, skills, and capacity to love and be a parent. Self-advocacy is a very important skill for trans people to acquire so that we have the capacity to defend ourselves in the wake of serious challenges that can be devastating to our lives. Examples of self-advocacy mentioned in the chapter include compiling a file to demonstrate one's capacities to parent, as well as working to ensure that one's children and family have the social support networks they need. This may also involve meeting with teachers and others with whom our children regularly engage.

CONCLUSION

My story ends with "happily ever after," after all. In September 2012, my daughter moved home. We transferred her to a school with a healthy environment, and all of our lives have improved dramatically. My son is an adult and on his way to university along with his girlfriend. My relationship with both my children remains intact and healthy, and, surprisingly, my relationship with their other mother isn't bad either.

I want to challenge trans communities to mobilize to protect the rights of trans parents, our children, and our families—whatever form the latter takes. As Richard Green informed an audience at Oxford University,

> During the protracted period of litigation ... the non-transsexual parent promotes a negative image of the transsexual parent and any positive images fade in the absence of continuing positive experience. With no hard data demonstrating harm to a child from continuing direct contact with a transsexual parent, and many anecdotal experiences of a positive nature, the time is overdue for the transgender community to fight for parental rights with the same intensity as other, more publicized, battles raging for equal protection and fair play. (Green, 1998a)

A WORD FROM JESSICA BOYCE

A Youth's Perspective on Transitioning Families

Sometimes children grow up in situations that are out of the norm or different from most families. Most families have a mom, dad, and a few children, and you live in one house where you get on a bus every morning to go to school and come home every day for supper. Not every child has this experience; I didn't. Yes, I woke up every day and usually took a bus. I had an older brother whom I tolerated as part of the family that I came home to every day after school. But the first difference between me and the world was, I had two homes. I know this isn't a very strange story; divorce is, sadly, a common thing among families, but my parents' divorce was a bit more complicated. It started when I was about three years old, and my (soon-to-be) mother took my brother and me camping with my aunt. There, among the trees and the campfires, my mom first told me she that she was a girl and that I should call her "Mommy" not "Daddy." I asked her why she wasn't "Daddy," and she told me it was because when she was born, some parts of her were born a boy and some parts of her were born a girl. Well, I understood that, so "Mommy" she was.

At school, when people asked me why I didn't have a daddy, I decided that it was more fun to make a game out of it than to just tell them. So they went through all the scenarios: Were you adopted? No. Did your dad die? No. And, the most common, Did you never know who your dad was? Nope. Who gave birth to you, your curly-haired mom or your short-haired mom? Short-haired. After that they didn't know what questions to ask. So after a few days of them continuously asking, I'd try to explain it to them. And when I was done telling them about how my mommy was a daddy, but she changed to a mommy, they would look at me and ask, "Why would she ever do that?" And little me didn't understand why she would do that, so I gave them the answer they would understand: well, when she was born, some parts of her were a boy and some parts were a girl. They always accepted that because they were kids, and kids don't tend to judge people the way adults do.

Slowly I grew up. I went to my curly-haired mommy every other weekend and every Wednesday, and I was with my short-haired mommy the rest of the time along with my brother. Living with a transgendered mom and another mom wasn't much different than living with divorced lesbian parents. I got everything my parents could afford to give me, and I lived a pretty much normal life. As I got older, I no longer referred to them as "curly-haired mom" and "short-haired mom." To both of their dismay, when I was around other people, I wouldn't call them "Mom" anymore because that got way too confusing with two moms. Instead I called them by their first names when I was apart from them, and Mom when I was with each of them. It worked fine for the most part.

If I was in the presence of someone from her "team," that person would correct me when I wouldn't refer to one of my moms as "Mom. " Yes, there were teams, of course—people who rooted for one of the two moms and didn't appreciate me not loving one more than the other. They were the people that frustrated me the most. As I got older, the more my family seemed to get along but the more the people around me judged. I lived in a small religious town where finding another non-religious person like myself was like finding a needle in a haystack. No, it's not that I didn't like religious people, but religious people didn't seem to like me. The sad part was that I was perfectly fine. I didn't believe in the Bible, but there were a few who didn't and they still had lots of friends. I tried to make friends my whole life, but I was always the one with the strange parents; the different one. But it wasn't that bad. Most of the kids didn't care, and I had a few friends, but most of the friends I had weren't allowed to come over to my house alone. They were only allowed to come over if there were a few other kids there. If I hadn't found it so frustrating, I would have found it funny instead. All these parents who thought my mom was going to kidnap their kids, or corrupt them—it was ridiculous! I always wondered if my bad school experience would have been different if I had lived in a city, where people were more easygoing, and I think I'm going to find out.

I'm in high school now, in the city, and my school is amazing. Being different in this school isn't a bad thing, and I'm thinking people won't care who my mom is here. Overall, I think having a transgendered parent is just like having any other parent. The only difference is how the child feels about it, and how the people around you respond to it. But come to think of it, the same thing could happen because your parent is less wealthy than the rest of the people around them. Personally, I think people just like to judge!

REFERENCES

Bauer, G., Boyce, M., Coleman, T., Kaay, M., Scanlon, K., & Travers, R. (2010, July 26). Who are trans people in Ontario? *Trans PULSE E-Bulletin*. Retrieved from www.ohtn.on.ca/Documents/Publications/didyouknow/july28_10/E-Bulletin.pdf

Bone, J.M., & Walsh, M.R. (1999). Parental alienation syndrome: How to detect it and what to do about it. *The Florida Bar Journal, 73*(3), 44–48.

di Ceglie, D. (1998). Stranger in my own body: Atypical gender identity development and mental health. London: Karnac Books.

Freedman, D., Tasker, F., & di Ceglie, D. (2002). Children and adolescents with transsexual parents referred to a specialist. *Clinical Child Psychology and Psychiatry, 7*, 423–432.

Gardner, R. (1998). The parental alienation syndrome. New Jersey: Creative Therapeutics.

Green, R. (1978). Sexual identity of 37 children raised by homosexual or transsexual parents. *American Journal of Psychiatry, 135*, 692–697.

Green, R. (1998a). Transsexuals' children: Divorce and the implacable spouse. The Third International Congress on Sex and Gender: An Inter-disciplinary Conference, Exeter College, Oxford University, September 18–20.

Green, R. (1998b). Transsexuals' children. *International Journal of Transgenderism, 2*(4). Retrieved from www.transparentcy.org/Resources-Refs-TSChldrn-RGreen.htm

Green, R. (2006). Parental alienation syndrome and the transsexual parent. *International Journal of Transgenderism, 9*(1), 9–13.

Ludmer, B. (2011, June 20). Divorce and parent alienation. *Between the Margins* [Radio show]. Retrieved from www.betweenthemargins.ca/archives/btm_parent_alienation_show_sm.mp3

Owens, A.M. (2001, February 2). Father's sex change does not alter custody, court says. *National Post*. Retrieved from www.nationalpost.com/news/national/story.html?f=/stories/20010202/461994.html

Sales, J. (1995). Children of a transsexual father: A successful intervention. *European Child and Adolescent Psychiatry, 4*, 136–139.

Tully, B. (1992). *Accounting for transsexualism and transhomosexuality: The gender identity careers of over 200 men and women who have petitioned for surgical reassignment of the sexual identity*. London: Whiting and Birch.

White, T., & Ettner, R. (2004). Disclosure, risks and protective factors for children whose parents are undergoing a gender transition. *Journal of Gay and Lesbian Psychotherapy, 8*(1-2), 129–145.

White, T., & Ettner, R. (2007). Adaptation and adjustment in children of transsexual parents. *European Child Adolescent Psychiatry, 16*, 215–221.

Part II "Changing the Way We Change": Critical Reflections on Doing Trans Activism

Trans activists have been working to create change in various socio-economic, political, and cultural milieus for decades. Contributors to Part II draw on their own experiences of struggling for social change to offer critical reflections on trans politics. The chapters in this section offer readers insight into the affective dimensions of "trans-" oppression and its impact on trans activism. Trans subjects are governed by the colonialist, capitalist, imperialist, hetero-patriarchal relations that frame Canadian society, despite the fact that a significant number of trans people are excluded from Canadian nationhood as what Benedict Anderson identified as an "imagined community." Part II examines the ways that trans individuals are impacted by structural, institutional, and interpersonal violence. This section emphasizes the impact that such violence has on trans activist networks and communities. The chapters included here also offer practical solutions regarding how to address this violence individually and as a community, as well as techniques to cultivate more vibrant, equitable, and socially just cultures of resistance.

Three key themes can be gleaned from the introspective work presented here. Internalized and lateral violence and its corrosive effect on activism constitute the first theme. Governing relations have what Judith Butler has referred to as a "psychic life." Racialized, dis/abled, impoverished, and non-normatively sexed and gendered bodies have been pathologized, criminalized, exoticized, and castigated for their "failure" to abide by bourgeois codes of morality. Trans subjects internalize this derogatory knowledge, which is intended to reproduce and legitimize existing systems of power. As Grey Kimber Piitaapan Muldoon (Chapter 8), Rupert Raj (Chapter 9), Marie-Marcelle Godbout (Chapter 12), and Devon MacFarlane and Tien Neo Eamas (Chapter 15) discuss, this creates feelings of rage, depression, and anxiety. These feelings are often turned inward, rendering these subjects as at risk and jeopardizing activist networks through lateral violence. Lateral violence refers to injurious behaviours perpetrated by trans individuals and/or networks toward other trans people and/or organizations.

The second theme relates to reflexivity as an ethical responsibility for social justice activists. As asserted by barbara findlay (Chapter 10), Calvin Neufeld (Chapter 11), and Grey Muldoon (see Chapter 8), it is necessary for individuals to evaluate themselves and their actions in relation to the social world. How is one's subjectivity and approach to politics influenced by privilege? How does privilege influence what is identified as an issue for trans politics? As Raj points out, reflexivity is not the same as harbouring liberal guilt. Critical introspection is work performed with the intention of opening one's mind, heart, and spirit to learning about oneself and others in relation to power, with a commitment to transformative movement. The insidious nature of whiteness, able-bodiedness, and masculinity, as well as the privileges afforded by middle-class location, geographical location, citizenship status, and, as Neufeld argues, being classified as human rather than animal, must be recognized, challenged, and unlearned.

Strategies to create, sustain, and strengthen trans networks represent the third major theme of Part II. As Godbout suggests in an interview with Viviane Namaste and Nora Butler Burke, "self-love" is a vital tactic that can work to strengthen trans individuals and communities. In his chapter, Raj articulates the need for trans activists to engage in self-care before they experience burnout, vicarious trauma, and other harmful effects of such intense socio-political engagement. Nurturing each other is another way that trans networks can work through challenges. MacFarlane and Eamas discuss their organizing of two free events open to trans community members and their friends, families, and allies. Through these events, they sought to uplift, inspire, and re/invigorate trans individuals and allies by shifting the focus from despair and hopelessness to joy and celebration. By focusing on the knowledge that trans people have much to be proud of, they worked to challenge internalized violence. In the round table discussion presented in Chapter 14, the participants demonstrate the ways that trans and queer youth with intellectual disabilities acknowledge each other's sex and gender identity and sexuality as valid, and ensure each other's belonging in the wake of social exclusion. In Chapter 13, members of the Trans Access team discuss how they address the psychological impacts of trans identities and embodiment coming under scrutiny when providing trans education for social service, health care, and education providers and agencies.

Contributors such as Raj, the Trans Access team members, and MacFarlane and Eamas emphasize the importance of adopting and exercising conflict resolution models to ensure the growth of trans networks, programs, and communities. They offer practical suggestions gleaned from their own experiences. Open communication, honesty, and holding each other accountable to standards of equity and justice serve as examples. A key to conflict resolution—and remedying the lateral violence that can often occur when privilege is not interrogated—lies in being open to change. Such openness is modelled through the shift in method halfway through Chapter 8, as the written text based on interviews conducted with trans subjects residing in Northern Ontario gives way to an interview in which Grey Muldoon discusses with his co-editor, Dan Irving, how activism can be compromised when particular voices are discouraged.

This section demonstrates the ways that critique must be directed inward. Trans subjects, networks, and communities are central actors in the production of knowledge that can propel or obstruct transformative change.

Chapter 8 A Sense of Place: Expressions of Trans Activism North of Lake Nipissing

Grey Kimber Piitaapan Muldoon[1] (with Dan Irving)

"Who are you?" cannot be separated from "Where are you from?" Place and a sense of what that place means is necessary for us to feel we belong—we belong somewhere, amongst, and in relation to. We are found in our human relations and in relation to all that is. To situate our identities without physical surroundings is to dissociate. Gender identity, counter identity, or lack of identity is experienced in place.

Written from a first-person perspective, this chapter presents portraits of eight two-spirit and trans activists currently residing in Northern Ontario. Meant as a piece of documentary artivism, the method of gathering these life stories, the struggle to prepare a text, and the format are crucial to the inquiry. The interviewees are respected collaborators in this work. It includes an interview between the author and editor Dan Irving, allowing further analysis of themes and reflections on affect, academia, and activism. The key question posed to collaborators was "What is it like to live here for you?" Themes of spirituality, families, and being "out" on the land, as well as isolation, hyper-visibility, substance abuse/recovery, and relocating for services or to meet other queer people, emerge. While this work addresses Northern Ontarian experiences primarily, the work also situates that experience in relationship to the "scenes" of larger cities. Refuting the universalizing idea of ignorant-unsafe locales, it asks where is gender un/expected or un/supported, and by whom/what? Against the erasure of the success, agency, and beauty special to each place, it seeks a subject-to-subject dialogue. The interviews were completed in 2009, took place in the communities, and were achieved without funds through hitchhiking and hospitality. Some additional interviews were held and all were reflected upon in 2012.

Most people, especially trans, two-spirit, and queer people, fear being confined by our past: many of us feel a need to deny our history daily to survive. I wonder about the possibility of continuity, bringing new meanings out of our past identities and circumstances.

Azilda is a hamlet on Whitewater Lake, near Sudbury, Ontario, where I grew up from 1982 to 2001. In the summer of 2009, I planned to return, queerly, after gender transition but before sex transition. My experience in Toronto's queer, social work, and activist spaces could not answer questions such as: "Are there (m)any other trans people in Sudbury?" "Will I get killed there?" "Can I be myself in First Nations spaces?" and "Does my desire to change my body relate to my spirit?" These questions were out of place. I yearned for my origins: for others like me.

I was not looking for those finding themselves out of place in a backwater. I wanted to question the idea of a backwater filled with ignorant "primitives," requiring enlightenment from the Silver City. So, I hitchhiked to Sudbury, North Bay, Thunder Bay, and Sault Ste. Marie, with analog tape and a recorder to interview seven people I did not yet know. These people had responded to a call out: "Looking for two-spirit, genderqueer, and trans people in the North to interview about their activism (gender identity–based or otherwise)."[2] I went to every community where someone had responded.

Please excuse my bias in language. This area is only "North" in its cultural relationship to the rest of the province, but "South" to many communities further north. Similarly, I refer to Toronto and Ottawa as "the cities," though they are only ones of greater magnitude. Sudbury, Sault Ste. Marie, Thunder Bay, and North Bay are commercial centres and cities in relation to other places such as Moose Factory or Gore Bay.

I conducted this research without institutional supports, needing my actions to speak for me rather than only my credentials. I hitchhiked and accepted hospitality where it came, encountering and responding to power dynamics and prejudices manifesting in others and myself. Struggling with material resources and relying on the people I met is not only a contribution to constructed images of the romantic and rugged Northern life; it also demonstrates an approach of pragmatism, honing practical relationship skills and emphasizing network development, which are *necessary* tactics for persons of poverty and those seeking good relation to the land.[3]

I set out with two ideas like stones carried in a hip-pouch on the road.

First, the dominating conception of a gender non-conforming life is native to the cosmopolitan, and natal to Toronto, New York, San Francisco, and other *specific* locations. Other forms become invisible. The male person that I felt myself to be was not Torontonian. My preferred way of life and surroundings that I felt most alive in are not necessarily the ones offering social networks, ideas, safety, and amenities to people with "strange" gender experiences. To become visible, did I need to change?

Second, being its own place, Northern Ontario has its own struggles and genders, and therefore its own experiences of gender non-conformity. I believed these unique experiences to be valuable to equity and freedom struggles, not as a broadening of thought for those in centralized locations that suggest a "true" centre to stretch away from toward distant things, but as an introduction to a whole other centre of experience. The other centres exist in relation to the urban-centred experience. I wanted a more dynamic model comprehending multiple centres.

Everyone that I met was brave and inspiring. Everyone.

PRESENTING PERSONAL NARRATIVES

1. *Starr Loon Danyals* is a trans woman in her early thirties who lives in downtown Sudbury. She has cats and offers me tea. She does presentations on trans experience and volunteers for the Women's Center and the Sudbury AIDS service organization. For her, activism is surviving and living your life as you are openly. She says that volunteering proves that she is a real person in the community because she contributes to it. When she was younger, she was going to be a Catholic priest. She still likes prayer and spirituality, but also thinks that what could be called God or a creator appreciates our using our freedom to be diverse. She never liked the hierarchy of the Church. It forced her out for being "gay" when she was 21. In her twenties she developed a drag queen persona named "Twilight Starr." Since 2007, she has been living

as a woman. The harassment was worse for her when she was in her drag role and outside the clubs or bars than it has been for her as Starr Danyals, yet she stays inside sometimes for weeks because of the staring, threat of violence, and "flabbergasting" ignorance. She is a big-boned, tall woman and does not think she will ever pass, yet she does not see a man in her face: while tall like the women in her father's family, she sees her mom and the women from that side in her facial features. She has a blonde wig and black wig. The black one reminds her of her paternal relatives; the blonde one, of her mom's. Both sides are bilingual French-Canadian Catholics. Her mom is important to her, so she is working to make her relationship with her a good one.

2. *Vincent Bolt* is a Sudbury FTM in his early twenties. He has given many presentations on trans issues in Sudbury, usually without pay, leads trans support groups, and worked with the Primed resource project in Toronto. A very keen Marilyn Manson fan, he meets me in a T-shirt depicting Manson's prettiest phase. He once had a black-furred rabbit named Phoebe, who is his Higher Power in AA. Phoebe died in 2012. He was raised a Catholic and started high school at an all-girls Catholic prep school. There, he experienced harassment for being a Goth and outspoken in temperament as much as for being a female with a girlfriend, which ultimately led to his activism. I spoke to him in 2009 and again in 2012 after coming across him at a queer-friendly eatery and artist hub in Sudbury. In 2012, he notes that he did not meet another trans person for a year after coming out. Things have already changed radically for people disclosing or coming out as trans in Sudbury since he did so. He passed as male in 2009, but now has found that the continued use of hormones and his chest surgery have helped him to lose weight and travel around the bathhouses of Europe with joy and ease. (He recommends the hot tubs.) He is seeking further medical transition. He was raised to feel like he most belongs to his Italian mother's family lineage. He also knew his two Anglo-Canadian great-grandparents, who have now passed on. He says, "They were wonderful. Great-grandpa made no fuss about me being Vincent." These grandparents adopted and raised his grandmother, who was of First Nations descent. Vincent is proud to be connected to these three relatives.

3. *Anonymous* is a two-spirit woman who is turning 30. She works as a queer health researcher and is married to a woman who is a teacher. They are moving further north immediately after this interview, and we lose contact in the move. From a low-income background, her parents were both members of Narcotics Anonymous. Her father quit NA and left her mom with four children when she was 6 years old. She remembers her mom surviving on $400 a month with four children: "I don't know how she did it." Her mom, an addictions counsellor, is Mi'kmaq and French, and the family has struggled for Aboriginal status. For my collaborator, Anonymous, this struggle is about finding out who she is. She feels pain, anger, and fire and wants to know what happened to put it there. She speaks poetically and brilliantly about historical trauma: she says it passes on through generations, spirit melding into spirit, transferring unresolved. She connects her experience of feeling not queer enough as a woman attracted to men and women with her experience of feeling not Native enough as a person of mixed heritage without "status." She has written a poem about a healing she had that was undermined by that elder telling her that lesbian love is a confusion of friendship: "Where do I belong?

Where is safety and security? Where is love?" Literally sitting as we are in a town where most people consider themselves Christian, she is aware that for some people around us the answer to these questions is in Jesus. While she thinks Jesus is "fucking great," she is "not interested in worshipping someone else." We discuss gender presentation, and she admits that she would present as more androgynous but feels pressured to present as pretty or feminine to be more accepted in the community, even by those who know her wife as her wife.

She describes her impression that "people are more beautiful in Toronto," with some embarrassment for her homely home. I am struck. Rather than reject her generalization, I think it's politically insightful: like many oppressed groups, we are made to feel ugly. Also, being Northern icons, like other things deemed inferior, we are appropriated for ironic urban currency. Appropriation tells me that something complicated is happening. We are discussing a ubiquitous queer whose glossy, trendy, mannered, and together impression—the messiness itself glamorous and calculated—denies the gritty, worn, shabby, openly mad, and neglected queer. I suggest that people here have different priorities, less access to health care, social support, disposable income, and fashionable goods and services. I insist: anyone with resources could learn to look that way. She says, "I've heard [people say] it's because of incest in small towns." So have I. Often.

Perhaps anonymity in the city explains the greater devotion to image management, in part—it is easier to achieve this type of beauty when you can avoid being seen at your worst. It also makes "beauty" more desirable when a glance in passing is often the only contact between individuals. I tell her that Northern people overwhelm me with their beauty, using a different rubric. Glittering city people can keep their inner lives guarded, even if they declare their political affiliations and gender in their outer appearance more than she does. This mimics how outliers can feel about political theory and language. They feel ugly, even gross or deformed, about their "imperfect" point of view.

4. *Treanor Mahood-Greer* was born and grew up in Southern Ontario (Hamilton region). A long-time activist in his mid-fifties, he is suffering burnout in 2009 and spending time as a "gardener"—meaning he is recuperating so he can be effective. I meet him, his partner, and their dogs at their home. He notes his motorcycle in the driveway, which is named "Sex Change," and jokes that it is a less expensive and more practical marker of gender identity. They give me moose steak. I show him that I have "fat-sacks" too, but I am in a (chest) binder. His partner orders one online immediately.

Treanor's dad has cerebral palsy and did any task expected of him anyway, providing an interesting example of performing masculinity for Treanor growing up. He remembers being ostracized at church as a kid and still can't tolerate the patriarchy in it. His lesbian feminist years gave him pagan and goddess models for spiritual action. A trans-positive minister who, along with the congregation, encourages Treanor to draw pictures while he's there, heads the church he goes to now with his partner. People appreciate his drawings instead of thinking he is being disrespectful by not paying attention, and he appreciates this. Treanor always wanted to be in the bush when he was growing up, and became a geological technician working with a "bunch of ol' boys." He was the only woman in the bush who was "different," as in looking like and working like the men (that is, "like the men" according to the standards in that environment). He describes how in the bush, being accepted as a man meant being seen as competent. This was achieved not only by actually being competent, but also by not being seen as nervous or uncertain when faced with dangerous or unfamiliar tasks, and was performed by language, gestures, or postures of acting like you knew what you were doing, and by watching first. This insight can be applied to many masculinities. In Treanor's case, he's a butch, just like The Duke (John Wayne). "For lack of a better word" he now identifies as a trans man. He's currently a social worker and has a chapter in this book (see Chapter 18).

A major goal of my project is to connect other people together. Treanor is seeking more mentorship, or open subject-to-subject communication from other trans people.

Treanor remembers when he was developing his lesbian social identity. A butch took him aside and magically explained all the words and customs of being butch. He remembers her smoking a pipe and how wonderfully impressive this was. Through this connection, he could learn gender competence in a personal, private moment.

Without a similar figure in transgender spaces, he has felt he is expected to know things or want things he does not. This mentorship is not about explaining Treanor to himself, but about a welcome introduction to the unaccustomed social milieu, and resource sharing. For example, he shyly observes that he is expected to cover his chest if he has not had surgery, even in a hot tub in a trans space, but he does not see why or like the implications. He feels out of place. In a case like this, someone willing and eager with whom to discuss feelings of disorientation prevents isolation and creates new insights for both people.

I think this is linked to Treanor's "John Wayne" gender and description of passing as "like a man" in the bush. Though other genders also wish to seem competent or not naive when entering a new social space, Treanor's stories connect this desire and masculinities. Asking lots of questions is contrary to some preferred ways of obtaining new skills.

Trans experience has grown through the Internet. People take off-line experience into online experience, and take online experiences back into their physical locations. But it is important to recall that even carefully crafted online relationships do not replace live sharing. You cannot work out your whole gendered life online. Online conversations might feel exclusive and far away, and simply lack elements that only occur when bodies are present in the same space, such as when sharing a meal of moose steak and poutine. Customs the urban dweller has had ample opportunity to explore are treated as basic to trans identity and experience. Non-urban dwellers may feel naive as trans people and activists while the unique knowledge not possessed by the urban person goes unnoticed and unsought.

Treanor does not lack experience, yet he quips that it's hard to feel respectable or take up space as a trans activist when your accomplishment might be having three people over to your house for a potluck. We need to celebrate these tiny gatherings for what they are: powerful. They take the same energy as larger ones because they mean doing the same amount of work. When Treanor's partner encourages him to move to where there are more trans people, Treanor believes he would perhaps be overwhelmed or even bored with all the trans-related activities in a central location.

He has developed and is working with a concept for approaching gender-based oppression as "genderism." It is my opinion that this insightful approach is inspired by his location. I hear a version of it from the other interviewees, and in myself. What Treanor calls genderism is often labelled as sexism, trans/misogyny, or transphobia. While these things are also occurring, genderism proposes an entirely different frame. Genderism, as I understand his concept, affects all persons who are treated or treat persons as inferior for reasons of "gender"—a set of expectations for congruence amongst behaviour/s, presentation/s, body, and internal experience/s of gender.

Specifically, genderism is rooted in a set of standard, acceptable social genders enforced structurally through not recognizing other genders or by not giving primacy to the individual's sense of their own gender. Genderism may cause one devastating effect, transphobia, in which people experience fear of people who transition, seek transition, or who otherwise are perceived to cross the dominating boundaries of established genders. "Sexism" is supported by and complexly related to genderism. To distinguish it from genderism, it might be described as the socially constructed inferiority of one sexed body, on this planet and in this era, usually female, intersex, and trans bodies. Treanor does not use "transphobia," as this term is often used to refer to genderism as a whole, implying that fear is the major manifest form of oppression and that trans people alone experience oppression through genderism. Genderism also oppresses cispeople, genderqueer people, women, and men.

5. *Ma-Nee Chacaby* is a two-spirit elder and lesbian woman who lives in Thunder Bay. Ma-Nee is wonderful to talk to. I highly recommend tea with her. She really likes being herself. She tells me so, over and over. Four years later, in response to her, I still think to myself: "How? How do I be myself, Ma-Nee?" Then I laugh at me. Her name, "Ma-Nee," was lost to her for a while, so she had to reclaim it. It refers to a hill covered in blueberries. Her apartment is covered in her artwork, mostly paintings. She likes to give these as gifts, creating a wealth of relationships through the presence of her work in other homes. She works in paint with the challenge of impaired eyes. She is in her sixties and has been working as an elder since she was 34. It was very hard for her to accept the need to do this work, as it means responsibility for others, and she has sometimes found it hard to be responsible even for only herself. She feels her two-spirit self in her work as a healer. It makes her able to empathize strongly with both men and women. She was raised speaking Cree and Ojibwe and learned English when she started school. She was raised to believe in a "higher power outside": "Like, trees. And, grass. And water. And rocks. Rocks are my stones—they're like my fathers and mothers, grandmothers. Rocks and stones are my grandparents."

Ma-Nee was a toddler when her grandmother (*kokum*) located her. She had been adopted into a French family. Her *kokum* raised her often miles away from anyone else, surviving by trapping, fishing, and eating moose near Ombabika, in the Lake Nipigon area. Her *kokum* told her about her own long life and about traditional roles for two-spirit persons before her death at age 104. Ma-Nee, then 15, wedded a man in a marriage arranged by her birth mother. The marriage was abusive and did not last long. Like my own family, there are many adoptions in Ma-Nee's. She has three children: two birth children and a daughter, Maya, whom Ma-Nee adopted when she was 15. Maya is now a language activist who lives in Toronto. Her daughter asks her to come to Toronto where it would be less lonely, but Ma-Nee likes being a 15-minute walk from the bush, and even Thunder Bay seems crowded to her. Her life has been full of activism and harsh retaliation. She was beaten up several times after coming out in 1988 on television during an interview about an equal rights protest action. Race was a factor in the attacks. Sometimes it was white people who attacked and sometimes it was Native people, who said they believed she was making it even worse for them, since they were already suffering racist attacks and did not need to be associated with gay people and suffer that violence (against gay people) too. Ma-Nee is an AA member and enjoys the (not queer) dances, but again feels lonely and rejected there. Most of Ma-Nee's chosen family are white gays and lesbians. (I meet some of them. They run the Women's Center, which welcomed trans people in 2009.) Yet she wishes there were more out Native gays and lesbians. They all leave, she knows, because life is too hard in Thunder Bay—but that is changing. She is trying to start a social group for cross-gender and two-spirit people with her friend Chris...

6. *Christian Thompson* is two-spirit (Nakota) and transgender. He had recently arrived in Thunder Bay from Regina. He arrives at the interview in a blue truck covered in canoes, and enjoys hunting, kayaking, hiking, and snowshoeing. He had not taken hormones but had undergone some chest surgery when I spoke to him in 2009. When I contact him in 2012, he informs me that he has now been on hormones for a year and is living as male. Especially before he could be read as male, it was very important to him that transgender be understood as an internal experience and as not having much to do with presentation. For him, this was linked to the fracturing of communities, as we tend to tell each other who we are or must be. His activist work, then, is an "examination of giving ourselves voice." Christian is working to develop resources for "outlying and rural" transgender people, working out of Northwestern Ontario. I am given a resource he is humble about having helped create called *Convergence*, a video document in which queer Northern persons are given voice. It resonates with me. Christian's work means that he knows many local trans people. He notices that people leave for years to facilitate transition and may not feel comfortable coming back, having resettled after being displaced.

7. *Wendy Houle* is a woman and a transsexual in her late fifties. She is a commercial artist, an ex-military marching musician, and a disability activist. As a child she suffered a brain injury, and while relearning how to speak, she would draw to communicate. With multiple disabilities, including a back condition, depression, and the complex effects of the brain injury, she has spent her life being told she could not do what others could and "being put down." Yet she has done many things in her community: she now works in civics and volunteers, advocating for better access for people with disabilities, including transsexuals. She has also faced other people's gender problems her entire life: "They have a gender problem, not me." First visiting Toronto's Centre for Addiction and Mental Health (CAMH) in 1991, she began living as Wendy full-time in 2002 and is excited to be finally going to Montreal for sex reassignment surgery (SRS) in 2013. After college, she married a woman who accepted her internal experience of gender but who later divorced her because she could not live with her depression.

The people at CAMH once told her that she should move closer to it. But Wendy has four children who were then living with her ex-spouse, and she wanted to stay where they were. Having lost custody on the basis of her experience with depression, she regained custody in 1993, performing as a single parent. Baptized Catholic, but with a Protestant mother, Wendy went through an agnostic phase. However, she began to associate the part of her that loved life with spirituality during her deepest depression. Now, especially as she can live more and more fully as Wendy, she feels the awareness of an inner spiritual life growing.

Wendy struggled with CAMH, who she says "have no clue about the North." By chance, we meet several women Wendy knows. None of the women are queer, trans, or butch, and none of them have long hair or wear skirts or makeup. Wendy says her presentation as a woman on these local terms made it difficult to access services in Toronto. Eagerly anticipating SRS this year, Wendy says that she is the same person she has always been: while she needs her body to change, she looks at people "on the inside" and would prefer it if others did too. For Wendy, the worst trouble is her loneliness related to her disabilities and gender.

Wendy has not experienced physical assault in Sault Ste. Marie for her gender. Indeed, for many people I spoke with, the worst and most prevalent violence seemed to be isolation and neglect. I found less direct violence being reported than was expected by my family and friends, who believed that I could not even survive here. Wendy comments that she finds avoiding physical violence possible because she is a sober person. Again, instead of taking her comment as indicative of her ignorance of assaults that do not involve intoxication, I find insights. Firstly, not everyone can easily avoid intoxication or spaces where others are intoxicated or prone to violence. Indeed, many experiencing depression and similar conditions also experience a disinterest in protecting themselves. So, while no one should have to avoid public spaces, this survival skill (sobriety and awareness of environmental factors) should be lauded. While there may be less area, literally, in which to establish demarcated queer "safe" space in a smaller place, people from cities with peaceable neighbours may forget that they avoid some places in their city to feel safer. Because people from elsewhere may not acknowledge local decorum or know where to go or how to escape danger, they may mistakenly conclude that a place is experienced the same way by locals. Secondly, activists in any location cannot ignore the relationship between violence, intoxication, and cultures of intoxication. Creating more sober space, engaging in reduction-of-harm tactics, and questioning cultural links between violence and intoxication are necessary to improve the lives of everyone. Almost all of the people I spoke to understood the connection between substance abuse activism and queer activism, such as the correlation of unsupported queer identities and mental health. Assaults happen everywhere within queer spaces and between trans people, and not only from external threats; often cultures of intoxication are involved and unquestioned.

REPRESENTING THE STORIES OF THE PEOPLE

To my great fortune, I presented this project at a panel discussion during the Sudbury Pride celebration in 2011 at an event that screened a documentary called *Does This Canoe Make Me Look Fat?* I presented alongside an old friend who spoke about bisexual activism, and was paid with a donated case of Pepsi and the cost of bus fare from Toronto. I felt so welcome in that room, which was "surprisingly" surprising. There were people there who had known me from before I left. Whisked out to a lake to swim under the stars, I found I could not relax and be there. I had only ever been seen as a woman in Sudbury and transitioned in isolation in Toronto.

I had originally hoped for a coherent research narrative, full of quotes from the interviews.[4] Perhaps I failed. But perhaps something more interesting happened in these five years. It is now 2013. In this very short time the experience of trans and two-spirit people in the North has changed dramatically. The Additional Resources listed at the end of this chapter address these changes.

In late 2012, I believed I could not afford to complete any version of this work. I wrote

Dan Irving to say so. Dan asked if he could interview me about my research instead. He was interested in "the affective obstacles" I had faced as a trans activist "when trying to communicate with other trans activists," and believed "the opportunity to transition to an alternative format of communication creates space to elaborate on experiences in Northern Ontario and also discuss openly the ways that our abilities to voice our concerns and listen to others are compromised by fears of judgment and tying ourselves in knots—due to our mutual commitments to equity and social justice—to ensure no one is offended."

I am not sure what Dan is talking about. Perhaps he is saying that activists are restricting voices by being so critical of one another, and that dialogue brings wisdom. I could appreciate that.

Part of that interview follows.

A CONVERSATION BETWEEN DAN AND GREY

Dan Irving (DI): Can you discuss your project and why you believe such research is important?

Grey Muldoon (GM): A sense of place in activism is important. I will explain why twice: once in an academic voice, once in another voice; both are important.

Voice 1: A sense of place is important in activism for the following reasons. First, gender variation exists everywhere, yet gender-based experience varies locally. Thus, basing theory and activism of gender on urban-based experiences only reflects forms of experience dominant in the city. Second, those with resources tend to control how knowledge is produced. Third, cities are in a colonizing relationship vis-à-vis less densely populated locations with less material infrastructure. Less dense locales are forced to support the aims of the cities. Cities benefit and yet posit themselves as benefactors, patronizing of and charitable to the marginalized margins. Fourth, the activism of the cities generally views other locations as a *terra nobilis* or as primitive (note: colonial language is intentional) places without valid cultures and resistance cultures of their own. And, finally, universalizing robs us of our specificity.

I was hoping to disrupt such theory and organizing strategies that threaten to erase contextualized experiences.

Voice 2: Dear City-Lover: A sense of place is significant to our sense of ourselves. Where do we come from? Where do we go? Gender is unique everywhere—each location has its own specialness in making gender. (This is like the variety in local cheeses.) Non-urban spaces have produced ideas of benefit to all and residents have "developed" thoughts of their own. We may actually like living here.

We have a context: without the anonymity of large cities, many have greater privacy needs. Without the supportive infrastructure or presence of others with trans and two-spirit experiences, we have a greater need for the support of the cisgender and straight people in our lives. This means we have interesting, fulfilling relations with non-trans communities and people, which those who do not could learn from. You might be missing something.

Speaking of which, you may not find us when you look or ask around. Maybe we do not dress like the people with similar gender or politics in bigger cities, or use the same labels, or have the same social activities or hobbies that you recognize as activism. Want to have tea instead? When we place other identities—such as parent, child, hockey coach, rape crisis counsellor, Catholic, Native—in priority above achieving gender recognition, we may need to make that choice. We might like to adopt or adapt some of your tools, but stop proselytizing, okay? Some of what you have—like those rainbow stickers, and synthetic hormones, and the operations—seem useful. Show us what you have to offer. We would like to decide what we need to take for ourselves. Thanks for listening, Backwoods and Bushy Trails.

DI: How did you go about getting people to interview?

GM: The call out I used was meant specifically to show knowledge and respect for Northerners in how it was worded. More generally, it had a non-medicalizing approach, offered direct one-to-one contact, and an open question format. I thought it was important to visit the communities in person rather than conducting the interviews over the phone or by using electronic media.

DI: What were some differences in organizing in the North to come out of the interviews?

GM: Mainly, it's more draining and less rewarded. There is no infrastructure for organizing—basic problems such as having nowhere to meet after 5 p.m. except a bar, so that before you meet, you need to find everyone, create the space, and by then you are tired. Meanwhile, you are expending energy getting needs met, travelling long distances for specialized services, or researching, or educating, or social contact. It is rare to get paid or compensated materially for activism. HIV/AIDS service organizations, some bars and restaurants, and some university and women's services are supportive while some rape crisis centres and shelters were unapologetically (I asked) inaccessible.

On a more positive note, participants shared complex thoughts combining their gender, activism, spirituality, and the local environment. Spirituality and the bush, even "solitude," are not things you hear much about elsewhere; things are not as parsed and cerebral as they are within many urban resistance efforts and initiatives.

DI: In 2008, Lucas Crawford wrote a piece for *Women's Studies Quarterly* where he argued that it is problematic to assume that non-urban, rural communities are "backward" or "lacking in community": while "trans" may not be visible as it is in Toronto and gender may be performed differently in rural Ontario, this does not mean that these areas are less developed. How do you respond to this? Did your conversations with folks in Northern Ontario produce similar findings?

GM: The question is problematic for two reasons. First, I did not speak to "rural people." Neither a trapline nor a mining/logging city is a "rural" space. That is a displaced English motif of the countryside, mismatched to the geography, ecology, and occupations of many non-urban places. Second, proving that non-urban places are not backward resembles proving that queer people are not perverts or that racialized people are not animalistic. To begin with, whose standards am I using, and why? It's an offensive thing to try to prove you are not inferior using someone else's concepts of value, isn't it?

The idea of "backward" is especially virulent and malignant with depictions of two-spirit people. Most definitions of two-spirit suggest time-travellers coming from the past. Depictions enshrine people as historical relics instead of presenting a tradition that is creating culture for the future.

Even more so, the word "community" in your query needs to be critiqued. A community is not the same as a shared identity. A community requires participation and not simply consumption of identity-related cultural products and theories. It involves contributing to shared resources. The greater the participation of each person and reliance on one another, the greater is the applicableness of the word "community." Northerners are entirely better at comprehending this interconnectedness. They are interested in being ordinary; they are interested in seeing their exceptional qualities honoured, not singled out.

It was not my intention to objectively prove that everyone desires to remain in remote places. In fact, most persons, regardless of identity, leave the North to find or follow opportunities elsewhere. What I am showing is that if some people want to leave, this does not prove that there is a problem with being "queer" or "different" in a small place *categorically*. I feel that it is a myth that keeps the opportunities in big cities, creating a sort of drain of power, talent, and energy. Often the person leaving is not actually interested in or suited to the city but must try to be to achieve their dreams and visions.

DI: Any further topics you want to discuss regarding your research?

GM: Yes. I would like to address two things that I think contribute to the idea that small places are oppressive. The first is the confusion of familiarity with understanding and acceptance, or the mistaken idea that familiarity leads to a positive relationship. It should be obvious that we can have a hateful and oppressive relationship with those we are familiar with. In fact, familiarity is often necessary to ingrain supremacy. We can have an open and respectfully curious relationship with things that are new to us, or a violent one. A violent one can arise from a horrific sense of dread and disgust that occurs in us when something strikes us as not fitting into the categories essential to our safety. Two-spirit, trans, or otherwise "strange" people can cause this response in others and amongst ourselves. This can certainly be overcome, but we would need to recognize its presence. The same is true for a response to the unknown. We may project and imagine things more in spaces unknown to ourselves and others, but what we project or how confident we feel is learned. Persons in the city continually confuse superficial familiarity and etiquette around "othered" people with respectful relationships.

The second idea is that the stereotypes perpetuate the status quo. People outside cities internalize the myths about small-town small-mindedness and no longer see counter evidence or fight against oppression in those spaces, considering it natural and hopeless. Meanwhile, small-town people who resent the domination of the cities amplify their stereotyped bigotry to protect their sense of distinction. They use their cultural location to defend and perpetuate this behaviour and the supremacy it maintains. Queers become associated with the city and its stereotyped features. The queers are then defined as out of place, for better and worse.

DI: Shifting focus, while the significant time lags on our part as editors impacted your ability to engage with your project in this particular written format, you also experienced affective disturbance in terms of writing. Can you speak to this?

GM: I have a fancy university education, so that my grassroots style and history of poverty with its linked chronic health conditions should not hinder my production of written output … but it does! Dan, you commented that you are aware of the challenges, contradictions, and benefits of performing trans activist labour within the milieu of scholastic publishing. As I find myself at odds with my love of scholarship, I appreciate that awareness. I fought hard to gain access to that world, and do not find it easy to dismiss it or devalue it. However, not everyone becomes equally educated in school, though they obtain the same credentials. And there are other ways to educate: I do not think education is the same as schooling. Some of this is about exclusion in activism in the popular sense of excluded categories (class, ability, fluencies, literacies), but more interestingly, I think we are talking about the failures of activism that takes schooling as a model. Our strategies emphasize rote learning, required reading, social literacy, propriety, perfection of lexicon and syntax, and ultimately credentialism. I do not think we can approach equity, justice, or even dignity with only the tactics of a system meant to reproduce marks of class. At the moment, to be queer and social is to be schooled and classed.

DI: So often we, as trans activists, speak of being rendered invisible or silenced by the government, the medical establishment, within social services, and so forth. However, we often silence each other. Can you comment on this?

GM: Thanks. Actually, I had not considered that all the apologists and their attempts to assuage their own fear, guilt, and shame had silenced me. Let me do so here.

Before I touched trans activism, I was involved in anti-poverty, mad, and feminist politics. Words are very important. But I do not want to foster superficial criticism of inclusion by adding one more thing to the list of things people can attack and degrade each other for "oppressing"—calling out people for their anti-rural prejudice, urban privilege, or problematically non-snowmobile-inclusive transportation statement.

To make word-based activism effective, we would need to *remember how to listen to each other*. I don't want to be one more speaking voice if the problem is that no one is listening, and I do not know if I can listen anymore after all that so-called "anti-oppression" training. I worry I will hurt people every time I talk now, yet I do not think anymore without attacking.

DI: When you wrote to inform me of your decision to pull your chapter from the reader, you articulated specific affective obstacles that prevented you from writing. Can you speak to your fears and anxieties in terms of the imagined audience you believed you were writing for, the criticisms that you believed you would face, and the pressure you felt to have your analysis be completely comprehensive and inclusive?

GM: Your question might be read as personally directed hostility or as priming the reader to see a weak person. I know this is not your intention, and knowing that it is not is what bothers me most.

Contrary to the chorus of *imagined* voices you depict, I know real people who have told me to stop speaking who will read this anthology. I was mainly dealing with despair; feeling ineffective. As a person of poverty, I also fear the shame of having to fight for my own voice in scholarship in a way my "peers" do not. But the things to fear from writing are not only "voices." People legitimately fear concrete backlash from other "activists": assault, harassment, loss of work, denial of funding or permissions, and withdrawal of social support tragically result from attempts to gain security and agency.

Then there are the imagined projections you infer. They begin with voices telling me to "get over myself and write." As if the problem is simply that *I* care how much people think of me personally. Then they start with gender. They tell me that I should see myself as 100 percent—"has always been"—MAN, or I should not call myself one. They tell me not to identify with my body/parts, that none of my embodied experience is like a woman's, and, as a man, I should not expect to talk about sexism as a personal experience. As a "trans" male feminist, I should be an adorable helpful child. Forever. Except in bed. I should fuck everyone who comes on to me, just like when I was an underpaid, big-busted blonde. Except, they insist, for a man, no sexual pressure or expectation can be coercive. They tell me I should be really mad at people who are seen as fitting within acceptable gender norms.

They do not stop at gender. They say I do not *really* have chronic pain or autism. They say that autism means I lack empathy. They require me to either perform as more disabled or overcome the pain. They do not care about depression. They tell me that I should not practice indigenous thought or spirituality because I have grey eyes, unless I can justify my location as an authentically racialized "victim" in *their* eyes. My family's poverty makes me icky or sexy or both, but *never* competent. They insist I'm a snob if I do not feel freer eating out of dumpsters. They advise that not relishing witnessing trauma is sheltering myself from life. PTSD is overreaction if it's *my* PTSD. My poverty is merely relative if I am "Canadian." Oh, and though they have never been further north than Barrie-North, they tell me it's not relevant to be from the North if you are now in Toronto, or that being trans and looking white in the North is not as serious a challenge to agency in this world as being a trans sex worker of colour in the city. They fragment and reify me. They tell me to fragment and reify myself too. They tell me to pretend that I do—or do not—know the word "reify." They demand I situate myself in reified fragments. And then they call me a liberal. But they also complain that I am erasing the violence and stifling the homogeneity they experienced as trans people in their own rural small-towny past, by my saying it's not horrible t/here now.

As if it's personal… And the last voice, my mom, is screaming: "Don't tell them you're poor! You had enough! Think you had it *real* rough, huh? I spoiled you."

I mutter: "I have been tired of hearing about who had it easier than whom since before I could speak."

Mom says, more quietly: "If you tell them what you don't got, then that is all they'll ever see. And you get to go nowhere—fast."

I say: "They see it anyway. Maybe I should tell them what it is they are seeing."

Then my real mom, not a haunting voice, but my real mom, who just happens to be dead, shows up with her short, cropped, vibrant red hair. She does not speak, but she places a light-coloured "piton" (token) for pichenotte (crokinole) in my hand.

Crokinole is a tabletop game in which two sides flick their pucks, trying to knock the other team's pucks out of the centre of the circle and leave their own. If you land flat in the centre, that puck is secure for the rest of the game. Do I want to be a token? Mom is reminding me of what I really want to say. I should get over myself, and maybe write: There is a grave misuse of political analysis to evade personal accountability or to avoid holding anyone personally accountable. We attack or defend people, naming them victim or perpetrator, when most people are both based on insider/outsider classifications alone. We make that "who we are." We do not ask what we have to gain by identifying as a defender.

Politically, we need to work out questions about how to expect personal accountability and to build our capacity to do that. Rather than sorting ourselves into responsibility tokens when deciding who we are, we can say "Where are we coming from?"

NOTES

1 Chi-Meegwitch, *merci beaucoup*, thank you very much—Michelle L. Pettis is invaluable. My interview participants enriched my life significantly with a single meeting. Thanks to everyone who gave me rides, especially the woman who said picking me up for a two-day ride helped her heal the damage from an abusive FTM ex-partner; that lonely francophone lumberjack who asked if I was "a guy, or a tomboy"; and the woman living in the North, hailing from Toronto, who explained Northern bigotry and ignorance of cultural diversity: "People up here wear plaid shirts, have no teeth. They collect welfare, spend it on beer and bingo, and then are prejudiced against hard-working Asians." Thanks to everyone who offered me a place to stay, especially Cynthia Coons and family, and whoever's blue bush plane I misappropriated in the Sault. Thanks to everyone who helped me find contacts, fed me, offered to meet with me, or lent me encouragement, especially Laurel O'Gorman, claro, Tyson, Luka, Leda, and mom.

2 The call out, intentionally constructed to receive a better response (than more generic call outs) from a remote or non-urban audience, and to demonstrate knowledge of and respect for local concerns, is available on request from the author to others hoping to reach similar goals.

3 Anyone interested in visiting or exchanging messages with me or with those I interviewed is welcome to be in contact. Persons of two-spirit, trans, genderqueer, or otherwise challenging gender experience from smaller industrial centres, remote or isolated communities, the bush or out on the land or on "reserves" are especially welcome: connecting subjects and their communities to resources and each other is what I consider to be my work.

4 Anyone wondering about the details of why this was not done may contact me directly.

ADDITIONAL RESOURCES

For people looking for work on two-spirit theory:

Driskill, Q.-L., Justice, D.H., Miranda, D., & Tatonetti, L. (Eds.). (2011). *Sovereign erotics: A collection of two-spirit literature.* Tuscon: University of Arizona Press.

Jacobs, S.E. (1997). *Two-spirit people: Native American gender identity, sexuality, and spirituality.* Urbana: University of Illinois Press.

For recent media coverage on the North and two-spirit and trans experiences:

Carpenter, L. (2012). Celebrating Gay Pride in Thunder Bay. *Wawatay News, 39*(19).

Pope, J., & Norwell, J. TransNorth. *CBC Radio.* www.cbc.ca/sudbury/features/transnorth [last accessed January 4, 2013].

Chapter 9 Zening the Art of Trans Activism

Rupert Raj

INTRODUCTION

As a trailblazing trans activist, gender specialist, consultant, published researcher, professional trainer, and psychotherapist supporting trans people and their loved ones, I write this chapter to offer personal and professional insights, and practical strategies for neophyte as well as veteran trans activists in Canada and beyond. The personal perspective I provide here is twofold: I speak as a trans man and trans activist (across Canada and in the US since 1971), and as a clinician practitioner and academic researcher. Specifically, the chapter focuses on six major areas that are quintessential to addressing transphobia, as well as developing tools to resist this ongoing and devastating problem: (1) "gender work," (2) community connection and empowerment, (3) transphobia and trans activism, (4) focusing, (5) anti-oppression, and (6) burnout, vicarious traumatization, and self-care.

The multifold nature of transphobia is defined as societal violence as well as internalized oppression. External transphobia can be individual and/or systemic; internalized transphobia may affect only the individual self or the larger trans community as well. In terms of the larger trans communities, internalized transphobia often manifests as projection (i.e., "the oppressed-as-oppressor," and "cannibalistic" infighting).

In the section of the chapter addressing trans activism, I will draw upon my own experiences as a trans activist, including my therapeutic client self-empowerment model and selected examples from various other trans activist approaches (Raj, 2007). Community connection (Adler's psychological principle of "social conscience") will be examined in terms of its empowering sense of "interconnectedness" and its correlation with positive mental health. The discussion of empowerment will incorporate the dualistic nature of power; that is, developing the personal power of the individual (the trans person), as well as the social power of the collective (the trans community).

Alongside burnout—or "compassion fatigue"—the chapter outlines the related condition of vicarious traumatization, which largely plagues health care and social service professionals working with trans clients, but may also impact peer workers within the trans community. Some theoretical understandings of, and practical strategies for, the prevention (ideally) and amelioration of burnout and vicarious traumatization will be offered in the section on self-care.

I. "GENDER WORK"

As a trans activist or "gender worker"[1] across Canada (first in Ottawa, then in Montreal, Vancouver, and Calgary, and now in Toronto) and to a limited extent in the US from 1971 onward, I was one of very few early trans-identified trailblazers advocating for the trans community. Comprising the first breed of transgender organizers, we were breaking new ground. In those days, prior to the availability of the Internet, we were quite isolated from one another geographically, culturally, and ideologically. We frequently fell into pitfalls as we attempted to navigate this uncharted territory, scrambling by the seats of our pants or skirts to stay both sane and effective. This task alone required some prodigious digging out!

One of the particular reasons I wished to embark on the book venture of *Trans Activism in Canada* was to address the still-prevalent issues of burnout and "vicarious traumatization" and the attendant need for effective self-care for professional health care and social service providers, community and peer workers, partners and family members, friends and allies who support members of the trans and two-spirit communities, and our loved ones.

I was not yet 20 when I decided to devote my life to being a gender worker, which, at that time, was referred to as a "professional transsexual." Such a position was much maligned by most of the "in stealth" or otherwise mainstream members of the trans population. Like most of my fellow trans activists, I was young and pretty green when it came to trying to change the world for the better for my trans sisters and brothers. In those days, and perhaps even now, if one made it through more than four or five years (never mind ten, twenty, thirty, forty, or more) of trans community activism, it was a major milestone marking exceptional emotional resilience, or perhaps masochism! Unfortunately, my propensity for masochism has been rapidly atrophying over the past few years in direct proportion to my degree of burnout.

It's a tragic irony that one of the most insidious forms of burnout for me, and very likely for others, is the effect of negativity promoted by some of my fellow trans activists. Indeed, at times, the trans community acts in "cannibalistic" ways. We tend to turn on one another rather than fighting the common enemy—a not uncommon socio-dynamic within marginalized populations. Such infighting can take many forms, including erasing, excluding, devaluing, disrespecting, distrusting, ridiculing, trivializing, judging, blaming, flaming, condemning, neglecting, and abusing.

Trans burnout and trans (vicarious) traumatization is a very real hazard when fighting "the righteous war" for social justice for gender transgressors and our loved ones. Consequently, trans self-care for we "gender warriors" is all the more needed. To counter this disabling burnout effect, I propose some strategies for self-care as a way to help minimize the probability of its recurrence and to help ameliorate its deleterious impact on psychological health. I burned out so badly after more than 19 years of straight gender work while going to school and/or working that I needed to take 9 years off, from 1990 to 1999. I got an unlisted phone number and "mainstreamed," or lived "stealth," in the heterosexual world. I worked for a major corporation, wore a three-piece business suit, and married a straight, post-transitional trans woman. I surely needed that 9-year break from LGBT communities (especially trans communities) as I was "trans saturated"![2]

II. COMMUNITY CONNECTION AND EMPOWERMENT

I have written on the critical importance of self-empowerment or personal agency and communal empowerment or social agency and the transferability of one to the other (Raj, 2007). Alfred Adler and psychologists onward have underscored the close parallel between community conscience (or "social interest," as Adler first termed it) and positive mental health. Community connectedness is one of the three "life tasks" for human beings according to Adler, and is the forerunner of what we today call "social justice" or "community activism." Just as self-empowerment is the keystone of healthy self-esteem, so is community empowerment. Both are the cause and the effect of communal advocacy because the more we value ourselves as trans people (including gender-dissonant,[3] genderqueer, and two-spirit individuals), the more we feel a sense of solidarity or interconnectedness. This, in turn, often motivates us toward empowering our individual and our collective lives. As stated earlier, such feelings of personal and communal power should hopefully transform into emotional well-being. Thus, community connection often leads to collective empowerment, which can lead to revitalized forms of community activism.

III. TRANSPHOBIA AND TRANS ACTIVISM

The reason for trans activism is simple: transphobia is a form of bigotry based on a fear of, and hatred toward, transsexual, transgender, and two-spirit people. The continuum of transphobic violence ranges from discrimination and harassment to emotional, verbal, physical, and/or sexual abuse, to murder or forced suicide. Such violence also includes familial and societal exclusion, inequitable access to human rights, lack of access to health care and social services, religious oppression, and police brutality (see Gapka & Raj, 2003). Transphobic violence can be perpetrated by individuals as well as systems, such as families, schools, workplaces, and ethnoracial and faith communities.

Transphobia is not only exercised by sources and forces of power external to sex- and gender-variant individuals. Transphobia is often internalized. This self-limiting process occurs when a trans person or a group of trans individuals internalizes society's oppressive attitudes toward hir or toward trans people as a whole. Internalized transphobia often leads to low self-esteem or self-hatred, poor body image, self-harming behaviours, high-risk behaviours, suicidality, anxiety, depression, substance use, alienation/isolation, and/or conflict with the law.

Activism and Trans Activism

Activism means advocating to improve the quality of life for a particular, often marginalized, population or community in the realms of human rights, accessible and equitable health care and social services, affordable housing, prison reform, economic access to higher education, job creation programs, and so forth. Trans activism is especially challenging due to societal and internalized transphobia, small numbers (less critical mass), and infighting amongst trans activists.

Some Key Watchwords

Trans politics is a terrain fraught with tensions and contradictions. Individuals often wish to address the injustices they face or witness others facing, but do not know where to start or how to be effective. Here is a checklist of some things to consider incorporating into your own activist efforts. Is your work: focused, strategic, effective, diverse, inclusive, anti-oppressive, culturally competent, realistic, healthy, balanced, trans positive (inclusive, sensitive, responsive)?

IV. FOCUSING

Focusing is a proactive way to prevent or ameliorate burnout and garner more effective forms of advocacy. Some ways to focus are to choose an overall type of trans activism, a general area of interest, a specific issue, and a particular segment of the trans population on which to concentrate. When activists embrace more than one of each of the above, they risk burnout or the significant decline of the effectiveness of their abilities. They are often forced to confront the effects of spreading themselves too thin.

Some key areas of trans activism on which to focus include: community activism; political activism (i.e., lobbying); legal activism (human rights, court challenges); educational activism (anti-oppression trans training in schools, etc.); scientific advocacy (research, recommendations); health care advocacy (best practices, standards of care); therapy-as-activism (clinical practice); social services advocacy (best practices, policy development); employment and workplace advocacy; religious activism (trans inclusion in faith communities); art-as-activism ("artivism": making videos, slam poetry); and media/public relations/government relations.

"The trans community" is a bit of a misnomer. There are multiple subpopulations or trans demographics with specific issues that require particular attention. Some examples of these include gender-dissonant children, trans teenagers, older trans people (50-plus); trans people of colour, trans refugees/immigrants, two-spirit and Aboriginal trans people, trans people with disabilities, homeless trans people, low-income trans people, trans sex workers, trans people with HIV, trans people in prison.

Some specific issues that trans people and allies face include: the inclusion of "gender identity" and "gender expression" as a protected ground against discrimination in provincial, territorial, and federal human rights legislation; access to affordable, equitable, and trans positive health care (sex hormone therapy, sex reassignment surgery, hair removal therapies, counselling services, etc.); access to equitable trans positive social services (including affordable housing); access to equitable and trans positive governmental services (including legal change of name and sex designation); inclusion and acceptance by our diverse ethnoracial and faith communities in Canada; improved trans positive governmental and community supports for two-spirit and Aboriginal trans people, and trans people with disabilities (including people with HIV, low-income trans people, and trans people of colour); improved trans positive immigration practices for trans newcomers and refugees; trans positive community and clinical supports for trans seniors, gender-dissonant children, and trans teens; penal reforms for trans prisoners; legal reforms for trans sex workers; and more information, resources, education, and supports for our loved ones, allies, and supporters.

V. ANTI-OPPRESSION

Anti-oppression frameworks are often employed by trans activists seeking to draw attention to the systemic power relations that shape our attitudes and behaviours. Such relations of power and privilege include colonialism, racism, ethnic and cultural oppression, classism, sexism, homo/bi/trans/intersexphobia; genderism, ageism, and ableism. Anti-oppression also highlights particular phenomena that result from such contexts, including the hierarchy of oppression ("oppressed as oppressor") and the need for letting go of guilt by those of the dominant culture. Furthermore, anti-oppression approaches encourage activists to understand political contexts and oppression by applying intersectional analyses to see how race, sex, gender identity, socio-economic class, cultural identity, religious faith identity, political identity, and sexuality are interconnected.

The following are principles of anti-oppression:

1. Power and privilege play out in our group dynamics, and we must continually struggle with how we challenge power and privilege in our practice.
2. We can identity how power and privilege play out only when we are conscious and committed to understanding how racism, sexism, homophobia, transphobia, and all other forms of oppression affect each one of us.
3. Until we are clearly committed to anti-oppression practice, all forms of oppression will continue to divide our movements and weaken our power.
4. Developing an anti-oppression practice is lifelong work and requires a lifelong commitment. No single workshop is sufficient to change one's behaviour. We are all vulnerable to being oppressive, and we need to continuously struggle with these issues.
5. Dialogue and discussion are necessary, and we need to learn how to listen non-defensively and communicate respectfully if we are going to have effective anti-oppression practice. Challenge yourself to be honest and open, and take risks to address oppression head on.

The following points address how anti-oppression can play out in practice:

1. When witnessing or experiencing racism, sexism, and so on, interrupt the behaviour and address it on the spot or later, either one-on-one or with a few allies.
2. Give people the benefit of the doubt. Think about ways to address behaviour that will foster change and try to encourage dialogue, not debate.
3. Keep space open for anti-oppression discussions and try focusing on one form of oppression at a time—sexism, racism, classism, and so forth.
4. Respect different styles of leadership and communication.
5. People with privilege need to take responsibility for holding others with privilege accountable.
6. Try not to call people out because they are not speaking.
7. Be conscious of how much space you take up or how much you speak.
8. Be conscious of how your language may perpetuate oppression.
9. Don't push people to do things just because of their race and gender; base it on their words and experience and skills.
10. Promote anti-oppression in everything you do, inside and outside of activist space.
11. Avoid generalizing feelings, thoughts, behaviours, and so forth to a whole group.
12. Set anti-oppression goals and continually evaluate whether or not you are meeting them.
13. Don't feel guilty, feel motivated. Realizing that you are part of the problem doesn't mean you can't be an active part of the solution!

VI. BURNOUT, VICARIOUS TRAUMATIZATION, AND SELF-CARE

Burnout

Burnout is defined as "emotional exhaustion resulting from the stress of interpersonal contact" (Maslach, 1982), especially when one is repeatedly engaging in difficult situations or circumstances, or with individuals whose quality of life has been severely compromised. A similar term is "compassion fatigue." High burnout rate in trans activists is due to overextending oneself, unhealthy boundaries, vicarious traumatization, volatile infighting within the trans community, poor self-care, lack of effective coping strategies, isolation, and a lack of effective supports.

The symptoms of burnout include physical fatigue and other somatic complaints such as migraines, ulcers, high blood pressure, malnutrition, and insomnia. Other symptoms are disorientation, inability to focus, memory loss, irritability, anxiety, frustration, anger, abusive behaviour, apathy, anhedonia (inability to experience pleasure), emotional numbness, depression, cynicism, unhealthy substance use, self-harm behaviour (e.g., cutting, burning), suicidal thoughts, and illegal actions.

Vicarious Traumatization

Mental health practitioners, peer providers, personal caregivers, and activists who work with traumatized individuals and communities are typically at risk to contract this indirect form of traumatization. Symptoms are similar to burnout and include frustration, irritability, anger, withdrawal, blame, and guilt (Pearlman & Saakvitne, 1995).

Vicarious traumatization can sometimes "infect" other providers or activists who come into contact with the vicariously traumatized provider or activist.

Self-Care

Proper self-care is critical to the well-being of the individual trans activist and also to the welfare of the trans community—and, even further, to the sustainability of the trans movement itself. Self-care strategies involve striving to achieve a healthy life balance that attends to the self, loving relationships, family life, friendships, community connections, school life, work life, volunteerism, leisure activities, nature, and spirituality.

Such a balance is possible if one knows their personal limits and develops healthy boundaries, has the support of fellow activists, engages in mindfulness meditation or other meditational practices, has access to massage therapy, employs other relaxation techniques, has mechanisms in place to work out their anger through therapeutic support, has proper medical/health care, strives for a healthy diet and sufficient sleep, and engages in time/space/financial management.

CONCLUSION

This chapter addresses six major areas of trans activism: "gender work"; community connection and empowerment; transphobia and trans activism; focusing; anti-oppression; and burnout, vicarious traumatization, and self-care.

It is my hope that it offers some personal and psychological insights, as well as some therapeutic and practical strategies and overall resources for the trans advocates of today and tomorrow, as we continue the "good fight" for social justice everywhere while re-channelling our "righteous rage" toward effective change. As agents of change, we have a responsibility to pass this gift of mentorship along to others.

I wish you well, fellow sojourners, as we travel together on our gender journeys, trying to make the world a safer and better place for gender-dissonant, genderqueer, trans, and two-spirit people and our loved ones. Sisters, brothers, and all those in-between, let us shout out in solidarity: Trans Pride! Trans Power!

NOTES

1 Gender Worker was the business name of the transsexual/transvestite counselling, educational, and peer-support service I founded in Toronto, which ran from September 1987 to July 1990. Prior to 1987, I did gender work under the auspices of the Foundation for the Advancement of Canadian Transsexuals (FACT) of which I was president from January 1978 through December 1981, and founded and edited *Gender Review: A FACTual Journal* from September 1978 through December 1981. I then founded and edited the *Metamorphosis* newsletter in that same month until May 1988. In 1983, I founded and incorporated the Metamorphosis Medical Research Foundation (MMRF) in Calgary, of which I was president until it folded (in Toronto) in May 1988.

2 I'm not using the phrase "trans saturated" in a derogatory way, but rather in the same way as "I'm burned out with work" or "I'm saturated with trans politics." Of course, there is just a hint of cheekiness.

3 "Gender-dissonant" (G-D) (a.k.a. "gender-divergent," "gender-diverse," "gender-variant," "gender-anormative," "gender-non-conforming") children, according to empirical research studies, do not all grow up to identify as transsexual or transgender. (See Peggy T. Cohen-Kettenis's *Transgenderism and Intersexuality in Childhood and Adolescence: Making Choices* [2003] and Kenneth J. Zucker and Susan J. Bradley's *Gender Identity Disorder and Psychosexual Problems in Children and Adolescents* [1995].) However, whether or not the G-D child later identifies as a trans man or a (trans) woman, or even if she/he does not, the real issue is whether or not the child is experiencing gender distress (and/or societal gender phobia) and how best to support her/him.

REFERENCES

Cohen-Kettenis, P. (2003). *Transgenderism and intersexuality in childhood and adolescence: Making choices.* Thousand Oaks, CA: Sage Publications.

Gapka, S., & Raj, R. (2003). *The Trans Health Project Report.* Toronto: Ontario Public Health Association. Retrieved from www.opha.on.ca/ppres/2003-06_pp.pdf

Maslach, C. (1982). *Burnout: The cost of caring.* Cambridge: Malor Books.

Pearlman, L., & Saakvitne, K. (1995). *Countertransference and vicarious traumatization in psychotherapy with incest survivors.* New York: W.W. Norton.

Raj, R. (2007). Transactivism as therapy: A client self-empowerment model linking personal and social agency. *Journal of Gay and Lesbian Psychotherapy*, (3-4; Activism in LGBT Psychology Practice). Binghamton: Haworth Press.

Zucker, K.J., & Bradley, S.J. (1995). *Gender identity disorder and psychosexual problems in children and adolescents.* New York: The Guilford Press.

Chapter 10 Acting Queerly: Ruminations on Being a Queer Lawyer and Activist[1]

barbara findlay[2]

barbara findlay's life and identity are affected by the racism, anti-Semitism, ageism, classism, professionalism, sexism, heterosexism, genderism, ableism, Judeo-Christianism, sizeism, and anglophilia of Canadian society. She is a fat, white, aging, cisgender, queer, relatively able-bodied anglophone woman lawyer and equality rights activist. She was raised working class and Christian by parents of British heritage, in Canada. She was locked in a mental hospital as a teenager because she was a lesbian. In 2001, she was adopted by the Wet'suwet'en people.

Kimberly Nixon was victimized by male violence: abused by her partner, attacked on the street. She received counselling from Battered Women's Support Services, an all-woman feminist agency in Vancouver, and became a peer counsellor there. Having recovered from the trauma of her own victimization, in 1995 she decided to volunteer at the Vancouver Rape Relief Society.

She had no difficulty with the screening questions; Kimberly is a feminist. But in the middle of the first evening of the volunteer training, the facilitators told Kimberly that she had to leave because she was not a woman. Kimberly filed a human rights complaint, and barbara findlay was Kimberly Nixon's lawyer. Rape Relief sought unsuccessfully to judicially review the decision to refer Nixon's complaint to a tribunal. Nixon was successful at the tribunal, and was awarded the highest human rights damages in BC history.[3]

Rape Relief initiated a judicial review of that tribunal decision.[4] *They won: the Court said that Rape Relief had the right to decide who was, or was not, a "woman." Nixon appealed to the Court of Appeal; she lost again. That Court said that because Rape Relief was an organization benefiting women, a group protected by the Human Rights Code, Rape Relief was not required to observe the Human Rights Code.*[5]

However, it was a case of losing the battle, but winning the war. Over the seven years of Kimberly's case against Rape Relief, she and barbara findlay embarked on a campaign to convince every women's group in BC and Canada to be trans-inclusive. Today, Rape Relief remains the sole women's organization in BC that does not welcome trans women.

To locate myself in the discussion (because we must always, I think, locate ourselves in the discussion), it's not that my experience is the touchstone of truth. But if a proffered truth cannot explain my experience, I doubt that experience. And I have found that if I am not explicit about my location in relation to a question, I am less likely to find a workable truth. I have often been at the margins of a centre. I entered the legal profession in 1977, when there were very few women practising law. I had to get a psychiatrist to certify me as sane before I could be called to the bar, because of my having been in mental hospitals.

When I realized I was a lesbian, in 1967, gay sex was still illegal under the Criminal Code and homosexuality was a mental illness under the DSM (the psychiatric bible of diagnoses). I always told my confidantes at the workplace that I was a lesbian, and I never denied it if asked. But the norms of the time dictated that the question was rarely asked.

I had gone to law school with the not-uncommon hope that I would be able to make a difference to people who needed a voice. As a feminist, I also went to law school with a healthy dread of the socialization process of a professional school. After I got called to the bar, I worked with a union-side labour firm, then with the Legal Services Society. I taught in the Faculty of Law at UBC, and have ultimately ended up in private practice, doing a general practice for queers with an emphasis on equality and human rights cases.

In my non-lawyer life, I worked as a feminist in a women's bookstore, women's health collective, women's study group, at women's conferences, and so forth. I had arguments with men, the basic, tiresome ones—why they should not call women "girls," why "he" did not include "she" regardless of what the grammar books said. I taught "Women and the Law," a law school seminar created shortly after I graduated from UBC.

In the seventies, lesbians were regarded as the *problem* of the women's movement: (non-lesbian) women were afraid that if people knew there were lesbians in the group, the whole group would lose credibility since people would think everyone was a lesbian. So although there were lesbians in every women's organization, often in leadership positions, lesbians were *sotto voce* in the women's movement. As a lesbian, I absorbed the societal view of myself as someone who was evil, or criminal, or crazy, or all three.

As a woman, the choices I was offered were very few. On our first day of classes in first year, a law professor said, "I feel sorry for the girls in the class. You can be fluffy and incompetent or ball-breaking, cigar-smoking bitches like Mary Southin." (The next day, all 13 of the women in the class had a cigarillo.)

Since I have been called to the bar, I have three times watched the Supreme Court of Canada find a reason to deny equality rights to lesbians and gay men. In 1979, it decided that a classified ad in a newspaper was not a public service, thereby avoiding the question of whether sexual orientation could be a proper basis for discrimination. In *Mossop,*[6] the Court decided that since the federal government had deliberately chosen not to include "sexual orientation" when it amended its human rights legislation, Mossop could not claim human rights protection as a gay man. In *Egan,*[7] the Court said that although a gay man was entitled to Charter protection from discrimination on the basis of sexual orientation, he was not entitled to relief because, in his case, the discrimination was permissible.

The experience of being a lawyer—and therefore a member of a privileged group in Canadian society—who did not herself have the same civil and human rights as everyone else in the country has been a central paradox of my life and my lawyering. It is a backdrop for my preoccupation with understanding how someone is both privileged and oppressed at the same time. In the early eighties, I went to an unlearning racism workshop. It changed my life in the same way that feminism had. I gained a conceptual framework that helped me to understand the way that I, as a white person, contribute to the establishment and maintenance of racism in this country. I began to co-facilitate unlearning racism workshops, hundreds of them over the next 20 years.

I belonged to a group called AWARE (Alliance of Women against Racism Etc., the "Etc." being all of the other oppressions). We had a policy that we would always have a woman of colour and a white woman as co-facilitators of the workshops, because we found that people listened differently to someone who was affected by racism in the same ways as themselves. White people trusted a white facilitator; people of colour did not. The opposite was true for the facilitator of colour. In AWARE, we also took as an assumption that racism, or any other oppression, was not only, or even mainly, an intellectual matter that could be changed by more or different information. We understood racism to be something that affected us—white people and people of colour—in every aspect of the way we understood ourselves, thought about ourselves, felt about ourselves, felt about others like us.

The focus of the white women in AWARE was on the ways that we had internalized a position of privilege. We called it "internalized dominance," a term coined by Janet Sawyer. Internalized dominance is the conceptual counterpart to internalized oppression. It is the messages that we absorb, osmotically, about the features of our identities that are "normal," "natural," "Canadian." For me, those features included the colour of my skin, my education, my relative able-bodiedness, my unaccented(!) English, my Christian heritage, my unambiguous gender, my professionalism, my age—a vigorous 35 at that time. I worked hard to notice the ways in which I took my privilege for granted. I assumed without thinking about it that I would never have trouble entering a room, anywhere in Canada, because of the colour of my skin. That no one would ask "where I was from" the first time they met me and mean "from what country did you come." That I did not have to call ahead to see if the meeting room was wheelchair-accessible, and if so, whether the washrooms were too.

People who are in a dominant group with respect to an aspect of their identities feel, and are treated as, normal. We feel and are treated as if we belong. We feel and are treated as if we are entitled to be well treated. People who are in the target group for oppression with respect to an aspect of their identities feel and are treated as not part of the norm. We feel, and are treated as if, we do not automatically belong. We do not expect to be well treated; often we are not.

The startling thing is that we are all, every single one of us, both privileged and oppressed in Canadian society. Canadian society bonuses white skin, male cisgender, heterosexuality; anglophones, non-immigrants, and non-Aboriginal people; able-bodiedness; a Christian heritage ... the list goes on. Canadian society penalizes skin of colour; female, trans, and lesbian bodies; non-English speakers, immigrants, and Aboriginal people; disability. But every individual person has some characteristics that are bonused and some that are penalized—if only because we were all, once, children; and we are all, now, adults in relation to children.

*****

I remember a three-day residential community workshop in which we were dividing people along other axes of oppression: gender and sexual orientation. When it came time to divide the straight people from the lesbians, the question arose about where the bisexual people belonged. We facilitators were taken by surprise, since it had not occurred to us to think about this question in advance. I was adamant: bisexual people did not belong in the lesbian group because they "participated in male privilege" and "did not share the same experience as lesbians." I am embarrassed to say that I "won" the argument, and the bisexual woman was put into a caucus group by herself.

I tell that story often, because I remember the absolute moral certainty of my position. The view I held was commonly accepted among lesbians at the time. We had, after all, carved spaces for ourselves at great personal cost. We had had to come out in women's groups who didn't want to acknowledge us; we had had to have confrontations and hurtful conversations with women we thought were our friends about why it was necessary to have lesbian caucuses in women's organizations, a place for lesbian women to breathe, to be able to be authentic with each other, to sort out our feelings and our fears. When I think about it now, I do not know what it was that made me so adamant. I think it was the feeling that I had so little space as a lesbian that I should not have to move over for someone who wasn't "really" one of us. We lesbians did not trust bisexual women. I think somewhere inside we believed that they would take the stories of our lives back to their men.

We were wrong. We were wrong because we did not understand that what united us was our common experience of heterosexism (the conviction that heterosexuality is the only natural form of human sexual expression) and homophobia (the fear and loathing of anyone not heterosexual). Women-only groups, lesbian-only groups, women-of-colour groups, women-with-disabilities groups ... all were absolutely critical to our understanding of ourselves. They still are. Nothing takes the sting out of the experience of being humiliated because you are female, or because you are lesbian, more than hearing other women describe the same thing happening to them. It is quite literally the only way to redraw the boundaries of self that were violated by the sexism or the homophobia. And it is one of the most effective and efficient ways for members of a group targeted for oppression to develop an understanding of how the oppression operates, in their own lives and in the lives of other targeted people.

That is why organizations like the Vancouver Rape Relief Society and Women Against Violence Against Women (WAVAW) and Battered Women Support Services (BWSS) started as women-only peer-support services for women who were victims of male violence: to offer a space where a woman could come to understand that the violence she experienced was not her fault, whatever her husband/boyfriend/date/stranger said. This was a space outside the gaze of male eyes, safe from mocking male judgment or threat.

But unless and until we learn to consider both the ways we are oppressed and the ways we are oppressive, we will continue to replicate the problem of oppression. Our "women's groups" or "gay groups" will continue to turn out to be mostly white, able-bodied, anglophone ... in other words, otherwise privileged.

The much more interesting, and much more difficult, conversations are across the differences among us: for example, when my heterosexual Wet'suwet'en sister and I talk about racism and homophobia in our relationship.

*****

Though I have watched the Supreme Court of Canada deny my rights as a lesbian, I have also watched that Court transform the legal situation for gay men and lesbians in the country. In *Vriend,*[8] the Court said that if a province was going to offer human rights protection, it could not protect only some marginalized groups: the Court read in sexual orientation to the list of protected grounds in the Alberta Individual Rights and Protection Act. In *M v. H,*[9] the Court held that it was contrary to the equality guarantees in the Charter to offer a protective regime on relationship breakdown to heterosexuals, but not to gay or lesbian partners.

And within 10 years, the law was transformed. Ten years ago there was not even protection against discrimination in the BC Human Rights Act: lesbian co-mothers risked losing all contact with their children if their relationships broke up; lesbians could access sperm from medical sources only by portraying themselves as straight; there were no inheritance rights on intestacy; two people of the same gender could not adopt a child together. Today there is no piece of legislation, federal or provincial, affecting gays and lesbians in this province in a discriminatory manner except for the anachronistic "homosexual panic" criminal law defence. So I believe in the power of law to work change.

*****

I came to transgender issues by coincidence. A trans woman phoned me in a panic the day before she was to leave for her sex reassignment surgery to see if I could speed the production of the necessary bureaucratic approval for it in time for the operation to proceed. I intervened with no clue about what I was doing or how the system worked. I was successful only because the approval had already been granted, and I was able to convey good news to my client. Shortly after that I was approached by the High Risk Project Society, an organization offering emergency services to transgendered street people in the Downtown Eastside (as documented by Sandy Leo Laframboise in Chapter 5 of this text). They wanted to write a report on transgendered people and the law. There was, at the time, exactly one piece of writing on that topic in all of Canada. It was 1994.

High Risk gathered together representatives from various parts of the gender-variant communities: cross-dressers, transgendered people, pre- and post-operative transsexuals. After examining what trans people were doing in other, primarily American, jurisdictions, the committee deliberately chose to use the word "transgender" as the umbrella term to include all gender-variant people. *Finding Our Place*, as the report was titled, concluded that trans human rights complaints could be advanced for transsexuals under the heading of "disability," since "gender dysphoria" was recognized as an illness in the DSM. But the risk of proceeding in that manner was that only transsexuals would be entitled to human rights protection. There was also controversy among the trans community about the claim that gender dysphoria—the diagnostic term for transsexualism—was a disability. Some thought that gender variance, like homosexuality, was not a "disability" at all, but a normal variation in the human condition. Others worried that if transsexuals described themselves as non-disabled, they would lose access to publicly funded gender identity treatment and sex reassignment surgery.

In American jurisdictions, trans equality rights were beginning to be advanced under "sexual orientation" and under "sex" pretty much equally. The report considered whether "sex" would be an adequate ground under which to advance human rights complaints, and concluded that it was not a surefire outcome since protection on the grounds of "sex" was customarily applied in situations that assumed a bigendered reality. Sexual orientation seemed inappropriate. And so the report recommended that "gender identity" be added as a protected ground under the Human Rights Code.[10]

*****

Language, the act of naming, is critical to the struggle of any marginalized group. It is critical that the group decide for itself what words come closest to describing their experience. I did not attend the committee meetings at which language was considered, because as a non-trans lawyer I would have had a disproportionate impact on that discussion.

Finding Our Place became an organizing document. When the BC Human Rights Commission held hearings around the province to take suggestions for amendments to the Human

Rights Code, there were submissions at virtually every session that "gender identity" be added as a protected ground. As it happened, British Columbia was the first Canadian jurisdiction to consider the question of human rights recognition. The language adopted by the community here became the language in other parts of the country, though laws in some places now include "gender identity and gender expression," for example.

Meanwhile, on the legal front, there began to be successes. The first BC case, *Sheridan v. Sanctuary Investments,*[11] concerned a pre-operative transsexual woman who had been denied the use of the women's washroom in a gay bar in Victoria, and on another occasion had been denied entry to the same bar because her driver's licence photo (still male) did not match her gender presentation (female). Her complaint was on the grounds of sex (gender)[12] and physical or mental disability. The respondent said that he was acting on complaints of other women, lesbians, patrons of the bar who objected to "a man in the washroom," and that he was entitled to refuse entry to someone without proper identification.

Sheridan won the right to use the women's washroom. But she lost the right of entry to the bar unless her ID matched her gender presentation.

There was both jubilation and consternation in the trans community when Sheridan was announced. From a legal perspective, a victory in the women's washroom was a significant victory: it was the quintessentially taboo place for a "man" to be. It was particularly significant since Ms. Sheridan had not yet had her sex reassignment surgery. But it was also deeply worrying that discrimination could be justified on the basis of someone's gender presentation.

The next thing we did was organize a conference about transgendered rights. I was the token non-trans person on the organizing committee. One hundred people showed up for the first-ever Canadian trans conference. The air was electric with the excitement of people discovering themselves.

*****

While helping to organize the Justice and Equality Summit, I was also attending meetings with representatives of the Attorney General. Hope was in the air; perhaps the Human Rights Code would be amended to include "gender identity." The main concern of the Attorney General was spaces where people were naked together—change rooms, that sort of thing—and they proposed that the exception for "public decency" remain in the Code.

I advocated for that solution. In meetings with trans people, and then at the Justice and Equality Summit, I argued strongly for that solution as a stepping stone to full equality. I explained that there were provisions with respect to "public decency" in the Criminal Code, and that we would never succeed in having the legislature pass an amendment to include gender identity without it. I was wrong. I was wrong for three reasons. First, it was my own transphobia that made me certain that a solution that included the possibility of a penis in a women's change room would not, and could not, fly. Second, it was not my place, as a non-trans person, to be advocating for one position or another. Third, my voice—my experienced lawyer voice—inevitably spoke louder than it should have. I was acting out of my privilege and, without intending to, silencing trans people.

*****

Coincident with these developments in the trans communities in BC, some women's organizations were beginning to object to the participation of trans women in women-only spaces. On September 8, 1999, the BC Human Rights Tribunal decided *Mamela v. Vancouver Lesbian*

Centre,[13] holding that the organization had improperly discontinued Susan Mamela's membership in the organization because, they said, she acted like a man. By the time the case got to hearing, the Lesbian Centre no longer existed, having disintegrated, in part, in reaction to the controversy over trans inclusion.

There began to be a groundswell of opposition to the participation of trans women in women-only spaces. Reminiscent in some ways of the lines drawn during the "porn wars" in the eighties—when some feminists decried pornography as the blueprint for violence against women and fought to have the standards of pornography reflect that harm, and others pointed to the liberatory aspects of explicit sexual materials, especially for lesbians—feminists queued on both sides of an acrimonious debate. Each side accused the other of essentialism. Each side suspected or accused the other of having abandoned their first feminist principles. The battles raged in national women's organizations—NAC (National Action Council on the Status of Women), LEAF (Women's Legal Education and Action Fund), NAWL (National Association of Women and Law)—and in national equality organizations such as the Court Challenges Program, which funds federal equality test cases. *Nixon v. Rape Relief* became the focus of those battles.

*****

It is the experience of coming to *Nixon*, of having the honour of being welcomed among trans people, in trying to understand my own reactions, my own transphobia, and then trying to figure out how to advocate for trans people in a legal system that barely acknowledged their existence—that is the challenge that I am trying to articulate.

Human rights legislation invites us to think in categories. Either male *or* female. Either white *or* not white. Either able-bodied *or* disabled. Decoded, human rights legislation directs "us" to treat "them" as if "they" were like "us." The unarticulated norm is a straight, white, able-bodied cisgender man who was raised Christian and middle class, who is neither too old nor too young, who is well educated and has neither a criminal nor a psychiatric record. Norm, and his wife, Norma. Human rights legislation constructs those of us with spoiled identities as like Norm, except for our race, gender, sexual orientation, religion, age, ability, and so on. We are offered neither language nor paradigms to understand our lives if we happen to experience—for example—racism and sexism and homophobia, because we are lesbians of colour.

Some people talk about the "intersection" of oppressions. Intersection has even grown a suffix and become "intersectionality." But if you unpack "intersection," you find a word that describes two lines crossing. Oppressions are not lines. Oppressions do not "intersect." I may live at an intersection, but I am not an intersection. To describe oppression in terms of intersections is worse than unhelpful. It is misleading, obfuscatory. It hides much more than it illuminates. We are offered neither language nor paradigm to understand the most complex facts about identity: that we are all part of the mainstream, the norm; and we are all, or have been as children, part of the disadvantaged minority. We are as adults both privileged and disadvantaged.

Any combination of privilege and oppression manifests differently than any privilege or any oppression on its own. For example, the privilege of education inflects the oppression of homophobia, so that I am seen as eccentric, and no longer as crazy. Racism manifests differently when compounded with poverty than it does compounded with wealth.

We are offered neither language nor paradigm to understand our lives if life changes parts of our identity. If we grew up being treated as white, and discover as adults that we were adopted from the reserve into a white family ... what are we? If we were married and had children before we came out as lesbians, does that mean we were always lesbians, though mistaken? Or did we "used to be" straight? What is a "disability"? If a person with poor eyesight can see with the help of eyeglasses, does s/he have a disability? In Canada, where eyeglasses are relatively available? In Rwanda, where they are not?

*****

Oppression has these characteristics. It is relational. Oppression does not exist except between people. Oppression exists in a country's ideology, or its commonly accepted view of itself. It is a socially sanctioned idea about who is better than whom.

That socially constructed merit–demerit system is one that we absorb as part of who we understand ourselves to be. We take in the disparaging ideas that a culture has of us as someone whose race is not white, whose sexual orientation is not heterosexual, whose religion is not Christian, whose language is not English. As a lesbian in the late sixties, I understood myself to be crazy, criminal, and evil. But I understood that I was the problem. I had no concept of a homophobic culture. Indeed, I was *unspeakably* crazy/criminal/evil. The only information about people like me was in courses called "Deviance." As a white person, I have been taught that I am "normal." A real Canadian. My ancestors, I was taught, were the pioneers, the settlers, bravely carrying the truth of Christianity to the Indians. I knew nothing of Canada's deliberate and systematic genocide of First Nations, or of Canada's policies that were meant to exterminate the cultures of Native people, to "civilize" them.

Oppression is not a one-way phenomenon. It is reflexively constructed by our individual and collective reactions to the experience of oppression, of ourselves and of others. I am not simply a passive recipient of the (mis)information of this oppressive culture. I am also a *participant* in that culture. Every time that I hear a racist or transphobic or classist or anti-Muslim remark and do not contradict it, I offer my agreement and support to the continuation of the racism and transphobia and classism and religious intolerance. Every time I hear a homophobic remark, or a fat joke, or a joke about people with disabilities and do not object, I am participating in my own oppression. So it is not *only* the case that I am oppressed; I am also an agent in the oppression of myself and others. I am an agent for, or an agent against, this society's oppressions. Those are the only choices, since there is no neutral place.

*****

Oppression is discussed as if it is about one person/many people oppressing one person/many people—perhaps discriminating against them; perhaps calling them names; perhaps simply not taking them into account. That description is fundamentally mistaken. Each of us who is oppressive has also been oppressed. This is not to say that *at a particular moment* one person is not oppressing, or harming, or assaulting, or discriminating against, or calling names at, another. But it is to say that to understand classes of people as oppressors, and classes of people as oppressed, oversimplifies and obfuscates day-to-day dynamics in a dangerous way.

I recall a situation that arose in an unlearning oppression workshop that I was co-facilitating with a white person who had a disability and an Aboriginal person who was able-bodied. The able-bodied Aboriginal person proposed to smudge and to acknowledge that the land we were meeting on was First Nations land. The disabled white person pointed out that smudging—smoke—could be harmful to anyone with compromised lungs. A heated argument ensued. The Aboriginal person said that they had never heard of anyone in their community getting sick from smoke, and in their view this was just one more way for white people to forbid Aboriginal people from performing their traditional rituals. The person with disabilities responded that disability issues were never taken seriously, that only issues of race seemed to count as true issues of oppression because no one ever thought about the physical consequences for people with disabilities of things like smoke and scents. Who was right? Who was wrong? I suggest that to answer that question is to fall into the trap of Western either/or thinking: that there is only one right answer. To ask that question is to put the question at the wrong level.

*****

Oppression is not simply bad treatment by one person of another. If that were so, then all mistreatment would resolve into "that's life"; "happens to all of us." A fundamental feature of oppression is that the oppressor is the person who, in relation to that feature of their identity, is in the dominant group. By definition, they start with the socially conferred power of being part of the norm. Conversely, a fundamental feature of being oppressed is that the person who is being oppressed is, in relation to that part of their identity, in the target group, the out group, the non-dominant group, the oppressed group, in society. By definition, they start with the disadvantage of being part of the marginal in society with respect to that aspect of themselves.

*****

Oppression is not simple. It is not the case that "homophobia is homophobia is homophobia," nor that "racism is racism is racism." Straight people react differently to gay men than they do to lesbians. White people react differently to rich people of colour than they do to poor people of colour. The reactions are homophobic/racist—but the treatment is likely to be different. Human rights legislation cannot touch those pieces of our lives. Unless and until we develop a conceptual analysis that is both usable and responsive to the complexity of the diversity of this society, human rights legislation will continue to become less and less relevant in Canada.

NOTES

1 The original version of this article was written in 2001.

2 I want to thank my teachers, Gloria Yamato, Ricky Sherover-Marcuse, Celeste George, Nym Hughes, Joanne Arnott, D.D. Bloom, Dorrie Brannock, Monika Chappell, Kimberly Nixon, jacquie allen, Leah Decter, and Haruko Okano. None of them is a lawyer. And I want to thank my partner, Sheila Gilhooly, without whose sense of humour and shared (un)reality, I could not do the work I do.

3 *Kimberly Nixon v. Vancouver Rape Relief Society* 2002 BCHRT 1.

4 *Vancouver Rape Relief Society v. Kimberly Nixon et al.*, 2003 BCSC 1936.

5 *Vancouver Rape Relief Society v. Nixon*, 2004 BCCA 516.

6 *Canada v. Mossop* [1993] 1 SCR 554.

7 *Egan et al. v. Canada* (1995), 124 D.L.R. 609 (S.C.C.).

8 *Vriend v. Alberta* [1998] 1 SCR 493.

9 *M v. H* [1999] SCJ No 23.

10 Since then, "gender identity" has been, or is being, added to several human rights codes, including the federal Human Rights Act; but not in BC.

11 *Sheridan v. Sanctuary Investments Ltd.* (c.o.b. B.J.'s Lounge), January 8, 1999.

12 At the time, "sex" and "gender" were used interchangeably in the laws of BC.
13 *Mamela v. Vancouver Lesbian Centre* [1999] BCHRTD No 51.

Chapter 11 Choosing Better Than Oppression

Calvin Neufeld

> There is no pre-given identity of form or function to be found anywhere in nature, [Darwin] argues; rather there is mutation, inconsistency, and radical connectivity that produces the identities and differences we recognize as individuals and species.
>
> —*Elizabeth A. Wilson*

What do vegetarianism and other forms of ecological politics have to do with trans- activism? Everything. This chapter is poised to engage with contemporary scholastic inquiry that problematizes the animal/human/ecological divide wherein humans are constructed as superior.[1] I argue that many trans and two-spirit people can relate to the devastating effects of being dehumanized. While individuals who don't look gender variant tend to have an easier time, those who are racialized, colonized, feminine, and impoverished occupy lower rungs of the hierarchy governing society. They are punished because they're perceived as different. Humans are not the only *beings* subordinated by hierarchical and binary thinking (i.e., "us versus them"): the bodies and spirits of non-human animals are grossly violated in Canadian society.

We are not powerless, however. We can resist hierarchical governing structures that impose themselves on us, as well as hierarchical mentalities that we internalize and enact on ourselves and Others everyday. To enact social justice for trans communities, as well as for non-human species, I'm challenging us to choose better than ways of so-called living that are oppressive to ourselves and Others with whom we share resources. As a "trans-" activist, I try to live my truth daily—this includes not eating animals.[2]

OTHER

The word "other" is used in so many ways that it's not easy to define. It denotes that those cast into the category of Other do not belong within the legitimate purviews of what is recognized as the nation or social as imagined communities. As a result of being constructed as not belonging, not only is the suffering of Others not given priority, but they are perceived as threats to the entitlements of those acknowledged as normative members of the social. An Other is always different in a way that qualifies it as less deserving. A woman who looks like a "man in a dress" is different in a way that is regarded as less deserving of dignity and respect. A non-human animal is different in a way that is regarded as less deserving of freedom and life. This is all part of the same problem.

In fact, there is a thin line between beings considered to be humans and those deemed to be animals. To justify the enslavement of African, Caribbean, and indigenous people, for example, they were rendered as less than human, as animal-like. They were considered so different as to lack the emotional complexity to experience suffering and as incapable of reason. Some even went so far as to claim that they were grateful for the security of their confinement.

When cast out from the category human, there is grounds for oppression. Animals that are farmed for food, held captive for our entertainment, and often the ones bred as pets are treated very cruelly because they aren't considered human at all. How can one form of oppression end without the other? If oppression can be justified somewhere, it can be justified somewhere else. Its eviction must be total.

PERSPECTIVE

I live in a rural environment. In the summer I sleep in a tent where distractions are minimal, and I'm reminded that I live, and depend on, an abundantly vegetative Earth. I can hear a chorus of eclectic sounds—mosquitoes, squirrels, crickets, birds. I'm surrounded by living Others who pursue their own interests and survival, as I am doing; who communicate with each other, as I am with you.

In this environment, I feel like an arrogant bumbler in the world of animals who is taking up too much space. I hear myself surrounded but all I see of animal life is me. And accompanying me, in stark contrast to all other life forms that are present, are *my* tent, house, outhouse, car, solar panels, trampoline, lawn chairs, and gazebo. Heaving through the sounds around me is a cow, or several cows, in what I interpret as distress. I've been told that there's a period each spring when farmers separate infant cows from their mothers and that the cows, both infant and mother, wail in response, often for days. I'm used to hearing cows out here as there are several farms in the area, but now these sounds have been given a meaning. They have become language, and I can no longer listen without grief. Critical scholars and other trans activists often choose *not* to witness the abjection or listen to the cries of species and the Earth suffering surrounding us. It makes me wonder whether human beings are a dysfunctional species.

HOW?

How is oppression justified? I find the question mind-boggling, but it's critical. Oppression occurs every minute of every day. I have engaged in the oppression of others and I have been an Other myself. The problem is real and it affects us all. It must be taken seriously.

The deepest roots of oppression, I believe, run right down to the fear that feeds on difference. Wrestling with difference begins at the earliest age, when we fear what we don't recognize or understand. I remember witnessing a little white girl meeting a black person for the first time. This child, too young to know what racism is or how to be courteous in a moment of surprise, reacted with a mixture of shock and fear to her unexpected encounter with a Haitian face. The innocence of her response, the slow, silent, backward retreat to safety, had us laughing, my Haitian friend and me. The girl's response revealed that there's comfort in the familiar, in faces whose expressions we understand, in language whose sounds carry meaning to us, in behaviours that are easy to predict. We're unsettled by the unknown.

But how do we respond to what we don't understand? For that's where the trouble begins. Do we retreat, as that little girl did, to the safety of the familiar? Do we distrust it? Do we fill in gaps of understanding with our own assumptions? Do we generate images that hardly resemble the subject? Do we devalue this hollowed-out version of a being?

This is how easy it is for the seed of oppression to sprout from the most natural conditions. How it moves from this to full-grown oppression—and cruelty—that's what boggles me. But that's the critical point, because trans people are being treated badly on the basis of their difference. Animals, all the more so, to say the very least. What could be powerful enough to justify cruelty? What is there to be gained from the restriction of health, happiness, freedom, life?

PRIVILEGE

I'm flabbergasted now at the eating of animal flesh. My compassion has been stretched to the most painful limits; I feel like a raw wound walking through a world of suffering and death served up for dinner. Humans have stepped beyond the category of innocent participants in a natural order. We don't need to eat animals. And our method of eating animals in terms of agribusiness and industrial farming is not only a massacre in itself, but a massacre of the Earth.

We self-aware omnivores face a crisis of identity (actually I consider myself biologically herbivorous, but generally speaking, "omnivore" is the identity of choice). From our dietary armchair we debate whether we're meant to eat meat or meant to eat plants as if that's the only relevant question. We overlook the knowledge of which is the *better* choice—a choice that transgresses concerns with our health and the affordability of meat products to embrace a more sustainable, non-violent, just, and compassionate politics.

We know that we can be healthier on a plant-based diet; those of us who can't face different choices (leaving room for hypothetical medical conditions, as well as those living in harsh climates). But most of us, possibly all of us, with the help of science and technology, would thrive as vegans. And the Earth's rivers, forests, pastures, and animal offspring would breathe a collective sigh of relief. It is the better choice.

Nature can't be used to justify our acts of unprovoked and unnecessary violence; these are almost exclusively human behaviours, and we have long since abandoned our submission to nature's codes of conduct. Nature doesn't dictate our actions; we must assume responsibility. In North America, the honest defence of our animal diet is that we love to eat meat. We love cheese and ice cream. This is particularly troubling considering the cost and how terribly we're affected by it. It isn't just the massacre of animals; to *enjoy* flavour that comes at such a cost—imagine the 50 to 1,000 cows whose flesh and fat can be found in a single hamburger—requires a moral immunity. It is this *moral immunity* that justifies oppression but compromises our capacity as socially just and ethical actors.

When it comes to eating animals, moral immunity is found in the subtle, yet ever-present, thought of our being special. We're consoled in our food choices by the notion that the rules we accept for our kind—don't kill, don't kidnap, don't confine (except the baddies), don't steal—simply don't apply to those other beings with which we share the Earth. "That's different," we say. *They're* different?

Our apathy and indifference grow ever more reprehensible as animal "processing" grows ever more aggressive to accommodate our palates and our disposable income. We find ourselves having daily encounters with injustice, yet we fail to recognize it. In our purchases we finance and in our attitudes we endorse forced confinement, physical violence, manipulated sexuality, the separation of mothers and babies, and the taking of life. We become oblivious or even partial to that which should grossly offend us.

Otherwise, we fear, there would be no cream in our coffee, no shrimp on the barbeque, no greasy pizzas to regret the morning after. But those luxuries, if we must have them, have plant-based substitutes, ones that come with a peaceful conscience over dinner. So why, I have wondered, are we so unwilling to relinquish our consumption of animal life?

History of hierarchical power relations reveals how fiercely privilege is defended by those who possess it. While social justice activists, especially those working with anti-oppression paradigms, problematize white, masculine, able-bodied, and class privilege, the privilege gained at the expense of animals remains peripheral to activist projects. Nevertheless this commitment to human privilege embedded in an erroneous sense of superiority is a significant problem in contemporary society framed by ecological crisis. It is the form of oppression that, even amongst the most compassionate of us, remains unwilling to die.

DECEPTION

In *The Dreaded Comparison,*[3] Marjorie Spiegel recounts a conversation she had with an egg "factory" worker:

> The conditions in the area where the chickens were housed were so abhorrent that I had to go outside every few minutes to breathe. The air was filled with dust and ammonia as the excrement pit beneath the rows and rows of "laying-hens" cages was emptied only once every two years. The chickens had part of their upper mandible cut off (de-beaking) and were living four to a cage a little larger than a record album. They lived in these conditions for two years until they were moved into trucks—their first and only experience of the outdoors—and driven to a slaughterhouse. Below is a portion of our conversation:
>
> *Q:* Do you think about the chickens much?
>
> *A:* Usually I don't.... The chickens here ... know where their next meal is coming from, and they don't have to worry about predators...
>
> *Q:* It seems like a lot of their natural tendencies are inhibited though, in terms of expression, a pecking order, being able to mate...
>
> *A:* Well, no, they don't mate. They do, oh ... they stretch; and they're happy. We see them, when we're walking through the place removing the dead ... and they stretch. The pecking order: I think they have it in their individual cages.
>
> *Q:* Well, not being able to walk, or turn around, or scratch...
>
> *A:* Well on the other hand, if we were to put them out on the floor, it would take a lot more labor to gather the eggs. And eggs would cost a great deal more.
>
> *Q:* But in terms of the chickens who are doing the actual work, producing the eggs. What would they be happier with?
>
> *A:* On the other hand, what's the alternative? Do we quit eating eggs?
>
> *Q:* Why do you have to de-beak them?
>
> *A:* The chickens will, in their pecking order, pick on the weakest chicken.... Once they draw blood, then they just keep on going. They're quite cannibalistic.
>
> *Q:* But when they're in a barnyard that usually doesn't happen.
>
> A: No, but then the one who's being picked on can get away.

> The comments of the egg-worker show how thoroughly a person is able to *internalize* propaganda.... [T]he interview reveals how it is possible to be confronted daily with reality, yet cease to see it. It's not easy, at first, to recognize the kind of deception that makes oppression of others acceptable, even "natural." (pp. 75–77)

REPEATING THE MISTAKE

Much suffering has been justified by the logic that mystifies difference. Trans activists are working to expose the deceit that differently gendered people are mentally ill, morally inferior, or less deserving of rights and privileges generally considered standard, such as health care, education, employment, and other factors that improve one's quality of life. This work stems from the conviction that we're deceiving ourselves when we regard difference as inferiority and then presume that those deemed inferior are not entitled to the rights extended to those whose embodied sex, gender, class location, citizenship status, and sexual practice are legible as "normal."

It's unfortunate, then, that we've been slow to understand what it means to be wrong to assign value to difference and to deny rights according to the value we've assigned. I say this because we're repeating this mistake, on a scale and of a severity that has no comparison. We're not like (other) animals, we say. We're superior. Or perhaps, if not superior, then different, unique in a way that carries exceptional value. But we're wrong as we've been wrong before. We're different, that's all; and we're the same, as much animal as any other.

As though in premonition of how his work would be misused, Darwin scribbled in the margin of his notebook that he should refrain from using the words "higher" and "lower." He looked closely into the book of nature and could find nothing to exempt human beings from that broad category of animals shaped equally though variously by a common history of natural evolution. We're a magnificent and unique species of animal (though we say it ourselves), but our evolutionary tree is every bit as ancient and phenomenal as any other. We're one of many magnificent and unique species of animal, and we've spent just as long in the evolutionary kettle. In other words, we're special, but not that special.

Anti-oppression and social justice activists know that difference is a social construct that legitimizes colonial, capitalist, and patriarchal systems of governance. In terms of trans activism, we fight for the freedom to self-determine our embodiment and crucial aspects of our lives. We struggle against confinement to strict sex/gender categories, as well as within institutions such as mental health facilities and prisons. And yet, while we acknowledge that it's unjust to assign value to some bodies over others based on difference, we justify assigning more value to the human species over non-human species. Because, we argue, we're different.

With the knowledge that we can choose otherwise, we imprison and slaughter animals of other species. We separate females from their infants and deny males the companionship of their mates (if we even let them live). We steal from their bodies. We inject hormones, antibodies, and dyes into them to manipulate their bodies for our consumption. We confine them to cages and stare at them at the zoo. Because, I believe the argument goes, they don't exhibit the ability to reason as we do, or to communicate as we do, or to experience the spiritual as we do, this somehow makes them inferior to us. And further, on the basis of their inferiority, we deny our obligation to recognize or honour their rights—although, by some twist of logic, we afford limited rights to those animals considered "cute" or "intelligent" or "human-like," in contrast to animals considered "vermin," or "stupid," or "tasty."

THE END OF OPPRESSION

It is unacceptable that the right to life, quality of life, freedom, and happiness should be possessed only by white people, or only by men, or only by hetero or cissexuals, or only by humans. As a transsexual, I continue to resist exclusion from the circle of deserving; I claim my belonging. To the extent that I've succeeded, it's been a bittersweet victory, because I look out and see those who remain excluded, suffering more than I will ever suffer on the basis of their species, while I occupy a conflicted middle space in companionship with the oppressors and in solidarity with the oppressed.

Oppression can only be overcome when it's overcome entirely. And we, of trans experience, who occupy some of the lowest echelons of society, can do better than demand for ourselves what we deny to others. If we hope to lift the weight of oppression from our shoulders, we must first learn how to exercise compassion for those who are considered beneath us. How else can oppression end?

NOTES

1 Hird, M.J. (2013). Animal trans. In S. Stryker and A.Z. Aizura, *The Transgender Studies Reader 2* (pp. 156–167). New York: Routledge; Chen, M.Y. (2013). Animals without genitals: Race and transsubstantiation. In S. Stryker and A.Z. Aizura (Eds.), *The Transgender Studies Reader 2* (pp. 168–177). New York: Routledge; Hayward, E. (2013). Lessons from a starfish. In S. Stryker and A.Z. Aizura (Eds.), *The Transgender Studies Reader 2* (pp. 178–188). New York: Routledge; Kier, B. (2013). Interdependent ecological transsex: Notes on re/production, "transgender" fish, and the management of populations, species, and resources. In S. Stryker and A.Z. Aizura (Eds.), *The Transgender Studies Reader 2* (pp. 189–198). New York: Routledge.

2 Such praxis continues to be on the fringe of trans activism; however, I am not alone. Transsexual, vegan, and prostitute rights activist Mirha-Soleil Ross has been making these connections for decades. In 2001, she brought animal rights to the forefront as Grand Marshall of the Toronto Pride Parade (www.youtube.com/watch?v=ik7n8CoRRF8). She also made these connections in a powerful performance piece entitled *Yapping Out Loud: Contagious Thoughts from an Unrepentant Whore* (Mirha-Soleil Ross, Dir. Nicole Stamp, 2004). She and Xanthra Phillipa MacKay would sell back issues of their 1990s 'zine *gendertrash* at the Vegetarian Food Fair.

3 Spiegel, M. (1996). *The dreaded comparison: Human and animal slavery.* New York: Mirror Books/I.D.E.A.

Chapter 12 "What Is Missing in Our Community Is Self-Love": An Interview with Marie-Marcelle Godbout, Founder of L'Aide aux Transsexuel(le)s du Québec

Nora Butler Burke and Viviane Namaste
Translated and revised by Natalie Duchesne

Marie-Marcelle Godbout founded L'Aide aux Transsexuel(le)s du Québec (ATQ) in 1980. She has given many media appearances, has run a telephone support line for decades, and is currently involved in a community organizing project concerned with the needs of elderly trans populations. Viviane Namaste interviews Godbout about their shared commitment to combatting the invisibility and systemic erasure of trans people.

Viviane Namaste (VN): To start things off, could you introduce yourself?

Marie-Marcelle Godbout (MG): My name is Marie-Marcelle Godbout, and transsexual issues have been dear to my heart since the early seventies. Those were the years when I started to be attentive to this community. At the time, I was an auxiliary nurse, and the only doctor that prescribed hormones [to transsexual women] would suggest that they come to my place to get their injections. And so that's how it all started; I would have a line of people at my door on Mondays. I was very attentive [to what they would say], because at the time I hadn't had my operation yet.

VN: And could you tell us about the beginnings of the L'Aide aux Transsexuel(le)s du Québec [ATQ]?

MG: Well, it all comes back to Christine. She was my greatest friend, and the discrimination that she faced on her deathbed pushed me to act. We had worked together as transvestites doing revues in cabarets. One night, I was walking home on rue Sanguinet [in Montreal], when I saw a hooded figure coming toward me. I got scared. Suddenly I'm thinking to myself: What do I do? Turn around? Run? In the end, I kept going, and when our eyes met I recognized Christine. She had just had a sex change operation. They had just operated on her and then let her go, just like that, alone on a November night. She was completely lost. She looked at me and said, "I'm alone in the world." So I grabbed her and said "Not anymore," and I brought her home. I was really a mother to her then. And it was at that moment that I realized what it really meant to change one's sex. You couldn't change your papers, you couldn't change your identity, and there wasn't a doctor that would treat [Christine] because "We don't touch that." It was awful.

Christine eventually ended up in Toronto with a very good job at Delta. She was such an intelligent person. She even had an international line at work. And then one day a man from Las Vegas fell in love with her, with her voice.[...] She decided to send him pictures from her days as a dancer. She didn't want to send anything recent because she had put on some weight. But then eventually the man from Las Vegas announced that he would be coming to Toronto for work and that they were finally going to meet in person. I remember she called me in distress because she did not look like the pictures she had sent him. Well, Christine decided to go see a surgeon to get her stomach stitched.[...] You have to understand that, for her, having a man in her life was the best thing that could ever happen. She had her surgery on November 6. I remember it was the 6th because I was also on an operating table in Toronto for my sex change surgery. But, her surgery didn't go well. [Her health kept deteriorating until one day] she fell and had a stroke. She spent 14 months at the hospital in a coma. I think that the lack of respect on the part of the staff just pushed her further into her coma, to the point where they declared her a vegetable. When I would go visit I could manage to communicate with her a little. I'd talk to her in French. And I'd bring my son. Oh, how he loved his Aunt Christine! He'd squeeze her tight, and she would open her eyes and squeeze my hand. For 14 months it went on like this, and my suspicion that the staff were not treating her right just kept growing. So one day, I showed up unannounced. When I arrived at Toronto General Hospital, there were two nurses in Christine's room telling her to "be a good little boy now." Her face hadn't been shaved in a while. You could see that she had been curling her upper lip to hide it. I was so angry! For them to disrespect her on her deathbed, after all she had been through. The whole way home to Montreal, all I could think about was that I had to do something, start something. That's where the ATQ came from.

VN: In what year was the ATQ founded?

MG: In 1980, at least that's when it became official; I started helping people before that.

VN: How did the women and men in the milieu react?

MG: Oh, they hated me! I wanted to be in the media, because as you know, back then all the media had to say about transsexuals was in relation to crimes, prostitution, drugs, and prison. I had a man in my life, a son, I was living the life of a normal woman of my generation, and I wanted people to know. But what you have to understand is that, back then, transsexuals faced a lot of rejection, usually from a very young age. We were a little effeminate or different, and it wasn't very well respected. The rejection was so great that all my generation wanted was to be able to fit in, to live like everybody else. In the end, we were hiding. But then I came along, and no, no, no! I called [television host] Jean-Luc Mongrain and told him that I wanted to do a television interview with him. He said sure. So there we were, the Minister of Justice, Dr. Ménard, a whole panel really. And the Minister of Justice explained that, in law, we are taught that we will never be able to make a woman out of a man, nor a man out of woman. Well I told him, "Just you wait and see, we'll take care of that!" And I remember Mr. Mongrain then asking me if I had orgasms like a woman or like a man. And this was in the eighties! So I replied, "I don't know what women's orgasms are like, I don't know what your orgasms are like, but I do have orgasms!" It was such a rush. I just wanted to be Mother Teresa, so all of a sudden I announced right there on television that a helpline now existed for transsexuals, and I gave them my home phone number.

VN: I love it.

MG: And that's how the helpline started, day and night. And back then the people who would call in were married, they had children, grandchildren even. They had tried to suppress all of that because they preferred to live the life that was expected of them. It was hell. Imagine the people calling in the night, [with] a big ball of emotion stuck in their throats. They had seen me on television and had secretly taken down my number. It took some people months to finally decide to pick up the phone and call. Oh, how I heard such suffering in the beginning! Now a little less, you know people today talk [about transsexuality], but in the beginning it was just horrible. They'd commit suicide. Bang! I'd hear the phone fall on the ground. And back then it wasn't like today. You couldn't send an ambulance or call S.O.S. Suicide. I'd be left there wondering if they were dead or alive.

VN: You made reference to the fact that things were different back then. What do you think that young people of today need to understand about the past?

MG: Young people today, when I talk to them, I know that they are not suffering any less than we did back then. Their suffering in the present is no less than mine [was] in the past. It's just that, back then, I'd be getting ready to go out and I would never know if I would make it home that night to sleep in my bed or if I'd end up in prison. It was like the Gestapo. And if someone decided that they were going to beat you up in the street, the police might very well encourage them: "Let's go, harder, give it to him!" We had nothing, we weren't citizens, we had no rights. We were second class, not even second class. At any moment they could arrest you. Once, I working as a server in a bar and the police arrived wanting to know who the pusher in the place was. I was so innocent. I had no idea and I told them that. Well the next night they came to arrest me for cross-dressing and solicitation. I was guilty long before I ever got [to stand] in front of the judge. Just because I was dressed in women's clothing, I was a criminal. It was associated with homosexuality, and homosexuality was criminal.

VN: In what year was this?

MG: Before 1969, the omnibus bill passed in 1969; after that they couldn't use homosexuality—if you dressed like a woman you were automatically a homosexual—as just cause for arrest. But even today, in 2012, people suffer. One person comes to mind: she can't find a place to live and this is happening in 2012, not the seventies. It upsets me. She may have behavioural problems, but she is still human. In another era they would have put her in a psychiatric institution. Now she is free, but really, she isn't any freer than if she had been institutionalized.

Nora Butler Burke (NB): What was the relationship between francophone and anglophone transsexuals back then? Did they go to the same bars?

MG: I don't know much about the anglophone side of things. Sometimes they would invite me when they wanted to start something. Here in Montreal, there wasn't much on the anglophone side in those days. There were bars on the West Side, but I can't really tell you about anglophone transsexuals. I guess the people we came across were either francophone or they could speak French. Like Christine, she was an anglophone but she spoke French.

NB: Maybe you could tell us a little about how the bar scene in Montreal evolved over time.

MG: It was outrageous how the police would treat us. I remember, I'd be sitting in a bar when all a sudden all the big lights would come on. It was surreal. And there you would have six beefy cops talking amongst themselves. They were pointing at people in the bar as they decided which one of us they were going to take with them to the police station to harass for a few hours. As you can imagine, it was torture, enough to make you go crazy. Sometimes, I'd be sitting there, and I wouldn't even be able to remember my name. I was so sure that it would be my turn and that they were going to point in my direction. This was a regular occurrence.

Before my time, there was Lana St-Cyr. Lana wasn't a transsexual, but I have a great deal of respect for this person because he opened up a lot of doors for us. This is before Guilda even. He was hired in the 1940s by Madame Pétrie. Now young people won't even know who she is, but she had a theatre on St-Laurent and she hired Lana to perform on stage dressed as a woman. As Lana started to become known in the bar scene, police would go see the owners and warn them that if they didn't kick *that* out immediately that they would lose their licence. Back then the morality police had a large influence on bar licences. Well, Lana fought for her right to work. She went to court and convinced the judge to give her permission to perform on stage dressed in women's clothing—not to dress as a woman in the streets, mind you. Lana was a homosexual, but homosexuals couldn't have a bar either. What they did to us, it was the same for them. It was criminal. If there were 15 of us in a bar, well that's 15 people that the police could take away. It was worse if you were wearing a wig. Not only were we accused of being homosexuals, we were also accused of disguising ourselves in order to commit a crime. And at the time there were a lot of bank robberies where people would wear wigs, so it was easy to make that accusation. But what happened with Lana is that she became somewhat of a public figure. And so when a club would open, they would solicit Lana to work for them. That way, they could put Lana on the advertisement outside by the door. Homosexuals then knew that this was a place where they could go and that they would be accepted without getting attacked.

Cléopâtre was one of the first clubs in Montreal where transsexuals would go. It was their bar. To this day, when we want to organize something, we go to Cléopâtre. It [started] in 1977. I remember that I wanted a job to buy a new car. Lana wasn't working. Things were on the decline. She didn't even have a phone. So, Lana came to me and said that some Greeks had just bought the Canasta, and that they wanted to give her the second floor. But since she did not have a phone, she gave them my number instead and asked me to pretend that I was her. One of the partners called me and explained, thinking I was Lana, that they had strippers on the first floor but that they didn't know what to do with the second. I'd worked at the Canasta, back in the day, as a magician, so I knew it well. Anyway, I told him that if it were me, I would open a bar for transsexuals, with transsexuals as barmaids, servers, and everything. He told me that he would have to talk it over with his partners. He later called back and said okay. And just like that I had a job. I got my car, and transsexuals had a bar they could call home. One of the first in the world, I think. To this day, I have friends from Europe tell me that they have never heard of anything like it. It was great. You would have the president of a company walk in wearing a business suit with a little bag, go into the washroom, and come out in nylons and high heels. It was a place where people could live out their fantasies and express their difference. It makes me happy to think about Café Cléopâtre. It was in the artistic sector of the city as well. Ah! How I would love to be 30 again. I have a few ideas of what I'd be up to in there!

VN: Having witnessed this evolution and the progress made in many sectors, what would you say are the priorities for the future? After all, you have a lot of experience and are a long-time activist for trans people.

MG: I think the number one priority, when looking toward the near future, is the fate of aging transsexuals. Many people have been in the shadows for 35 or even 40 years, and they are frightened by the thought of losing their anonymity. They would rather commit suicide than go to an old age home. It really demonstrates how limited the progress has been. They managed to escape suicide by going into hiding 40 years ago but now they are again ready to commit suicide to avoid being exposed. I think the biggest thing would be for more acceptance *within* this community. That people accept themselves the way they are. I ran into someone this last Saturday or Sunday. I had known her when she was 14 years old and I was already in my thirties. But I didn't recognize her. It wasn't until she took off her glasses that I finally recognized her eyes. She was like an old woman of 80 years, and yes we can pass for an 80-year-old woman. I said, "What happened?" She told me that she had never been able to accept not being a woman, a real woman. The thing with being transsexual is that the more you try to get away from it, the more it chases you, and the more you confront it, the more it disappears. I know from experience. I did the media and everything. It never chased after me. I never heard my neighbours say anything about it, because everybody already knew, so there was nothing left to gossip about. I've been married for 40 years, I have a 36-year-old son, and two grandkids. And I never hid who I was. I would not want to be anything other than transsexual. If you were to tell me that I had a chance to do it all over again, I would say leave me as I am. I worked hard to get here. This acceptance does not come on its own.

Many were not so lucky. I'll get a call: "Nobody loves me." You know, if you want others to love you, you have to start by loving yourself. What is missing in our community is self-love. It's very, very rare that you will meet [a transsexual] that is proud and happy to be who she is. So that's what the work ahead looks like, which is more about consciousness than therapy and evaluation. Even if you had your operation 50 years ago, it will always follow you.

For example, I once got a call from Lise,[1] the first transsexual woman to get a sex change operation in Montreal. It was done at the Notre-Dame Hospital, and they made her sign papers saying that if she ever talked about the surgery they were going to take her to court. A nice start to life, eh? You have this secret and then on top of this you have the doctors, the specialists, telling you that if you ever talk about it, they will take you to court. So she went and worked for the nuns. And since it was illegal to remove a functional organ, they declared her a hermaphrodite to justify the surgery. And they got the Catholic Church to change her baptismal certificate on the grounds that she was a deformed woman. Lise got her baptismal certificate, kept her job, and got married in the Catholic Church. And she thought that the man she had been living with for years did not know.

So one day, I'm on Clair Lamanche's television show, and she asks what I think it must be like for women who got the operation and then decided to turn the page and not come back to it. I told her that they must be like prisoners. The next day Lise called me. She was unable to even say the word "transsexual." She told me that she did not live like a prisoner; rather she lived like a fugitive with dark tinted glasses, always worried that somebody would recognize her. Imagine the solitude. At one point, she had taken an appointment with a psychologist in Verdun, thinking that at least she could talk about it with him. But as soon as she told the psychologist that she had had a sex change operation, he kicked her out of his office, yelling at her as she passed through the waiting room. It was something like "You people who get the operation to do prostitution, I'll never deal with one of you!" As you can imagine, it took a few more years before she would try talking to anybody again. Do you understand how awful the torture this woman went through was? And now she was calling me, telling me that she never even told her husband or her doctor. So I introduced to her to a doctor whom she could be honest with. He sent her for tests, and when the results came back, he informed her that her only kidney was severely infected. Well, she thought she was dying. On the way home, she told her husband: "You know that little wooden locked box? Well if I die, once you read what's inside, promise me you will burn it." Well, he answers, "You mean your sex change papers?"

It's like I always say, the more you run away, the more it chases you. And stuff happened to her. She had the house that dreams are made of, right down to the little flowers, the whole nine yards. One day it started to get around; people were saying that she was not a woman. And people would walk by, you know those little old ladies in flowered dresses, and they would say things like "No wonder there are no birds left, the scarecrow has scared them away," and the like. It drove her husband crazy, her as well. So they sold it. But then, behind their new home, there was an old age residence. A couple of ladies were out back, and one tells the other, "That's the one that got the sex change operation." But the other lady was deaf, so she had to repeat it over and over, louder and louder. Oh, the shame! You can't keep fleeing. I think the most important work ahead in the trans community is to give people a sense of pride. Be proud of yourself, and then you will have the respect of others.

NB: These days, we see the kind of work you have done increasingly take place within government-funded non-profit organizations. What strikes me is that for all these years you have done this work from a truly grassroots approach, without ever being paid.

MG: Well, I may not have been paid in money, but life has rewarded me! Working without a salary, it hasn't been a penance. I don't regret a thing.

NOTE

1 Fictionalized name.

Chapter 13 Trans Access Project: Running the Gauntlet

Kyle Scanlon, Jake Pyne, Dani Araya, Alec Butler, Jazzmine Manalo, Evana Ortigoza, Julissa Penate, Yasmeen Persad, and Kenji Tokawa

A note on terminology: we are using the word "trans" in its broadest definition to include those who identify as transgender, transsexual, two-spirit, intersex, genderqueer, male-to-female (MTF), female-to-male (FTM), cross-dresser, and so on.

With 9,164 social service staff and students trained, 488 workshops over eight years, and covering geographic territory as diverse as Halton, Etobicoke, Oshawa, Barrie, Hamilton, Guelph, Waterloo, Belleville, Durham, Peel, Orillia, Ottawa, Kenora, Kingston, Peterborough, Dryden, Hamilton, Kitchener, and Toronto, the Ontario-based Trans Access Project team has been pretty busy. And on top of that, we've had speakers present at conferences in Philadelphia, New York City, Seattle, Montreal, and Las Vegas.

Since participating in Trans Access workshops, 25 Toronto shelters have created trans access policies for their agencies. In 2002, project staff assisted the City of Toronto to change the Toronto Shelter Standard Guidelines so that trans people would be served in the gender in which they identified to best preserve their safety. In 2005, Trans Access won the Major Leonard Frost Award from the Ontario Association of Hostels for "Outstanding Work on Behalf of Homeless People." In 2008, the project won the City of Toronto Public Service Quality Award for Excellence. In a nutshell, agencies all across Ontario that could not serve trans people back in 2001 have since opened their doors to trans service users. There's no doubt the Trans Access Project has had a tremendously significant impact within social service sectors that has improved the lives of many trans people. But rarely does anyone ask: What has been the impact on us?

The Trans Access Project is a community development initiative. The project began in 2001 under the stewardship of Christina Strang, the Meal Trans Coordinator at The 519 Church Street Community Centre. Programming for trans people at the centre was exploding. In addition to the meal program, it offered outreach for sex workers and had organized a youth group. The result was that Christina heard more and more stories of trans people facing barriers while trying to access basic services.

The first incarnation of the project was as the Trans Community Shelter Access Project, and it was Christina and Kyle Scanlon (who would eventually become the Trans Programs Coordinator at The 519) who began the first "train the trainer" round. Jake Pyne was one of those first trainees, and it was Jake who, in 2002, became the Project Coordinator.

The Trans Access Project sends out a diverse range of trans-identified individuals into the social service field to deliver trans awareness/sensitivity/anti-oppression training. The goal of these workshops is ultimately to reduce the barriers that keep trans people from accessing services that most people take for granted. The team has trained staff members at a range of services, from shelters to detoxification centres, AIDS hospices, housing services, sexual assault centres, youth services, legal clinics, employment centres, addictions services, hospitals, and settlement services.

But conducting this training has its price. For every triumph, and every aha moment of considered reflection when staff suddenly "get it" and it feels certain that service will be positively impacted, there are also defeatist days that sink a trainer down into the depths of despair. This chapter will explore the experiences of Trans Access trainers in doing their work and the unanticipated impact the work has on them.

In preparing this chapter, some current and former members of the Trans Access Project team came together to be interviewed and share stories, laugh, vent, and ruminate on the project's impact on their lives. Quotes from team members come directly from the interviews that took place during two team meetings.

To fully appreciate the impact of this project, it is important to understand the philosophy behind it. Trans Access is first and foremost a training project for service providers, but it is also a community development project. The project could have simply hired two qualified "trainers" to go into the field and deliver training to service providers if that were the only goal, but instead the project drew together a team of trans people who had no previous experience conducting training. The project taught them facilitation skills and the vocabulary used in social services to give them the background and credibility they needed to deliver training. This was a great opportunity to hire trans people without formal education—some were trans sex workers and homeless trans people—who wanted a shot at changing the course of their lives. The project made an active decision to use only trans-identified presenters. Jake and the Trans Project staff wanted to avoid the appearance of "non-trans professionals" who carried more influence and status than their trans co-presenters. We wanted to ensure this was more than a glorified speaker's bureau.

We also wanted to challenge the classic service-provision model in which a trans person will always/only be a "recipient" of service. In our framework, these presenters shifted to becoming service providers, and we insisted they take on all the responsibilities attached to that title. We did not want them to be perceived as "charity cases," and aimed instead for service providers to have a transformative experience by engaging with trans people (and often sex workers) as colleagues rather than as clients. Having gone through the hiring process in this project, we knew that our trainers were intelligent, thoughtful, compassionate human beings who had the kind of insight one can achieve only through personal experience. These experiences were considered highly valuable to the project, and these trans people only needed an opportunity to show themselves (and the world) what they could accomplish if they set their minds to it and if they were given the right supports. As proof that these team members were highly prized and to further demonstrate that there was no "charity," the trainers were well paid for their time. It was a priority of the project that team members know they were as valued and respected as other professionals were in the field.

This model, however, required a delicate balance of responsibilities. There were our responsibilities to the presenters themselves, to ensure they were given sufficient training to provide them with the "language" of social services so they could connect professionally with their audiences. We had responsibilities to our funders, to complete the trainings they had funded us to provide. We had responsibilities to the agencies we trained, to provide high-quality presentations that would help to shift agency practices that discriminated against trans people. There were responsibilities to The 519 itself, to ensure our trainers behaved professionally and upheld The 519 mission any time they acted as representatives of the agency. And, ultimately, we had responsibilities to the trans community members who would be using the services of the agencies we trained, because, bottom line, if our trainings did not facilitate a process of creating access, then the project would have failed.

For the most part, trainers were appropriate, professional, and respectful while delivering workshops. But occasionally there was a slip. A presenter would make a wrong—perhaps it is more accurate to say "politically charged"—statement of some kind. For example, a facilitator once made an offhand comment about a particular agency being "transphobic." Word got back to that agency, and there were repercussions for the project and The 519. Presenters had to work to manage the fallout from these kinds of instances. Diplomatically addressing an agency to discuss their institutionalized transphobia is a delicate and sophisticated art and a highly specialized skill. While recalling this incident, Jake Pyne, who has now left the project, said, "Dealing with transphobia in a professional context is different than in day-to-day life. [The facilitator] wasn't wrong—it was just a different skill that was needed there."

Another way that presenters were responsible for their words had to do with the issue of representation, and the recognition that anything a presenter said about their own experience would likely be generalized to the whole trans community. It became imperative that presenters ask themselves "Whose needs am I meeting if I tell this story?" and determine the context under which any particular story is relevant, meaningful, and useful. Presenters learned to describe "common" experiences and place less emphasis on their specific personal experiences unless those experiences helped to illustrate a key message of the workshop.

Another issue that presented an ongoing challenge was that of visibility as a trans person and disclosure of trans identity. At any time, someone could walk into a training classroom and throw a presenter for a loop. In our team meeting, presenter Alec Butler described having just such an experience while conducting a workshop for shelter staff: "My neighbour who lives across the hall walked in. As I am not out as trans in my building, I found this very disconcerting to say the least. The next day I called his boss … and explained about my neighbour who had no idea I was trans. She assured me that one of the main messages of the workshop—to keep a person's trans status confidential—is primary in work. With the trans community she assured me she believed her employee/my neighbour would follow this policy in regard to our shared living situation."

With staff trainings, we could usually expect that there was some kind of commitment to anti-oppression and human rights underlying their interaction with us. We could surmise that they would act professionally (at least to some degree) both inside and outside of our trainings. However, despite assurances that things would go smoothly in workshops, the safety of the presenters was never absolutely guaranteed. And there was some reason for fear. An agency having policies was no guarantee that its staff would follow those policies. As presenter Kenji Tokawa described in our team meeting: "I have fears around outing myself on such a regular basis to complete strangers who have given me no reason to trust their actions once the workshop is over and the street lights come on. I often wonder if it is actually safe enough yet for trans people to be putting themselves out there like this."

Staff workshops were not the only situations where visibility/disclosure could be an issue. The Trans Access program also offered training for residents of shelters, and these workshops presented their own particular challenges and benefits. Residents were accountable to themselves, to each other, and to the guidelines of the shelter in which they resided, but unlike staff, they had no professional code of conduct to which they had to adhere. Some facilitators felt unsafe about this lack of policy. Kenji Tokawa elaborates: "Although I have been privileged enough to not yet experience a violent encounter because of my trans identity, I know I am always at risk for violence in the future. This knowledge worries me, particularly going into these workshops in order to reverse the tide of transphobic violence."

But for other Trans Access presenters, the residents' workshops provided a refreshing change of pace. With residents, interactions were often seen as being "more genuine" and real. Some project facilitators also felt they could relate much better to the residents, since their backgrounds sometimes held common elements. One fascinating insight was that, while the staff at shelters routinely explained that the largest barrier to trans access was the attitudes of shelter residents, the residents themselves often pointed to the staff to say the prejudice against serving trans people came from them.

Another significant difference with Trans Access workshops for residents is that they were asking something very different of the residents than from the staff. Staff were being asked to provide access and service; essentially, to do their job. However, shelter residents were being asked to live with and sleep beside trans people with whom they might be profoundly uncomfortable. Residents had much more at stake personally than the staff. And with this recognition, some project trainers decided to allow the residents a wider berth in terms of the kinds of questions they could ask and the language they used to ask them. Ultimately, trainers found that the same question could be invested with a very different meaning depending on who asked it and in what spirit it was asked.

Being open to answering questions could be challenging. One perceived benefit of the project was the allure of being imbued with "expert" status. In the beginning, it might have felt affirming to be asked questions, to have the attention of "professionals," to feel as though we as community members had something worthwhile to offer. And it definitely was empowering to be the ones in control of the message, rather than the media and the so-called psychiatric experts who had defined the trans community for so long. But there was a downside. Project presenters were commonly asked very personal and intimate questions.

Early on in the project, trainers related to these kinds of questions differently from the way they related to those same questions after the project matured. Initially it was a validating experience to be asked, to capture the interest of staff members and residents, and to believe personal confessions could help to stamp out transphobia. Over time, however, Trans Access trainers developed a deeper analysis of transphobia and the recognition that transphobia was played out through power dynamics. When trans presenters were expected to answer every question posed, no matter how personal, it reinforced a power dynamic that promoted transphobia: that trans people were specimens to be poked and prodded and that the bodies and sexualities of non-trans people were normal and unremarkable. For instance, a staff member at a conference demanded answers to questions about one of our team member's genitals. She felt the team's presenters were there to educate her and she had a right to an answer. This perception that a trans person had no right to privacy once they walked up to the podium was pervasive. Workshop facilitators had to either develop a very thick skin or find another way to handle these situations.

One unanticipated outcome of these messy moments was that trans presenters became expert at deflecting offensive and overly personal questions. Part of this was due to the initial process of training, which placed a priority on exploring issues related to "boundaries." The team carefully thought through the implications of what it might mean to answer questions. For instance, someone in the audience might be your future neighbour or future employer. How comfortable were you with sharing that information? And even if you personally were okay with answering such a personal question, were you just reinforcing the dynamic that trans people are compelled to answer incredibly invasive questions about themselves at the behest of anyone who asked? To ensure that no question surprised them, the project team came up with a comprehensive list of questions that covered issues related to genital configuration, family issues, experiences of violence, sexuality, passing, religion, and so on that they might not respond to.

And trans workshop facilitators also decided to explain why they weren't going to answer a question. This allowed for more learning for the audience. Presenters might say they weren't going to answer a question about their sex life because it was too personal, or a question about their genitals because it's not appropriate for anyone other than a health care provider or a potential lover to ask that. Similarly, service-provider audiences were reminded that the only questions they should be asking their service users were questions that related directly to the service they received at that agency. But if service providers could not use their trans clients to explore their own curiosity, who could they use? It was often the Trans Access trainers themselves.

When asked to describe their feelings about working on the Trans Access Project, our team recounted mixed feelings. One team member used the phrase "emotional roller coaster." Presenters bravely faced a new audience at each workshop, putting themselves in the spotlight to be scrutinized and judged. Invariably, workshop attendees would say things that made our team members cringe. Hurtful and callous words were frequently said that hindered our presenters' ability to keep their self-respect. For instance, staff in trainings would sometimes comment on the appearance of trans people in general, and of our presenters in particular. One team member was once told that the agency staff could "tell" that he was trans because of various physical aspects of his body (height, hand size, voice, hips, etc.), and on one occasion an agency staff member commented that a male-to-female presenter passed well and was "pretty." This constant scrutiny was one of the most negative aspects of the work. At other times, staff made generalized comments that were also hurtful, such as asserting that trans women are just "men in women's clothes." In one workshop, a staff member from an agency compared trans people to monkeys. These comments were perceived as cruel and demeaning, and they left presenters feeling defensive, angry, and sad.

Trans Access presenters went into these trainings with a fervent wish to impact society and with the hope that the service providers they trained were coming to the table with the same goal. However, that was not always the case. Trans Access facilitator Julissa Penate explains:

"At times I [got] mad and frustrated at some of the comments and reactions of the crowd, but I stay[ed] calm and [found] a way to deal with it in the most appropriate and professional human way. I once had a guy say 'That's the way it is in society,' meaning 'Get used to it and deal with it.' I got very upset and I had to ask the audience how we as social service providers expect to make people feel equal with that kind of mentality. I mean, aren't we the ones [who] want to make [a] difference? So if you don't feel that way, maybe you shouldn't be in this field of work." Julissa's faith was somewhat restored in the next moment when, she said, "People clapped."

But there were times when the audience just wasn't responsive. As Dani Araya describes: "They were so dead, they might as well have been corpses, and they gave off a vibe like they were ready to get this workshop done so they could [just] go home. I did feel a few of them [were] gawking and gossiping about us." All of these experiences were degrading and disempowering. Workshop facilitators carried these emotions with them long after the workshop was over.

Workshop presenters felt demoralized when the workshops did not ultimately deliver on their expectations, and when changes to agencies or systems were barely plodding along. In 2004, for instance, it seemed as though the possibilities were endless and that this project was going to completely transform the shelter system overnight. But it didn't. Not only did some agencies stop progressing, some were even regressing. This was a key moment of realization for one member of the Trans Access team, Jake Pyne, who served as the Trans Access Coordinator until 2008. He recounted these experiences as having a huge impact on his decision to return to school. He realized that the trainings, while highly valuable, only represented one piece of the larger puzzle in the process of change. Other pieces beyond our control included the need to develop trans positive policies, acquire committed funds for site renovations for some facilities, address the lack of social justice work within the men's hostel system, and advocate for the weight of human rights law to come down hard on the side of justice—access and inclusion—for trans people.

Also frustrating were those issues that were not being fully addressed through the workshops. For instance, one specific piece of work in the Trans Access Project was providing workshops for staff at agencies serving women who were survivors of violence. While it was a fairly straightforward argument to say that trans women identified and lived as women and should receive services at women's agencies, it was far more complex to discuss the issue of trans men and FTMs who were also survivors of violence but did not identify or live as women. In general, discussion of FTMs in any women's shelter or service was a challenge because it required a rather sophisticated analysis of gendered services and access barriers. Our hands were frequently tied in the politically charged climate of women's services, so we had to make the decision to pursue the accommodation of FTMs in other ways, including a research project that eventually created the report *Invisible Men: FTMs and Homelessness in the City of Toronto*. One FTM workshop presenter commented on how agonizing it was to find himself biting his tongue in a workshop when this politically divisive issue was raised because he knew that the process of accommodating FTMs would come at a much slower rate.

Other challenges included the issue of horizontal hostility. Horizontal hostility could be described as a situation where groups of marginalized people begin lashing out at each other rather than joining forces to lash out against their true oppressors. In the Trans Access Project, horizontal hostility sometimes played out in the way presenters interacted with one another. The response of the project was to intervene immediately and try to use the conflict productively. Together the team developed strategies to give each other honest feedback that was both critical and supportive. Coming to understand the concept that conflict could be dealt with openly and productively was a huge learning experience for many project team members.

Many of the trans women on the project had never met a trans man before, and vice versa. As well, this was the first time that some of the trans presenters had been exposed to sex workers. These presenters had the opportunity to learn from each other and, despite their differences, operate as a team. That concept of being a team was crucial to the success of the project. Kenji Tokawa explains: "I hear it in the laughter of camaraderie around the folding table at our monthly team meetings, the community it forms for us trans folks, and the value it adds to our hard-come-by identities. This is why I come back to work, week to week, month to month, and hopefully year to year."

As a team, Trans Access trainers agreed to work within a framework of anti-oppression and anti-racism. That analysis only deepened over time as the presenters on the team became more diverse, incorporating MTFs, FTMs, people of colour, sex workers, two-spirit trans people, self-identified cross-dressers, people with experience in the shelter system, people with experience with substance use, and intersex people.

Some of the presenters in the project gained in personal confidence. Julissa Penate says, "I used to be so quiet and now I have more confidence to talk in all areas." After months with the project, facilitators showed other signs of increased self-confidence and self-respect. Many of them began applying for community positions that they never would have applied for if it had not been for their experience with Trans Access and the credibility they attained as social service workers.

For all the frustrations and challenges, everyone involved with the project recounted numerous successes. Many of the presenters commented on how important it was to them to pass along an understanding of trans issues and to feel a moment of connection when they recognized that the staff were "getting it." Kenji Tokawa comments: "I feel it in the smiles of appreciation from participants who thank me genuinely for taking the time to come and facilitate." In those moments they knew that they were creating change in the way Toronto social services agencies handle trans access.

The presenters also commented on the importance of developing relationships with the staff at the agencies where the workshops were held, and how it allowed them to become resources to their friends, family, colleagues, and service users. These relationships also allowed service providers to see the real humanity of trans people. Evana Ortigoza says, "I'm proud to be one of the facilitators in Trans Access going around to different agencies to let them know we have the same skin, heart, and feelings [as] everybody else." Jazzmine Manalo explains: "It gives me self-fulfillment when I know in the end I have paved the way for the next trans woman who will access the service."

After exploring all the ways that the project impacted our team, there needs to be an acknowledgement of how much these Trans Access team members brought to the project themselves. In many ways, as Jake Pyne said, "All we really did was provide a platform for them to get out there and really shine." While these individuals may have lacked "professional credibility" before joining our team, they were brimming with heart, compassion, intelligence, dedication, and courage.

And it didn't take long before these facilitators were leading the project. Once these trainers got up and going, the learning cycle shifted, and the roles all changed. The trainers began to take control of the project, to feel ownership of it, to rewrite the workshop content, to bring in new handout materials, and to move it in new directions. Yasmeen Persad, for instance, began coordinating all the work on the trainings we provided to sexual assault centres and anti-violence agencies. Alec Butler began delivering trainings for the team on intersex and two-spirit issues. Kenji Tokawa came to the table with a list of changes that needed to be made to the definitions. All of our presenters weren't just "on" the project, they "were" the project. They had at least as much of an impact on the project as it did on them. And they're still having an impact.

These trans, intersex, and two-spirit presenters have become role models to members of the trans community and are the de facto next generation of trans activists. These trans people have developed valuable social service credibility, and they've gone on to be service providers in their own right, offering their knowledge, insight, and experience to shelters, health centres, and community centres across the city.

To be specific, there is now a long list of agencies in Toronto that are employing (either through paid or volunteer work) members from the Trans Access Project: the Sherbourne Health Centre, the Griffin Centre, The 519 Church Street Community Centre, Asian Community AIDS Service, Voices of Positive Women, Jesse's Place, 2 Spirited People of the First Nations, Street Haven, Delisle Youth Services, Hassle Free Clinic, Alliance for South Asian AIDS Prevention, Rainbow Health Ontario, LGBTQ Parenting Network, Black Coalition for AIDS Prevention, East Mississauga Community Health Centre, and the Centre for Spanish Speaking People. Some projects have also benefited from the input of these people, including Invisible Men: FTMs and Homelessness in the City of Toronto, Creating a Place Where We Are All Welcome, Trans PULSE, and the International AIDS conference.

Despite the challenges of this project—fear of violence, of being asked invasive personal questions, of being hurt with cruel words—the Trans Access Project has helped to change the face of service provision to trans people in Ontario. More importantly, it has forged a new group of trans service providers who have confidence in their abilities, a deep analysis of the way transphobia asserts itself in organizations, an understanding of how to dismantle that transphobia, and a sense of their own worth.

Let's give the final word to some members of the Trans Access team about the lasting impact the project has had on them:

> I like flexing my muscle as an educator for my community and letting non-trans people know that we have full lives, a rich history, and much to contribute to society now and in the future.
>
> —Alec Butler

> I like the feeling of bringing out our pride and sticking up for our community, the feeling of being able to share my experiences with others. I also like to hear—and at times, laugh—at some of the comments or topics that come up from the service providers we train. I have also gained a lot more confidence talking in public, and I really enjoy the opportunity to educate others.
>
> —Julissa Penate

> When the audience is eager and open, I always get a sense of satisfaction and that everything you say will be listened to and absorbed. It gives me a small chance to be a teacher and enlighten blossoming minds. I like being a proud representative and opening up people's minds and hearts to our struggles and challenges. The more we can share our wisdom, the better the world can be for trans and non-trans people.
>
> —Dani Araya

To sum up: Trans Access = deep impact. For everyone.

For more information about the Trans Access Project, please contact The 519 Church Street Community Centre at 416-392-6874 or info@the519.org.

Postscript

It is with great sadness that we share the news of author Kyle Scanlon's passing. Kyle committed suicide in July 2012 after a long struggle with his mental health. We share this openly and honestly because Kyle would have wanted nothing less. Kyle left behind an adoring community, loving friends and family members, fiercely loyal co-workers, and many questions. We wish for healing and peace for everyone who was touched by his important life, and we wish for justice for everyone who struggles in this difficult world.

Chapter 14 A Conversation about Art and Activism with Trans and Genderqueer People Labelled with Intellectual Disabilities

Zack Marshall, Marcus Burnette, Sonia Lowton, Rainbow, Romeo Dontae Treshawn Smith, Jay Tiamo, Onyinyechukwu Udegbe, and Tess Vo
Illustrations by Elisha Lim

INTRODUCTION

In this chapter, we aim to amplify the voices of trans and genderqueer people labelled with intellectual disabilities and to recognize the ways these activists are making change in their communities. We invite you to join us in a conversation about gender, disability, art, and activism.

In 2005, a group of lesbian, gay, bisexual, transgender, queer, and questioning (LGBTQ) young people labelled with intellectual disabilities came together to start a group called "Compass" at Griffin Centre in north Toronto. Griffin Centre is an accredited, non-profit, charitable mental health agency that has provided flexible services to youth, adults, and families since 1975. The agency is dedicated to delivering innovative services and developing creative partnerships that enhance lives and communities. Within Griffin Centre, we sought to create a space in Compass where our lives and experiences would be represented and celebrated. To our knowledge, no other group of its kind existed within or outside Canada at the time. Our efforts to link sexuality, gender, and critical disability perspectives were subsequently enacted through two key projects—sprOUT and *Our Compass*. Both sprOUT and Compass include active partnerships with people labelled with intellectual disabilities, including roles for peer educators who are paid employees and sprOUT consultants who are compensated with a monthly honorarium. All of this happens under the umbrella of reachOUT, a program for LGBTQ people at Griffin Centre.

Funded by the Ontario Trillium Foundation from 2008–2012, the initial goals of sprOUT were to build community with LGBTQ people labelled with intellectual disabilities across Ontario, to provide training and support to educators and service providers who work with people labelled with intellectual disabilities, and to document and disseminate best practices for working collaboratively with people with intellectual disabilities and their allies. The creation of sprOUT was in many ways a radical departure from typical ways of working with people labelled with intellectual disabilities. As noted in a recent program evaluation, the project's commitment to collaboration between service providers and LGBTQ people labelled with intellectual disabilities made it particularly unique (Marshall & Vo, 2012). A number of arts-based projects using film, theatre, animation, and photography have come to life through sprOUT and Compass. This includes *Our Compass*, a 30-minute documentary that was co-written by eight youth to highlight their personal stories and how they were drawn together as a "Rainbow Family."

It is important to understand the context in which these activities operate. sprOUT draws together people labelled with intellectual disabilities and service providers to focus on disabilities, sexual identity, gender identity and expression, and oppression. As such, the project is positioned within both the LGBTQ services sector and the developmental services sector. The developmental services sector includes organizations that provide services to people labelled with developmental disabilities (also referred to as intellectual disabilities). These usually operate separately for children, youth, and adults and include a full range of programs, such as education, employment, recreation, residential services, and day programs, in addition to more clinical supports such as counselling and support groups.

Addressing sexuality within the developmental services sector is often taboo (Marshall & Vo, 2012). This is linked to stereotypes and misunderstandings about people with disabilities as well as long histories of involvement with the service sector, including institutionalization and forced sterilization (Brady, 2001). sprOUT forged a new direction in the developmental services sector by actively engaging youth and adults labelled with intellectual disabilities in the creation and development of community-based initiatives (Marshall & Vo, 2012). Hiring LGBTQ people labelled with intellectual disabilities as sprOUT consultants and as co-leaders of training workshops for service providers and other people with intellectual disabilities was a significant departure from traditional clinical and behavioural models.

LGBTQ people with intellectual disabilities experience intersecting and compounded forms of marginalization and oppression. Resources and policies related to gender and/or sexuality are not always clear or accessible to people with cognitive differences. Most often these materials are not developed with these communities in mind. sprOUT's goals are directly tied to these circumstances and emphasize the creation of sex-positive spaces where people with intellectual disabilities can explore their sexuality; accessible and positive sexual health materials; the increased visibility of LGBTQ people labelled with intellectual disabilities; and supporting service providers both from the LGBTQ and developmental services sectors to gain new knowledge of how best to support LGBTQ people labelled with intellectual disabilities.

This chapter demonstrates our commitment to these values and includes the voices of eight people who have been actively involved with sprOUT and Compass: Jay, Marcus, Onyii, Rainbow, Romeo, Sonia, Tess, and Zack. The experience of cognitive differences, such as intellectual disabilities, may or may not be obvious in interactions with others. Combined with stigma and other forms of ableism, this can contribute to a lack of recognition of people who have been labelled with intellectual disabilities. In order to challenge these representations, we worked with visual artist Elisha Lim, who transformed self-selected photographs into graphic illustrations that serve to increase our visibility in a more concrete way. In the group picture on the following page you can see how interconnected we are and the types of roles we have played. To develop the content for this chapter, a draft set of 31 questions was initially developed by Zack. The questions were then reviewed with Jay, Rainbow, Romeo, and Sonia until we came up with a final version of 19 questions to ask in group and one-on-one interviews. These interviews were recorded and transcribed. Onyii, Tess, and Zack then developed a first version of the chapter, which was reviewed and revised by Sonia, Romeo, Rainbow, and Jay. While we were working on this, Elisha Lim created the illustrations that are an integral part of the chapter. The illustrations were also reviewed and revised with feedback to ensure that everyone was comfortable with the way their image was portrayed.

FIGURE 14.1: THIS IS HOW WE'RE CONNECTED

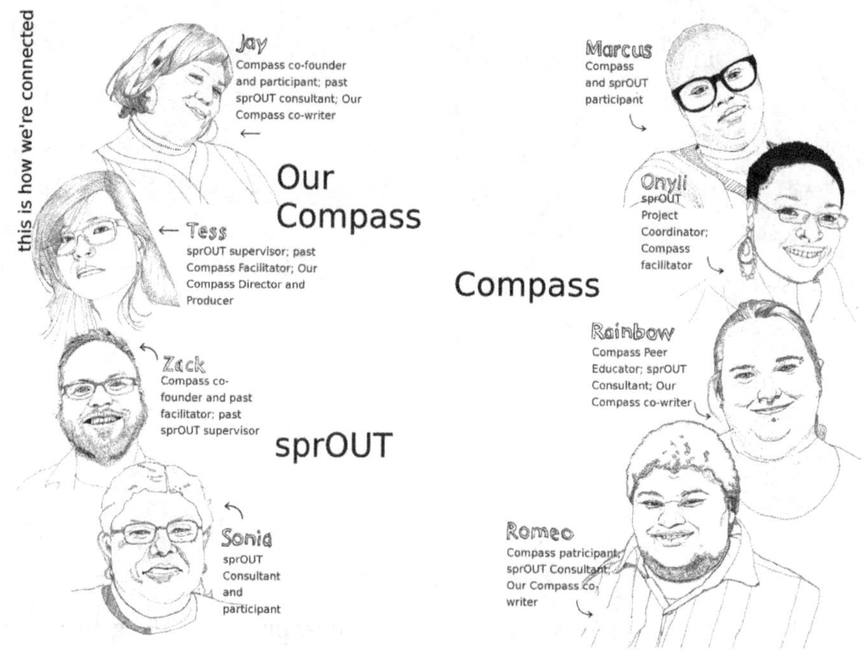

THE CONVERSATION

***Tess*: What would you like the people reading this book to know about you as a person?**
Jay: Being genderqueer, there's a lot of discrimination because a lot of people think, "Oh, you're just confused about your gender," or "You're confused about your orientation." I don't like to go by gender or orientation.
Romeo: As somebody who is trans, I can say that trans people get harassed and trans-bashed a lot—which needs to stop.
Rainbow: I want people to know that I am a healthy transgender person, who was raised by a really supportive family, and that I have an intellectual disability, and that I am not letting that stop me from doing things like other people. I face a lot of barriers in my life that I'm trying to pass, but I am struggling through.
Marcus: I'm transgendered; I'm a normal person like everybody else.
Sonia: I'm a lesbian, and I am proud to be a lesbian.

***Zack*: What would you like to tell people about your gender identity?**
Jay: That's difficult for me because I don't specify as a gender. I am who I am, so if you want to call me by gender-neutral pronouns like "they," "ze," or "hir," I don't care. Gender should be more fluid and more accepting; it shouldn't matter what gender you are. I consider myself a

FIGURE 14.2: JAY

"stem," which is another word for saying masculine and feminine mixed together.
Rainbow: I go by "she," and I am attracted to guys more than girls—but I am attracted to both. Basically, I'm a bisexual trans female.
Sonia: I only date women.
Romeo: I'm a straight trans guy.
Marcus: I'm a trans guy. I'm attracted to females.

***Onyii*: What would you like to tell people about your sexual identity?**
Jay: That's a complicated question. I can say that I'm genderqueer and that I like men, women, and in-between—I would date any gender or orientation. I think everyone has a different definition of what trans or genderqueer or gender fluid means. Because there are people who don't believe that someone can be genderqueer or gender fluid, there's an off-balance in the queer community. A lot of things about genderqueer and gender fluid people get thrown away; a lot of people are afraid to come out as genderqueer. On the other hand, you have us in a little corner.
Marcus: I identify as male. I am attracted to women.

***Zack*: You identify as male, and you're attracted to women. Do you have any trouble meeting women? How do you usually meet women?**
Marcus: I have trouble meeting women. [Laughter.] It's just one of those things—you just can't find nobody.

***Zack*: Do you think that is because you are in more of a rural area?**
Marcus: Yep. That's part of it and the fact that I have a lot of disabilities.
Rainbow: I'm mostly attracted to bisexual guys.

***Onyii*: Why?**
Rainbow: Why? Do you want me to be honest? The reason I like dating bisexual guys is because they're not as feminine as gay men.
Jay: Rainbow, do you really consider all gay men to be feminine?
Rainbow: Somewhat, yeah. I'm being honest; I like to date bisexual guys and girls—but I change every time, from liking gay guys, and then not liking them, to being friends with them. I'm attracted to bisexual guys, somewhat straight people, and some trans men.
Jay: I have a question; it's about stereotypes in the queer community. When people say "All lesbians are all butchy," is that always true? Are all lesbians mostly butch or is there a mixture? I've noticed that in the queer community everyone is put into a category. For example, "All gay men are feminine." I've met a lot of gay males who are very straight acting. I have a lot of lesbian friends who are very feminine, and I have others who are masculine. So when people say that "All gay men are this way," or "All transgender people are one way or the other," it kind of complicates things. Not every person is all feminine or masculine. You have people that are going to be in the middle. Like me, I'm in-between.

***Zack*: For trans and genderqueer people, "transition" means different things. What does transition mean for you?**
Jay: I don't really have an answer—it's complicated. You know, I'm still a little kid! I still don't even know what's up from down sometimes. Transitioning is a really big step for me, because I'm afraid that if I transition I can't transition back. It kind of worries me. I want to be happy being who I am. But at the same time I'm happy being in the body I'm in. I love being a male. But sometimes I have those days where I wish I was a girl. This is a hard question to answer.
Sonia: Transitioning for me is changing my sex over to a beautiful sexy woman, because when I was born I was put in the wrong body. I feel more drawn to the woman's side instead of the man's side. If you saw me, you would never know that I was a "man." I look like a woman; I feel like a woman; I can pass as a woman. I'm looking forward to the sex change. I'm having the sex change to correct the body that god has put me in—he's put me into the wrong body and I am uncomfortable. That's going to be corrected and I am excited about the operation, you know? No matter what I have to go through, the pain, I'm finally going to be who I am. I'm going to be happy about who I am, finally, for a change. That's it.
Jay: I really like that answer. I just don't know if transitioning is for everyone. It's a really big decision. Because after you get it done there's no turning back. Do you guys think it's going to be an easy thing to do, or do you think it's going to be challenging?
Rainbow: Let's just make people feel encouraged to get it done, Jay. A lot of people might feel bad if someone said, "Do you really want to get this done? Do you want to get your penis removed, because it's a lot of work."
Jay: Yeah, but are you guys scared? That's what I'm asking.
Rainbow: No, I'll cut off my own dick, with scissors, at my own house.
Jay: For me, it's scary to think about going through surgery.
Rainbow: To be honest, it's not scary.

FIGURE 14.3: SONIA

Sonia: I'm kind of scared. But I'm getting help with it from my psychiatrist, going through what I'm feeling.
Romeo: I'm all for transitioning. I have strongly believed that I was in the wrong body since I was born. I was placed in the wrong body and deep down there's a little boy—or an older gentleman—who wants to come out, and just needs to find a way out of being in a body that feels uncomfortable.
Marcus: I really want to do it—it's just getting down to Toronto to do it.
Zack: Have you had a referral to the CAMH[1] clinic?
Marcus: No, not yet. I'm seeing my doctor in a few weeks, so I'm going to talk to her about it.

***Zack*: What do you have in mind in terms of transition? What kinds of things do you want to change?**
Marcus: Well, I want to change everything on me. The whole works, the boobs and the vagina. Hormones, too, I really want to start doing that soon.
Tess: What are the barriers to transitioning?
Marcus: Just the fact that I keep forgetting. I forget to talk to my doctor about it, or I get too scared.

***Zack*: What kinds of things are you worried about?**
Marcus: Just the fact that she might reject me or something.
Romeo: Money. Money plays a big part in it.
Jay: But doesn't CAMH actually pay for your surgery?

FIGURE 14.4: MARCUS

Sonia: You're wrong about that. They don't pay for everything.[2]
Jay: Apparently, if you want to get the surgical stuff done, you have to live as the opposite gender for a year.
Romeo: I've been living it for more than a year.
Sonia: But there's a trick to it. When you go to CAMH, depending on what gender you are, you have to dress as who you are. If you're not doing that, they give you a hard time. They push you around, you know?

***Jay*: Being trans, what are your struggles?**
Sonia: Nothing is easy in this life—you have to fight for what you want.
Romeo: Homophobia. For me, it's homophobia.
Marcus: Struggles … right now I don't have any struggles.

***Onyii*: What would you like people to know about you as a person labelled with an intellectual disability? Do you tell people about it?**
Marcus: It is very hard to sit down and actually do things that I like to do because of my disability. If you're my best friend then I will tell you about it, but I don't want people to know me as my disability.
Romeo: I don't really tell people that I have a disability because I think that they would look at me as less of a person—I wouldn't want them to … call me names. When I'm dating somebody, I only let them know two or three weeks into the relationship.
Rainbow: I want people to know that I have a mild intellectual disability, because I think it's important to be honest with people, especially friends and family. Then you have support

FIGURE 14.5: ROMEO

when you're having an issue. People can say what they want, but my heart tells me to be honest and open. I want to be normal, and I am—we all are. Before I came out as having a disability, I felt like I was the only one, then I came to Compass. I feel that I'm not alone in the world—I'm happy to have the support.

Sonia: I don't like telling people I have a disability. I have a hidden disability. When you look at me, you wouldn't know that I have a disability. I can pass as not having one, so I usually fake it. I'm good at acting; I can pull it off.

Jay: I want to push the stigma. Even though I have an intellectual disability, I know that I can work and go higher—I'm trying to empower myself. People say that if you have an intellectual disability you can't love; you can't have sex; you can't cook; you can't do certain things. You have to crush the stigma and say "I'm a queer male with an intellectual disability. I have sex. I party with my friends. I go to work. I have a job."

***Onyii*: This chapter is about art and activism in our communities. When you hear the word "activist," what do you think of? What does the word "activist" mean to you?**

Romeo: Advocating for people who don't know how to use their voices or advocate for themselves.

Rainbow: An activist is someone who joins a fight for anti-bullying, gay rights, same-sex marriage, and stuff like that. People who want to see change.

Jay: An activist is a person who takes a stand for what they believe in. I think that can mean

FIGURE 14.6: RAINBOW

different things for different people. It can mean being strong or teaching people about different things. I'm an activist. I teach people about homophobia and transphobia.
Sonia: An activist is someone who stands up for other people and teaches them stuff.
Marcus: When I hear the word "activist" I think of Martin Luther King. He gave up a lot for the black community. He gave us our rights and our freedom.

***Onyii*: Would you call yourself an activist?**
Sonia: Yeah, I would.
Rainbow: I would call myself an activist.
Romeo: Yes, I call myself an activist. We're here to advocate for people who don't have a voice and to let everyone know that we are people too. Don't hate, appreciate. Don't criticize, show them and give them knowledge.

***Tess*: Could you tell us more about your own work as an activist?**
Jay: I started a youth group called Compass when I was 13. I think of myself as an activist because I brought together a lot of queer youth who had disabilities. For the past seven years, we've had the only group of its kind in Toronto, and in Ontario.
Marcus: I talk to people about my life. Yesterday I sat on the side of the road for a good hour and a half telling my story. Some guy was like, "So are you a girl or a guy?" I was like, "I go by guy but I'm technically a girl." It just started a whole conversation.
Rainbow: Since I got hired as a peer educator in 2009, I've been doing a mix of activism and

self-advocacy. I bring fun ideas to Compass, I lead presentations, I do outreach, and I am learning more about how to speak in front of people.
Romeo: When I was a sprOUT consultant, we would go to different places and do workshops on homophobia, transphobia, and sexual health. Also with Beatz to Da Streetz, I was the assistant coordinator and a participant. Beatz to Da Streetz is a music group that I was in; our goal was to empower youth through urban music. In my role as the assistant coordinator, I would hand out transit tokens, make phone calls, tell them when and where we were going to have practice, and do outreach. I really enjoyed working with Beatz to Da Streetz and sprOUT. I wish there were more roles like that ... being an assistant coordinator of something.
Sonia: Being in sprOUT, I like going and doing different things: role-playing, putting on skits, and talking about homophobia. I love teaching young people how to make the world a better place to live. I also work in a food group in my neighbourhood—I really like plants and growing food. Last summer, I set up a rooftop garden on my girlfriend's building. The people in the building really like it, and we give the food away for free—I think it means a lot for people to be able to get healthy food. We grow tomatoes, sweet potatoes, okra, and pineapple. I love teaching people how to eat healthy.

***Zack*: What is sprOUT?**
Rainbow: We do workshops for service providers and groups that want to learn about homophobia and transphobia.
Romeo: sprOUT is all about connecting LGBTQ people labelled with intellectual disabilities across Ontario. We do fun stuff. We've made buttons and T-shirts. We've done forum theatre, and workshops on homophobia, transphobia, and sexual health. I really loved doing the role plays, I loved doing everything. There is also a documentary, *Our Compass* (2010), and a claymation film, *Her Sparkly Lov* (2009), which I did the soundtrack for. I'm looking to do more soundtracks.

***Tess*: Can you tell me more about the documentary *Our Compass*?**
Rainbow: I am one of the co-writers of *Our Compass*. It's about eight youth labelled with intellectual disabilities and their stories. It talks about real-life issues and concerns, and how Compass came together as a rainbow family, and how it helps to block all the negative stuff—like a shield, a rainbow shield, a rainbow family.
Romeo: I was in the documentary and a co-writer. We each had different themes. My theme was Power.
Rainbow: Other themes were Pride, Confusion, Freedom, and Family.
Jay: I was part of the documentary too. I talked about my life, family, and relationships as a queer Asian male going through ups and downs, having a disability. My theme was Love.

***Tess*: How did you feel when we screened the documentary?**
Romeo: Awesome. Also, I was nervous, but I don't think I let it show. I love the film. Unconditionally.
Rainbow: It was fantastic. I just really loved watching it and having the opportunity to go up and introduce the film with everyone. Seeing it makes me emotional.
Jay: I get annoyed about it sometimes because I'm not a big "out there" person, like Romeo and Rainbow. When I watch it, it makes me cry, and then I start to get really, really shy, and I start being quiet—it's not really a good thing because I end up not talking.

Romeo: There were a few times when watching the film when I had my hood over my face—each time it got to my part. As my part finished, the hood came off my head.
Jay: I've grown up so much since we made the film.

***Zack*: What advice would you give to other trans and genderqueer activists who are just getting started in this work?**
Romeo: If your goal is to reach out to people who don't have a voice, then definitely do it—never give up.
Rainbow: Follow your heart, not your brain.
Sonia: Stand up for your rights and believe what you believe in.

***Tess*: Anything for service providers that you think they need to know?**
Romeo: Get to know the people you're working with. Speak up and don't discriminate.
Jay: I think you should get to know your youth, bond with your youth. Social workers teach youth, but youth also teach social workers—more than they actually expect.
Rainbow: About proper pronouns, for anybody—trans, gender fluid, or genderqueer—who may go by a different name or who might not like to be called "he" or "she," get educated and call people by the pronoun they prefer.
Marcus: Just be open.

NOTES

1 In order to obtain access to gender recognition surgery (also called sex reassignment surgery or SRS), such as chest reconstruction or vaginoplasty, paid for by the Ministry of Health and Long-Term Care through the Ontario Health Insurance Plan (OHIP), the Government of Ontario currently requires people to undergo an assessment and approval process through the gender identity clinic at the Centre for Addiction and Mental Health (CAMH).

2 CAMH does not pay for SRS, the government does. What the provincial Ministries of Health will pay for depends on trans individuals obtaining an official diagnosis from an accredited gender identity clinic, as well as on whether or not the specific procedures are covered under provincial medical insurance plans.

REFERENCES

Brady, S. (2001). Sterilization of girls and women with intellectual disabilities: Past and present justifications. *Violence Against Women, 7*(4), 432–461.

Marshall, Z., & Vo, T. (2012). *Griffin Centre's sprOUT Project Evaluation Report*. Toronto: Griffin Centre. Retrieved from http://bit.ly/127bggU

Nocera, F. (Director). (2009). *Her sparkly lov* [Animated film]. Canada.

Vo, T. (Director/Producer). (2010). *Our Compass* [Documentary]. Griffin Centre, Canada.

Chapter 15 Happy Tranny Day

Tien Neo Eamas and Devon MacFarlane

HAPPY TRANS PEOPLE ARE REVOLUTIONARY

In 2008 and 2009, a group of trans[1] people and allies in Vancouver organized what we described as "revolutionary events" based on the radical concept that trans people can be happy. We (Tien and Devon) were familiar with the dominant ideas and conversations that frame our lives as trans people as miserable and full of rejection, depression, and despair. We've seen movies and TV documentaries, heard conversations in support groups, and read research that focus on the difficulties trans people face, and we've faced some challenges ourselves. Because of how prevalent these stories are, it sometimes seems as if pain and difficulty are the only experiences that trans people could possibly have. We don't deny that there is tough stuff—loss of friendships and family, violence, barriers to employment, and barriers to transition, just for starters. And, we don't want to deny that, at times, trans people have had to lie and pretend that all is well—when, in fact, nothing might be further from the truth—to obtain and maintain access to medical care. However, we wanted to focus on aspects of our communities' experiences other than pain and difficulty. We wanted to create space for authentic conversations about trans people being strong, about trans people finding joy in coming into ourselves and connecting with our communities, and about trans people's courage, creativity, and resourcefulness. In our bold opinion, trans people rock!

This chapter addresses two very inspiring events—Happy Tranny Day in 2008 and Gender Euphoria Day in 2009. We discuss how the organizing team worked together to conceptualize and organize these events, as well as describe the events themselves to inspire others to find ways to promote the revolutionary idea of celebrating trans people.

VANCOUVER BEFORE THE HAPPY TRANS REVOLUTION HIT

It is important for readers to know a bit about what was going on in Vancouver for trans people (that we knew about) when we began conceptualizing Happy Tranny Day. For some years, up to and including 2007, public trans events had been related to the Trans Day of Remembrance, which memorializes trans people who have been murdered. The other publicly known and advertised gatherings for trans people in Vancouver were support groups. Advocacy and activist groups—particularly Trans Alliance Society—had been present in the early 2000s, but had become fairly dormant by the mid-2000s. In the mid-1990s, there had been two trans awareness marches, and some protests regarding trans women's exclusion from women's spaces. Kimberly Nixon's well-known human rights case against the Vancouver Rape Relief Society occurred during this period. In 2002, the Gender Clinic at Vancouver General Hospital had announced that it was closing, and trans communities responded to that by advocating for ongoing trans care. This resulted in the founding of the Transgender Health Program in 2003, with Joshua Goldberg as its first coordinator. Joshua led the Trans Care Project, which resulted in the development of a series of clinical care guidelines that are sometimes referred to as the "Vancouver Guidelines." From 2003 to 2008, there were occasional spates of organizing and activism in relation to access to care—particularly access to surgery—in the province. Additionally, some trans films were screened each year at the very popular Vancouver Queer Film Festival. In Vancouver during this period, there were no trans-specific events that we were aware of that happened in relation to Pride, and there were only occasional trans-focused bar nights that were held as fundraisers, generally for the Trans Youth Drop-in or as surgery fundraisers. Many social activities happened in people's homes, in friendship and in social support networks of trans people. Gathering in public locations, such as restaurants and cafés, was not always safe or supported by businesses; furthermore, one needed to know other people in trans communities to learn about these events. Across all of these forms of organizing and activism, we were not aware of any events that were primarily focused on celebrating trans experiences.

A SNAPSHOT OF THE AUTHORS

It is important for readers to know a bit about us. We have known each other for over 15 years, transitioned at about the same time, and have similar philosophies about mindfully cultivating and living fulfilling and happy lives as trans people. We have both followed Gandhi's tenet of "Be the change that you want to see in the world" for many years. Happy Tranny Day was Tien's brainchild, which he developed because of his interest in promoting the happiness, wellness, and joy of trans people. Tien is an Asian trans guy who is a jewellery designer, an interior designer, and a feng shui consultant. He has lived as male since 2003; before that, he was active in lesbian-of-colour communities in Vancouver, where he was practised in "fighting the straight, white, middle-class man." As a new immigrant, this helped him to build community and a sense of belonging. When he came out as trans, he carried on with this same "fighting" mentality, focusing on transphobia, cisgenderism, and ignorance. In early transition, Tien had struggled with feeling that there was something wrong with him because he was not happy being in a female-sexed body. He thought that fighting his surroundings and changing how people perceived him would make him happier. However, he later found this to be painful and difficult. At this point, he was consumed with unhappiness and upset, rejection, disappointment, anger at others, self-pity, and depression. For Tien, peace and happiness arose from a combination of physically transitioning, Buddhism, and other spiritual practices that enabled him to love himself completely the way he was. Given this, he was looking to contribute to the well-being and happiness of trans communities in Vancouver in ways that were different from what he was witnessing at that time.

Devon is a white, middle-class trans guy who has been connected with trans communities since the late 1990s. He tends to use a range of words to describe his gender identity, including trans, genderqueer, and sometimes "female to other." His transition process began in 2000, and he is not sure whether his transition is complete or not. His work background includes community development and program development in health and social service settings, and he describes himself as a social justice activist. He has been "queer by profession"—his paid work has focused on LGBT issues—on and off since 1996. One of his accomplishments in serving trans and queer communities was founding Prism Alcohol & Drug Services, which is discussed in a different chapter in this book (see Chapter 19).

HOW DID WE DO THIS?

Together, we wanted to create an event that was going to celebrate trans happiness. From early conceptualizations, we knew that we wanted the event to be enjoyable and to draw together very diverse parts of trans communities. From our perspective, people on the FTM and MTF spectrum, genderqueer people, people who were involved with drag queen and king communities, and cross-dressers—along with their partners, families, and friends—were seldom in the same spaces together and did not seem to interact with one another often. It was also important to us to create an event that was inclusive, appealing to and reflective of the ethno-cultural and class mix found in Vancouver, and as accessible as we could make it, given our awareness of the range of abilities within trans communities in Vancouver. We ensured that we booked a wheelchair-accessible space. However, we failed to consider the possibility of developing materials in Braille or of hiring ASL interpreters. We also wanted to promote the opportunity for people to connect and talk with one another. Because of this, we did not want the event to have an overtly activist or political feel so that it would attract those who did not generally go out to events that had an activist approach. Our preliminary idea for the event was to have a "fun fair" during the afternoon, a light dinner and entertainment, along with a sober, all-ages dance.

We pitched this idea to a few people we knew and invited them to get involved in an organizing committee. We also pitched the idea to a few funding bodies and businesses, and secured small grants, sponsorships, and donations. Later in the chapter we will talk about both the organizing committee and the resources we accessed.

DRUMROLLS, PLEASE... THE EVENTS

The venues for Happy Tranny Day (2008) and Gender Euphoria Day (2009) were decorated with streamers and balloons, and recorded music (mostly by trans artists) provided a relaxing soundscape. Posters covering the gender designations on the washroom doors depicted a cartoon toilet and read "May all pee in peace." Large sticky notes featuring the names of local, national, and international trans people whom others found to be inspiring and positive role models covered the walls. More names and valued characteristics about these people were added throughout the day. Paper tablecloths in the refreshment area featured questions such as "What truly rocks about being trans?" and "What are the gifts from trans people to our communities?" and "How is my life better, my world bigger, for having trans people in it?"

All who attended were welcomed by smiling volunteers and given a ticket for door prizes. Trans and gender-variant people, cross-dressers, and drag kings and queens of all ages, abilities, and ethnicities came out for the event. Some people brought their cis friends, partners, kids, and parents. Happy Tranny Day was attended by 125 people, while well over 200 attended Gender Euphoria Day.

Both events were organized to be a constant hive of activity with some quiet spaces for people to just sit and take it all in. Depending on when individuals arrived and how long they stayed, they could take part in the afternoon fun fair, which included volunteer-run stations (e.g., making millet-stuffed packers and falsies; crafting stickers, stencils, and silk-screened T-shirts with trans positive slogans and affirming statements; having your fortune told; receiving tips on makeup, hair, and other aspects of gender presentation; playing games at a table hosted by the facilitators of the Trans Youth Drop-in; getting a free massage from registered massage therapists; picking up information from community groups and agencies). They could eat a buffet-style dinner at long tables conducive to conversation, or attend the evening performance featuring drag performers, comedy acts, musicians, and people doing readings—all of whom were part of local trans communities.

HOW WE MADE THE EVENT EVEN MORE FABULOUS

The organizing committee knew that we could take something great and make it even more fabulous. We invited people to complete an evaluation at the conclusion of each event, and we also circulated an online survey early in the planning process for the second event. After each event, we discussed what worked and what we could do better. We also reread the notes we had made at the first planning meeting for each event during which we had defined success and how we would measure it. We reviewed the feedback we received after the first event, Happy Tranny Day. Generally, people had found the event to be very welcoming and inclusive, and were thrilled that we had put it on. However, we could have advertised more widely that the event was in a wheelchair-accessible location, and the accessible door should have been used as the main door. We also heard that holding the event on a Saturday would have been better than on a Sunday, and that the organizers could have been more easily identifiable during the event. We made those changes for the second year.

In the survey, we asked people in trans communities to rate our ideas, share what would absolutely make them attend the event, and give us suggestions as to what would make it better. We asked people to vote on options for the event name, and as a result of the vote and the feedback, we changed the name to Gender Euphoria Day. We also asked people to share the names of people in trans communities whom they saw as positive role models—and why. Most of the names that were put forward were local trans people, along with a few well-known trans celebrities such as Kate Bornstein and Leslie Feinberg. We used this to generate many of the names that went up on the Trans Wall of Fame.

THE MAGIC BEHIND THE SCENES: HOW WE MADE THIS HAPPEN

We realized that if the event was going to be as exciting and make as much of a difference as we envisioned, we needed to pay attention to our own intentions, actions, and process. We knew we needed to be mindful on many fronts so that we did not directly or indirectly perpetuate the notion that trans people must be miserable. Throughout all aspects of organizing, we were attentive to walking our talk regarding happy trans people; to creating a space where people could be excited and new ideas about trans people could emerge; to connecting with the community in a different way; and to learning new things and applying our learning.

Walking Our Talk

For Tien to walk his talk, it took being happy himself. He was used to swimming in the pool of unhappy conversations, and he needed to get out of that pool to create something new. He knew that to create the event and have it live up to his vision, he needed first to be able to be happy, empowered, and feel great about his own life. He was used to having disempowering thoughts about his body, his transition, and his life. He realized that he needed to change the way he thought about himself; then, he could be happier. Tien, as a trans individual, started the deliberate practice of looking after and loving himself—including his body—and valuing everything in his life and his surroundings that brought him joy. This took a commitment to having joy and love be present always—something that he describes as a continuing journey.

Tien was clear that it is possible for trans people to be happy, to be empowered, and to live an awesome life. He knew that as he became increasingly happy about his own life, he could contribute to others' peace, joy, and well-being. As he engaged in conversations with others about Happy Tranny Day and Gender Euphoria Day, he practised having humility, and having love and respect always be present—particularly for trans people whose work had enabled trans people and communities to move forward as far as we have. He committed himself to being inspiring and bold, and to creating whatever was required for Happy Tranny Day and Gender Euphoria Day, regardless of obstacles, concerns, or fears that arose.

For Devon, co-organizing and co-leading the Happy Tranny Day and Gender Euphoria Day events was a natural fit. From his experience working as a community developer—both within queer and trans communities, and within a geographic neighbourhood—he had a substantial background in working with groups and organizations, and in leading the development of partnerships and coalitions. Devon strives to always build on strengths and assets in communities, a basic community development principle (Kretzmann & McKnight, 1993). He had not been to, or heard of, events that focused solely on celebrating trans people, and for him, the time had come to include fun and celebration as part of the repertoire of events that trans communities might organize. Devon first learned about the concept of the personal being political when he was a young dyke taking Women's Studies courses, and he found this very applicable to his experience as a trans person. He was aware that many trans people struggle with a lack of role models, social isolation, and challenges to establishing positive self-esteem, and he saw Happy Tranny Day and Gender Euphoria Day as having the potential to contribute to greater joy and well-being in trans communities. In co-leading these events, he took his usual approach of identifying and acting on values that would enable a project to come to life, and on questions that would guide the project. The values he identified were inclusion and collaboration. He was also very mindful of what behaviours he modelled in the context of an event celebrating trans people.

Together, we identified a number of trans people whom we invited to join the organizing committee. We sought people who had connections to diverse parts of trans communities—for instance, people on the MTF spectrum; genderqueer people; drag and other performers; ethnocultural communities; youth and older adults; and people with disabilities. We also sought people who had skills and experience that would be helpful in organizing an event, who were excited by the vision of the event, and who would find joy in bringing it to life.

See the Dream and Get It!

At our first organizing committee meeting, Tien and Devon oriented the group as a whole to the preliminary plans for the event. We emphasized that the intention of the event was to celebrate trans people's courage, strength, and creativity—traits that are often found amongst trans people, our families, and our communities as we weather adversity. We worked as a group to identify what a successful event would look like. We recorded the ideas on a flip chart so that we could see the ideas that had been generated. For the group, success included the following: diversity, inclusion, and accessibility—reaching *all* areas of trans communities, including genderqueer people, cross-dressers, people involved with the drag scene, people who had transitioned, and people of all ages, ethnicities, abilities, and incomes; reducing barriers to participation; seeing people at the event whom we did not know and who did not normally tend to participate in trans community events; everyone feeling welcome and respected; an event that could lead to new partnerships; everyone experiencing the strength and power in trans communities; generating more support both for the idea of trans people being happy and for this idea come to life; and people having a great time.

The organizing team also identified what a successful and sustainable working relationship would look like. We took steps to ensure that that no one took on too much and burned out, that each organizing member was motivated and excited about the tasks we took on, and that we would follow through on our commitments or ask for support. Some of the organizers had learned through previous experience that good communication and behaving with integrity was vital to success, and the group as a whole agreed to work together in this way. Collectively, we decided to share the leadership for tasks and areas of responsibility, and so we defined clear roles within the organizing group, and clear tasks that volunteers would take on.

When challenges arose, we checked in with each other and stayed focused on the event and experiences we wanted to create. Consistent with empowerment as a living praxis, we identified *solutions* to current challenges, rather than dwelling on the problem or upset. Collectively, we asked each other to take on tasks that we personally found enjoyable. This worked very well, because the organizing group had people with a broad range of interests. We rotated the task of minute-taking amongst people who were interested in this task, emailed the minutes as quickly as possible, and set the next agenda before a meeting ended. This supported good communication and ensured that everyone was clear about the decisions made, next steps, and action items, and that we could come prepared to focus on the work at hand at the next meeting. We spent some time checking in at the beginning and end of each meeting, asking how people were and how the meeting had gone for them. This helped us get to know one another a bit better and to understand more of the context if someone was feeling unheard, agitated, or frustrated. It also enabled us to reflect on and learn from what worked well in a meeting to continually improve the organizing process. In the first year, we used a flip chart to take notes during the meeting to help make our thinking as a group visible to one another, and to promote good communication and reduce the likelihood of unnecessary conflict. Using a flip chart was also helpful in directing our thoughts toward creating new concepts and new ideas that inspired us. We posted the flip chart page that contained our ideas about what success looked like at each meeting to help keep us on track.

The group made sure to keep joy, excitement, and positivity present at our meetings—that we were walking our talk in this. Tien was aware that the revolutionary conversation (that trans people can be happy) takes practice and commitment, including for each of us in the organizing group. Tien tended to be the person who brought us back to the vision for the event as needed, and ensured that our conversations in the organizing meetings were also supporting all of us in being happy trans people. At each meeting, we shared what we were excited about, what was working well in planning and in getting work done for the event, and what we wanted for the event. We made sure to continuously ask "Will this promote trans happiness?" and "Is it fun?" and "Is it playful?" about every aspect of the event. We also asked ourselves: "How do we create an event that's really engaging and accessible for a diverse group of people?" This was important as we knew that some trans people are quite isolated, some struggle with anxiety, some may have concerns about presenting as their preferred gender in public, and some may not know many (or any) other people at the event. We needed to make it welcoming, and physically and financially accessible to all.

CHALLENGES

In the first and second year, the organizing committee determined what was more effective and efficient for us, and what did not work as well.

Names, Names, and More New Names

A significant challenge arose regarding the name of the event. The trans women on the organizing team were uncomfortable with the name of the first event—Happy Tranny Day. We had addressed these concerns the first year by using Happy Tranny Day as a subtitle for the event: the full name was "Celebrating Gender Diversity: Happy Tranny Day." We saw this as a trial to see if the name would work. However, what was used in practice—as in this chapter—was simply the subtitle. We also realized through feedback about the event that the level of discomfort with the name was greater than some members of the organizing committee realized. The committee as a whole came to recognize that, for many trans women, the word "tranny" had painful connotations—ones often associated with verbal, physical, and/or sexual assaults, dehumanization, ridicule, and the denial of a person's identity. Even though some people on the committee felt ready to *reclaim* the word "tranny," we were more committed to the event being accessible and inclusive. Tien took an approach of deep compassion, of being able to honour the people who brought forward these concerns, to hear them and thank them for being a part of the process of laying the foundation, so that collectively we could do the work that we were aiming to do in the event—to create happy trans people. Devon's approach was to have us look at the underlying interests and the collective values we had agreed upon regarding respect, inclusion, and what supports celebration. Another organizer suggested that we do a community survey and invite people to help us find a name for the event that would feel inclusive and celebratory.

We could not satisfy everyone, yet this did not dampen our passion for the event. We did not let challenges regarding the name become a barrier to us organizing an impactful event. How fitting, since many of us go through quite a process in finding a name that fits us well!

Where, Oh Where, Shall We Meet?

When planning the first event, we met in the homes of organizing committee members. However, some people's homes were not physically accessible. For the second event, we met in a café , which meant that we could not easily use the visual tools that increased our effectiveness. When we considered a third event (which has yet to happen), we secured a meeting space at a community health centre that was free, physically accessible, and had both white boards and flip charts.

To Invite or Not to Invite

Questions arose concerning inviting the Vancouver Police Department to attend the event. As we explored this, we recognized that a police presence would be intimidating and alienating for some trans people for many reasons, including the criminalization of sex work and other aspects of the street economy, experiential knowledge of police engaging in racial profiling, the negative experiences of some newcomers with police and military in their countries of origin, the possible former arrests of older trans people under laws related to cross-dressing, and the potential for police harassment upon the presentation of a driver's licence that did not match a person's chosen name or gender identity. Some trans people would choose not to come or would leave if they knew or found out that on-duty police would be there. This did not align with our vision; therefore, the organizing group decided not to invite the police. Of course, if trans people or their partners happened to work for the police, they could attend—though not in their work roles or uniform.

The Importance of Orientation

In planning our first event, we continually oriented new planning members to the purpose of the event and to our collaborative decision-making processes. This ensured that people were always clear about our intent. In planning for our second event, we failed to be as diligent in this vital process. This resulted in a new member arranging for a community survey that did not support the purpose of the event. During this potentially contentious conflict, the members of the organizing committee were careful to maintain positive relationships with one another and with the external groups who were approached to partner on the survey.

BRINGING HOME THE BACON AND TOFU WIENERS

We were clear that the event was not-for-profit, and that we were going to break even; any extra funds would go toward the budget for the following year's event. We were able to put on an amazing event with a small budget. We made arrangements with a trans group that was a registered non-profit organization and whose mission sufficiently aligned with ours to have them be a sponsor of the event. This arrangement enabled us to use their non-profit registration number in our funding applications. We approached VanCity Credit Union in both years, and TD Canada Trust only in the second year, to sponsor the event. Both institutions are known for providing funds to queer and trans community projects. In the second year, Prism Alcohol & Drug Services (an initiative serving LGBT2SQ communities) provided a $500 sponsorship. Our total budget for the first year was $2,000; for the second year, $4,000. The event was free, but donations were encouraged at the door, which resulted in from $600 to $1,000 in contributions each year. The bulk of the funds went to paying for the hall rental, performers' honoraria, food and catering, and supplies for the fun fair. Food and catering costs were the largest single element of the budget, followed by the hall rental and honoraria for performers. Based on prior experiences, members of the organizing committee recognized that sharing a meal can be an invaluable means to building community. Also, as poverty is such a common issue for trans people, dignified access to a healthy meal and snacks can support well-being.

Members of the planning committee divided up the work of securing donations for food, door prizes, and printing, ensuring that people took on work that they were happy to complete. There were key go-to people on the organizing committee who were responsible for sourcing other volunteers to support the aspect of the festival they were leading. The roles of these key go-to people were to coordinate volunteers, food and refreshments, the fun fair, and the performance.

GRINDING TO A HALT

We (the organizing committee) held the event twice. A number of factors contributed to a decision to put the event on hold. First, there were changes in the availability of key people. Tien—the originator of the event—moved out of town. Devon and another organizer had gone back to school and were not able to commit much time. Second, conflict regarding the original name and the use of the word "tranny" resurfaced, and this appeared to affect some organizing committee members' interest in continuing to be a part of the event.

We were unable to find new people who would commit to taking on the work and moving the event forward. At a community meeting, 12 new people expressed interest in helping to organize an event. However, none were able to follow through. This may have had to do with our very limited ability to inspire, motivate, and support new members to join the organizing committee.

GETTING BACK IN THE SADDLE

We have heard from community members that they would love to see Gender Euphoria Day happen again. If we organize another event, we would ensure that we have a clear vision and mission statement and that co-organizers were willing to embrace it. For the organizing team to be most effective, we would ensure diversity in the team, including in skill sets. In bringing an organizing team together, we would begin with conversations that help to build awareness of one another's backgrounds, interests, and what had drawn everyone to be involved in the event. We would definitely ensure that we diligently oriented people to the vision and mission—that of promoting trans happiness.

In the early stages of bringing a refreshed organizing committee together, we would engage in conversations about how we would work together and how we would handle conflict. We would lead the group in co-creating expectations of the organizing committee as a whole. We have considered what we would request of co-organizers, and co-organizers would likely have other suggestions. We would request that co-organizers be willing to be accountable to the group; to think about issues from a community perspective; to work through conflict; to step back from taking hard and fast positions; and to listen to and honour one another's concerns, as well as to actively engage in self-care.

WRAPPING IT UP WITH A LITTLE GENDER-DIVERSE BOW

A small, dedicated group of trans people and a few allies created revolutionary events that were solely committed to promoting trans happiness. Tien believes that if we continually strive for peace, joy, and love for ourselves and others, then—and only then—peace, joy, and love can be available for our communities, families, and the world. There were many successes and challenges in putting on these events as we applied our learnings and fine-tuned everything. Gender Euphoria Day is the beginning of many more events that celebrate the beauty, joy, creativity, strength, courage, and love of amazingly diverse communities—the trans communities. Here's to much joy for our communities!

NOTE

1 We use "trans" as an umbrella term that includes people who identify as genderqueer, gender variant, trans, transgender, transsexual, drag queen, drag king, cross-dresser, bigender, pangender, gender fluid, and more, as well as people who have transitioned.

REFERENCES

Kretzmann, J.P., & McKnight, J.L. (1993). *Building communities from the inside out: A path toward finding and mobilizing a community's assets* (1st ed.). Evanston, IL: Institute for Policy Research.

Part III Transforming Institutions from the Inside

The chapters in Part III address ways that trans activists work with, and within, various organizations to achieve concrete social change that will improve the quality of life for trans subjects. While there is significant thematic overlap between chapters in this section, we have divided them into two sections. Chapters included in "Part IIIA: Tranformations in Bureaucracy" are written partially as reflection pieces by trans activists situated within education, social services, and shelter organizations. Trish Salah (Chapter 16), j wallace (Chapter 17), Treanor Mahood-Greer (Chapter 18), and Devon MacFarlane, Lorraine Grieves, and Al Zwiers (Chapter 19) provide readers with an understanding of the challenges of evoking change in often deeply rooted institutional cultures, funding mandates, and official policies. They offer practical tips and best practices for navigating bureaucracies based on their own successes and current struggles. Chapters included in "Part IIIB: Transformations in Health" address trans activist engagement with health care organizations and providers, including gender identity clinics, sexual health clinics, and hospitals.

Three key themes are woven through the chapters in Part III. The role that bureaucracy and organizations play in the production of sex/gender discourse serves as the first theme. Discourse refers to organized systems of knowledge that determine what we know and how we come to know it (Adams, 1997). Grounded within Foucauldian theoretical frameworks and other materialist theorizations of power, power is exercised through the production of knowledge. Knowledge is produced through various means, including bureaucratic and organizational operations, as well as our individual everyday interactions with various institutions. Dominant knowledge concerning binary sex/gender, and the ways that such understandings are mediated through colonialist, capitalist, hetero/homonormative, nationalist, and ableist logics, emerge from and are reproduced in significant part according to the operations of social institutions. As the authors in this section demonstrate, the organizational production of normative or proper notions of sexed embodiment and gender identity and expressions occurs continuously.

Epistemic violence is the second theme of Part III. Violence is not limited to physical, emotional, spiritual, and sexual harm, but occurs through the production of knowledge and the erasure of other—and competing—ways of understanding. Readers recall contributors to Part I, such as James and Laframboise, discussing their "discovery" of their two-spirit identities and indigenous cultures. The fact that indigenous knowledge of multiplicity and difference amongst sex, gender, and sexuality is not readily available is an example of the way that colonial governance—including ongoing attempts at cultural genocide—functions through the production of knowledge. The ignorance and misunderstanding of trans identities and experiences that are often present in every layer of bureaucracy, organizations, and institutional sites, such as education, is injurious to many trans individuals and communities. Authors such as Trish Salah (Chapter 16), Silvia Tenenbaum (Chapter 21), Ayden I. Scheim and colleagues (Chapter 23), and Judith MacDonnell and Robin Fern (Chapter 25) respond to the following question: How can trans activists work to disrupt dominant discourses of sex/gender mediated by colonialism, racialization, and hetero/homonormativity, as well as bourgeois codes of morality? Authors including j wallace (Chapter 17), Treanor Mahood-Greer (Chapter 18), Will Rowe (Chapter 20), Wallace Wong (Chapter 22), and Kathy Chow and colleagues (Chapter 24) provide insight into a different inquiry: How can the advocacy and educational work performed by trans activists cultivate the creation of new and alternative forms of knowledge that enable the improvement of trans people's quality of life?

The third theme explored in this section relates to the politics of inclusion. The chapters included here enable readers to think through which strategies and best practices to use when engaging with bureaucracy and other institutional dynamics to achieve the inclusion of "trans-" subjects. Readers may want to take note of the ways that subjects function within many of these texts in reference to trans individuals, as well as political issues. Given the long history of trans erasure, which has denied many marginalized subjects access to basic and trans-specific health care, education, essential social services, housing, and employment, it is imperative that interventions be made within institutions to ensure trans-inclusive policies.

Chapters by Trish Salah and Will Rowe serve to problematize the ways that we think about the inclusivity of trans subjects. Rowe's text urges trans activists to consider the ways that trans subjects themselves are implicated in reproducing knowledge through their participation in, and interaction with, institutions. Focusing on female-to-male trans men, Rowe demonstrates the ways that they perform normative masculinity to obtain approval for state-funded medical transition procedures. Salah discusses the ways that integrating trans identities into institutions such as the labour movement can have coercive and colonizing effects, given the fact that particular understandings of trans identities and experiences are presented. This, of course, leads to the exclusion of trans individuals and issues deemed non-normative, such as sex work.

Other chapters, such as Chapters 23 and 24, discuss the merits of community-based research as a more socially just way to produce alternative knowledge, based on the needs identified by marginalized members of trans communities who also form the organizational research team.

REFERENCES

Adams, M.L. (1997). *The trouble with normal: Postwar youth and the making of heterosexuality.* Toronto: University of Toronto Press.

Chapter 16 Gender Struggles: Reflections on Trans Liberation, Trade Unionism, and the Limits of Solidarity

Trish Salah

In hir 1992 manifesto, *Transgender Liberation: A Movement Whose Time Has Come* (1997), Leslie Feinberg invited transgender and transsexual people to join lesbian and gay people in a revolutionary political movement modelled on, as well as metaphorically and materially linked to, the historical struggles of working-class and colonized people worldwide. With this manifesto, as well as subsequent fictional and political writings, Feinberg attempted to fuse old left and labour politics of solidarity with identity political organizing models constellated by the encounter of civil rights and other new social movements with the liberal and representational politics of the academy. At the same time, Feinberg attempted to create the *conditions of possibility* for trans and queer people to infuse modes and nodes of leftist organizing that historically have been dominated by white working-class and middle-class heterosexual men.

It has been only recently that leftist and labour movements have begun to show signs of including heterosexual white women, people of colour, and lesbians and gays in anything more than constrained, instrumental, and tokenizing roles, and if that process has begun, its progress has been uneven, peripatetic, and subject to more than occasional setbacks. Situated in and between left-labour and women's and gay and lesbian liberation movements, Feinberg's work both attests to the presence of feminist, gay liberationist, anti-imperialist, and civil rights activism within socialist and workers movements of the US in the 1970s and 1980s and attempts to move forward a revolutionary articulation of identity-based and workers' struggles.

Feinberg's writing is amongst the best known of the new transgender literature of the last 20 years, and despite hir position outside of the academy, hir books have become canonical within newly established and emergent academic fields of women's, gender, queer, and trans studies. This is a significant achievement, but given Feinberg's political project, it begs a certain question. That is to say, what is the relationship between circulation and legitimation within sections of the progressive academy and broader social change, particularly in the context of left and labour organizing? And how has this relationship contoured the ways in which Feinberg's political vision has been realized, if it has? In other words, if Feinberg's work has been taken up by leftists and unionists, by queer, trans, anti-racist, and feminist movements, how might hir currency within queer and feminist academic circles determine how and by who, and to what effect?

In this chapter, I explore some questions about the relationship between feminist and queer discourses on transgender, the politics of recognition and social negation within identity political and left organizing, and gender politics on the left, and offer some narratives and analysis of attempts made to realize some of the allegiances called for in Feinberg's 1992 manifesto in the context of Canadian labour organizing during a period of intensifying neoliberalism. These narratives and analyses draw upon my own experiences between the years of 1999 and 2005, when I was actively involved in local trans community cultural and political organizing, as well as organizing within my union, the Canadian Union of Public Employees, Local 3903, and its national LGBT equity body, the National Pink Triangle Committee. In each of these contexts, I collaborated with allies to create conditions of possibility for trans solidarity and inclusion. But when is inclusion coercive, colonizing even? When does our desire for recognition, to recognize ourselves in others, to be in solidarity, to rescue ourselves in others, misfire, and to what ends?

I hope to offer some documentation of, and reflections upon, these attempts to meet trans people's needs through the creation of separate spaces, strategies of "trans inclusion" in LGBT caucuses and committees, the use of non-discrimination instruments and collective agreements, and alliance building with marginalized and criminalized trans workers. I also reflect upon the conditions under which these processes stumbled or failed. In these collaborations, we saw impressive gains but we were simultaneously confronted with the limits of that solidarity and inclusion within these organizations. Or, perhaps I should say that we came up against the limits inherent to a politics that understood trans inclusion chiefly in terms of a politics of representation, one that understood trans workers as members of a sexual minority, analogous to lesbian and gay workers and in need of similar protections and supports. Implicit within this analogy was a failure not only to understand the specific forms of social exclusion and erasure faced by trans people, but also to apprehend the ways in which homonormativity and governance feminism function to regulate systemically de-privileged women and trans people within progressive institutions and left spaces. These processes constituted at times an effective block to both trans inclusion and solidarity, particularly in the context of a neoliberal move away from social unionism and toward a much more limited program of business unionism.

Before moving into that discussion, I would like to situate Feinberg's intervention historically and consider the ways it functions rhetorically to model a transgender-inclusive, materialist analysis. Additionally, I call attention to the rhetorical strategies Feinberg employs to make the case for a politics of solidarity between workers; socialists; colonized peoples and people of colour; women; and lesbian, bisexual, gay, transsexual, and transgender people. I argue that, ironically, it may be precisely the rhetorical strategies that enabled Feinberg's impressive influence within emergent queer and trans academic literatures that delimited the potential impact of hir call for transgender liberation within leftist and trade union contexts.

TRANSGENDER RHETORICS, QUEERING DISCOURSES

Virginia Prince,[1] the author of *The Transvestite and His Wife*, is often credited with introducing the term "transgender" to describe those persons who are, for Prince, largely male-assigned at birth and heterosexual within their sex of assignment, invested in long-term full- or part-time cross-dressing and cross-gender living. Bridling against the clinical designation of transvestism with its implication of sexual fetishism, Prince advocated a desexualized—and hence, more respectable, because asexual—understanding of cross-dressing. She asserted that transgenderists did not simply *trans*vest but crossed gender as well. Attempting, with limited success, to destigmatize an abject position, Prince's "liberal" contribution was to articulate a transgenderal identity that could articulate, however uneasily, with heterosexuality and marriage. More problematically, Prince was also concerned with differentiating transgenderists from practices of drag that she associated with homosexuality, garish outrageousness, and prostitution, as well as from transsexuality, which Prince viewed as a mental pathology.[2]

Transgender was, in turn, rescued from its "effeminate" and epicene association with Prince and middle-class cross-dressers by Leslie Feinberg's *Transgender Liberation: A Movement Whose Time Has Come*, a 20-page pamphlet that lays out the broad contours of much of Feinberg's subsequent political writing, combining a sweeping historical materialist narrative of transgender lives, oppression, and struggle with a call to arms that invokes transgender as the name for *all* gender non-conforming people. There is, also, a subtle reconstitution of the term around the heroic masculinity of the passing woman and the working-class butch.[3] We will return to this last point when discussing the import of Feinberg's uptake in the context of gender studies and queer and trans theory, but first I want to think a bit about the other ways in which Feinberg's text functions in revolutionary terms.

Transgender Liberation: A Movement Whose Time Has Come was first published by World View Forum, the publishing arm of the World Worker's Party. It is worth noting that at the time of publishing hir piece, Feinberg had been writing for the World Worker's Party newspaper for nearly 20 years. Under the nom de plume of Diane Leslie Feinberg, as well as Diane Feinberg and Diane Steinberg, ze addressed issues ranging from police violence to workers' rights, and indigenous, feminist, and anti-racist struggle.[4] This is significant as it locates Feinberg squarely within the discourses of international communism and left anti-imperialism. This is important to recall, given how frequently hir work is articulated with that of other foundational texts of trans and queer studies produced at the same moment, whether the post-structuralist feminism of Judith Butler's *Gender Trouble* and Sandy Stone's "The Empire Writes Back: A Post-transsexual Manifesto," or the postmodern liberal individualism of Kate Bornstein's *Gender Outlaw*.

Reading this manifesto as emerging out of left and anti-imperialist worker's discourses makes the centrality of the working-class butch legible in terms of left masculinism even as it allows us to appreciate how engagement with early forms of transnational, anti-racist, and socialist feminisms leads to an attempt to hold class politics in tandem with a commitment to intersectionality.[5] Poised between the gay and lesbian reclamation of a repressed past, and the post-structuralist deconstruction of transhistorical sexed subjectivities, Feinberg attempts to produce a dialectical history mapping the conditions of possibility for transgender lives in relation to shifting modes of economic production, class relations, religious governance, and imperial/colonial projects. Drawing upon modernist, feminist, womanist, and gay historical reconstruction of the agrarian matriarchy and matriline, through cross-cultural anthropology, Feinberg attempts to write transgender subjects into history and across cultures. Ze also attempts to rebut those constructions of transgender in lesbian feminist narratives that constitute trans as oppressive, though through a somewhat dubious manoeuvre ze avoids directly confronting either Marxist or lesbian feminist transphobia. Within hir narrative, passing emerges as a symptom of gender oppression, framed as a survival strategy under a gender-intolerant patriarchy. This effectively contests the disparaging of butch and femme within lesbian feminism, celebrates gender-variant and third-gender roles across cultures, and combats rhetorics of authenticity within transsexual medical discourses that frame non-passing trans people in problematic ways. On the other hand, it colludes with feminist and Marxist condemnations of transsexuality as artifice and complicity with patriarchal values.

While this might, at first glance, appear strategic in crafting the possibility of shared ground for transgender–feminist and/or queer anti-capitalist conversations and possible coalition building, it may also have consequences for who is able to participate within a coalition. Margaret Deirdre O'Hartigan first called attention to the fact that Feinberg's publisher for *Transgender Warriors*, Boston's Beacon Press, had also published Janice Raymond's anti-transsexual screed *The Transsexual Empire: The Making of the She-Male*. And as several have noted in the wake of Adrienne Rich's passing, in *Transgender Warriors*, Leslie Feinberg acknowledges the support of the lesbian feminist poet and revolutionary thinker, who was also a friend and mentor of Raymond and whom Raymond acknowledges for her assistance and support in writing *The Transsexual Empire*.[6] In drawing attention to these associations, I do not mean to indict the invaluable work done either by Rich or Feinberg, or indeed the many good books published by Beacon Press; I do mean to pose the questions of (1) how Feinberg's trans butch identity and transgender politic might have freed hir to enter into associations from which transsexual women and perhaps men would have been excluded, and (2) how such associations might have implications for the form of transgender coalitional politic ze calls into being.

As an exemplary instance and metonym for the transgender warrior, the figure of the heroic working-class butch runs throughout Feinberg's work, and in a certain way collapses hir fictional work, such as *Stone Butch Blues*, with hir explicitly autobiographical and movement-building writing. Though not universalist in hir iteration, Feinberg's sweepingly inclusive and coalitional use of the term "transgender" came to reference a broad panoply of sex- and gender-variant individuals, including intersex persons, cross-dressers, transsexuals, and ultimately anyone who saw themselves as in any way at odds with their sex or the gender normatively attributed to it. We might here observe the evolution of "transgender" from Prince's emphatic, multiple differentiations, operating as a narcissism of minor difference, to the assimilative, aspirationally incorporative ambitions of Feinberg's revolutionary history.

In another register, the interventions of Prince and Feinberg suggest how, and under what conditions, transgender(ism) has been and is being produced as an "emergent identity" or as an occasion for the proliferation of identities. They invite consideration of how the transgendered figure comes to represent closed or more open-ended categories, and invite the question of how one might occupy an identity that is less an identity than an occasion for identity transgression and proliferation and/or transgressively gendered sexual practices. Paradoxically, they also beg the question of what it might mean to anchor gender transgression and/or proliferation to one preferred figure, such as the respectably heterosexual and bourgeois matron, or a heroic, working-class, trans butch. Beyond such emblematic figures, and within the more variegated and various identificatory itineraries of differently positioned trans subjects, we might ask what work of transference infuses figures of rhetoric and narrative with the affective attachments of familial cross- and same-gender identifications. I think we need to think about these effects and interactions, not only in terms of their political ramifications, but also in terms of the socio-psychical affects they engender and the differences they make for imagining communities. On the one hand, it is important to attend to the various ways in which certain representations of transgender and transsexuality are appropriated by political agendas that are either actively hostile to transsexual and transgender persons, or opportunistically engaged in projects with effects that are detrimental to the well-being of transsexual/transgender persons. On the other hand, we need to think through the stakes, appeals, and consequences of a culturally and psychically inhering demand for a figure for the transgression or transcendence of sexual difference that occludes, erases, and contours the possible subjectivities of gender-variant individuals.

Within such "agonistic" and ambivalent histories, figures of elsewhere and elsewhen, gleaned from medical, anthropological, philosophical, political, and historical texts, activate a mobile archive of genre crossing and blurring intertextual traffic between transsexual and transgender memoirs, social histories, and political tracts. Indeed, in Patrick Califia's *Sex Changes*, and Jason Cromwell's *Transmen and FTMs*, these figures are as frequently wrest from their prior recuperation as emblems of transhistorical and cross-cultural gay or lesbian subjects.[7] As Viviane Namaste (2000) and Katrina Roen (2001) both show, it is unclear whether contemporary Western trans scholars who repudiate these forms of ethnographic and "global gay" colonization avoid making similarly appropriative manoeuvres when describing hegira, "hermaphrodites," and "two-spirit" people as precursors and analogues to transsexual and transgender identities. In other words, indigenous forms of gender variance are relegated to the past by virtue of their presence in the practices of lower-class, rural, non-English speaking, or Native subjects, even as they are understood to have been surpassed by middle-class and/or cosmopolitan subjects with access to and participation in global human rights and cultural and leisure networks that implicitly or explicitly privilege Western-style queer and trans modes of being. The reiteration of the Eurocentrism of global gay discourse in transsexual and transgender critiques of its transphobic erasure attests to the difficult problematic of elaborating a counter-discourse in relation to one axis of identity-based oppression while remaining genuinely attentive to the interplay of economic and social capital, transnational identification, and rhetoricity operating within identity formation and social location.

Whether they tell of exceptional cross-living individuals, or of societies and genders that have "disappeared" as a result of colonial violence or historical movement, the "berdache," "passing woman," "hegira," and other-cultural "third-gender" subjects are variously cast as noble ancestors and as disappearing prehistory to contemporary Western activist modes of transgender life, community, and history.[8] Ironically, repeating the errors of the lesbian and gay anthropologies and activisms they hope to correct, some scholars engaged in the knowledge production of transgender liberation, of formulating a counter-discourse, have substantially constituted that discourse through a Eurocentric progress narrative, one that looks to racial and cultural others as raw materials for its own elaboration. Such "genealogy" functions as well as family romance, narrating fantasies of parenting and youthful rebellion, of sibling rivalry, of love and hate. Consider Leslie Feinberg's periodizing account of "progressive struggles" in hir *Trans Liberation*:

> [M]any today who are too young to remember what life was like before the women's movement need to know that it was a tremendously progressive development that won significant economic and social reforms. And this struggle by women and their allies swung human consciousness for-

> ward like a pendulum.... Now another important movement is sweeping onto the stage of history: Trans Liberation. We are again raising questions about the societal treatment of people based on their sex and gender expression. This discussion will make new contributions to human consciousness. (1998, pp. 4, 5)

This passage from *Trans Liberation: Beyond Pink or Blue* echoes narratives animating hir earlier works, such as *Transgender Warriors* and *Transgender Liberation: A Movement Whose Time Has Come,* as well as the personal-historical narrative of *Stone Butch Blues.*

So here we see some of the broad movements involved in the mobilization of a transgender counter-discourse and counter-public, a mobilization that occurred through the performative reiterations of transgender both as a heroic female masculinity and/or the ludic subversion of gendered norms, implicitly articulating transgender as and through key political and theoretical figures of queer and radical feminisms. In Feinberg's history, transgender folks are both located at the "origin" of the modern gay rights movement, figured through the presence of drag queens of colour at the Stonewall Riot, and marked as "those left behind" or abandoned by the progressive movements of the 1960s and 1970s. Curiously, though there is an acknowledgement of trans political activism dating back to this beginning, and narration of lesbian-feminist and gay liberation exclusions of trans people, Feinberg's narrative seems to elide the development of trans activism during the ensuing decades, and downplays practices of active exclusion and anti-trans discrimination in gay, lesbian, bisexual (GLB), and feminist contexts. This historical rhetoric, with its implication of generational inheritance between progressive movements, and concomitant erasure of trans activism and lives between Stonewall and queer liberation, is to be found in a wide range of transgender writing (e.g., Bornstein, 1994; Califia, 1997). In this narrative, transsexual and transgender folk disappear from the political stage and struggle, perhaps succumbing to political quietism and fear of exposure. A variation of this narrative suggests that male-to-female (MTF) trans people may have pursued individualist, civil rights–based reform, but in ways that were non- or anti-feminist, liberal, single issue, less than sexy, and so forth. This narrative, locating trans people as existing but marginal, adds and stirs us in to the history of gay, lesbian, and feminist struggles.

Following Rubin (1998) and Elliot and Roen (1998), we might see this as an instance of transgender discourses' recapitulation of some of the central themes, points of reference, conceptual figures, and analytic movements of a queer theory that, looking to revitalize itself but anxious not to stray too far afield, embraces and folds into it. Namaste (2000) suggests as much when she casts the problem as one of sourcing: writers such as Feinberg (along with Kate Bornstein and Rikki Anne Wilchins) became representative transgender figures because their accounts of transgender were and are repeatedly cited by queer and feminist theorists and activists *as representative.*[9] Because queer activist and academic networks enjoy a high degree of integration with—or, at least, access to—the institutional apparatuses of public culture (print and broadcast media, schools and universities, political lobbies, etc.), the accounts of transgender that circulate in these networks accrue a currency that transsexual accounts lack.

Attempting to forge larger solidarities, Feinberg reconfigured the anti-transsexual, anti-transvestite rubric of Virginia Prince to both contest and have a conversation with the anti-transsexual, anti-gender-variant discourses of an earlier generation of (lesbian) feminists.[10] In hir work, transgender counter-publicity was generated and sustained through reterritorializing and transvaluing elements of feminism and lesbian and transgenderist subculture, and accessing queer and feminist publishing and campus networks. But to the extent that transgender discourses articulated themselves through and with feminist and queer discourses, Feinberg also primed and framed trans politics in lesbian, queer, and feminist terms, adopted or intervened in queer and feminist problematics, and empowered queer and feminist allies as interlocutors and potential experts on trans issues. This had significant consequences inasmuch as it shaped the terms under which trans issues would become articulate and intelligible in the context of North American trade union activism. As Dan Irving notes, it has often been feminists within unions who have brought trans issues and politics forward. Given the amply documented histories of feminist and queer transphobia,[11] this fact should give some pause; however, my point is simply that if Feinberg's early pamphlet has not been widely read by trade unionists, hir politic has significantly shaped feminist and queer accounts of transgender, and has been significantly shaped by feminist and queer ambivalence around transsexuality as well.

TROUBLING INCLUSION, IMPOSSIBLE SOLIDARITIES?

I have spoken to some of the ways in which Feinberg's manifesto is historically situated and functioning rhetorically as an invocation of a radical and radicalizing call for a transgender politics of struggle and solidarity. Now I would like to discuss some attempts to enact such a politic within the Canadian labour movement. I should say that I don't claim such politics are exclusively inspired by Feinberg's early pamphlet, but that they participate within a tradition it substantially formalizes, one of thinking of the Marxist critique of capitalism and the state in tandem with the situation of gender-variant or gender-minority subjects. Further, I believe they carry forward the discursive burden of transgenderist, lesbian, and feminist "transsexual-phobic"[12] histories that Feinberg necessarily negotiated. So, *Transgender Liberation* is not the origin but is perhaps a text signalling a certain tipping point into "mainstream" visibility.

Indeed, in "We Are Family: Labour Responds to Gay, Lesbian, Bisexual, and Transgender Workers," diversity scholars Gerald Hunt and Jonathan Eaton (2007) suggest that "transgender activism has been late to emerge as a social movement, building to a large degree on openings created by gay, lesbian, and bisexual activism" (p. 142). Though I do not have the space here to document a longer history of trans activism in the Canadian or international context, and as such accounts exist elsewhere, I will suggest that such an assertion, one not at all uncommonly made, is a consequence of mistaking what Henry Rubin (1998) has named "queer paradigmed" transgenderism for trans in its umbrella sense, and does function precisely to forget the history of transsexual, transgenderist, transvestite, and other gender-diverse subjects' activism. For example, in the Canadian context, from the 1980s onward there is a significant linkage of transsexual political organizing and sex worker activist networks, facilitated by the neglect of both overlapping constituencies in HIV/AIDS prevention services, social services, and mainstream/gay activism (see, for example, Highcrest, 1998; Ross, 1995).

That said, though trans people undoubtedly have long been active in Canadian labour, Hunt and Eaton (2007) are correct to suggest that labour's *explicit*[13] engagement with trans workers got underway in the mid-1990s and gained momentum in the early 2000s. One form this engagement took in the 1990s was the first Solidarity and Pride Conference of the Canadian Labour Congress (CLC), held in 1997. The conference was organized by the Solidarity and Pride

Working Group, established in 1994 to represent LGB members in CLC-affiliated unions and provincial federations of labour. Gail Owen, a member of the Public Service Alliance of Canada, was one of the first out trans activists in Canadian labour and, to the best of my knowledge, the only out transsexual activist at the first Solidarity and Pride Conference.[14] Until that time, the main issues addressed by the Solidarity and Pride Working Group were issues of legal equality for lesbian and gay workers, homophobia in the workplace, and solidarity with "other" equity-seeking groups. Thanks to Gail Owen and those who supported her, there was some acknowledgement of the work to be done on trans issues, though it was not until 1999 that the Solidarity and Pride Working Group formally added transgender issues to their mandate. Initiatives undertaken between 1997 and 2000 included the formation of regional Pride working groups, some provincial Pride labour conferences, a CLC-wide positive space campaign, work with affiliated organizations such as EGALE Canada and the labour caucus of the NDP, work done through resolution to conventions (to fund positive space campaigns and educationals, and to develop model equity language for contract negotiations). As Hunt and Eaton (2007) note, the CLC also undertook to consult with members of trans communities in three provinces (British Columbia, Saskatchewan, and Ontario).

At the second Solidarity and Pride Conference in 2001, there were 11 of us who identified as trans and felt able to be out about it. Survey questions for the discussion paper were distributed in that context, and we were invited to bring them back to our communities. And in Ontario, trans activists in and out of labour worked to see that those questionnaires reached as wide a representation of the trans community as possible.[15]

But let me backtrack, and explain how I came to be involved in this work. Surprisingly, my involvement in union activism around trans inclusion did *not* begin with my union local, CUPE 3903, which organizes teaching assistants, contract faculty, and graduate assistants at York University. It was through activist contacts in the trans community that I was invited to participate in the trans community consult in Ontario in 2000, and at the urging of a friend who also happened to be a queer labour activist that I made my way as a (non-delegated) attendee to the Ontario Federation of Labour's "Labour Behind the Rainbow" conference in 1999. Out of that consult, and others in British Columbia and Saskatchewan, the CLC Solidarity and Pride Working Group developed a transgender discussion paper, which was circulated in the months leading up to the 2001 Solidarity and Pride Conference. It was the startling and dismaying disjuncture between several of the recommendations made at the Ontario consult (which in turn reiterated demands made by trans activists at the Labour Behind the Rainbow conference) and the contents of the discussion paper that inspired me to request my local delegate me to represent CUPE 3903 at the second CLC Solidarity and Pride Conference that took place in June 2001.

By this time, I had become active in the local. In 2000 and 2001, we were involved in a 76-day strike (which ran from October 26, 2000, to January 10, 2001). That strike took place during the Harris years, which is to say during the intensification of neoliberal policies that substantially undermined Ontario's social safety net, and attacked the entire public sector and almost every marginalized group in the province. It also coincided with the rise of local struggles against poverty and the post-Seattle attention on the part of big labour to a global justice movement that was just then beginning to mobilize for the Free Trade Area of the Americas (FTAA) summit in Quebec City. It seemed that union militancy was on the increase across North America, and unions such as CUPE, CAW, and CUPW seemed open to a vision of social solidarity with all working people, and not simply their own members. Linda Briskin (2007) argues that an increase in social unionism at that time was also tied to an increase in equity work within the union movement.

In any case, in the lead-up to CUPE 3903's 2000–2001 strike, the union enjoyed a very high level of support and mobilization within its membership. Strike votes regularly returned with strong mandates to strike, and in previous years the threat of striking had allowed the union to make significant gains. At that time, CUPE 3903 union activists were active on multiple fronts, organizing with other locals within CUPE and with other unions, as well as with feminist, anti-capitalist, and anti-poverty movements. The union was characterized by strong and transparent communication with membership, and a support for member activism. So, in the spring of 2000, when our union was soliciting input into what our bargaining priorities should be, I met with members of my local's Women's Caucus to discuss how the union could work for trans members. At that time, there were a number of high-profile struggles impacting trans communities: most visibly, Mike Harris's Conservative government's then-recent de-listing of funding for sex reassignment surgery, and Kimberly Nixon's human rights case against Vancouver Rape Relief. And these seemed to suggest some places where we could start our work: guaranteeing access to gendered services and spaces for trans members, preventing discrimination on the basis of gender identity and expression, and providing some form of economic support for transitioning members. We were also aware that the hardships our members might face were symptomatic of the larger interlocking systems of neoliberal capitalism, sexism, heterosexism and transphobia, and racial and neo-colonial rule.

At the time, in the Women's Caucus, there was a somewhat fuzzy but positive idea that trans women would be welcome in that space, though it was not declared formally through policy or even enacted through common practice. To the credit of the co-chairs and other active members of the caucus, the change was implemented fairly painlessly, and we quickly moved on to the question of how the caucus could advocate for trans members. At the local level, our discussion touched on a number of possible avenues for change to the union's bylaws and constitution to prohibit discrimination on the basis of gender identity and/or expression, to recognize trans people's self-identification (specifically in regard to gendered spaces), and to fight transphobia. We also developed bargaining language guaranteeing paid transition leave, non-discrimination and accommodation language in the collective agreement, and the increase of monies to the Ways and Means Fund, with a specific allocation toward providing financial support to transitioning transsexuals within the union. Along with other more celebrated gains, these demands were part of what we won in the 2000–2001 strike.[16] That contract language became the boilerplate bargaining language for union locals within CUPE and set precedents for the Canadian Labour Congress and the American Federation of Labour and Congress of Industrial Organizations. Not only in Canada, but in the US, contract faculty, teaching assistant, and graduate assistant unions use it as the basis for crafting their own trans inclusion language.[17]

CUPE 3903 activists also committed energy to trans advocacy outside of the context of the union local. In June 2001, I was one of two representatives from CUPE 3903 (along with Spenser Rowe, a two-spirit union activist) who attended the second CLC Solidarity and Pride Conference where a group of trans delegates and allies pushed to make transsexual and transgender worker's issues central to the conference agenda.

The Trans Caucus met twice over the course of the conference, once on our own and once with CLC staffer and ally Sue Genge. The purpose of the meeting was to articulate strategy and goals for our work with CLC and its affiliates in terms of trans rights work. The group also functioned as a safe space for trans people who felt unable to be out, even in the context of the Solidarity and Pride Conference. Though this may seem surprising, several delegates recounted experiences of being patronized, insulted, and/or shunned by lesbian and gay co-workers, who seemed embarrassed by, uncomfortable with, or disapproving of their queerly gendered/gender-transgressive behaviour. In terms of goals, we articulated several, which we committed to working with our locals, our unions, and the CLC and affiliates to meet: the allocation of resources for the development of a trans/workplace educational package, with training to be given by trans educators (1 FTM, 1 MTF); the completion of the CLC policy paper on trans issues to be submitted for adoption at the CLC conference in 2002; the election of trans members to the Solidarity and Pride Working Group; the circulation of model contract language throughout the CLC, and strong lobbying on the part of the CLC for all affiliates to work toward benefits and non-discrimination language in their collective agreements and in their constitutions and bylaws; the convening of a "trans in the workplace" conference before the CLC convention in 2002; the adoption of a convention resolution calling for full funding of transsexual/transgender gender transitions under public health care across the country; and the adoption of a convention resolution supporting trans and non-trans sex worker activists' call for the decriminalization of sex work, and working with the labour caucus of the NDP to introduce such a motion to Parliament.

The following year, however, at the 2002 convention of the Canadian Labour Congress, trans issues, and LGBT equity issues more generally, took a decided backseat to more "mainstream" campaigns, and, of course, the election. Our two wins, a resolution in support of Mark Hall,[18] and an early intervention to get transgender included in our non-discrimination statement, while important, barely scratched the surface of what needed to be done.

Within CUPE, we had somewhat more success at our 2001 National Convention. Local 3903 sent a large delegation to the convention, bringing motions that called upon CUPE to incorporate trans representation in its equity bodies and non-discrimination into its constitution and bylaws, to develop and put into use trans positive educational materials, to create a national trans workers working group,[19] to challenge the privatization of health care and the de-listing of transition-related medical expenses, to take leadership in the fight to decriminalize sex work, and to support the unionization of sex workers. Surprisingly, through a combination of smart and strategic work by advocates and allies, strong affective attachments to an ideal of worker solidarity among the delegates, good timing (unions were riding high on mid-1990's gains in lesbian and gay rights, and more open to a view of social unionism than they became in the post-9/11 climate), and good luck, all of those resolutions were passed at the national union level. Their implementation, however, was another matter. Predictably, when I found myself as the only trans member of the National Pink Triangle Committee (for the first year and a half of my tenure there), the hardest sell, both to my fellow committee members and the union leadership, was solidarity with sex workers.

TRANS LIBERATION WITHIN OR VERSUS UNION BUREAUCRACY

Gerald Hunt and Jonathan Eaton (2007) describe the process of trans advocacy in the union context as proceeding less through grassroots mobilization among the membership than through a process whereby trans activists and GLB allies got the ear of leadership and then secured equity commitments that were operationalized in top-down fashion. They make the argument that transgender activists' gains have been dependent upon and benefited from foundations laid, and networks established, by gay, lesbian, bisexual, and feminist activism. Relatedly, in an interview with Gary Kinsman (2007), Dan Irving makes the argument that the passage of trans and sex worker rights resolutions at the CUPE National Convention has transpired in ways that have bypassed member engagement.

For example, in 2001, the Solidarity and Pride Committee drafted a series of motions for the 2002 CLC National Convention that specifically addressed the concerns of trans workers within the union movement. And while these motions were all passed, they were passed by the national executive in camera and not debated on the floor. The agenda was filled primarily by executive elections. Representatives from locals nationwide did not have the opportunity to hear, discuss, debate, or vote on these resolutions. This has a tremendous impact on trans education and awareness within the labour movement. Furthermore, it raises issues concerning the implementation of trans positive policies at local levels. These motions passed on paper, but how were they brought to the attention of representatives expected to report back to their local? What systems of accountability are in place to ensure that these motions are understood and implemented? (Irving, in Kinsman, 2007)

From my perspective, Irving (in Kinsman, 2007), and Hunt and Eaton (2007) raise some important issues regarding processes of grassroots mobilization and education, autonomy, and consensus within progressive organizations and movements. In particular they highlight, in different ways, the challenges of (sexual) minority activism within a left framework at a time when labour's commitments are split between left solidarity, equity struggles within a neoliberal "diversity management" frame, and survival of neoliberal backlash. I believe, however, that they miss important features of the situation they describe.

Hunt and Eaton (2007), and Irving (in Kinsman, 2007) are certainly correct to highlight the way in which GLB allies, networks, and conferences worked with trans activists to raise the profile of trans issues with union leadership up to a point. That said, I would disagree that this involved bypassing debate on the convention floor, member education, accountability, or solidarity building with non-GLBT union members. For example, Gail Owen's activism at the first Solidarity and Pride Conference resulted in relatively broad-based consultation with trans workers in unionized environments in the development of the CLC trans discussion paper. When that paper was circulated at the Ontario Federation of Labour convention, and trans activists discovered that it did not reflect the input they had given during consultations, trans activists worked to see that the paper and questionnaires reached trans workers and community members, both within and outside of unionized workplaces, who provided additional critical feedback. We consulted independently with our communities, which led to pushback from trans communities against the representation of our issues that was being produced by non-trans, but possibly GLB, equity activists, staff, and policy-makers within the upper echelons of the CLC. We also worked with allies, both hetero and homo, feminist and leftist, within our union locals to garner support to send trans activists and resolutions to various conventions. Doing so involved writing reports, lobbying, and giving workshops at the local level, that is to say, education and movement building, not only for our local executives, women's caucus, and stewards council, but in the context of general members meetings. It is also worth noting that conferences such as Labour Behind the Rainbow and Solidarity and Pride are large gatherings, rivalling the size of Divisional and National Conventions. And while they are attended primarily by GLB and T members and allies, many of these members do not identify primarily as activists or leftists but rather attend looking for support from their union. As well, they draw non-GLBT equity activists, leadership, educators, and staff. Finally, recall that unions are also embedded in sectoral, cross-sectoral, and identity-based organizations and institutions. Drawing only upon my own experience, and the activities of CUPE's National Pink Triangle Committee during my tenure as a trans rep, I can point to presentations, debates, and educationals on trans workers' and sex workers' rights made at community-based conferences ("Sexin' Change," the Philadelphia Trans Health Conference), international GLBT gatherings (International GLBT Human Rights Conference of the Gay Games in Sydney in 2002, and International GLBT Human Rights Conference of the Outgames in Montreal in 2006), and national and international labour conferences of the Canadian Labour Congress and Public Services International (PSI), as well as to presentations on trans and sex worker rights given to both CUPE's Ontario and National Women's Committees.

In regard to the question of debate on the convention floor, the situation is also more complex than it might at first appear. It is true that at the CLC National Convention in 2002, elections and a range of other agendas predominated, and equity issues received short shrift. Nonetheless, trans activists and allies did "work the convention floor," intervene at microphones, and lobby behind the scenes in ways that built cross-constituency alliances and led to the passage of some trans and sex worker positive resolutions (albeit by the executive, following the convention, as Irving correctly points out). However, such resolutions did hit the floor and receive debate at CUPE Ontario's Divisional Convention that year. And at CUPE's 2001 National Convention, a transsexual activist called out the national president on the backburnering of LGBT and equity issues from the convention floor. The president's public misgendering of that activist became an occasion for a public trans pedagogy observed by the assembled delegates. That in turn led to the adoption of non-discrimination language for trans workers in CUPE's constitution later in the convention (which required debate on the convention floor) and to the passing of trans positive resolutions. It is worth noting that a resolution committing the union to working in solidarity with sex workers, particularly trans sex workers, to end the criminalization of prostitution in Canada, was not debated on the floor, but was referred back to the National Executive, which passed it in their first meeting of 2002.

It is hard to know whether our solidarity with sex workers' struggles would have been better served by a debate on the floor of the convention that year. I don't know if we were quite prepared for that discussion yet. As a trans rep to CUPE's National Pink Triangle Committee over the following four years, that was where I discovered the greatest resistance to our work, from both union leadership, and GLB and feminist activists and staffers. This resistance raises another difficulty with overly simple accounts of trans activism's relationship to GLB and feminist networks and gains: often it was queer and feminist members and staff who opposed this work, either on ideological grounds or out of fear of a public outcry.

The impasse around sex work had to do with the pitfalls of a narrow identity politics, as well as sex work stigma, and arguably a failure of labour analysis; that is, a failure to engage sex work as a labour issue. Several issues were bound up in that failure. First, in the movement away from social unionism to business unionism, there was a decreasing commitment to social solidarity with all workers and marginalized groups. This transpired at the level of union leadership, and was indeed imposed in top-down fashion through the neoliberal rhetoric and logics of the 2003–2005 Strategic Directions Plan by which then-national president Paul Moist reoriented CUPE politically. Second, in the increasing homonormativity of gay and lesbian rights activism, both outside and within the union movement, there was a prioritizing of the fight for "equal marriage" over virtually all other GLBT issues, to the extent that, for instance, one staffer requested that 50 percent of his paid time be given over to that dossier, despite a number of pressing and time-sensitive issues, such as the not-yet-defeated Kimberly Nixon appeal. Third, a combination of sex worker stigma and abolitionist feminist opposition to sex workers' rights contributed to opposition from multiple sectors within the union. Fourth, the call for sex worker solidarity came from trans sex workers who were not "out" as unionized workers, and so there was a persistent doubt as to whether they were legitimately representing sex workers, trans people, or trade unionists, and skepticism about what "they" had to do with "us."

This objection to sex worker solidarity was made despite the fact that transsexual sex workers were demonstrably some of the most courageous, hard-working, and effective advocates for trans people in the country, setting up peer-run services for street active and poor trans people; documenting trans peoples' social exclusion from homeless, youth, and women's shelters and public health care, particularly HIV/AIDS services; and advocating for and developing harm reduction programs (see Sandy Leo Laframboise in Chapter 5 and Jamie Lee Hamilton in Chapter 2 of this volume). This objection came despite the observably high percentage of trans women involved in sex work, and the documentation of trans peoples' effective exclusion from many areas of more socially validated forms of employment, and it came despite multiple requests to the Canadian Labour Congress, as well as CUPE, specifically, for solidarity in the decriminalization campaign from transsexual as well as cissexual sex workers. In fact, it came despite the trans community's input to the CLC trans discussion paper, despite the fact that the union passed resolutions committing itself to working in solidarity with sex workers, and despite the tremendous unpaid effort to educate CUPE members by activists from the Canadian Guild for Erotic Labour as well as by individual trans sex worker activists.

Despite some pro sex worker statements by individual union activists such as CUPE Newfoundland divisional president Wayne Lucas, who called for decriminalization and unionization for sex workers in 2004, Canadian labour backed away from its solidarity commitments to sex workers. While it is tempting to suggest that this is primarily reflective of an unwillingness to endure public outcry, it is instructive to think about how sex worker solidarity was backburnered in the CUPE context. In the first instance, it was deprioritized in relation to an ostensibly more "core" issue (the fight for gay marriage), which was framed as a crisis situation that demanded all of our resources (ironically, this crisis occurred precisely as gay marriage came closer to being won). In the second instance, sex work was redescribed as a women's issue, and therefore an issue for the Women's Committee to take leadership on (and sidelining the Pink Triangle Committee, which had brought the issue forward). In both cases, a politics of identity were deployed in ways that not only trumped solidarity politics, but also enacted unspoken identity politics at the same time. The gay and lesbian issue of gay marriage became more "core" to the concerns of the GLBT committee than the trans issue of "sex work." Likewise the redescription of sex work as an issue for the Women's Committee effectively played off gender against sexuality, erasing a rich history of lesbian, bisexual, and transsexual women and gay men in sex work, and effectively suggesting as well that the identity of "woman" is in the last instance the property of cissexual and heterosexual women. In both cases, there was a failure to acknowledge the status of sex workers as workers.[20]

In his "Normalized Transgressions: Legitimizing the Transsexual Body as Productive," Dan Irving (2008) draws attention to the extent to which a focus on identity politics within trans advocacy has relied upon narrative tropes of self-actualization, particularly in the civil rights sphere, whether focused on non-discrimination language, health care, violence, or, indeed and especially, employment. As both Irving (2008) and Joanne Meyerowitz (2002) point out, self-actualization narratives have been deployed strategically, but to ambivalent effect, by marginal trans subjects seeking recognition within the American/US context, cohering as they do with narratives of national exceptionalism. Irving suggests that these tropes, and the strategies that accompany them, are especially amenable to our current moment of neoliberal governance. Trans masculine self-fashioning, in particular, often invokes competence as a worker, a breadwinner, as "economic man," in short.

Neoliberalism is flexible, and is engaged in feminizing workforces (Marchand & Runyon, 2000) while requiring stoic, producing, and consuming bodies. It required belt-tightening for the good of the national body following the economic crash of 2009, but also within the wartime climate of intensified homo/nationalism post-9/11. It is of course singularly unsympathetic to the communal anti-economic activity of feminine communities and sexualized communities, such as those formed by trans sex workers. Materially challenging the monosexual and monogamous model of the couple, whether hetero or homo, trans sex worker communities remain disparaged and subalterned by contemporary trans, queer, and feminist politics, including union politics (see Salah 2009, 2013; Gillies, Clamen, & Salah, 2013). And as Canadian unions have turned toward a business union model after the brief radicalizing romance with the anti-globalization movement between Seattle and Quebec, they have found it convenient to redeploy muscular and heteronormative as well as homonormative strategies to contend with internal difference, cutting back on social union commitments to solidarity with precarious, youthful, racialized, feminized, and criminalized workers.

CONCLUSION

To conclude, I want to return to Leslie Feinberg's *Transgender Liberation: A Movement Whose Time Has Come*. The revolutionary coalition of GLBT people, working people, and people of colour that Feinberg promoted was envisioned within a lesbian, feminist, anti-imperialist, and intersectional frame. Nonetheless, the transgender rights discourse that inherited it (as trans rights activists negotiated trans exclusion in feminist spaces, and appealed to Feinberg and queer theory for common ground) radically circumscribed its revolutionary ambitions. The iconic appeal of the figure of the working-class butch, and the inheritance of an anti-surgery position from both Prince and lesbian/queer feminisms, colluded with leftist and broader (trans) misogyny in downplaying the importance of trans sex worker voices (as women's voices, as trans worker's voices) and marginalizing trans women's voices within labour and left organizing. The movement toward business unionism rendered practical logics for managing diversity and dispensed with social solidarity. Union leadership, for instance, turned to the legal branch and the Women's Committee to adjudicate whether to follow through on commitments to sex worker solidarity or to support Kimberly Nixon's appeal against Vancouver Rape Relief.

Despite substantial gains, CUPE and the CLC let trans workers down, and did so precisely through treating GLB and feminist allies as arbiters of trans realities. To think about trans inclusion, then, also means to think about the intersections of psychic, cultural, discursive, and political economic formations around the lives of trans workers, including trans sex workers.

Space where self-identification is taken as a given is, to me, one of most powerful gains made in regard to the politics of identity; much of the credit for this work goes to mixed-race women and queer women of colour, who worked to deterritorialize the borderlands of identity by testifying to the violences of identity regulation. Identity politics draws our attention to our collective belonging around a shared attribute—race, sexuality, gender, and ability. Identity politics might also recall us to the fact that we are always more than one thing—gay Muslims, fags with chronic illness, lesbian feminist trans prostitutes. Identity enlists our knowledge of ourselves, raises our voices, consolidates a collectivity in its difference from others, and may turn as well toward internal differentiation. Identity wants a mirror, and perhaps, resentfully, to crack it.

Leslie Feinberg's work reminds us of labour activism's foundation in solidarity, the shared bond of workers, and it is the extension of trust and support to others. In thinking about trans inclusion, we must consider not only the significant question of queer as a paradigm that leads to the devaluation of transsexuality, but also the question of what a feminism that does not undermine sex workers might look like.[21] Perhaps more fundamentally, we must ask how we might make less violent use of one another. To do that, though, we must contend with the difficult conception that we make use of one another—even as we may act in solidarity, we are enacting our desires, fantasies, and effectuations of identity, mobilities of power, and blockages or preoccupations of our oppression. It seems it is still far easier to lament violence against trans people, or inveigh against tricks and pimps, than to collaborate with sex workers and trans people in addressing the conditions of our work and lives. If intersectionality helps us to recognize the interconnections of oppressions and calls upon us to self-situate and recognize our privilege, investments, and locations, then by being attentive to appeals to our affect, we can notice what is being appealed to in appeals for our solidarity: our self-importance, our identification, and all too often the confirmation of our identities in rescue narratives. Intersectional thought made attentive to the registers of our affective investments offers both possibilities and problems but not guarantees. Ultimately, for solidarity to be meaningful, it must be based in self-representation, self-organization, and true respect for local autonomy.

NOTES

1 Prince founded *Transvestia* magazine and the earliest North American cross-dresser support organizations, and, between the 1950s and the 1980s, was a prominent organizer in heterosexual MTF transgender contexts. Leslie Feinberg cites Prince as the originator of the term "transgender" in *Transgender Warriors* (1996). Richard Ekins and Dave King (2006) suggest Prince coined the term "transgenderal" in an article for *Transvestia* in 1969, and modified the term to "transgenderist" in a 1979 publication in

the same magazine. Prince was a friend and associate of Harry Benjamin, "the father of transsexualism," and Benjamin acknowledges her influence upon his thought and reprinted her taxonomy of trans identities in his influential book *The Transsexual Phenomenon* (1966). Prince was a lay sexologist with a doctorate in pharmacology, and the distinctions she made in her terminology drew upon Magnus Hirshfeld's (1910) distinction between (male) homosexuality and (male, heterosexual) transvestism, and echoed Havelock Ellis's association of transvestism with "aesthetic emotion" (Ekins & King, p. 2).

2 Prince's distancing of transgenderism from an erotic component distinguished it against gay drag and prostitution, fetishistic cross-dressing, and transsexuality, as well as from sex in "the feminine role." In this way, Prince actively restigmatized those practices and identities. In Ekins and King's (2006) account, Prince regarded the 1990's use of transgender as an umbrella term as a "hijacking" of her language. I want to thank Dan Irving for his insightful suggestion that in Prince's normative taxonomy (and its concomitant disparagement of prostitution, "fetishistic" pleasure in cross-dressing, homosexuality, and surgical transition), we can see an early index to tensions between trans as ontology of selective intelligibility (or social viability) and trans as figuring a socio-diagnostic of power.

3 Arguably Feinberg's laudable attempts to promote transgender as an expansively inclusive rubric encompassing all forms of gender variance may echo, even as it would contest, the phallic inscription of "man" as a universal signifier, with a particularly masculine privileged signified.

4 Hir earliest writings on trans subjects appeared anonymously; for example: (1978, June 2). "Transvestite Tortured by Cops, but Wins Court Battle: 'It certainly took a lot of courage,'" p. 10.

5 In this light, Feinberg's practice at this time seems to enact a version of the intersectional politic called for in some 1970s black feminist thought, most famously, the *Combahee River Collective Statement* (Combahee River Collective, 1978).

6 See O'Hartigan (1997). Namaste draws upon O'Hartigan to make a slightly different argument in her *Invisible Lives* (1990). For discussion of the knowledge politics around the mourning of Adrienne Rich and the significance of her transmisogyny, see "Adrienne Rich and Transmisogyny: We Can Begin by Acknowledging That It Matters" (Tenderqueer, 2012).

7 See, for instance, Cromwell's extensive reading of the erasure of trans masculine subjects in the anthropological and historical mainstream, as well as in the reclamatory work of gay and lesbian historians and anthropologists, in *Transmen and FTMs* (1999, pp. 44–83) and Patrick Califia's critiques of Jonathan Katz's *Gay American History: Lesbians and Gay Men in the U.S.A.* (1976) and Will Roscoe's *Living the Spirit: A Gay American Indian Anthology* (1988), in *Sex Changes* (1997, pp. 120–162).

8 This historical schema is consolidated in and disseminated by Feinberg's *Transgender Liberation: A Movement Whose Time Has Come*, and hir *Transgender Warriors*, but, to be fair, predates hir interventions. Speculative historical and cross-cultural surveys of transgender ways of being and forms of oppression are an underexamined and common, if not requisite, generic feature of transsexual and medical case study, suggesting both transsexual patients and their clinicians felt compelled to keep up with, and legitimate their own narratives through, ethnographic and historical studies. See, for instance, Benjamin's *The Transsexual Phenomenon* (1966), Millot's *Horsexe* (1990), and Beth Elliot's *Mirrors* (1996).

9 Personal conversation with Viviane Namaste, but for elaboration on this point, see *Invisible Lives*.

10 One of the earliest transsexual critiques of Feinberg was authored by Lou Sullivan, deceased founder of the *FTM Newsletter* (later *FTM International*), and gay transsexual "pioneer." Sullivan's open letter to the editor(s) of Worker's World regarding their 1980 publication of Diane Leslie Feinberg's *Journal of a Transsexual*, framed it thusly: "This pamphlet was the only piece of information available on the subject

of transsexualism in this [the San Francisco Gay Freedom Day] largest of gay assemblies ever." Sullivan goes on to describe the pamphlet as portraying "transsexuals as confused, doomed, and hopeless people for whom there is no possibility of peace" and being "misrepresentative of the transsexual condition, and anti-transsexual in effect" and suggested "future editions of your pamphlet should be entitled 'Journal of an Androgyne' or 'Journal of a Gender Dysphoric,'" allowing that while Feinberg's narrative might be reasonably representing the failure of social and surgical trajectories for hirself, that ze was not in a position to indict transsexual lives and choices (Sullivan, n.d., pp. 14, 15). Sullivan's review of Feinberg's pamphlet does some complicated historical, affective, and positional work. Sullivan's career as the "first gay FTM activist" and the founder of the contemporary FTM community, in tandem with his review of Feinberg's pamphlet, demonstrates that one does not need to advocate the merger of queer and trans constituencies to pursue an anti-homophobic trans politic, and suggests the terms of coalition on offer from some in the queer community may work to specifically anti-transsexual effect. Symbolically this is achieved in part through simply indexing the existence of Feinberg's early publication, which, explicit in its denunciation of surgical and hormonal trajectories, demonstrates the roots of Feinberg's transgender vision in a politic that both confused transgender and transsexual identities, and rescued the former by repudiating the latter.

11 For representative accounts, see Elliot (1996), Elliot and Roen (1998), Namaste (2000, 2005), Rubin (1998), Serano (2007), Stone (1991), and Jake Pyne et al. in this text (see Chapter 13).

12 The term is Xanthra Phillippa's.

13 I say explicit only to make the point that this period marks labour's engagement with workers who were "out" as trans, whether by choice or in response to being "outed" or challenged on their gender identity.

14 Of course, labour had been dealing with trans issues before that conference but often in reactionary ways. For example, in 1995, Leslie Ferris was censured following an anonymous complaint about her using the women's washroom. Local 15 of the Office and Technical Employees Union was ordered to pay Ferris $6,000 by the BC Human Rights Tribunal in 1999. So labour unions' support for trans workers' rights was often preceded by trans union members working to force labour to acknowledge trans people's rights, sometimes through the courts.

15 For instance, they were distributed at an OFL/CLC sponsored consult, as part of a conference track focused on trans people and labour that I organized at the "Sexin' Change" conference, and through SOY (Supporting Our Youth) in Toronto.

16 I should say that bargaining language was developed not only internally within the local, but also in dialogue with an activist at the York Women's Centre, who was working toward transitioning that space.

17 Though I cannot here treat, in any substantial way, the development of university-based trans labour activism in the United States, I want to at least mention the remarkable work of André Wilson. Drawing inspiration from our gains at York, Wilson, then a graduate student in Architecture and an organizer with the American Federation of Teachers union local 3550, went on to become the first out trans lead negotiator for an American union and to win inclusive health insurance coverage ("no exclusion" clauses and explicit coverage of at least some surgeries). Subsequently he's worked in a variety of settings across the US to leverage changes in coverage for others. Successes include trans inclusion in the health plans at the University of Michigan, the University of Washington in St. Louis, the University of Washington (Seattle), and the University of California at Santa Cruz.

18 Oshawa teen Mark Hall's 2002 fight to be permitted to bring his boyfriend to his high school prom made headlines and engendered widespread support in LGBT and mainstream media, as well as drawing support from trade unions.

19 In the end, this resolution was rewritten to suggest the addition of three transgender representatives to the National Pink Triangle Committee.

20 For a more detailed and multifaceted account of this process, see Gillies, Clamen, and Salah, 2013.

21 In fact there are many, many examples of both, and many queer and feminist union activists, staffers, and friends deserve appreciation and thanks for being invaluable allies and supporters in the fight for trans inclusion and sex worker solidarity in the Canadian union movement.

REFERENCES

Benjamin, H. (1966). *The transsexual phenomenon*. New York: Julian Press.

Bornstein, K. (1994). *Gender outlaw: On men, women, and the rest of us*. New York: Routledge.

Briskin, L. (2007). Afterword. In G. Hunt & D. Rayside (Eds.), *Equity, diversity and Canadian labour* (pp. 244–255). Toronto: University of Toronto Press.

Butler, J. (1990). *Gender trouble*. New York: Routledge.

Califia, P. (1997). *Sex changes: The politics of transgenderism*. San Francisco: Cleis Press.

Canadian Labour Congress Solidarity and Pride Working Group. (2003). *Transgender discussion paper* (pp. 1–15). Ottawa: Canadian Labour Congress.

Canadian Union of Public Employees. (2004). *Sex work: Why it's a union issue* [Background paper]. Retrieved from http://cupe.ca/EqualityPride/samesexworkbackgroundpaper

Combahee River Collective. (1978). *Combahee River Collective statement*. Retrieved November 20, 2012, from http://circuitous.org/scraps/combahee.html

Cromwell, J. (1999). *Transmen and FTMs: Identities, bodies, genders and sexualities*. Urbana: University of Illinois Press.

Ekins, R., & King, D. (Eds.). (2006). *Virginia Prince: Pioneer of transgendering*. Binghamton: Haworth Press.

Elliot, B. (as Geri Nettick). (1996). *Mirrors: Portrait of a lesbian transsexual*. New York: Masquerade Books.

Elliot, P., & Roen, K. (1998). Transgenderism and the question of embodiment: Promising queer politics? Special issue of *GLQ*, *4*(2), 231–261.

Feinberg, [Diane] L. (1980). *Journal of a transsexual*. New York: World View Forum.

Feinberg, L. (1993). *Stone butch blues*. Ithaca: Firebrand.

Feinberg, L. (1996). *Transgender warriors: Making history from Joan of Arc to Dennis Rodman*. Boston: Beacon.

Feinberg, L. (1997). Transgender liberation: A movement whose time has come. In R. Hennessy & C. Ingraham (Eds.), *Materialist feminism: A reader in class, difference, and women's lives* (pp. 227–235). New York: Routledge.

Feinberg, L. (1998). *Trans liberation: Beyond pink and blue*. Boston: Beacon.

Gillies, K., Clamen, J., & Salah, T. (2013). Working for change: Sex workers in the union struggle. Chapter 8 in E. van der Meulen, E.M. Durisin, & V. Love (Eds.), *Selling sex: Experience, advocacy, and research on sex work in Canada*. Vancouver: University of British Columbia Press.

Highcrest, A. (1998). *At home on the stroll: My twenty years as a prostitute in Canada*. Toronto: Vintage Books Canada.

Hunt, G., & Eaton, J. (2007). We are family: Labour responds to gay, lesbian, bisexual, and transgender workers. In G. Hunt & D. Rayside (Eds.), *Equity, diversity and Canadian labour* (pp. 130–155). Toronto: University of Toronto Press.

Irving, D. (2008). Normalized transgressions: Legitimizing the transsexual body as productive. Special issue of *Radical History Review*, (100), 38–59.

Katz, J. (1976). *Gay American history: Lesbians and gay men in the U.S.A.* New York: Avon Books.

Kinsman, G. (2007). Trans politics and anti-capitalism: An interview with Dan Irving. *Upping the Anti Journal, 4.* Retrieved on November 27, 2012, from http://uppingtheanti.org/journal/uta/number-four

Marchand, M., & Runyon, A. (2000). *Gender and global restructuring: Sightings, sites and resistances.* London: Routledge.

Meyerowitz, J. (2002). *How sex changed: A history of transsexuality in the United States.* Cambridge: Harvard University Press.

Millot, C. (1990). *Horsexe: Essay on transsexuality.* K. Hylton (Trans.). New York: Autonomedia.

Namaste, V. (2000). *Invisible lives: The erasure of transsexual and transgendered people.* Chicago: University of Chicago Press.

Namaste, V. (2005). *Sex change, social change: Reflections on identity, institutions and imperialism.* Toronto: Women's Press.

O'Hartigan, M.D. (1997). *Our bodies your lies: The lesbian colonization of transsexualism.* Pamphlet on file with author: P.O. Box 82447, Portland, Oregon, USA, 97282.

Prince, V. (1967). *The transvestite and his wife.* Los Angeles: Argyle Books.

Raymond, J. (1979). *The transsexual empire: The making of the she-male.* Boston: Beacon Press.

Roen, K. (2001). Transgender theory and embodiment: The risk of racial marginalisation. *Journal of Gender Studies, 10*(3), 253–263.

Roscoe, W. (Ed.). (1988). *Living the spirit: A gay American Indian anthology.* New York: St. Martin's Press.

Ross, M. (1995). High risk project: Dancing to Eagle Spirit talks with Mirha-Soleil Ross. *Gendertrash,* (4), 5–10.

Rubin, H. (1998). Phenomenology as method in trans studies. The Transgender Issue. Special issue of *GLQ, 4*(2), 263–281.

Salah, T. (2009). *Writing trans genre: An inquiry into transsexual and transgender rhetorics, affects and politic.* Unpublished doctoral dissertation. York University, Toronto, Canada.

Salah, T. (2013). Notes towards thinking transsexual institutional poetics. In. E.C. Karpinski, J. Henderson, I. Sowton, & R. Ellenwood (Eds.), *Trans/acting culture, writing and memory: Essays in honour of Barbara Godard.* Waterloo: Wilfrid Laurier University Press.

Serano, J. (2007). *Whipping girl: A transsexual woman on sexism and the scapegoating of femininity.* Emeryville, CA: Seal Press.

Stone, S. (1991). The empire strikes back: A posttranssexual manifesto. In K. Straub & J. Epstein (Eds.), *Body guards: The cultural politics of sexual ambiguity.* New York: Routledge.

Sullivan, L. (n.d.). *WillyBoy, 7,* 14–15.

Tenderqueer. (2012, March 29). Adrienne Rich and transmisogyny: We can begin by acknowledging that it matters. *You're Welcome.* Retrieved November 27, 2012, from https://yrwelcome.wordpress.com/2012/03/29/adrienne-rich-and-transmisogyny-we-can-begin-by-acknowledging-that-it-matters/

Chapter 17 Trans in Class: Trans Activism in a Suburban School Board

j wallace

For all students in Halton, but with great honour and admiration for the ones who have done and continue to do this work.

In the fall of 2012, the Halton District School Board opened two new high schools, Garth Webb Secondary School in Oakville and Craig Kielburger Secondary School in Milton. Both schools include single-stall all-gender washrooms. Sometimes this is what victory looks like—no fanfare, no mention in the official press releases, but a quiet improvement that means anyone, regardless of their gender identity, their gender history, or their trans status, can go to the bathroom while at school. And still, when I mention this to people outside of Halton, the answer I get is "Really? In Halton?" I've been hearing this response for seven years, and in reply to the doubters, I say the same thing I have consistently said: "Really. In Halton."

I began bothering the Halton District School Board over matters of gender in September of 1984. I was 10, and an avid soccer player. My school in South East Oakville had decided it was too small to support two soccer teams, and come tryout time, they announced tryouts only for the boys' team. I was incensed, and I remember storming angrily into the Physical Education office to complain. We eventually reached a compromise: there would only be one team and it would play in the boys' league, but I could try out for it. I played on the boys' team for two years. I don't remember where I got changed for the games, and I don't remember other teams complaining. I remember only two moments of upset—the first, when I walked onto the field for tryouts, and the second, when I made the team that first year and a number of boys did not. As an adult feminist, I recognize that this solution was imperfect, but as a young person, playing on the boys' team felt absolutely right.

The Halton District School Board is a suburban board, part of the 905 belt around Toronto. It includes the communities of Oakville, Burlington, Milton, Georgetown, and Acton, each of which has strong commuter transportation ties to Toronto but very little inter-community connection. I grew up in Halton, attending schools there from 1979 to 1990, and then, in the way of queers, I left.

In July of 2005 I returned to Halton to work on a partnership between the school board and a local NGO, the Halton Organization for Pride and Education (HOPE). What was originally intended to be an 18-month contract addressing homophobia became seven years of changing school culture and climate around sexual orientation and gender identity.

INVISIBILITY

When I started work in Halton, my supervisor at HOPE had several pieces of advice. The first was "Start in Burlington; they are more ready than the rest of the board" and "Save the north (Georgetown and Acton) for last." When I did start working in the north I was further advised to "Always carry a cell phone" and "Try to be gone before dark." This kind of advice from the only LGBTQ group in the region prompted me to reach out to other service providers. I knew there were other LGBTQ people there, and I wondered what kind of services were available to them. Peer Outreach Support Services & Education (POSSE), a peer-support organization based in Georgetown and Acton, was involved in supporting LGBTQ youth. It also engaged in public advocacy, and after years of requesting that the township fly a flag for Pride week, POSSE staff finally launched a human rights complaint against Halton Hills for their refusal. However, they were the exception—all other service providers I spoke with responded with a variation of "If someone comes out to me, I help them get to Toronto."

The original project entailed bringing together students from all the public high schools in a community, running a 10-week training program with them, and then supporting them as they went on to train the high school staff. In the initial phase, I would introduce the project to area principals and seek ways to inform students about the project. There was some money to provide transportation and snacks, but the actual content of the training program was left entirely up to me. Once students had been recruited, and were coming to meetings, I would go back to the principals and try to get a two-hour block of time in a staff meeting or Professional Development Day for the students to present back to staff.

Despite the Halton District School Board being an official partner on the project, principals were initially reluctant to engage with me or the project. My phone calls were not returned. Repeatedly I was told that there was not much need for this kind of work, as principals were unsure if they had any gay students. One principal I met with demanded to see my Police Background Check and questioned me aggressively: "Why should I give you, a gay man, access to children?" People weren't sure what transphobia was, let alone whether actual trans people existed.

Viviane Namaste writes that "transsexuals and transgendered people are produced though erasure, and … this erasure is organized at a micrological level, in the invisible functions of discourse and rhetoric, the taken for granted practices of institutions, and the unforeseen consequences of social policy" (2000, p. 53). Indeed, the experience of students was one of erasure—from the provincial Trillium student registration system that offers only "male" and "female" options in its "gender" field and requires surgery to change someone's gender, to the lack of bathroom access (Alamenciak & Green, 2012), to pressure on trans students to leave the school system altogether—and schools continued to deny our existence.

Except, we were there. Of six young people attending one of HOPE's youth groups in north Halton, three of them identified as trans.[1] In the fall of 2006, Nicki Ward had signs across Wards 2 and 4 in Milton, asking people to vote for her in the municipal election (Hennessey, 2006). Her signs did not say she was a trans woman, but her slogan, "If we don't manage the change, the change will manage us,' which appeared on all her signs, was a nod to those who knew. While the focus of the project was "homophobia," I immediately included "gender identity and gender expression" in the work.

In December of 2005, I wrote HOPE's first trans rights brochure to accompany one about sexual orientation, and I started taking the conversation public. In the spring of 2006, I opened a presentation at Oakville Trafalgar High School with the line, "I last was at O.T. as a student in 1990—a great deal has changed since then. You've got a whole new school building, and I've got a whole new sex." The students in the group were incredibly committed to the presentations, and patiently responded to questions from teachers about the difference between transgender and transsexual.

Coming out as trans did not actually clarify who I was for people—it simply paved the way for further conversations. Again and again, I had to explain that I was not a gay man who sometimes performed in drag, or even a gay man who wanted to be a woman; I was a queer man who had been a woman. By the spring of 2007, people were clear enough about the existence of trans people that, when the board convened a policy team to update their human rights–related policies, I was asked to join and work on developing a policy on "gender identity and gender expression." The policy was drafted, circulated, commented upon, and shared with other school boards, although it was to remain at the draft stage for years. The policy addressing gender identity and gender expression finally entered officialdom in the fall of 2012 as an Administrative Procedure.[2]

One of the concerns repeatedly expressed to me was that there was zero Canadian data on how many trans students there might be in high schools, and even less about what their experiences might be. When I used US-based data, often from the Gay, Lesbian and Straight Education Network (GLSEN) who biannually survey students across the US, it was often dismissed outright as irrelevant as "Things are different here." In January of 2008, a group of students I was working with in the north of Halton District decided to create their own data. They created a lengthy list of questions and began surveying teachers and students in Acton, Georgetown, and Milton. In under a week they collected 244 completed student surveys and 44 teacher surveys. Three of the students surveyed said they identified as trans—and suddenly we not only had Canadian data, but Halton data. Student reaction on the surveys to the idea of trans students was intense, and the comments included the following:

- "The idea of someone physically changing their body so they can be someone else is stupid to me."
- "I feel that that is a dumb decision to make."
- "How utterly disgusting."
- "You are how you are born and should be proud of your gender."
- "The way they act would be unappealing to me."
- "It's gross."
- "It would be really weird and not normal."
- "Because I think you are born the sex/gender that you were supposed to be born. God made you the way you are."

When teachers were asked what they would do to ensure a trans student had safe access to bathrooms, 61 percent said they would consult an administrator for advice. This last question and response made administrators particularly nervous. When I shared these results with them they looked distinctly worried; they didn't have the answers either, and realized that they needed them. The student researchers concluded that clearly both staff and students needed more education on how to better support trans people in schools.

MAKING CHANGE

One of the things that has always been true is that in order to create a cultural shift, you need strong allies. When the initial Educating Our Educators project was conceived, it was to be only me working with the students, with very little support coming from elsewhere. Immediately upon starting, I had the good fortune of meeting Abi Salole of Community Development Halton. She was inspired by the project and agreed to give me office space at Community Development Halton and to co-facilitate meetings with me. Abi had also grown up in Halton, and had recently completed her Master of Social Work degree research there, specifically in the area of youth activism. Her connections and support proved invaluable. Co-facilitating with Abi not only gave the youth two different sets of experience, but also two facilitators with different identities: Abi identifies as a ciswoman and as a person of colour. We were careful to position the work we were doing within a broader social justice movement. Our first group was considered exceptionally diverse for Halton and included two refugees, two people of colour, a Jewish student, and a person who is deaf.

While in some areas anti-homophobia work has been seen as "a white thing," we were able to quickly overcome that and make it clear to LGBTQ student activists that they needed to be advocates, not only for themselves, but for social justice more broadly. Among other things, this meant that the inclusion of trans issues was already a part of the work and did not depend on trans students being part of the group. This broad commitment to social justice also made it easier to partner with other organizations. For the duration of my time in Halton, one of the strongest partners of the work has been the Halton Multicultural Council, a community-based settlement agency. I trained and worked with their settlement workers annually, which meant the work reached a much broader audience and was much more accessible in schools.

Another significant ally and a steady advocate has been the Halton District School Boards's Equity Coordinator, Suzanne Muir. Suzanne's portfolio includes addressing all equity issues at the board level—she consistently advocated on behalf of LGBT people, hired me for the work, and referred staff to me. Suzanne is also a Muslim woman who wears the hijab, and we found that doing trainings together was very powerful. People were in awe of our working together. We were both interested in addressing social justice broadly, including Islamophobia, homophobia, and transphobia, and the students attending the trainings would model their actions on that. While I'm naming Abi and Suzanne as champions of the project, it is also true that there have been many student, teacher, and administrative champions. Trustee Donna Danielli deserves both honour and recognition for her work at the board level, beginning with ensuring that the students were able to present to trustees in 2008, sharing information about this work and why it was needed, and pushing the board two years in a row to actually fund the work. As much as I sought to be seen as part of the board and as an agent of change from within, many other people contributed to that change. Movements do not consist of one person, and I did none of this alone.

In June of 2007, as the Educating Our Educators project came to a close, we were able to secure three years of funding from the Halton Healthy Community Fund to continue doing anti-homophobia and anti-transphobia work in the schools. This funding allowed for three days of work per week to launch Gay-Straight Alliances (GSA) in all 15 high schools in Halton District. At the time, only one Halton high school had a GSA. At the same time, the nature of my work began to change. When a trans girl in grade 7 identified herself to the school and complained that she was being targeted for harassment by her peers, I was asked by the school board to work with the student, the school, and her community. In addition to doing group projects in partnership, I began doing casework specifically for the board. Part of this was strategic—the more closely I was seen to be "part of the board" by staff, the more what I said and did was seen as credible and as something that staff needed to pay attention to. Also, taking on contract work with the board meant that I had access to a school board email address, which significantly increased the number of people who would respond to my messages and the speed with which they would respond. The responses started to shift too. At the close of a presentation in Oakville, a principal approached me and talked about two "young women who thought they were men. They had a really hard time and neither one of them survived high school." It was part confessional, and part grief for the two young women. He asked me what else he could have done and what else they might have needed, and was willing to make changes in how trans students experienced his school.

One of my strategies for trans education and trans inclusion was to make sure that it was seen as a broader social justice issue and not just part of forming GSAs. The 2008–2009 school year offered a powerful opportunity for me to demonstrate this. Based somewhat on the success of the first "Halton Inside and Out" conference (a conference I had initiated for staff and students who were already involved or wanted to be involved in challenging homophobia and transphobia in schools) in 2007, the school board planned to host a social justice conference on December 11, 2008, called "Making the Change," for students in grades 7–12. I proposed that S. Bear Bergman,[3] a trans person, come and perform hir solo theatre piece *Clearly Marked* as the keynote event for the conference, a proposal that the committee accepted. I circulated Bergman's website, biography, and some of hir writing to the group, and nothing more was said until the Friday before the conference. In *Clearly Marked*, Bergman talks about the labels that are applied to hir, labels that include queer, trans, and Jewish, and about how challenging it can be to get people to see the person behind the labels. The piece is performed by Bergman with the assistance of a local volunteer, in this case, a student I had previously worked with.

The Friday before the conference, Bergman and the student volunteer arrived at the school that was hosting the conference to do a tech rehearsal. I was working elsewhere, but the rest of the planning committee was present. The committee members, who had not paid much attention to the material I had given out earlier, suddenly realized that the word "transgender" was going to be said repeatedly from the stage, and all hell broke loose. They seized the script; there were panicked calls; I was told the show could not be performed as it was "not appropriate." I did what I often did in moments like this: I called the board's Equity Coordinator, Suzanne Muir. Suzanne asked if I thought it was appropriate. When I said yes, Suzanne said, "Tell them I said it's too late to change things; they need to go ahead with it." While I was on the phone with her, the student volunteer was in discussion with the organizing committee, urging them to proceed as planned, and reminding them that "we hear language worse than this in an afterschool special any day of the week—at least let them hear something appropriate."

Ultimately, the performance did go ahead. Near the end of the show, Bergman skips through the audience, asking any boy who has ever cried, any girl who has ever been told she is too angry, anyone who has ever felt constrained by gender roles, to stand up, and like a transgender fairy, Bergman waves hir wand and says "Transgender, transgender, transgender." They all stood up, cheering. They were all moved. Not a single parent complained. This really was a turning moment both for me and my allies on the board. For me, this was a clear lesson that "our communities are more ready than we think" and a direct lesson in not letting educators' fears of parental complaint prevent us from doing our work. For other staff, it was a moment where they confronted their fear of being openly seen advocating for trans people, their worry that this would impact their careers. They pushed through it to find themselves commended for including trans issues. Committee members independently apologized to me, Bergman, and the student volunteer.

TRANS STUDENTS AND TRANS PARENTS

In September of 2009, the GSA work officially moved from HOPE to the school board, from a community organization to inside the institution. This meant that I now had a school board phone number as well as an email address and that the work looked far more official. The most frequent request from schools was for help in supporting individual students. Calls from elementary schools were primarily about children who had been identified as male at birth and were expressing themselves in more feminine ways. Calls from high schools were more broadly about trans students. A significant number were concerned with bathroom access, although students were also looking for access to medical services, and parents were looking for support with name changes. Referrals for support around gender identity and gender expression was the most frequent request to the Equity Office at this time. The first calls were along the lines of "This student has a problem." I knew that we were making a difference when the calls began to be more along the lines of "There's a trans student at our school, and we want to do better at supporting the student."

Many students I worked with reported feeling extremely isolated. We tried offering online groups, but the students were very clear that they actually needed to see each other in person. While there was support from a number of social workers, it was not until June 2012 that we managed to host a one-day conference for trans students called "Being Me." By then, I knew of 11 students in Halton high schools who identified as trans. While the highlight of the day for the students was being able to see and connect with other trans people, they also shared their disturbing school experiences. FTM students said that they had had male students grope their chests while saying things like "This shouldn't bother you if you are a guy," that harassment was commonplace, and that lack of bathroom access led to some trans students dropping out. One student confessed that he left the school to use the bathroom at a nearby community centre. Another reported going to a store that had a single-stall bathroom. Yet another reported going home. Following the conference, I followed up with schools to make sure all students had access to appropriate bathrooms. I toured one school with a principal who had assured me that the school did not have a bathroom that could be made accessible. By the time I arrived for the tour, he had found one.

Requests for support from schools began to include proactive work—in two schools, a parent was transitioning, and the schools requested training for staff and resources for the students. Always, our annual GSA conference included a significant number of trans people (trans women, trans men, and genderqueers) as presenters. After the fourth annual conference, one student told me that he'd been to the trans workshop and felt he could love his cousin again. After the fifth conference, I heard back from a student who had a parent who had transitioned. The only trans person the student had known before the conference was her mom, but by the end of the day, she'd seen six different trans people in leadership roles. When she got back to school, she asked her trans mom to come pick her up there for the first time. Her mother had not entered the building before as a woman, at the student's request. After the conference, the student found she could have her mother come in, and the mother felt welcomed by staff.

GETTING IT ON PAPER AND MAKING IT LAST

In the spring of 2012, the provincial government told all school boards to reduce the number of teachers they employed in non-teaching positions. This was a significant disappointment, as the premier, Dalton McGuinty, had championed himself as "the education premier." While he was premier, the Ministry of Education had released a report called *Shaping a Culture of Respect in Our Schools: Promoting Safe and Healthy Relationships* (Ontario Ministry of Education, 2008). The strategy document *Realizing the Promise of Diversity: Ontario's Equity and Inclusive Education Strategy* (Ontario Ministry of Education, 2009), which detailed equity benchmarks that all school boards in the province were to achieve over four years was also released. And Bill 157, the Educational Amendment Act (Keeping Our Kids Safe at School) was passed in June 2009. However, "the education premier" had decided that equity was not as central to education as those documents and legislation indicated, and there were cuts across the province. In Halton, the entire Equity team was declared to be surplus. While most of the positions were restored before the beginning of the 2012–2013 school year, the GSA position was lost. This was particularly galling as, that spring, the same government had passed laws explicitly stating that boards needed to support students who were interested in addressing transphobia (Bill 13, Accepting Schools Act) (Broten, 2012) and had added "gender identity and gender expression" as protected grounds under the Human Rights Code. The provincial policy framework was stronger than ever, but the people implementing the policy were cut.

While I believe that the differences this work made in the lives of individual students matters, I am also reflecting on what the lasting changes are. In Halton, I left a commitment to having all-gender-inclusive washrooms in schools; books with gender-independent and trans characters in all school libraries; clear procedures on how to support, accommodate, and include trans and gender-independent people in our schools; and a system-wide belief that this is part of social justice—you can't have social justice without trans people. Since I left, the board has been taking the recommendations from the "Being Me" conference seriously. In addition to all-gender bathrooms being included at the planning stage in new buildings, at least two high schools have being retrofitted to include them. Throughout the spring of 2012, I'd worked with staff, students, and parents to improve the *Draft Administrative Procedures: Gender Identity and Gender Expression* that I had first prepared in 2007. I circulated the policy as widely as possible, and ensured that even if it had not been passed, it was being used. Since I left, the Administrative Procedure has been included in the *Inclusive Language Guidelines*. In the fall of 2012, it passed as its own document.

Over the six years, some things got better and some things got done, but it's also very true that the work is not complete. Frequently, I would find myself telling students that they are not receiving the affirmative and celebratory education that they deserve, but that I would work with them to help bring that about, and that the skills they would learn in that work would be valuable to them their whole lives. It's absolutely true, and it's also a cop-out. Education is a steady stream of daily acts and individual moments, and as long as teachers are still starting their classes with "Good morning, boys and girls," there is work to be done. The dual goals that gender-independent children and trans children be celebrated in schools and that no learner be limited because of their sex or gender are still a long way off.

Looking ahead, it's difficult to determine what kind of advocacy path Halton will have for the next five years. I can see the moment shimmering on the horizon when gender-independent and trans students are a celebrated part of school populations, but it's very much a work in progress. The 2012–2013 school year has been a difficult one for student activities as a result of government-imposed contracts with teachers, and union job action that has meant no student activities for the majority of the year. When students heard that the GSA conference, "Halton Inside and Out," would not be held, they petitioned to get access to the funds earmarked for the conference and ran it themselves. They invited me to give the closing keynote address and included two other trans people as presenters. The "Being Me" conference was held for a second time, and two trans people from outside the board were hired to facilitate the day for students. Students are finding ways to continue the work.

As has been pointed out more than once by my colleagues, trans students in Halton started coming out in school once the school culture around homophobia and transphobia had shifted enough in their direction. While there is still much to be done, I'm buoyed by the fact that moving toward a more positive school culture made it safe for some very brave gender-independent and trans people to be visible, and that they—in their turn—will pave the way for even more trans students, faculty, and staff. I remain deeply hopeful that the board will continue to provide the training, physical spaces, and resources needed for this.

NOTES

1 Logan, Marcus. (2005, September). Halton Organization for Pride and Education (HOPE). Board report.

2 An Administrative Procedure is a board-approved procedure that directs how staff should address an issue. Administrative Procedures (APs) are approved by Administrative Council (all superintendents and the director of the board). Policy must be approved by the Board of Trustees, and the trustees are generally more conservative than Administrative Council.

3 For further reading, please see Bergman, S. Bear. (2009). *The Nearest Exit May Be Behind You*. Vancouver: Arsenal Pulp Press; and Bergman, S. Bear. (2010). *Butch Is a Noun*. Vancouver: Arsenal Pulp Press. Also see Bergman's website at http://sbearbergman.com

REFERENCES

Alamenciak, T., & Green, J. (2012, November 13). Transgendered student denied access to men's washroom. *Toronto Star*. Retrieved from www.thestar.com/news/gta/article/2012/11/13/transgendered_student_denied_access_to_mens_washroom.html

Broten, Hon. L.C. (2012). Bill 13: An act to amend the Education Act with respect to bullying and other matters. Retrieved from www.ontla.on.ca/web/bills/bills_detail.do?locale=en&Intranet=&BillID=2549

Hennessey, M. (2006, October 10). Candidate wants to shake things up a little at council. *Inside Halton*. Retrieved from www.insidehalton.com/print/423324

Namaste, V. (2000). *Invisible lives: The erasure of transsexual and transgendered people*. Chicago: University of Chicago Press.

Ontario Ministry of Education. (2008, December 11). *Shaping a culture of respect in our schools: Promoting safe and healthy relationships.* Safe Schools Action Team Report on gender-based violence, homophobia, sexual harassment, and inappropriate sexual behaviour in schools. Retrieved from www.edu.gov.on.ca/eng/teachers/RespectCulture.pdf

Ontario Ministry of Education. (2009). *Realizing the promise of diversity: Ontario's Equity and Inclusive Education Strategy.* Retrieved from http://edu.gov.on.ca/eng/policyfunding/equity.pdf

Chapter 18 A Very Brief Discussion of Social Work and Gender[1]

Treanor Mahood-Greer

INTRODUCTION

In 2002 I lost my job. At the time, I worked as a therapist in the violence against women program at a feminist counselling centre in Northern Ontario. It was within this space, dedicated to challenging various forms of gender-based violence, that I was targeted. I wondered why social workers occupying managerial positions believed they could harass me, and why my co-workers who supported me from the sidelines never addressed the harassment that resulted in my job loss. I realized that my experience was not unique, given the multiple problems that many trans people face on a daily basis. This led me to question whether the attitudes of my managers and co-workers were similar to other social workers' conceptualizations of gender. Given the significant role social workers play in the lives of their clients, their understandings of gender will either legitimize the oppression of transgender/transsexual (TG/TS)[2] people and subjugate them further, or aid in empowering them.

In this chapter, I present a brief discussion of social workers' conceptualizations of gender and the therapeutic relationship that they may or may not have with TG/TS people in Northern Ontario. This discussion is informed by my experiences as a trans-identified individual, my graduate studies in social work, and conversations I have had with cisgender colleagues concerning my gender identity, as well as other embodied gender identities. These conversations revealed significant unfamiliarity with non-normative expressions of gender, which leads my cisgender colleagues to ignore gender issues or to merely "tolerate" trans people. I argue that this inadequate response shapes the calibre of non-normatively gendered people's experiences when attempting to access social work services. I hope this chapter will encourage those in the helping fields to reconceptualize gender to better assist trans clients.

REVIEW OF THE LITERATURE

The bulk of the scholarly literature with which social work students engage reinforces the sex and gender binary based on the categorical separation between men/women and masculinity/femininity affixed to each respectively. There is no allowance for other gendered possibilities within this governing system (Ekins & King, 1997; Namaste, 2000).

Furthermore, feminist research comparing differences between men and women (Harder, 1999; Lynn & Todoroff, 1998) tends to document women's experiences of workplace discrimination and harassment and inequality within broader society. Research focusing solely on women's rights cannot address the ways being trans impacts our efforts to attain or maintain employment, as well as to access social services. As a trans man, my workplace harassment and subsequent job loss was due to problematic responses to my self-determined transgender identity.

When other gender performances, such as those of butches or masculine females, are acknowledged within social work curriculum, these subjects are often referred to as "she" or "butch women"; rarely are they comprehended in terms of another gender (Rifkin, 2002). TG/TS people continue to be silenced and their daily experiences are erased (Israel & Tarver, 1997; Namaste, 2000). This does not bode well for creating trans positive social services (Carroll, Gilroy, & Ryan, 2002; Mallon, 1999a, 1999b, 1999d; Pazos, 1999; Raj, 2002; Wilchins, 2004).

Clearly, social work commentary needs to reconceptualize gender as a power relation to better reflect how forms of trans oppression emerge and are manifest. Gender needs to be broadened to include embodied identities that transgress dichotomous knowledge. Enriching social workers' knowledge of gender will enable them to recognize violence inherent within binary notions of gender that negatively impacts both trans and cisgender people.

I approach notions of "transphobia" or "genderphobia" as terms reflective of a broader analysis (Califia, 1997) used to critique homophobia. "Homophobia" refers to socially constructed discriminatory practices against gay, lesbian, and bisexual people to maintain "hegemonic heterosexism" as a social relation (Kinsman, 1994). It is problematic to define sexual- and gender-based oppression as a phobia because such conceptualizations individualize people's fears regarding difference. Furthermore, phobia locates such variance within the individual, thereby pathologizing their identities and experiences instead of acknowledging them as erased by governing systemic gendered discourses.[3] When oppression is viewed as a personal problem, it hides from public view the ideological matrices and ruling apparatuses that lie beneath gender (Kinsman, 1994; Namaste, 2000).

If social workers fail to grasp how genderism impacts everyone's lived experience, then they will continue to impede change in trans people's lives, which is what happens when social workers fail to acknowledge the lived experiences of trans people. There needs to be a personal and professional motivation amongst social work students, as well as those working within the field, to reconceptualize gender, to illuminate the functioning of hegemonic gendered regulations, and also to challenge the discursive practices that legitimize genderism.

RESEARCH METHODS

My research framework consists of feminist research methodologies, trans theories, and qualitative grounded theoretical methods that recognize the impact that race, gender, class, and sexuality have on the formation of gender-based subjectivities (Cromwell, 1999; Fonow & Cook, 1991) and allow for participant experience (Berg, 2001; Cresswell, 1994). I used a reflexive approach (Hertz, 1997), so my trans experience and standpoint as a researcher (Berg, 2001; Kirby & McKenna, 1989) could engender social workers' understanding of the lives of TG/TS people.

Participant selection was carried out by purposive sampling that is consistent with grounded theory (Cresswell, 1994; Kirby & McKenna, 1989). I interviewed eight social workers, and I required them to have, at minimum, a BSW, but six also had an MSW. All were practising in a variety of social work services, such as a private practice, addiction clinics, community mental health, community education, psychiatric services, general counselling, and violence against women. They worked as a private counsellor, a case manager, a supervisor, a manager, and an executive director, and all worked with individuals, couples, and families. The participants were between the ages of 40 and 60 years with multifarious practical knowledge. Two participants were francophone, two identified as lesbian, four as heterosexual or straight, and two did not identify or clarify their sexuality. They either responded to an invitation sent to agencies to recruit potential participants or heard about the research through word of mouth. It should also be noted that one participant identified as Anishinaabe (Ojibwe) and the others identified as white, which is consistent with the demographic composition of Northeastern Ontario: largely white with a significant indigenous population.[4] It should be noted that none of them self-identified as TG/TS as some did not reference their gender while others gave themselves an individual gender self-identification, such as "unique." I conducted one-hour semi-structured interviews to enable spontaneous questions and more open discussion concerning the participant's understanding of gender variance, the experiences of TG/TS people, and how they applied such understandings to their social work praxis.

CONCEPTUALIZING GENDER AND TG/TS PEOPLE

The participants mainly conceptualized gender as only male or female, despite thinking that people create their "own gender." Participants described gender as being like a soup, with different processes comprising the base. One individual explained: "I think gender is formed and then starts changing the minute it is ... whether it fits or not." One participant felt gender was formed through parental authority: "What are the parents' expectations of you, right? And societal authority—and then, how you act and behave in society in general." Others thought it was constructed through biological and societal factors: "It's part biological, and part how you're socialized by the family ... and if you're born a boy, you play with trucks."

For some research subjects, biology stood as the "real" aspect of gender, rendering it unchangeable or at least hard to change. The social aspect of gender was less real, a part that is changeable by either outside or internal influences. For others, a cultural ingredient was added to the bio/social soup: "We are also assigned gender based on the environment around us. And it depends on who is around you and what cultural impacts are influencing the people around you ... gender is going to shift accordingly." So gender is understood as a phenomenon formed out of biological features and then congealed by social and cultural factors.

Social workers participating in the study struggled to discuss gender beyond the binary. They also confused gender practices with gender identity. They recognized the existence of different genders; however, they could not identify them. Similarly, participants reported knowing transsexuals but could not address the specificity of transsexual identities, issues, or experiences. When they spoke of personal experiences interacting with trans individuals, they often mislabelled their gender identities as being gay or lesbian.

Research participants tended to find it much easier to identify their own gender than explain their performance or embodied expression of gender. One individual explained: "Well, I know I'm female, I guess, you know.... I guess I have a lot of ... I don't even know how to explain this. I mean I don't see myself as being a very feminine woman." She said "I'm a woman" because she related her gender to how she feels. However, as she conceptualized gender her thoughts were muddled, which echoed the confused and roundabout responses provided by most participants. For instance, one interview subject explained:

> If you start from the biological framework, then you are going to go down the road of describing gender in very clean lines … [F]rom a cultural or social perspective, then, you may lead to something different. I see gender … um … on a continuum and on that continuum are many … are many sides to gender or many types of gender demonstrations. So I don't know how I would define gender, other than to say that it is not a clear-cut concept.… [O]bviously gender on the one side is formed biologically so that at birth you are assigned by … um … by nature. You are assigned a particular gender, and then … um … that may shift over time.… Um, so what was the question?

The minimalization of one's gender stems from the practice of seeing the "person first," which is one of the principles of social work. So someone's gender is only important if the client presents it as problematic. Some participants attempted to imagine a gender alternative beyond the binary: "Some person who doesn't really identify with either/or, and they're androgynous. You know, they're just a neutral." When the participants lacked words to describe plural gender identities, they resorted to familiar descriptors such as "he looks like a she"; furthermore, any gender expressions they identified in terms of "neutrality" were curiously still framed as male or female. As they discussed gender, they would mix up ideas and put them into a pattern that made sense to them but misrepresented a trans positive notion of gender (e.g., "a man dressed in women's clothes"). This pattern is problematic for anyone who might seek counsel from a social worker concerning trans-related issues. The ways in which their comprehension of gender remains unchallenged reveals how gender as a ruling relation is legitimized through interactions between social workers, who occupy a position of power, and their clients, who are more vulnerable.

Some of the participants recognized their fallibility by acknowledging that a barrier of misinformation existed between themselves and trans people. One participant spoke honestly about making a past reference to a "guy in a dress." I asked if they would make that kind of comment again and received the following response:

> Well, I'm not sure I wouldn't [say "Who's the guy in the dress?"].… [I] hope that I would have a different language than that. If it looks, if the individual looks male and is wearing a dress, I'm really not convinced that I would have other language in my head. I may not use it … I understand the individual can be trans, and I understand that there can be cross-dressing issues.… You don't see the guy in the dress in terms of your first immediate thought? See, I do.

Once again, knowledge about TG/TS people or their issues does not guarantee that specific trans identities and expressions will not be erased. Social workers have to continuously work to deepen the ways they conceptualize gender and apply it to TG/TS people.

Other social workers were so accustomed to gender difference that they failed to acknowledge it. In their attempts to recognize "the person" first, they framed gender variance as unimportant. One can critique this main principle of social work vis-à-vis working with trans clients in our contemporary context in two ways. First, client-centred approaches can limit social workers' ability to address every issue. As identified in my research, there is an institutional ordering of agencies, and this ordering constricts social workers' everyday practices. Social workers often work through their client's most current issue or the one that can be solved the quickest. Given these restrictions, social workers often fail to address gender identity and oppression as they see gender as unrelated to issues of placement within shelters, obtaining job training, or counselling. Second, the desire not to offend their clients often renders social workers silent regarding gender identity. One participant spoke of the awkwardness they felt when they recognized someone they believe to be a trans person: "Why is it not important to not notice them? Well, I think that it's a [matter of] comfort level ... something that, you know, I don't feel uncomfortable with them, [to] be staring at them and noticing them." A few participants spoke about not wanting to hurt or embarrass their clients.

While both these issues are important—and will not be remedied through judging social workers—my experience has revealed that the all-encompassing nature of gender, and the way it is embedded, presents challenges that may seem altogether unrelated to gender. All aspects of our lives as trans people are mediated through sex and gender variance; therefore, trans identities and experiences must be incorporated into the commitment of social workers putting the person first.

GENDER IN PRACTICE

The social worker's knowledge of gender, the way such understandings are incorporated into the therapeutic frameworks that guide their practice, and how such understandings influence their attitudes toward gender expression in the workplace are all important when considering ways to address the impact that current social work practice has on trans people and to develop trans positive therapeutic practices and services. Trans and sexuality studies literature on trans embodiment and oppression has not transferred successfully to social work programs and non-academic sites. One participant spoke of receiving limited anti-oppression training, while another, when asked about trans education, noted that "we didn't even learn about gays or lesbians!" As a result of this void in social work education and subsequent training, practitioners had no proper language to discuss trans people as embodied subjects; instead, many participants consistently misused terminology when referring to TG/TS people. Other participants' discomfort around offending clients prevented them from gaining knowledge through inquiring about issues related to gender identity, such as what terms or pronouns service users preferred:

> *Participant*: I think I would try to avoid using a pronoun to him/her. If I was talking about this person to someone else and that person was there, I would go "Marla, Marla." Yeah, I would try and avoid using a pronoun.
>
> *Interviewer*: Would you not just ask her how she would like to be referred to?
>
> *Participant*: That would not occur to me.[5]

Additionally, the participants revealed the need for education so they could recognize differences between trans identities and experiences. Their therapeutic framework has to be pliable enough to address this distinction.

FRAMEWORK FOR PRACTICE

The frameworks guiding participants' social work practice in Northeastern Ontario were rooted in feminist perspective or eclectic approaches based in empowerment, eco-feminism, cognitive behavioural theory, systems theory, and solution-focused and/or harm reduction models. While many participants were unfamiliar with trans theory, they believed their feminist politics could enable the development of trans positive approaches to serving clients. Others spoke about the ways indigenous philosophies and teachings can enrich social work praxis. Furthermore, all participants believed they could engender change for trans-identified clients when starting from the client's perspective. In addition to their theoretical frameworks, participants thought that their skills were sufficient to serve trans clients.

However, when social workers are working with trans people, they need to do more than just address service users' social locations and the specific issues, needs, or wants that the trans client might identify to the social worker. While feminist and indigenous perspectives are indeed useful, social workers must acquire trans-specific theoretical knowledge as well. Such working knowledge of trans identities and oppression will enable them to anticipate structural and political obstacles that trans people may encounter and intervene on their behalf when necessary. It is also crucial for service providers to have the knowledge and experience of working with trans people in positive spaces so that together they can challenge barriers to gender self-determination.

INCORPORATING OR EXCLUDING GENDER PERSPECTIVES IN PRACTICE

Results of my study showed that when social workers' personal perspectives become intertwined with their therapeutic practice, they could not separate out their personal beliefs. For example, one social worker explained how they would work with a trans client and would relate to them as either male or female, depending upon their interpretation of the service user's presentation:

> *Interviewer*: But if this person can pass as a woman—"Hi, my name is Sally." Would they become a woman then?
>
> *Participant*: Only in my perception.

This social worker's gender perspective remains unchanged, so a male-bodied person identifying as a trans woman might be perceived as a woman but conceptualized as male. Contrary to their client-centred approach, some participants made their client's gender problematic even if the client did not identify it as such. One social worker shared how they would help a male-bodied person with a drinking problem who says in session that s/he wears women's clothes: "I would effectively investigate how that is impacting on them. You know, what function does this serve for you? How long have you been doing, behaving, in that way?" The service provider's questions related to the clothing their client said they sometimes wear and not to the problem of alcohol abuse.

Questions such as "How long have you been drinking?" or perhaps "Is there a relationship between the drinking and the stigma a male-bodied person who wears a dress might face?" are not posed. The chosen line of questioning impacts the direction this social worker will take by concentrating on the biological properties of sex rather than on alcohol consumption—the concern for which the client sought counsel. This participant's reaction appears to come, at best, from a place of curiosity concerning gender-variant identity rather than an approach of harm reduction or of working to ascertain appropriate services for their clients.

One participant who felt it was important to figure out their client's gendered past spoke of a discourse that erases trans people's narratives of their gender identity: "I think I can tell what anatomy they ... possess under their clothes.... I don't know if it is some false notion that I have in my head that, if I saw an individual whom I might label androgynous, I could tell whether they have male or female physiology—if it wasn't obvious." Why does this social worker believe is it important to have intimate knowledge of their client's anatomy? The quote above signals the cisgender entitlements that service providers often exude when working with trans clients. The notion that they can detect one's anatomy reproduces the notion of trans people as dishonest and deserving of scrutiny. This participant is indicating that they are on guard to spot a "phoney." Other participants admitted to similar types of surveillance: "I remember once I followed a trans person to see which washroom [they] used. That was many years ago, and now I realize the washroom one chooses to use does not indicate their gender anyhow."

Rather than playing guessing games regarding which washroom a trans person might use, it is more critical for social workers to understand the dangers that trans people face, which include interacting with service providers. This is especially the case for those who cannot "pass"[6] as men or women. Some participants provided indications of more trans positive approaches to service delivery. One social worker discussed a more open way to approach work with trans clients: "I see myself as an empathetic listener. [I want] to see where the person wants to go and what's stopping them from going where they need to." An awareness of trans people's everyday practices to become visible is an excellent start to honing such an approach. As social workers explore what prevents many trans people from accessing care and services necessary to transition, they can begin to strengthen their practice as allies who can easily identify and explain the obstacles their client might face and follow through with interventions and solutions.

WORKING WITHIN THE CONSTRAINTS OF THE WORKPLACE

Many spaces are inaccessible to trans people due to workplace constraints, policies, or the attitudes of service providers. Social services as employers or community organizations either outright exclude trans people or do so through the erroneous assumption that TG/TS people are included by default because the doors are open to serve the public. My research indicated that social workers' level of comfort regarding being able to work with gender-variant people is influenced by the policies held by the organization with which they are employed. Other participants noted that there were no official trans policies, which left them to figure out their own approach: "I'm not sure how. I think it just flows in a conversation and I always try to have respect ... so I got this kind of, I'm always open, but I wouldn't know. There's no rule. There are no guidelines."

There *are* guidelines for working with TG/TS people (Cooper, 1999; Mallon, 1999c; Pazos, 1999; Raj, 2002), many of which are influenced by anti-oppression models (Bishop, 1994) and other approaches to popular education that help people to unlearn gender (Arnold et al., 1991; Graveline, 1998). Such critical frameworks and approaches are easily adaptable; however, education and organizational commitment are required.

In addition to the presence or absence of trans policies, participants spoke about having to follow the mandate of their program. Many attempted to provide services to demographics that fell outside organizational or program mandates. One participant spoke about the difficulty of gradually trying to introduce a solution-focused therapy model into their practice, let alone include a whole new clientele. Social workers "hands are often tied" concerning what kind of models they can bring into practice due to organizational cultures and policies.

Some participants used feminist models that erase the gender identities of TG/TS people or exclude people on the basis of their "biological" gender or childhood gender, as is the case with women's shelters or a treatment centres for men. Erasing gender identity most often comes through misnaming trans identities (Namaste, 2000). Intake forms represent one way that the erasure of trans identities manifests itself concretely. Trans clients who identify as male/female or man/woman will want to check off M/F boxes; however, this is not the case for all trans-identified people. For others, the need to be acknowledged will not be recognized on forms that legitimize the gender binary. One participant discusses registering a client in their intake system as a male despite there being an opportunity to record their identification as transgender:

> *Interviewer*: Would you not have checked off the transgender section?
>
> *Participant*: Um, no. I checked off male.
>
> *Interviewer*: Checked off male?
>
> *Participant*: Because he presented with a male name.
>
> *Interviewer*: So if this person walked in and said, "Hi, I'm Jane"?
>
> *Participant*: Then I would probably check off female.

This erasure, social in nature, legitimizes dominant knowledge of gender within the workplace. Such narrow approaches to intake forms—one of the most common tools used within these particular workplaces—reproduce limited understandings of gender. Subsequently, our access to statistics regarding sex and gender alternatives that could potentially be gathered from intake forms is significantly restricted. Another participant addressed how the lack of recognition of transgender issues excludes trans people because it fails to provide proper referral resources to support gender-variant clients. In one particular case, one of the social workers with limited experience tried to admit a MTF into an addiction treatment centre, but problems arose because their organization did not recognize the client's trans identification:[7]

> [For] example, the client I had ... I couldn't put [the client] into the woman's detox because [they said] "It's a he." It's not a he, it's a she! And it's a she, and this is her name, and she should be [in the women's treatment group], not [the men's group]! How is she going to react with all those men? She is a woman. She told me so. I treat her like a woman. I offered her [women's detox and treatment], and I couldn't even get her the service.

In Northeastern Ontario, we lack resources for gender-variant clients. This dearth causes some social workers to work subversively around the rules to allow special cases to access services. As the facilitators of a group or treatment program, we can break the rules and sneak in trans people. This, of course, is a temporary and inadequate solution. This process requires a lot of work because one cannot sidestep agency rules all the time. Other group members have to be educated and have to agree to allow the "special case." This process also puts a negative or deviant slant on the participant who is "sneaking in." They become the "special case" who has gained access through the *consent* of those in power. The political and organized way genderism is maintained is not recognized in social work by clients, social workers, or the organizations for which they work.

Another problematic agency rule relates to public washroom usage. Problems often arise when clients are directed to the washroom that is presumed "proper." All but one participant reported handling this situation by being very evasive. They usually left the decision to the gender-variant client. This response was common: "I would just say 'Over there,' and let them choose [laughing]." The laughter is evidence of the awkwardness of such a strategy. Another social worker explained how they would direct questions concerning the location of the washroom and implied gender meaning on the trans person: "I would point generally." The rest of my research participants had an easy way out because the washrooms were either side by side, or they had only single-use washrooms, which are often assumed to be gender-neutral. They believed they were off the hook because it was not an issue for them, but ironically they never considered how control over bathroom access functions as a form of social regulation. Such social norms create a daily terrain of danger that trans people have to navigate, and those norms become reflected in the norms of the agency.[8] One participant felt washroom use was a non-issue and provided a very simple answer when questioned about the subject: "Where does society stand on that? ... [M]y guess is that even if you are in a dress, you are a man, [and] you use the men's washroom." This participant could not bring their understanding of a trans identity into practice despite noting earlier in their interview that an MTF should be seen as a woman. However, their response to the washroom question, "Even if you are in a dress, you are a man," did not put that belief into practice. Who decides if the person in a dress is a man? The person who is wearing the dress, the person ahead of them in the washroom, the other person about to follow them into the washroom, or the person passing by?

CONCLUSIONS AND RECOMMENDATIONS

My research project investigated two matters of gender: how a group of social workers personally conceptualized gender, and how they incorporated that understanding of gender into their practice. Based on the eight participants working in a variety of social work practices in Northeastern Ontario, I conclude that there is a direct relationship between their personal understanding of gender and the application of that conceptualization to their practice, which is also affected by the institutional barriers put forth by the lack of administrative and programming policies. I found most of the participants understood gender as a binary of male and female components that led to the erasure and exclusion of differently gendered people in their practice. It seemed their understanding of trans issues came from personal experience rather than from what they had learned as social workers. I also discovered that they often confused gender variance with sexual orientation.

Over the course of my study, it became apparent that it is important to have knowledge about trans theory, especially theorizations of trans identities, and to be able to apply such knowledge within social work practice. A lack of knowledge equals, in significant part, a lack of language, and this impedes social workers from developing mutually beneficial relationships with TG/TS clients. Problems with knowledge transfer and with terminology become intertwined in the relationship between social workers and their agency. Like the children's game "Simon Says," the participants demonstrated that if their agency does not recognize trans identities and experiences as valid by providing trans positive services, the participants most often lacked the motivation to make a change in their everyday practice. If they tried to initiate change in the absence of organizational policies and mandates, they risked being disciplined. One interview subject shared her experience of allowing a transsexual woman to join a group she was facilitating in the absence of a trans inclusion policy: "She came to my group, though. I made sure she was able to. They kind of, they told me, they didn't slap me too hard, because I was new."

The lack of, or limited, trans positive workplace education that participants received is linked significantly to whether or not they incorporated gender diversity into their practice. Social workers have a false perception that they can separate themselves from their practice. Most thought they could help a trans client because they were starting from the client's perspective and they had the right skills to effect change for a gender-variant client. Clearly, these participants could not separate their personal ideas of gender from their practice. This was demonstrated by my purposeful use of stereotypical images of what TG/TS people are presumed to look like because they are "visible" in Northeastern Ontario. An MTF trans person who looks like singer Adele or any other woman who embodies normative standards of beauty within Western society will never be seen as a "guy in a dress." This is not the case for many others, whose gender expression does not adhere to the racialized, ableist, and heterosexist standards of beauty that produce what it means to be feminine within contemporary Canadian society. So when one participant personally felt there was a third gender of "neuter" (a term they culled from the dictionary), they "neutered" any trans identification in their practice by not acknowledging or validating someone's gender identity or by not giving them permission to be the gender they believed they were.

The participants felt, erroneously so in my estimation, that their agencies were relatively trans positive because they occasionally provided services to transgender or transsexual clients. In addition, if they thought trans people had a right to services, they believed they could engender trans positive workplace changes regardless of agency norms or policies. In fact, many participants assumed they had gender positive policies: "I think that we probably, um, ...[we've] got very liberal policies, you know." It is important to note that liberal policies or even feminist polices are not equivalent to trans positive policies. Managers who participated in my study knew their organizations lacked trans positive policies, whereas the non-managerial participants did not. If social workers are the front-line gatekeepers for trans people who access services, managers have to be the gatekeepers to either help shift or maintain the organizational culture (Mallon, 1999b). Managers are the policy-keepers, as they mind the budget and the keys to the front door.

This research demonstrated that cisgender social workers have only a minimal understanding of genderism and of the social location of gender in their organizations. They were unfamiliar with the methods TG/TS people use to negotiate services, such as navigating publicly funded health care with an OHIP card that has the "wrong" gender marker on it. Making changes to implement trans positive options for practice can, of course, cost money and take time. However, making changes can be reasonable, and the implementation will vary with what an agency tries to do.

Some recommendations for change include gender sensitivity training for board members and staff, as well as clinical education to develop transgender affirmation when working with TG/TS people. Strategies could also be developed to build bridges between the cisgender and trans communities, such as language in the collective agreement to define TG/TS expression, transsexual transition status, and gender identity, which could encourage the hiring of TG/TS staff. Agencies could also support and encourage the usage of proper pronouns (depending on how trans people wish to be identified) when referring to TG/TS clients or staff. By supporting the hiring of trans workers, managers would ensure a safe space for trans clients. All of this combined would contribute to zero tolerance for genderism and heterosexism. It is recognized that there are problems with this particular dream list, because in Northeastern Ontario, not all trans people feel safe to come out or they do not identify as trans—they are "men and women." It is important to note that gender-variant people who are "seen" in social work settings are really the ones that "don't pass." None of the participants recognized that they could be helping men or women who have a trans-identified history, and because they are invisible, they are off the social workers' "trans radar." This would also apply to employees who are "invisible" and not out about their trans history, who wouldn't stand up and say they want to be recognized as a visible trans worker. For example, although I have been told there are trans people working where I do, they are not out to me nor do they represent themselves as the token or visible trans ambassador of the hospital.

Finally, agencies should guarantee safe restrooms for all people to use when accessing social work services. In my previous place of employment, I was told to use the "handicap" washroom, a single-room toilet facility with a disabled sticker on the door. The intention was to prevent women from seeing "a man" in "their" washroom, but also to keep me out of the men's washroom. All the participants' agreed that a TG/TS person could use a disabled washroom. They also believed that it was acceptable to simply point and let gender-variant clients pick their washroom. This will prove to be ineffective when someone in the washroom tells them they are in the "wrong" one. Social service agencies need to develop policies to support the spirit of a trans positive space. Adding trans positive signs/stickers on the doors of the washrooms would desegregate the social location of toilets from "Men/Women" only. This would encourage TG/TS people to use the restroom of their choice but also normalize their use for cisgender people. They could also distribute trans positive educational flyers or posters throughout the centre to demonstrate a genuine commitment to trans inclusion.

As a last recommendation, TG/TS people need to voice their identities. Namaste (2000) reports that there is a lot of research on the whys of transsexualism and transgenderism, but very little information on how trans people live their everyday lives. Further research should ask how TG/TS people operate in Northeastern Ontario with such a lack of services. For example, let's say I'm having relationship problems with my wife, and we decide we need marriage counselling. Well, I am sure that what we will want to talk about will be totally different from my cisgender neighbours. However, the counsellor that we will go to see will be expecting us to be like other heterosexual couples. It is important to know where these particular trans people go for help and what kind of help they are seeking. These are important matters that need to be considered. In order to deconstruct the bulwark of gender, we need to break it down and open up ranges of political possibilities to facilitate changes. This can be done in large part through dialogue about how the professional helping services provide and limit services and how transgender and transsexual people live their lives. By doing that, we can all work together to find common ground on which to stand to fight gender oppression.

NOTES

1 This paper is a brief summary of my 2008–2009 Master of Social Work thesis, *De-constructing the bulwark of gender: Social work practices and gender variance in Northeastern Ontario*. Laurentian University, Sudbury, Ontario. It is available at the Laurentian University J.N. Desmarais Library, call number M. ESS. MAHO 2007.

2 "Transgender/transsexual" (TG/TS) or "transgenderist/transgenderous" or "trans persons/trans people," "trans," or "gender variant," or "gender queer" are all terms that represent the amalgamation of a variety of non-conforming gender possibilities that are located outside the notion of a binary gender system. It is important to note that these categories are constantly changing and cannot be applied to all people, all of the time. In addition, the attempt to use the umbrella term of "transgender" can be very problematic for some transsexual people, because the word does not incorporate the living relationships between sex and gender (Green, 2004; Namaste, 2000). Transsexuals state that they are not changing their gender, but their bodied sex (Kotula, 2002). The term "transgender" was originally a catch-all term (Stryker, 1998), but it should be used simultaneously with transsexual to recognize similarities and differences between these groups. Despite all attempts to be inclusive, language practices limit our ability to define ourselves, so we are left with problematic terms that narrow the scope of people's understanding of their identity and their vision of gender. However, this chapter is not about transgender or transsexual people; rather, it is about anyone who is gender variant and who has a gender expression or presentation that puts them outside the notions of the binary of male and female, man and woman, whether they identify as trans or not. It includes male-to-female transsexuals—as well as the bearded lady who identifies as a woman—and it includes women who identify as women, regardless of a trans history. Since this is a "brief" discussion, I am trusting that the limitations of our language will not silence our diversity.

3 Gender discourses are mediated and objectified on paper; these texts are not how gender occurs in the everyday world. Consequently social workers may take them as truth and apply that knowledge to transgender and transsexual people. Gender is much more subjective. A method of deciphering that knowledge is to listen to the words of transgendered and transsexual people (see Smith, 1991).

4 This is similarly reflected in the demographics of social workers in Northeastern Ontario, as racism and colonialism ensure that all of the social workers I know are white and only a few are Native or African-Canadian, Asian, or disabled. Racial or disabled social workers remained unidentified or declined to participate in this research.

5 According to Audre Lorde (1984), that is an evasion of responsibility by the dominant people who do not learn about and make change for the oppressed group.

6 Passing is a discursive practice that is complex and organized, and conceptualized in many different ways. Generally, passing is the attempt by a member of one group, such as one gender identity or sexual orientation, to be assumed by others to be a member of another group, or the other gender or sexual orientation. Passing is one part of the regulated acts of gender imperialism. For example, I have heard (and I acknowledge that I have used it as well) the term used about women who do not "look like lesbians." For example, lesbians who have long hair and wear makeup and dresses are said to be passing as

heterosexual women, but actually it is their gender marking their visibility. They are accused of passing as heterosexual women because they are seen as trying to avoid the discrimination that "the visible"—to be read as those who are "butches" or "dykes"—lesbians face, rather than seeing them as lesbians who like to look "pretty" and "feminine." This is certainly a suppressive discursive practice that is used against femme lesbians, lipstick lesbians, and bisexual women to enforce the binary constructions of sexuality. The oppression that people who "pass" face demonstrates the colonialistic nature of gender oppression; this is relevant to all those who are "caught" trying to pass because they are often beaten, tortured, or killed. Gender oppression can affect anyone, even those who do not have a gender-variant expression, because they cannot be themselves and are pathologized and discriminated against because of their own self-identity and gender expression. Another example is the actress Dot Jones, who plays Coach Shannon on the *Glee* television series. Dot's gender expression and the biological features that she has been "given" make her life complicated, as reflected in her character of Coach Shannon. She identifies as a woman, but is often harassed as being a man.

The dualistic subjugation of gender passing is reflected in the way it is practised and constructed by transgender or transsexual people who attempt to pass or succeed in passing as the opposite gender. Someone with an assigned female gender at birth may be able to "pass" as an adult male. This creates a hierarchy of oppression as those TG/TS people who cannot pass experience more discrimination by cisgender persons, and the TG/TS community often devalues their gendered status. In other words, many transgender or transsexual people who were assigned a male gender at birth have physiological structures that would not fall within the stereotypical physiological categories of their desired gender. The consequence of this is that they might always look like "a man in women's clothes," and their physiological makeup denies or erases their experience of having their transgender embodiment acknowledged. Passing, assimilation, and "stealth" can be synonymous. If someone can pass completely, with very little intervention, they are said to be "in stealth mode." Many transgender/transsexual people who can pass are "coming out" as transgender. Some within the transgender or transsexual communities are beginning to recognize how their cultural identity has been lost by their assimilation into the binary gender system. However, some transgender and transsexual people who have struggled hard to accept their true gender feel that the binary gender system is essential for their self-determination. So, in the case of this research, the social workers are only giving identity to those who are not passing. The discussion will continue.

7 Organizations are organized and managed, not just for saving or making money, but to control ideological practices. So, in the example of social workers trying to introduce transgender or transsexual issues into their practice, if the agency does not want to spend money, or if they are genderist to trans people (like my former place of employment), they will encourage an official discourse of silence or ignorance of trans people. The way an agency is institutionally organized will obviously influence the staff, so they too will remain silent or ignore transgender or transsexual people and trans issues. And if they do know about trans issues, the official discourse of the agency will direct them from behind the curtain to keep quiet (see also O'Brien, 1999).

8 The norms of the agency are discussed by Dorothy Smith (1991). I find Smith's definition represents an accurate picture of the norms of the agency that I worked for, and the norms of the agencies as described by these participants. Smith writes that norms are the common beliefs of the people—in this case in the agency—that guide behaviours. But Smith takes that one big step further by recognizing the institutional ordering of the agency. There is work that is going on behind the scenes that remains hidden, yet it affects everything that happens around it. Smith writes:

> The normative analysis misses how this local course of action is articulated to social relations. Social relations here mean concerted sequences or courses of social action implicating more than one individual whose participants are not necessarily present or known to one another. (p. 155)

Consequently, within the context of the workplace, single stalls are seen as gender-neutral. But just like the social workers who have an easy way out and don't have to challenge their gender comfort level when they only have single-room washrooms, it is also an easy way out for agencies, which then don't have to address gender in the workplace (as in my former place of work, where my manager told me, "You can make (transgender) policies for clients, but not for staff").

REFERENCES

Arnold, R., Burke, B., James, C., Martin, D., & Thomas, B. (1991). *Educating for a change.* Toronto: Between the Lines.

Berg, B.L. (2001). *Qualitative research methods for the social sciences.* Needham Heights, MA: Allyn & Bacon.

Bishop, A. (1994). *Becoming an ally: Breaking the cycle of oppression.* Halifax, NS: Fernwood.

Califia, P. (1997). *Sex changes: The politics of transgenderism.* San Francisco: Cleis Press.

Carroll, L., Gilroy, P., & Ryan, J. (2002). Counselling transgendered, transsexual and gender variant clients. *Journal of Counselling & Development, 80*, 131–139.

Cooper, K. (1999). Practice with transgendered youth and their families. In G.P. Mallon (Ed.), *Social services with transgendered youth.* Binghamton, NY: Harrington Park Press.

Cresswell, J.W. (1994). *Research design: Qualitative and quantitative approaches.* Thousand Oaks, CA: Sage.

Cromwell, J. (1999). *Transmen & FTM's: Identities, bodies, genders, and sexualities.* Chicago: University of Illinois Press.

Ekins, R., & King, D. (1997). Blending genders: Contributions to the emerging field of transgender studies. *International Journal of Transgenderism, 1*(1). Retrieved from www.iiav.nl/ezines/web/IJT/97-03/numbers/symposion/ijtc0101.htm

Fonow, M.M., & Cook, J.A. (1991). Back to the future: A look at the second wave of feminist epistemology and methodology. In M. Fonow & J. Cook (Eds.), *Beyond methodology: Feminist scholarship as lived research* (pp. 1–15). Bloomington and Indianapolis: Indiana University Press.

Graveline, F.J. (1998). *Circle works: Transforming Eurocentric consciousness.* Halifax, NS: Fernwood.

Green, J. (2004). *Becoming a visible man.* Nashville, TN: Vanderbilt University Press.

Harder, L. (1999). Women, human rights and the development of the neo-liberal state in Alberta. In D. Broad & W. Anthony (Eds.), *Citizens or consumers? Social policy in a market society* (pp. 155–168). Halifax, NS: Fernwood.

Hertz, R. (1997). Introduction: Reflexivity and voice. In R. Hertz (Ed.), *Reflexivity and voice* (pp. vii–xviii). Thousand Oaks, CA: Sage.

Israel, G.E., & Tarver, D.E. (1997). *Transgender care: Recommended guidelines, practical information and personal accounts.* Foreword by J.D. Shaffer. Philadelphia: Temple University Press.

Kinsman, G. (1994). Constructing sexual problems: "These things may lead to the tragedy of our species." L. Samuelson (Ed.), *Power and resistance: Critical thinking about Canadian social issues* (pp. 165–188). Halifax, NS: Fernwood.

Kirby, S., & McKenna, K. (1989). *Experience, research, social change: Methods from the margins.* Toronto: Garamond Press.

Kotula, D. (2002). *The phallus palace: Female to male transsexuals*. New York: Alyson Publications.

Lorde, A. (1984). *Sister outsider*. Trumansburg, NY: The Crossing Press.

Lynn, M., & Todoroff, M. (1998). Women's work and family lives. In N. Mandell (Ed.), *Feminist issues: Race, class and sexuality* (pp. 208–232). Scarborough, ON: Prentice-Hall Canada.

Mallon, G.P. (1999a). Knowledge for practice with transgendered persons. In G.P. Mallon (Ed.), *Social services with transgendered youth* (pp. 1–18). Binghamton, NY: Harrington Park Press.

Mallon, G.P. (1999b). A call for organizational trans-formation. In G.P. Mallon (Ed.), *Social services with transgendered youth* (pp. 131–142). Binghamton, NY: Harrington Park Press.

Mallon, G.P. (1999c). Practice with transgendered children. In G.P. Mallon (Ed.), *Social services with transgendered youth* (pp. 49–64). Binghamton, NY: Harrington Park Press.

Mallon, G.P. (1999d). Appendix B: A guide to staff self-awareness. In G.P. Mallon (Ed.), *Social services with transgendered youth* (pp. 147–149). Binghamton, NY: Harrington Park Press.

Namaste, V.K. (2000). *Invisible lives: The erasure of transsexual and transgendered people*. Chicago: University of Chicago Press.

O'Brien, C. (1999). Contested territory: Sexualities and social work. In A. Chambon, A. Irving, & L. Epstein (Eds.), *Reading Foucault for social work* (pp. 131–155). New York: Columbia University Press.

Pazos, S. (1999). Practice with female-to-male transgendered youth. In G.P. Mallon (Ed.), *Social services with transgendered youth* (pp. 65–82). Binghamton, NY: Harrington Park Press.

Raj, R. (2002). Towards a transpositive therapeutic model: Developing clinical sensitivity and cultural competence in the effective support of transsexual and transgendered clients. *International Journal of Transgenderism, 6*(2). Retrieved from www.iiav.nl/ezines/web/IJT/97-03/numbers/symposion/ijtvo06no02_04.htm

Rifkin, L. (2002). The suit suits whom? Lesbian gender, female masculinity and women-in-suits. In M. Gibson & D.T. Meem (Eds.), *Femme/butch: New considerations of the way we want to go* (pp. 157–174). Binghamton, NY: Harrington Park Press.

Smith, D.E. (1991). *The everyday world as problematic*. Toronto: University of Toronto Press.

Stryker, S. (1998). The transgender issue: An introduction. *GLQ: A Journal of Lesbian and Gay Studies, 4*(2), 145–158.

Wilchins, R.A. (2004). *Queer theory, gender theory: An instant primer*. Los Angeles: Alyson Books.

Chapter 19 One Step at a Time: Moving Trans Activism Forward in a Large Bureaucracy

Devon MacFarlane, Lorraine Grieves, and Al Zwiers

INTRODUCTION

Have you ever struggled to figure out how to get equity and social justice issues on a bureaucracy's radar? Have you ever wondered how to advance trans issues *meaningfully* within an LGBT2SQ (lesbian, gay, bisexual, transgender, two-spirit, and queer) initiative operating on a shoestring budget? How progressive networks or organizations can create positive change that exceeds singular projects, workplaces, or milieus to build a more just society? These are the questions that we have grappled with throughout the process of advocating for, developing, and sustaining what has become Prism—a LGBT2SQ-focused initiative of Vancouver Coastal Health (VCH).

We are Devon, Al, and Lorraine. We have all played key roles within Prism. Devon worked as the community developer supporting the Lesbian, Gay, Bisexual and Transgender Population Health Advisory Committee (LGBT PHAC) from 1999 to 2002. He led community consultations that catalyzed the development of Prism Alcohol & Drug Services and served as the founding coordinator. Working with queer and trans people for several years as an addictions counsellor, Al has facilitated a number of counselling groups affiliated with Prism and currently serves as the program's clinical supervisor. Lorraine currently manages Prism and a number of other programs and services at VCH.

Devon self-identifies as trans and has been connected with trans communities for over 15 years, while Al and Lorraine have cisgender privilege. All three of us have substantial personal connections within trans communities and work experience with trans people. In light of racial, ethnic, economic, linguistic, sexual, and gender difference, we acknowledge that our efforts to be trans allies require significant attentiveness to diversity of trans identities, experiences, and needs.

In this chapter, we describe the temporal, material, and political contexts that enabled Prism's emergence, what services Prism provides, how Prism addresses trans issues in LGBT2SQ spaces, and strategies for creating and maintaining positive change within large bureaucracies. We also highlight approaches we have found effective in cultivating significant change regarding trans-specific programming and social service provision. These approaches include focusing on being patient, tenacious, and persistent; the importance of identifying and seizing opportunities; and the need to cultivate individual, programmatic, and organizational capacity and commitment to ensure that trans issues materialize in practice.

A NOTE ABOUT LANGUAGE

Prism currently uses "LGBT2SQ" (lesbian, gay, bi, trans, two-spirit, queer) to reflect the range of individuals and communities with whom Prism works. Given the evolution of language within trans and queer communities, we only use "LGBT" (lesbian, gay, bi, trans) when it is part of the proper name of a group or organization, or within direct quotations. "Two-spirit" is a term that has multiple nuances and is used in multiple ways. Coined at the Third Annual Intertribal Native American/First Nations Gay and Lesbian Conference held in Winnipeg in 1990 (Jacobs, Thomas, & Lang, 1997), Aboriginal people use the term "two-spirit" as part of reclaiming and reconnecting with "traditional First Nations gender diversity, which includes the fluid nature of sexual orientation and gender identity and its interconnectedness with spirituality and traditional world views" (First Nations Centre, 2012, p. 2); as a descriptor for LGBT and queer people of First Nations descent; to refer to a person who is in traditional, spiritual, social, or cultural roles where these roles may have no connection to a person's sexual orientation or gender identity (Ristock, Zocolle, & Passante, 2010); and to describe a person who has both masculine and feminine spirits (First Nations Centre, 2012), among other uses. "Queer" best reflects our approach to our work and the language used by the local community we serve.

THE LANDSCAPE

VCH is a large, publicly funded health organization with over 20,000 employees working across several cities, as well as in rural settings. While Prism is Vancouver-based, we also work to build capacity in other geographic areas. Prism originated as an initiative of VCH's Addiction Services program, and has a capacity-building role within VCH, providing education, information, referral, and health promotion for LGBT2SQ communities. Along the way, because of the cross-program nature of the work and in order to reflect the range of health service areas where trans and queer competency is required, the name was shifted to "Prism." Notably, Prism itself does not deliver direct counselling services. Our approach is detailed later in this chapter.

Vancouver has a growing trans population, as many people relocate here to access transition-related care. Common concerns amongst this diverse demographic include un/deremployment and poverty, safe and affordable housing, and issues arising from the criminalization of sex work and the social stigma surrounding it. These issues are compounded by racialization and colonialism. Prism recognizes that these and other forces, such as minority stress (Meyer, 2003), result in significant health inequities for LGBT2SQ communities. Thus, Prism takes a population health approach, seeking to influence and create change in relation to the particular factors that have a strong impact on the health and well-being of LGBT2SQ individuals and communities.

BEFORE THE BEGINNING...

Although Prism was launched in 2007, a constellation of factors that occurred more than a decade earlier created the conditions for the development of Prism. These factors included decisions made within the Ministry of Health and health care organizations throughout the Vancouver region, as well as advocacy by LGBT groups who spotted and seized upon significant opportunities. Such advocacy and activism within and beyond government departments and health care organizations required a commitment from many people to "walk their talk" about diversity and inclusiveness regarding LGBT2SQ communities. The work to move from rhetoric to tangible services that meet the concerns and needs of diverse LGBT2SQ people required leadership from management within the health care system. It also demanded persistence, tenacity, and an immense amount of patience on the part of activists working within the health care system.

Getting a Seat at the Table: The LGBT Population Health Advisory Committee

In the 1990s, the BC Ministry of Health regionalized and decentralized the delivery of health care services, striving to ensure that health care organizations were accountable to the communities they served. This reorganization resulted in the formation of the Vancouver/Richmond Health Board (V/RHB), which, in 1995, developed a series of neighbourhood and population-based committees that advised the Board of the V/RHB. The absence of an LGBT2SQ committee sparked lobbying efforts by members of the December 9th Coalition, a grassroots LGBT2SQ advocacy group. Their efforts served as a catalyst for the creation of the Lesbian, Gay, Bisexual and Transgender Population Health Advisory Committee (LGBT PHAC) in 1997 (Egan, 2005). The LGBT PHAC was unprecedented on a number of fronts—to our knowledge, it was the first committee of its kind in North America and the first instance where grassroots activism resulted in changes to the governance structures of public services to better reflect community needs in Canada (Egan, 2005).

The LGBT PHAC engaged in public consultations to identify priority health issues. The top three issues included the lack of access to competent health care, the lack of research regarding LGBT2SQ health, and issues relating to addiction and problematic substance use. Although the LGBT PHAC experienced challenges maintaining a full slate of trans members (i.e., a minimum allocation of three seats out of fifteen to trans people), it demonstrated an ongoing commitment to trans issues. For instance, the V/RHB was the first health care organization in Canada to include gender identity in its human rights and employment equity policies; this success occurred due to pressure from the LGBT PHAC.

Seizing Opportunities to Address Priority Health Issues

The degree of receptiveness of key decision-makers toward LGBT2SQ issues often relates to their prior knowledge of the issues, willingness to learn, and willingness to champion issues facing marginalized communities. In 2000, the LGBT PHAC learned that Addiction Services were being transferred from the Ministry of Health to the V/RHB. The LGBT PHAC approached the director and manager of Addiction Services to determine their interest in hearing from trans and queer communities concerning how LGBT2SQ people seeking addiction services could be better served. Management informed us that they would value the communities' perspectives; while bureaucracies are reputed to be slow-moving, the LGBT PHAC was also asked how quickly consultations could be completed to ensure that LGBT2SQ communities' perspectives were included from the beginning of the planning process. Such responsiveness stood in stark contrast to the years of advocacy required for formation of the LGBT PHAC just three years earlier. This may have been due in part to the High Risk Project Society, which Sandy Leo Laframboise addresses in Chapter 5 of this text. The High Risk Project Society had increased management's awareness of issues and barriers for trans people engaged in sex work, many of whom were street-involved and dealing with addictions.

Peer activists in drug user communities, people in recovery from addictions, counsellors, and community organizers joined with LGBT PHAC members to form a Substance Use Working Group to plan and organize the consultations. This group deliberately emphasized diversity and inclusion regarding group composition and its work; a significant portion of the membership were trans and two-spirit people. The consultations were led by facilitators who had taken part in training to build the necessary skills and knowledge to lead focus groups. These facilitators were trans and two-spirit people, as well as lesbian, gay, bisexual, and queer people from various cultural and linguistic backgrounds, who reached out to their peer groups and social networks to promote participation in the focus groups. Across the consultations, 65 community members and 17 service providers participated in focus groups and interviews held in over five languages. The process took two and a half years from the time LGBT PHAC met with the management of Addiction Services through to the release of the final report from the consultations (MacFarlane, 2003).

Meanwhile, Elsewhere in VCH...

In 2003, the Transgender Health Program (THP) was launched in response to community advocacy following the announced closure of the gender clinic a year prior. The THP was effective in building awareness of trans health concerns and in supporting trans-friendly health providers to increase the clinical knowledge they would need to provide competent care. The THP formed a partnership with the Transcend Transgender Support and Education Society to conduct the Trans Care Project funded through the Canadian Rainbow Health Coalition, which made a significant contribution to the health and well-being of trans people around the world through the development of a series of clinical care guidelines (VCH, 2006), sometimes referred to as the "Vancouver Guidelines." While it is not possible to reflect on the evolution of this important program here, it has and continues to play a critical role alongside committed others in working toward improved access to competent and quality transgender health care within the BC context.

Synergies emerged between the THP and the work stemming from the report *LGBT Communities and Substance Use—What Health Has to Do With It!* (MacFarlane, 2003). Responding to recommendations in the report, the THP launched a drop-in for street-involved trans sex workers in 2004. Additionally, the THP developed and delivered workshops relating to various issues identified in the report and through other community surveys (Goldberg, Matte, MacMillan, & Hudspith, 2003). Both consultations identified that trans people faced distinct issues concerning accessing shelters, supported housing, and residential treatment, as well as significant barriers to employment. This research prompted Prism's development of the Shelter, Housing and Residential Program Access Project, described later in this chapter.

Catalyzing Action

What Health Has to Do With It! placed trans and queer substance use issues on VCH Addiction Services' radar. This resulted in management and front-line service providers taking steps toward preliminary action to ensure meaningful services for LGBT2SQ people. Beginning in 2002, the manager for Adult Addiction Services in VCH–Vancouver made a point of hiring counsellors from LGBT2SQ communities, as participants in public consultations identified the importance of seeing themselves reflected in the staff. Over the next decade, at least nine trans individuals and five partners and family members of trans people worked in various capacities within Vancouver Addiction, HIV/AIDS, and Aboriginal Wellness Services.

The timing was not appropriate to move forward in the development of Prism in 2002, as extensive changes were being made to the scope and philosophy of Adult Addiction Services. However, it was possible to take small steps to enact some of the recommendations from the community consultations. Such steps included forming drop-in counselling groups for gay and bi men dealing with addiction, and creating a networking group for service providers working with LGBT2SQ people dealing with addiction. Although people on the FTM spectrum were welcome at the gay and bi men's counselling groups, FTM's who identified as gay, bi, or queer never attended group as out trans men and rarely stayed in the groups for long. This helped amplify an awareness of trans people's need to discuss substance use issues in relation to their trans identities and experiences.

DEVELOPING PRISM: DOING LGBT2SQ INSIDE A BUREAUCRACY

In 2006, the Director and Manager of Addiction Services believed the timing was right to develop Prism. Open to experimentation and learning from what had worked and what could be done differently, they were willing to take well-considered risks. Management also enabled the coordinator to identify areas for Prism's growth and act upon such opportunities. Five major principles guided Prism's development: (1) Prism would not be a "siloed" or stand-alone service; (2) Prism would strive to build competence throughout Addiction Services; (3) means would be created for staff with Addiction Services to self-select to participate in Prism, including through being identified as having competency and interest in working with one or more parts of LGBT2SQ communities, and through these counsellors developing and facilitating specialized groups and programming as clinically necessary; (4) Prism would also support other agencies, as much as possible, to build their capacity; and (5) Prism's work would be framed by a community development approach, thus supporting health promotion and capacity building within LGBT2SQ communities. As Prism has evolved in scope, these principles still guide its work.

Across time, we have worked consistently from an understanding that people have a constellation of experiences emerging from their social locations and identities. To provide competent and accessible services, it is vital that we pay attention to such differences and how they lend themselves to the complexity of those we serve. As stated by a participant in community consultations: "[W]hen we're looking at services that are accessible to the LGBT population, we're also looking at services that are ... accessible to people with disabilities, who are queer, who are First Nations, who have children ... because those are sometimes all one person" (MacFarlane, 2003, p. 41). Given that we strive to align our actions with our values—inclusion, justice, equity, and transparency—Prism has deliberately ensured that trans communities remain a significant focus. Prism's work in serving trans communities has benefited from synergies and greater opportunities for consultation, collaboration, and support that have arisen through the Transgender Health Program (THP), which provides peer support, information, and referral services, as well as the more recently developed Trans Primary Care Consultation Services. The latter collaborates with and supports family physicians, nurse practitioners, and other health care providers to provide competent care for trans people.

A LOUD "T" IN LGBT2SQ

Trans people often approach LGBT2SQ organizations with caution. We know from personal experience and from discussions with trans communities members that many LGBT2SQ organizations add the "T" as an inclusive gesture without changing the way they provide supports and services or the types of supports and services. Some trans people and allies describe the failure to integrate trans inclusion as "LGBT with a silent T."

We believe that it is crucial to take a multi-faceted approach to change if organizations are to become genuinely trans inclusive. As a result of having very limited funding, Prism has relied upon creativity and thoughtful consideration to determine how to most effectively create change and meet the needs of trans people who use substances. The approaches Prism took included fostering learning and education; building on personal knowledge in the department; cultivating commitment to trans issues; building awareness and reducing barriers to care; and creating opportunities for staff as well as programs to step up. Supporting information sharing and referrals—both amongst service providers and within trans communities—as well as "upstream" health promotion were other ways we strove to improve health outcomes for trans people and communities.

Fostering Learning and Education

Fostering learning is a vital part of organizations working toward becoming genuinely trans competent. For an LGBT2SQ organization to address trans issues in ways that will benefit trans people's actual lives, we believe that the organization's leaders, as well as staff, must cultivate knowledge regarding:

- The differences between sexual orientation and gender identity. Within many trans communities, "queer" is understood as an umbrella term referring to sexual orientation, not to gender identity.
- The diversity of trans communities and experiences. As an umbrella term, "trans" includes transsexuals, or those who desire to transition medically, socially, and legally, as well as genderqueers and cross-dressers who are predominantly heterosexual men and other non-binary identified people.
- The points of connection and differentiation between trans and intersex people's experiences.
- Points of overlap and distinctions among lesbian, gay, bi, and queer (LGBQ) and trans populations. Most LGBQ people are not trans identified, many trans people are heterosexual, some trans people seek connections with queer communities, while straight partners of trans people may not consider themselves part of queer communities.
- Issues often specific to trans populations that need to remain priority issues for organizations to address. These include the differences in current legal and social status of trans people (e.g., the lack of explicit human rights protection for trans people), severe barriers to employment, and rates of poverty, depression, and suicidality that are often substantially higher amongst trans than queer populations. Substance use, which may become problematic, is a common coping mechanism for dealing with these challenges.
- How cisgender privilege, cisnormativity, and transphobia can manifest within individual service providers' practices (as demonstrated by Treanor Mahood-Greer's chapter on

social workers in this volume; see Chapter 18), as well as throughout queer communities.
- The importance of involving trans people in priority-setting processes.

Prism takes an approach of providing training, consultation, and ongoing clinical supervision to groups to support learning. We recognized that training opportunities would need not only to change providers' understandings of trans issues and build empathy, but also enable them to practice differently. As much as possible, we have provided ongoing consultation and mentoring, as we are aware that people retain a small fraction of the content of a workshop. The nature and extent of learning opportunities Prism offers have evolved over time, and have been strongly influenced by the availability of funding. For instance, Service Canada's Homelessness Partnership Initiative funded Prism's Shelter, Housing and Residential Program Access Project (SHARP) between 2008 and 2012. Adapted from an initiative of the trans program at The 519 Church Street Community Centre in Toronto, which is discussed in Jake Pyne and colleagues' chapter "Trans Access Project: Running the Gauntlet" (see Chapter 13), this funding permitted SHARP to deliver 170 workshops to over 2,400 participants—primarily staff and tenants, residents, and clients of agencies operating emergency shelters, supportive housing, and residential addiction and mental health services—and also to present at 15 conferences. As with the consultations that led to Prism's development, and as with the initiative of the Trans Access Project at The 519 Church Street Community Centre, building the capacity of community members was a vital component of SHARP. SHARP provided training and part-time employment to peer facilitators who themselves had experienced homelessness or precarious housing, and who had lived experiences of accessing shelters, supportive housing, and/or residential addiction or mental health services. The BC Non-Profit Housing Association also partnered with Prism on SHARP; BC Non-Profit Housing Association's focus was on building awareness and support for LGBT2SQ housing issues within their sector.

Prism also created clinical supervision and consultation groups to meet twice monthly to support VCH staff in their learning, as well as with the challenging and sometimes emotionally painful aspects of their work. These groups created space for trans and queer issues to be regularly addressed within a large bureaucracy. These conversations helped counsellors and other service providers—both trans people and people with cisgender privilege—address whatever challenges were on their plates; integrate knowledge and theory relating to trans issues into their practice; and support them in becoming more aware of the patterns of issues that trans and queer people struggle with based on societal oppression. In turn, these conversations helped service providers in building relationships with their clients, in finding strategies to help their clients resist the internalization of societal problems, and in supporting their clients to make changes in accordance with the client's goals. Staff were also able to access individual supervision with Prism's clinical supervisor around issues that were not appropriate to bring up in group supervision sessions. Casual conversations outside the supervision groups between trans and non-trans colleagues also provided many opportunities to learn and deepen knowledge and practice.

Building on Personal Knowledge

A strength that Prism has been able to draw upon is that a number of core staff within Prism or Addiction Services have been trans identified or have trans individuals as partners and family members. At the same time, Prism also recognizes the importance of trans people and their partners and family members being *aware of the limits of their knowledge and experiences*. Everyone—including trans people—needs to engage in ongoing learning and unlearning activities to be able to act as informed allies for trans people who have different social locations, experiences, identities, and access to privilege than ourselves. Prism has also strived to create spaces for trans people who are very marginalized to be able to share their experiences, strengths, needs, and priorities in meaningful ways.

Cultivating Commitment

In the context of a health authority, trans issues tend to be more marginalized and less understood than issues facing queer, lesbian, gay, and bi people. More work is often required to cultivate a commitment to serving trans people, especially regarding residential services. We have found that using case-by-case examples, and walking service providers through the issues facing trans people, the barriers to care, and the tactics for overcoming them, can make a significant difference. It takes time to explore service providers' comprehension of access to washrooms, sleeping quarters, and gender-specific groups and programs, and to disrupt common forms of resistance to trans inclusion. These are often framed as concerns regarding the safety and comfort of cisgender clients, which can be quite problematic for trans folk seeking care.

Building Awareness and Reducing Barriers to Care

Trans people commonly face significant barriers to receiving competent health care, and many have had negative experiences (e.g., Feldman & Bockting, 2003; Kitts, 2010; Sperber, Landers, & Lawrence, 2005). It is important to ensure that trans and queer communities are aware of Prism, what to expect when accessing care through Prism, that some staff affiliated with Prism have experience working with trans populations, and the processes through which one can file a complaint should they have an unsatisfactory experience.

As an illustration, Devon had been approached by a trans woman who knew he was trans and worked at Prism. She felt like she could trust him enough to ask for help, even though it was very difficult for her to do so. Devon advised her that there were several counsellors affiliated with Prism who had worked with many trans women and had good reputations with trans clients. Knowing that she could be referred directly to trans-competent counsellors whom she would not need to educate greatly alleviated her anxiety about seeking care. Devon informed her that there was a complaints process should any concerns arise about the care she received; that trans individuals had experienced respectful treatment by those investigating complaints; and that a number of the patient relations staff had significant experience with LGBT2SQ communities. Again, this was reassuring for her, and empowered her to seek care.

Creating Opportunities for Staff, as well as Programs, to Step Up

Prism does not function as a "siloed" initiative. With the support of the manager for Adult Addiction Services, Prism is empowered to advance competent and specialized care in an integrated manner *throughout* Addiction Services. Prism accomplished this by making it attractive and easy to become involved in the initiative and by inviting counsellors to participate in concrete ways. An invitation was extended within Adult Addiction Services for counsellors to add their names to a referral list for Prism; counsellors are asked to self-rate their competency with different parts of LGBT2SQ communities and to include any additional areas of specialized knowledge to better match clients and counsellors. Thus, as a part of their everyday job, these counsellors see clients who contacted Prism seeking counselling for addiction-related issues. Counsellors were also invited to develop and initiate specialized groups for different parts of queer and trans communities. Some have also participated in developing and delivering training sessions and presentations, developing clinical practice guidelines, and writing articles (e.g., Boon, 2010; Everett, MacFarlane, Reynolds, & Anderson, 2013; MacFarlane et al., 2010; Zwiers, 2010).

Prism has also supported some programs and services in building access and competency at a program level, and not just at the level of individual service providers. We have developed recommendations for how to build and renovate facilities to promote access for trans clients and staff members, and have provided consultation to teams to help identify how they can step up together in not only becoming more competent, but also in building broader awareness of their commitment to serving trans and queer people. In this manner, with minimal funding, Prism has been able to catalyze significant change.

Supporting Information Sharing and Appropriate Referrals

We have learned that the availability of accurate current information is vital to support trans and LGB2SQ people who are accessing competent care. Both directly and indirectly, Prism helps match people up with appropriate competent services within VCH and with those provided by contracted and community agencies. A listserv supports the LGBTQ service providers networking group within Prism to circulate information about new groups and emerging issues, and to serve as a forum for posing questions. Some staff spend significant time developing and maintaining current information regarding the nuances of accessibility for trans people across programs and agencies, while others approach core Prism staff for suggestions for referrals. More recently, Prism launched an online platform to share resources and materials to promote ongoing learning (www.prismcop.ning.com).

"Upstream" Health Promotion, Addiction Prevention, and Earlier Health Action

Where resources have permitted, Prism has supported work to foster the development of healthy trans communities. In 2010, Prism received funding from Health Canada's Drug Strategy Community Initiatives Fund for Creating Action Learning and Leadership—or C.A.L.L. Out—initiative. This three-year project involved working with LGBT2SQ youth groups in urban and rural communities across BC to build community capacity, develop leadership skills in youth, and engage in health promotion and resiliency-focused substance use prevention activities. C.A.L.L. Out takes an approach of being youth-driven; youth participants stepped up within the project to determine the direction and participate in organizing activities and events. The final phase of the project involved youth being funded to lead mini-projects (hosting safe and substance-free youth events) in their home communities with the support of adult allies, and a youth conference at the end of the project term (March 2013). On occasion, Prism has sponsored community-driven initiatives whose focus and purpose align with its mission, and where a small injection of funds (generally under $500) will make a substantial difference. We prioritize sponsoring community-focused initiatives that reach trans people and other facets of LGBT communities with less access to financial resources.

ACTIVISM WITHIN A BUREAUCRACY

We in Prism have deliberately taken a range of approaches to cultivating positive change. Key approaches include understanding the organizational and broader political context, looking for policy levers, cultivating broader organizational commitment, exploring mutual benefits, and being vigilant in maintaining gains.

Organizations tend to change and evolve over time. In BC, as health authorities derive their mandate from the provincial government, the government of the day influences organizational priorities and the degree of progressiveness or conservativeness within an organization. The Canadian health care system as a whole is facing challenges related to sustainability, and it tends to respond to crisis and focus attention on hospital-based care. As activists working within a bureaucracy, we find it very important to be able to articulate clearly how our goals and priorities fit with and advance broader organizational mandates. We have also found that when advocating for a particular course of action, having a good understanding of the interests and priorities of the organization determines how we articulate our agenda. In some instances, we may emphasize the financial benefits of a course of action; in others, we may emphasize positive human outcomes.

Where possible, we have identified existing leverage points in policies, and have advocated for or supported the development of new policies that would help advance our work. For instance, the BC Ministry of Health requires all health authorities to work toward 15 areas of improvement, including reducing health inequities. Prism staff have met with a number of senior leaders to explore how initiatives advancing these key areas could better address the needs of trans and queer communities.

We have also taken steps to develop policies and practice guidelines that support staff affiliated with Prism in doing their work (Everett et al., 2013). Shortly after Prism was launched, we realized that some trans and queer counsellors were experiencing ethical dilemmas relating to encountering their clients outside of the office and were feeling that they needed to constrain their social lives for fear of being—or being perceived to be—unprofessional. Codes of ethics for many health professions require members of their professions to avoid dual relationships wherever possible. For counsellors from trans and queer communities who are working with members of their own communities, however, this is often not possible. In response, Prism convened a working group, including one of VCH's ethicists, to identify and take action on the most pressing issues. This working group developed an internal document, *Multiple Relationships: Establishing Professional Relationships and Maintaining Appropriate Boundaries When Working with Clientele from Small and/or Marginalized Communities* (MacFarlane et al., 2010), to support counsellors in their work. This clinical guideline also helps to protect queer and trans counsellors—as well as other counsellors working within their own communities—from negative evaluations regarding boundaries and professionalism from their supervisors and managers.

We have also found it necessary to review policies as they are released to protect gains. In 2007, VCH developed a "respectful workplace" policy regarding grounds that were protected from discrimination. A careful reading of the respectful workplace policy revealed an omission of gender identity, despite its inclusion in the organization's human rights policy in 2000. This omission was corrected through approaching management, who took the issue forward through the appropriate channels. In 2010, on the 10th anniversary of gender identity being covered, the VCH staff e-newsletter profiled the significance of gender identity being included in the human rights and respectful workplace policies in an article co-authored by Prism's coordinator and published under the vice-president of Human Resources' name. Since Prism's launch, our trainings have consistently mentioned that gender identity is protected within VCH policies, both to support trans clients and staff, and to build and maintain awareness of this aspect of the human rights and respectful workplace policies.

SUSTAINABILITY: SUPPORT, AND HOW WE CULTIVATE IT

As Prism has never had easy access to funding and resources, creative methods have been needed to catalyze positive change. It has been important to identify people who have positions of influence and power to champion Prism. In establishing and developing Prism, director-level support was critical, as was support both from managers who have had direct responsibility for Prism and managers for programs and services within which we sought to build capacity.

A key approach we have taken has been to build relationships. At times, strong and knowledgeable allies have shown up, as have people who want to do the right thing but who may not yet know what exactly that is and are excited to learn. We have worked with them to support their ability to be effective advocates and champions for Prism and the health and well-being of LGBT2SQ communities overall. At other times, we have had to work hard to cultivate relationships and to develop awareness of mutual benefits. We have found that developing relationships can require significant amounts of time, a great deal of patience, and an ability to create an environment safe enough to support dialogue, learning, growth, and change. We have found that it is very important to have strong interpersonal skills and to know one's own limits and triggers. It is also very important to be able to look after oneself and to have support systems to cope with what can be, at times, very problematic conversations and behaviours from colleagues, staff at partner organizations, and people in positions of authority over us.

We have also learned that when there are opportunities to secure ongoing funding or reallocate funding within a portfolio, it is important to seize them as quickly as possible because the fiscal climate can shift rapidly. As it is currently challenging to obtain sustainable funding for initiatives such as Prism within the context of health care, we have found that securing external funding, as well as internal one-time funding, has been an effective means to advance Prism's strategic priorities.

CONCLUSION

Across our work with Prism, we have found that it takes a substantial amount of time to create lasting change. Identifying and seizing opportune moments, as well as recognizing when the time and circumstances are not favourable for moving forward; being patient, persistent, and tenacious; and finding creative means to mobilize other's resources to achieve mutual goals have all contributed to success in advancing the well-being of trans people in an LGBT2SQ context, in a large bureaucracy.

ACKNOWLEDGEMENTS

Prism would not exist without the work of the members of the LGBT Population Health Advisory Committee, the members of the LGBT Substance Use Working Group, the participants and facilitators in the community consultations, and the director and manager who supported Prism in getting off the ground. We acknowledge the many managers and directors who have supported and championed Prism, the first clinical supervisor for Prism, the current and past core staff team for Prism, and practicum students who contributed their time and energy. We also recognize and celebrate the work of the many clinicians who have chosen to be affiliated with Prism. Finally, we acknowledge those who have advanced trans work within VCH—the coordinators, managers, and directors of the Transgender Health Program, and the staff and physicians involved with VCH's Trans Primary Care initiatives, among others.

REFERENCES

Boon, S. (2010). Same but different: Substance use in queer and trans communities. *Visions: BC's Mental Health and Addictions Journal, 6*(2), 12–13.

Egan, J. (2005). Nearly queerly: The life and death of a queer health advisory committee. *Canadian Bulletin of Medical History, 22*(2), 299–311.

Everett, B., MacFarlane, D., Reynolds, V., & Anderson, H. (2013). Not on our backs: Supporting counsellors in navigating the ethics of multiple relationships within queer, two spirit, and/or trans communities. *Canadian Journal of Counselling and Psychotherapy, 47*(1). Retrieved from http://cjc-rcc.ucalgary.ca/cjc/index.php/rcc/article/view/2658

Feldman, J., & Bockting, W. (2003). Transgender health. *Minnesota Medicine, 86*(7), 25–32.

First Nations Centre. (2012). *Suicide prevention and two-spirited people.* Ottawa: National Aboriginal Health Organization.

Goldberg, J., Matte, N., MacMillan, M. (Transgender Community Coalition), & Hudspith, M. (VCHA Coordinator). (2003). *Community survey: Transition/crossdressing services in BC.* Final report. Retrieved from http://transhealth.vch.ca/resources/library/thpdocs/0301surveyreport.pdf

Jacob, S.E., Thomas, W., & Lang, S. (1997). Introduction. In S.E. Jacob, W. Thomas, & S. Lang (Eds.), *Two-spirit people: Native American gender identity, sexuality, and spirituality* (pp. 1–18). Champaign, IL: University of Illinois Press.

Kitts, R.L. (2010). Barriers to optimal care between physicians and lesbian, gay, bisexual, transgender, and questioning adolescent patients. *Journal of Homosexuality, 57*(6), 730–747. doi:10.1080/00918369.2010.485872

MacFarlane, D. (2003). *LGBT communities and substance use—What health has to do with it!: A report on consultations with LGBT communities.* Vancouver, BC: LGBT Health Association of BC.

MacFarlane, D., Everett, B., Marlow, M., Hutchings, A., Spicer, B., Clifford, D., ... & Barlow, R. (2010). *Multiple relationships: Establishing professional relationships and maintaining appropriate boundaries when working with clientele from small and/or marginalized communities.* [Internal document]. Vancouver, BC: Vancouver Coastal Health.

Meyer, I.H. (2003). Prejudice, social stress, and mental health in lesbian, gay, and bisexual populations: Conceptual issues and research evidence. *Psychological Bulletin, 129*, 674–697.

Ristock, J., Zoccole, A., & Passante, L. (2010, November). *Aboriginal Two-Spirit and LGBTQ Migration, Mobility and Health Research Project: Winnipeg final report.* Retrieved from www.2spirits.com

Sperber, J., Landers, S., & Lawrence, S. (2005). Access to health care for transgendered persons: Results of a needs assessment in Boston. *International Journal of Transgenderism, 8*(2-3), 75–91. doi:10.1300/J485v08n02_08

Vancouver Coastal Health. (2006). *Clinical protocol guidelines for transgender care.* Transgender Health Program. Retrieved from http://transhealth.vch.ca/resources/careguidelines.html

Zwiers, A. (2010). LGBT people and mental health: Healing the wounds of prejudice. *Visions: BC's Mental Health and Addictions Journal, 6*(2), 10–11.

Chapter 20 Auditioning for Care: Transsexual Men in Ontario Accessing Health Care

Will Rowe

This chapter is based on a research project I undertook as part of completing my master's in Social Work during 2008–2009. Since writing this thesis, there has been a slight shift in the Ontario landscape regarding trans-specific health care, as well as in some of the language and terminology. The World Professional Association for Transgender Health (WPATH) released the newest version of the Standards of Care (SOC, Version 7), and the nomenclature of "gender identity disorder" has been replaced with "gender dysphoria." Although WPATH acknowledges that reparative therapy is not a modality it supports, the SOC in many ways continues to perpetuate a narrow reading of what constitutes trans intelligibility, keeping trans identities firmly tied to psycho-medico discourses.

The "old guard" that ran the gender identity clinic (GIC) at the Centre for Addiction and Mental Health (CAMH) in Toronto have moved on. Trans positive mental health practitioners have taken their place and ushered in a more progressive approach to medical transitioning. As evidence of this significant shift, the infamous questionnaire was updated in 2011 for the first time since its inception in 1970. And although far from the official apology that many trans individuals in Ontario would like from CAMH, in 2012 the GIC announced that their requirements for qualifying as "credibly" trans were now on par with every other GIC in North America. These changes include lowering the age eligibility requirement from 21 to 18; changing such terminology as "Real-Life Experience" to the more encompassing and appropriate "Gender Role Experience" (GRE); allowing access to hormones and chest surgery prior to 12 months of continuous GRE; and eliminating the need to legally change one's name to make it gender-identity congruent—what was perhaps the most contentious eligibility requirement for many—thereby making space for those who may be more fluid in their gender presentation and/or identity.

Very few trans-identified individuals are unaware of the incredibly transphobic history of CAMH's GIC, whether one transitioned 30 years ago or is just beginning the journey. We have all heard the "horror stories." As a trans-identified man and a social worker, there has been a hopeful shift in the stories I now hear as wait times and negative experiences of the GIC decrease and approval rates exponentially increase. It continues to appear that race and class are still informing the "credible trans trajectory," however. White, middle-class trans individuals are negotiating their way through the system with fewer stumbling blocks, intimating that social and cultural capital is manifesting as credible and capable.

Shifts in the landscape of care were not limited to the approach taken by the GIC. Community-based organizations, such as Rainbow Health Ontario (RHO), were also being established to address the multiple needs and issues associated with trans health care. Perhaps one of the more important occurrences in the shifting landscape in Ontario has been the community-based research project Trans PULSE (transpulseproject.ca). In 2009, 433 trans Ontarians were interviewed for the project, providing for the first time a thorough understanding of the complex lives that trans-identified individuals negotiate daily.

The institutional and community-based shifts within the landscapes of care were in part a response to the shifting identities and lives of many individuals within sexual and gender minority communities. During the summer of 2006, after having worked within women's services for 13 years, I was coming to the conclusion that the identity that I had laid claim to 20 years previously no longer adequately (if it ever had) represented me, and was often at odds with how I experienced myself in the world. The categories of "female" and "dyke" began to make less sense as I became aware of a burgeoning new language being made available via trans activism within Toronto and a more globalized world. Trans men were becoming vocal within this context, and trans masculinities and embodiment were rendered increasingly visible. This increasing representation opened spaces for me to explore potentially viable identities that made the most sense.

Along with lesbian, gay, and bisexual activism, trans communities—including those who identify as transgender and transsexual—have, over the past few decades, become large, vocal, and visible entities demanding rights and access to competent, sensitive, and trans positive services, particularly services involving the health care system.[1] As with other historically marginalized communities, access to these services and continuing barriers has often made manoeuvring through the health care system a difficult task for trans-identified individuals, especially transsexuals who often want or need to use the health care system to facilitate their transitioning process.

I began to physically transition from female to male when I left women's services and became coordinator of an LGBTQ service agency. As noted in the Introduction to this book, transition occurs on multiple levels, whereby one's personal transition vis-à-vis the embodiment and performance of one's sex and gender identity often informs their professional praxis. It was while working as coordinator of this agency that political activism became much more central to my social work practice. I became very involved in trans politics within the context of supporting institutional-level policy changes. Such involvement was my attempt to utilize the incredible amount of cultural capital I embodied, especially now that my subject position had shifted to the more privileged (precariously so, but privileged nonetheless) site of white heterosexual male (though still very much queer-identified).

As I negotiated and manoeuvred through institutional bureaucracies while attempting to legally change my identity and medically reconstruct my body, I began to realize that *the dominant, readily accessible trans narrative or discourse was increasingly becoming a part of my own narrative of trans identity*. This trans discourse highlights "how ideas from elsewhere penetrate everyday life, organizing people's relation to health care and affecting their everyday choices about how to act" (Campbell & Gregor, 2002, p. 43). In needing to access the psycho-medical institutions that assist us with aligning our experienced selves with that of our born selves, trans people have learned to adapt our lived experiences to reflect the meta narratives created for us by those within the psycho-medical field. As Christopher Shelley (2008) describes,

> Narrating the body becomes a necessary skill, and self-narration is a key element in persuading the authorities to permit SRS. The interiority of memory, and the need to ex/press trauma in a cohesive storied form, intersects with negotiating the exterior social world and its institutions. The self as an integrating story is re/called in pursuit of healing or repairing the mis-sexed body. (p. 28)

Such psycho-medical discourses serve as a powerful organizer of people's actions and interrelations.

Psycho-medical discourses play a significant role in creating and perpetuating knowledge of certain trans embodiment as intelligible or socially recognizable bodies. At this same time, we have been erased from the social world due to our lack of access to institutional health and social services, and the bureaucratic burden of attempting to match our lived experiences with that of our legally defined and identified birth documents. I was left still wondering about the everyday material reality of trans experiences and our engagement with the psycho-medical institutions we were reliant upon to create the feminine or masculine bodies we needed to be in the world. I became particularly interested in how transsexual males were not only learning to negotiate these systems but how in fact our everyday lives and understandings of ourselves had become entangled with these systems in ways of which we may not even be aware, let alone wary. How does our access to health care unfold? What are the implications of such governed access for the formation of trans identities?

These are the questions grounding my master's-level research project in Social Work.

CRITICAL ENTANGLEMENTS: A GRADUATE STUDY

My explorations of these questions are framed theoretically by institutional ethnography (IE) and theory grounded in Marxist and feminist critical social science. According to Mykhalovskiy & McCoy (2002),

> Unlike much ethnographic research, IE is not empirically focused on "experience" or "culture." Instead, it addresses processes of social organization. Institutional ethnographers are primarily concerned with exploring and describing the various social and institutional forces that shape, limit and otherwise organize people's actual, every day/night worlds. (p. 19)

IE's focus on the work of health care access with linkages to broader social movements renders it an important theoretical framework to illuminate the ways that transsexual males learn to negotiate access to trans-specific health care in Ontario. My research focuses on how the work that transsexual males do to meet our transitioning needs is shaped by, and linked to, institutional relations within the health care system. "Work" is defined as everything that people know how to do and what their daily lives require them to do (Campbell & Gregor, 2002). The specificities of the work required are formed by social and institutional processes functioning as invisible "ruling relations." According to Dorothy Smith (1987),

> They are those forms that we know as bureaucracy, administration, management, professional or-

> ganization, and the media. They include also the complex of discourses, scientific, technical, and cultural, that intersect, interpenetrate, and coordinate the multiple sites of ruling. (p. 6)

It is within these governing relations that our experiences not only of medical transition but also of ourselves as trans men are embedded.

Historical Context

A particular identity formation of "transsexual" arose out of a Westernized medical and psychiatric discourse during the early to mid-twentieth century, at a time in which psychiatry and medicine were establishing and securing a dominant role. Although trans people existed before the advancement of medicine and psychiatry, our lives became entangled within these establishments as we struggled with our inability to fit into our birth-assigned sex category and attempted to live with our sense of self via the use of clothing and "opposing" or "alternative" sex-based roles. At this time, the concept of gender used specifically to delineate that which was not biological had yet to be integrated within these discourses.

With the advancement of surgical techniques and the discovery of sex hormones, sex reassignment surgery (SRS) became an option for trans people. In a North American context, however, access to SRS became largely controlled under the domain of psychiatry. This was solidified during the 1952 development of the *Diagnostic and Statistical Manual of Mental Disorders* (DSM). The culminating entanglement of medicine and psychiatry occurred with the Harry Benjamin International Gender Dysphoria Association Standards of Care for the Hormonal and Surgical Sex Reassignment of Gender Dysphoric Persons, created and published in 1979. Currently known as the World Professional Association for Transgender Health Standards of Care (SOC), these guidelines proceeded to give mental health and medical practitioners complete control over access to hormones and SRS for trans people.

Although the need to access crucial health services to embody some trans identities created a reliance upon psychiatry and medicine, trans folks have not been completely passive agents. Trans people also became savvy consumers of the psycho-medical industry and learned to mimic the very narratives created about us to gain access to surgery and hormones (Namaste, 2005). According to McCoy (2006),

> [A]cquiring this level of expertise usually means that [trans people] assimilate the institutional gaze; they come to know themselves … as objects of institutional settings. They work on themselves; they produce their actions in ways that more tightly articulate the institutional process. Learning the discourse carries the intentionality of the discourse into the personal spaces of people's lives. (p. 119)

Trans people also exercised their agency through developing efforts to challenge the dominant gatekeeping role of medical-psychological institutions and the impact of these dominant discourses on transsexual people's understanding of themselves. As explained by Eve Shapiro (2004), "Transgender issues have become a site of activism, resistance, and social change … from a pathologized transsexual population that existed around support and informational groups to a politicized transgender community that challenges society's gender paradigms" (p. 166).

In 1968, the Ontario Ministry of Health began providing funds toward the development of a specialized gender identity clinic through integrating monies into the budget of the Clarke Institute of Psychiatry[2] located in Toronto. In 1970, sexual reassignment surgery was listed under the Ontario Health Insurance Plan (OHIP) for the first time. The Ontario Ministry of Health designated the Clarke as the only site authorized to evaluate trans people who wanted access to hormones and SRS. SRS for Ontario residents would not be covered under OHIP without authorization from the Clarke. The Clarke's gatekeeper role, however, went beyond the borders of Ontario to include all other provinces except PEI, Quebec, the Northwest Territories, and the Yukon.

During the 28 years that the Clarke functioned as gatekeeper—from the listing of SRS in 1980 to the de-listing of SRS by the Harris government in 1998—psychiatrists working at the Clarke became infamous for their sexist, classist, and masculinist views on trans issues, as well as the harassment and abuse that trans clients referred to the Clarke often experienced (Namaste, 1995, 2000). Unlike other gender identity clinics in North America that recognized the WPATH Standards of Care (SOC) as recommended guidelines for treatment, the Clarke employed a stringent reading of the SOC. Psychological and medical professionals at the Clarke modified the guidelines to impose rigid controls over eligibility criteria and to render the recommendations set out in the Real-Life Experience (RLE) or Real-Life Test (RLT) a mandatory requirement. The RLE requirements were as follows:

> The GIC [at the Clarke] has established guidelines for patients to be eligible for sex reassignment surgery. The individual must live in the chosen gender (the "opposite sex") full-time for at least two years. The GIC requires that this person provide written documentation supporting this claim. People can work, study, or do volunteer work full-time in order to meet this requirement. People can also engage in a variety of these activities, as long as the total is equivalent to full-time work or school. This guideline is commonly referred to as the "real life test."... After one year of cross-living, the individual is eligible for hormones. There is an endocrinologist associated with the GIC, who monitors the health of people who obtain their hormones through the GIC. After two years of cross-living, the individual is eligible for surgery. Before an individual is recommended for surgery, however, several other conditions must be fulfilled: he or she must be legally divorced, if once married; the person must be at least 21 years of age; there must be no evidence of psychosis; and there should be no recent record of criminal activity. (Namaste, 1995, p. 17)

Namaste (2000) has also reported that sex work was not deemed as qualifying work, and anyone who was seropositive for HIV was at risk of being disqualified. Female-to-male trans-identified clients rarely qualified for services at the Clarke. Even once phalloplasty and metoidoplasty became accepted SRS procedures, the Clarke still issued fewer than one female-to-male SRS recommendation per year compared to the four to six SRS recommendations for male-to-female transsexuals. During an Ontario Human Rights Tribunal Hearing in 1998, Dr. Dickey, one of the psychiatrists from the Clarke, conceded that 90 percent of trans clients seeking publicly funded SRS and access to hormones were denied.

Despite its very significant limitations and the oppressive ways in which it operated, from 1970 to 1998, the Clarke enabled *some* trans people to access state-subsidized hormone therapy and SRS procedures. In 1998, that access ended when the Ontario Provincial Conservatives de-listed SRS as an OHIP funded service. According to Shelley (2008),

> De-listing SRS as a procedure that can be publicly funded is a policy issue with concrete impacts on trans people's every day/night worlds and embodied lives. The neo-liberal favouring of private, consumer models of health care exacerbates class divisions that privilege those with the economic ability to pay for private services. (p. 70)

Access to trans-specific health care had been limited to those who successfully met the Clarke Institute's narrowly interpreted version of the Standards of Care. As such, Ontario provides a unique problematic and disjuncture. Hormones and SRS were publicly funded for trans people upon their recommendation alone. This changed during the decade following the de-listing of SRS. Transsexual individuals, particularly those residing in urban centres such as Toronto, employed a number of alternative routes to access transitioning health care services. For example, the Sherbourne Health Centre, which opened in downtown Toronto during 2001, rendered the provision of a holistic approach to health care for the LGBT community as part of its mandate. To date, the Sherbourne Health Centre has approximately five hundred trans-identified clients (www.sherbourne.on.ca).

For trans identified people outside of Toronto, the path to health care continues to be more tenuous. However, trans individuals have managed to find sympathetic family physicians who have been either willing to write prescriptions for hormones or give referrals to endocrinologists to enable their trans clients to access hormones. Trans men have, and continue to, pay out of pocket for "top surgery," and there are now a handful of plastic surgeons in Ontario willing to perform this surgery without a referral from a mental health and/or a primary health care physician, thus creating space for trans men to have surgery without an official diagnosis of gender identity disorder.

The Trans Health Lobby Group consists of members of the trans community and ally organizations, such as the Ontario Public Health Association, the Sherbourne Health Centre, the Canadian Union of Public Employees, the Canadian Federation of Students (Ontario), EGALE Canada, and the Rainbow Health Network. This group has been one of the main advocates for publicly funded SRS and related procedures as well as the education of media and politicians on issues of health care needs for trans communities.

In the spring of 2008, the Ontario Liberals re-listed hormones and SRS as funded under OHIP and, once again, reinstated CAMH as the gatekeeper to this funding source. The Trans Health Lobby Group has demanded to be part of implementing policy changes to ensure that CAMH does not continue as the sole gatekeeper. Many trans women and men are again seeking referrals to the GIC at CAMH especially for SRS due to the financial cost of the procedures, and not because they necessarily support or have had positive interactions with CAMH.

Literature Review

Research on access and barriers to health care services is often framed within a "social determinants of health" model and uses concepts of vulnerabilities and risk factors to explore issues of social marginalization, including poverty, homelessness, violence, increased susceptibility to using drugs and/or alcohol, the need to engage in survival sex work, and HIV/AIDS (JSI Research & Training Institute, 2000; Kenagy, 2005; Lombardi, 2001; Rachlin, Green, & Lombardi, 2008; Ware, 2004).

An issue in the literature is the often non- or cursory distinction made between the specific health care needs and issues of trans women versus those of trans men. The research often uses the term "transgender" or "transsexual" without demarcating whether participants in these studies have been female- or male-identified, lumping us together as a homogenous group with the implication being that members of the trans community have the same experience with health care or the same health care needs. When clarification as to participant identities has occurred, male-to-female transsexuals have predominantly been utilized within the research, with often very few or no female-to-males participating. This has further perpetuated the invisibility of trans men. The everyday reality for many trans men can be quite different than that for trans women.

The Trans Health Project, sponsored by the Ontario Public Health Association, provides evidence of similar themes emerging; that is, the need for health care services to become comprehensive and trans-inclusive, for health care providers to become educated on trans specific health care and trans positive to limit discriminatory practices, and for trans people to be a meaningful part of input into the health care process (Gapka & Raj, 2003).

Namaste (1995, 1999, 2000, 2005) has provided important groundbreaking studies of transsexual experiences, particularly within the Quebec and Ontario contexts. In *Access Denied* (1995), Namaste reports on a project in which 33 trans-identified individuals—only two were male-identified—were interviewed about their everyday experiences of social services and health care within Ontario. Namaste framed this study within an institutional ethnographic framework to demonstrate

> that the experience of transgendered people contradicts an "official" version of reality, in which all Ontario residents have the same rights and opportunities to access health care and social services. This report clearly documents that transgendered people are habitually refused the services they seek to live their bodies as they choose. Furthermore, my study indicates the situation is perhaps most serious for transgendered people with few resources. (p. 42)

Namaste's research looked specifically at access to and knowledge of hormones, primary care physicians, the gender identity clinic at the Clarke Institute, experiences with hospitals and emergency rooms, time spent in shelters, relations with police, and incidences of violence.

There is little research that considers the day-to-day reality of the work it takes to find competent, knowledgeable, trans positive health care, and the ongoing work of building relationships with health care providers to educate and convince them of our credibility as knowing bodies. To get the medical treatment we need, trans people will go to great lengths to prove to their health care providers that they are credible, real, and deserving of treatment, knowing that the providers play a large gatekeeping role to trans-specific care such as hormones and SRS.

How do we come to know what is a credible trans narrative within health care services? From where do we learn the discourses that provide us with the knowledge to access the services we need to transition and maintain our health? Discourse is defined as follows:

> The term "discourse" ... does not refer to discussion or dialogue as it does in everyday speech. Rather, discourse [means] a systematic way of knowing something, that is grounded in expert knowledge and that circulates widely in society through language, including most importantly language vested in texts. (Bresalier et al., 2002, p. 39)

It is this definition of discourse that grounds the analysis within the Marxist framework that IE is built upon. According to Smith (1999), "I know this discourse as an 'insider'; I am a participant; I know it as a local practice in my own life" (p. 134). My personal knowledge of being transsexual and transitioning services affords me the ability to spot the originating site of much of the discourse that has socially organized trans-specific health care in Ontario—the WPATH Standards of Care.

My Findings

During the summer of 2009, I conducted four semi-structured interviews with self-identified transsexual males who resided within a 100-kilometre radius of Hamilton, Ontario. Ranging in age from their mid-twenties to early forties, Thobias, Jason, Henry, and Wayne (all pseudonyms) were white and able-bodied, with English as their main spoken language. Through these interviews, I sought to illuminate the ways that participants' everyday experiences were connected to, and shaped by, the rules and policies of the health care professionals and organizations with which they engaged. As pointed out by Campbell and Gregor (2002), "When it comes to interpreting data, institutional ethnography relies on, explores and explicates linkages that are lived, brought into existence in time and space by actual people doing actual things" (p. 85). Participants were asked to share their experiences of accessing transsexual-specific health care services in Ontario, including how they became aware of these services, the steps they needed to take to access these services, their initial contact with the professionals and organizations providing transitioning services, and any steps they needed to follow afterward. Throughout the course of the interviews, and later, during further (re)reading of the interview transcripts, the data was subjected to the following line of inquiry:

> What is the work that these informants are describing or alluding to? What does it involve for them? How is their work connected to the work of other people? What particular skills or knowledge seems to be required? What does it feel like to do this work? What are the troubles or successes that arise from doing this work? What evokes the work? How is the work articulated to institutional work processes and the institutional order? (McCoy, 2006, p. 110)

Two main kinds of work emerged—the material work and the emotional work involved in accessing trans-specific health care. I defined "material work" as that which involved physical activity, such as phone calls, Internet research, attending support groups for information, attending various appointments, filling out forms, completing blood work, finding needles, injecting hormones, and educating health care providers about trans bodies and specific health care needs. "Emotional work" refers to the psychological energy that must be enacted by trans men to complete the various tasks and stages of transition. Such labour as having to be convincing and credible as trans or having to endure negative or puzzling interactions with health care providers takes a psychic toll on trans people.

The material and emotional work performed by trans men was explored in conjunction with the specific services they were attempting to access. As such, these experiences of work were mapped onto the main areas of access that emerged—the family doctor, and the gender identity clinic at the Centre for Addiction and Mental Health. The Ontario Ministry of Health has organized access to health care in such a way that a referral from one's family physician is required to access specialized health care services. Trans identification complicates the organization of how access to health care unfolds. In this instance, a family doctor who is familiar with the psycho-medical discourse often relies on such dominant understandings of gender identity to both set the criteria for who counts as transsexual and to inform their patients' treatment options.

The trans men I interviewed demonstrated that the family doctor is the site most often considered the access point for trans people who are interested in transitioning medically, as every participant opted to find service via this traditional health care route. For some trans people, informing one's family physician of their gender identity and wish to transition can produce levels of discomfort that provoke refusals on the part of their doctor to maintain them as patients. Not all cases are this severe. For many trans men, a family doctor's discomfort and/or lack of knowledge regarding trans-specific health care needs often leads to trans patients having to shoulder the burden of doing further material work to get the services requested. One of my research subjects, Wayne, compensated for his doctor's lack of knowledge regarding trans health by offering to do the material work of researching the health care options available to him. The knowledge Wayne provided to his doctor contributed to her willingness to write a referral for him. However, the referral for trans-specific care did not result solely from the information Wayne provided to his general practitioner. It was due significantly to the material and emotional work Wayne performed as evidence of his investment in transitioning medically. He explains:

> It had been two years since I initially asked her for testosterone, maybe over two years, and she said, "Fine, that's enough, you've jumped through enough hoops. Let's get you started."

Jason began inquiring about transitioning services in Toronto just before SRS was de-listed by OHIP in 1998. His family doctor was supportive, despite not being knowledgeable about trans-specific health care. Nevertheless, she did not extend her support toward offering Jason any practical assistance, such as finding appropriate referrals for him. Like Wayne, Jason did this work on his own:

> I had done my own research. I did go to an FTM support group out of The 519 twice when I was looking for hormones. At that point, Dr. —— was sort of the doctor that people were seeing. And I did see Dr. —— as an access point.

Because Jason's family doctor was uninformed, he chose to take it upon himself to find ways to access the service he needed to fulfill his desire to begin on hormones. Via a support network of other trans men, Jason managed to get the name of a doctor who was familiar with trans health care and willing to provide the treatment he wanted.

All four men familiarized themselves with what was needed to gain access to trans health care by knowing both what information to relay to their doctors and how to present themselves to the family doctor. They perform such labour even when the particular medical practitioner they are seeing is known within trans networks to be familiar with transsexual identities and experiences. If the doctor is unknowledgeable about transsexuality, as was the case for Wayne, Jason, and Henry, even more work is required of trans individuals to bring forth this mutual understanding of how trans-specific health care is socially organized to unfold. This knowledge comes directly from the language and concepts embedded within the WPATH Standards of Care.

Once a knowledgeable and willing family doctor is located, the next step in the process of transitioning medically is often to begin hormone replacement therapy to "change one's physical appearance, and aid in an individual's level of comfort with one's body. In the case of female-to-male transsexuals, the administration of testosterone has dramatic effects: the voice lowers, facial and body hair develops, muscles develop, and menstruation ceases" (Namaste, 1995). Without access to hormones, it is difficult for many trans men to be perceived by others as male. Therefore, the work to access hormones and to administer them effectively is a crucial part of transitioning. If access is difficult due to trans men having a doctor who is unwilling to prescribe testosterone or who lacks the appropriate knowledge required to administer hormones, the work undertaken by the men becomes increasingly arduous.

Some trans men want a hysterectomy, as they do not want to have female reproductive organs. Fallopian tubes, a uterus, and/or ovaries can be constant reminders of a sexed body that does not match their gendered body. Henry described the work he did in convincing his trans knowledgeable family doctor that a hysterectomy was an important health care issue for him. Although Henry was eventually referred to a specialist, it still took much dialogue and convincing on his part that this surgery was necessary for him and other trans men:

> [My doctor] went through a period where she didn't believe that hysterectomies were necessary.... She felt that it was very drastic, that it was kind of unnecessary, that it could be managed ... but I kept pushing for it.

The Gender Identity Clinic (GIC) at CAMH

For many trans men, sex reassignment surgery (SRS) is not financially feasible. During the 10 years that SRS was de-listed, trans men who had access to financial resources opted to pay for these procedures on their own, bypassing many of the criteria laid out in the Standards of Care (SOC). Unfortunately, this produced a two-tiered system within the domain of trans-specific health care in Ontario.

CAMH is the sole gatekeeper to SRS publicly funded by OHIP. As previously noted, this has been a point of contention amongst many trans activists who have lobbied to diminish the control maintained by CAMH. With the re-listing of SRS under OHIP in 2008, energy has been directed toward enabling other health care agencies across the province to become alternative recommendation sites. Whether one has had any personal interactions with CAMH or not, "the Clarke" (which CAMH is still often referred to as) has come to signify, within trans communities, the largest hurdle to overcome in having the transitioning process fully covered. This site that has controlled access to hormones and SRS has had a negative impact on the lives of many trans women and men. According to the men I interviewed, this has not changed. It would appear that interactions with the health care practitioners at CAMH's GIC continue to be difficult and often degrading.

Each participant alluded to the GIC at different points during their interview. They revealed that the actual process of moving from the decision to consider CAMH as a service option to an on-site appointment requires an incredible amount of work. These distinct areas of work that emerged during the men's engagement with CAMH began with considering CAMH as an option for service. For those deciding to pursue SRS via the GIC, additional labour includes completing the initial intake package. All four men had filled out the intake questionnaire that is sent out by mail. This text, which has gained much notoriety amongst trans communities, is the access point to CAMH's GIC and to the initial consultation with the psychiatrists who decide whether one is in fact a transsexual as defined by the criteria outlined in the *DSM-IV* under "gender identity disorder." Questions that are asked in this text are those pulled directly from the *DSM-IV* gender identity disorder criteria as well as from the SOC, particularly concerning the Real-Life Experience. Other work that trans men must do includes undergoing the consultation process and coping with the outcomes of their interaction with CAMH.

The men I interviewed had put much material and emotional labour into considering CAMH as a possible site for them to receive care. They spoke at length about the work they did to come to terms with their decision to, as Thobias stated, "give the Clarke a go and see what happens." He also spoke about the reactions he has received from other trans men who questioned his decision:

> And I've been ... sort of challenged by other trans guys. [And I have been wondering why I chose CAMH.] Why? I guess I don't feel very vulnerable. I'm out everywhere, and my life is pretty secure, what are they going to do to me? I'm not in an emotionally fragile space, I'm not in a financially fragile space, I've got lots of family and friends' support, I work in a job that everybody knows, and they all support it. What are they going to do to me?

Aware of this gatekeeper role of CAMH and the negative attitudes expressed toward other trans clients, Henry decides he does not have "the capacity or the energy" to confront the psychiatrists directly: "Like, how do you even begin to go to war with someone like that? How do you begin to intellectually compete with somebody who has established themselves in their mind as whoever they are?" Rather, he decides to "play along" during the process, choosing to be "just as cheeky and ridiculous as the psychiatrists are." Neither Henry nor Thobias has entirely disappropriated the discourse of CAMH as the site for trans specific health care. Henry is certainly aware of the power their program wields, and he is still willing to do the work, as frustrating and oppressive as it is to access publicly funded care.

The intake process utilized by CAMH represents another site where work is generated for trans men. The layout and questions comprised by the intake questionnaire come directly from the Standards of Care. The intake forms are framed to capture the qualifying nomenclature of gender identity disorder and to ensure that the Real-Life Experience (RLE) is underway. As mentioned previously, the RLE is used very inflexibly by CAMH. If trans people cannot demonstrate that they have begun living full-time in their chosen gender, they will fail to qualify for the services at CAMH and hence fail to realize the possibility of having their SRS expenses subsidized.

For some trans people, the RLE is much more complicated than it is for others, as it extends beyond being invested in transitioning. There appears to be little room afforded by CAMH for the consideration of possible extenuating circumstances. One aspect of the RLE involves choosing a first name appropriate to one's gender identity. To have one's name legally changed requires securing original birth documents and filling out government paperwork. To obtain government documents and to process changes to one's identification requires payment of administrative fees. For some trans individuals, this is not financially feasible. In addition, some men experience the requirement as unnecessary or inappropriate. Jason had done what he felt was necessary: he had shortened his female name such that it was gender-neutral. Unfortunately for him, this neutrality disqualified him from receiving services from CAMH. Jason was told at the only appointment he had with the psychiatrists at the GIC to come back when he could make a commitment to a masculine name or, as stated in the RLE criteria, "a gender identity–appropriate first name."

Wayne's situation is complicated by having dual citizenship and, therefore, having to navigate a different legal reality:

> I'm a US citizen and in the US the process is very different. You have to do, I mean it's almost ironic, but it's flip-flopped, you have to have done something that permanently changes your body before you can legally change your sex.... So if I start changing Canadian documents, I'm going to be in a situation where I have mixed documentation for a while.

CAMH's role as the site of the very strict gatekeeper to funded SRS is further illuminated via these comments by Wayne:

> They had set questions. There were correct answers to the questions. Some of the questions I knew the right answer [to] because I could just guess. So, yeah, the whole thing was really, like I said, it was not health care and it was not treatment, it was an audition.

Furthermore, CAMH's strict gatekeeper role extends to their interpretation of the text. Namaste's research (2000) demonstrates that CAMH privileges a heterosexual version of trans narratives. This is what counts as credible. According to Wayne,

> There were questions [where] they wanted to know about my childhood, my relationship with my mother, my gender identity when I was a child. They wanted to know about my sexual relationships, my sort of romantic history. Whether I dated men or women. The longevity of my relationships. They asked me whether or not I stand up when I pee. They asked me if I was binding my chest. They asked me when I have sexual fantasies, do I fantasize about penetrating or being penetrated?

CAMH's narrow interpretation of the Standards of Care prohibits Wayne and Jason access to trans-specific health care and, in turn, disavows their official status as (trans) men. Although trans identity has shifted over the years since the GIC was first developed, the intake questionnaire is still shaping and privileging a trans narrative that for some is no longer valid or relevant. As pointed out by Matte, Devor, & Vladicka (2009), "The SOC should recognize a wider range of potential identities among transgendered people, acknowledging that the concept of binary origins and destinations is not universally applicable" (p. 50).

CONCLUSIONS

Trans men do material and emotional work when they engage with various aspects of the health care system in Ontario. This intensive labour begins the moment these men decide to access specific services to facilitate their transition. My research showed that the family doctor was the initiating site for beginning to access transitioning services. However, what also became clear was the amount of work that occurred leading up to the initial visit with the family doctor. These men attended support groups to gather information on which family doctors were prescribing hormones; they researched the Internet to become familiar with the hormone replacement therapy (HRT) protocols and the physical and psychic effects of cross-gender hormones. They learned the criteria for meeting eligibility requirements to obtain a gender identity disorder diagnosis from CAMH. All of these material and emotional efforts were undertaken to ensure they arrived at the family doctor's office fully "armed" with the knowledge of, and the willingness to, reproduce the dominant transsexual narrative to access trans-specific health care. Together with psychological and medical professionals, FTM's produce the meaning behind who counts as a credible transsexual.

As previous research (Matte, Devor, & Vladicka, 2009; Namaste, 1995, 2000;) confirms, trans people are well versed in regard to the psycho-medical discourses that have created the credible trans narrative and perpetuated common trans trajectories toward treatment. Not every trans person is aware of the WPATH Standards of Care and its history. They do know, however, that there is a specific text that exists and has circulated to become part of an accepted discourse, and they know that this discourse gives us access to services.

Access is quite variable. Trans men often had to jump through hoops—sometimes for up to two years—before transitioning services were provided. In other cases, trans men would walk out of the doctor's office with a prescription for hormones after only one or two appointments. The men in my study were willing to take the informed risks associated with HRT because of the often central role that hormones have in the transitioning process. Nevertheless, they were concerned about the effects of cross-gender hormones on their bodies. My research subjects were more familiar with the protocols and the health research on the effects of testosterone and the potential for side effects than most of their family doctors. As a result of side effects, it is imperative that baseline blood work, pelvic, liver, and kidney exams are completed and regular follow-up monitoring occur (Namaste, 1995). The trans men I interviewed were interested in working together with their health care practitioners, especially given the fact that these physicians had little consistency regarding administering HRT and monitoring its effects. Initiating trans-specific health care practices and monitoring of such procedures was often prompted by the trans men participating in my study and not by their health care practitioners.

Some men were offered virtually no information with respect to administering hormones. Trans men at times must do their own work to figure out the correct gauge and type of needle to use for injecting testosterone, where to access these needles, and the appropriate bodily sites to administer the testosterone. Others, situated in large urban centres such as Toronto, have access to nursing care to assist with administering hormones.

My research also suggests that the gender identity clinic at CAMH is continuing to play a fairly large role in the lives of trans men. In the 10 years that SRS was de-listed in Ontario, other sites, particularly in larger urban centres, became available to trans people seeking trans specific health care services. Hormones for transitioning purposes are now much more readily available to trans men. As well, there has been an increase in the number of family doctors willing to work with trans clients. SRS, such as top and bottom surgery, for many, is still not financially feasible without OHIP coverage. For now at least, CAMH is still the only site in Ontario designated by the Ministry of Health to recommend these surgeries. Completion of the GIC program at CAMH is a necessity before SRS is insured as a benefit under OHIP.

It would have been quite easy to focus this project on the often discriminatory and derogatory reactions trans men cope with when attempting to acquire both general health care and trans-specific health care. Transphobia can be a debilitating part of everyday existence for trans people, and the trans men I interviewed and the academic research confirms this. My research suggests, however, that some of what is deemed a barrier to access that manifests as transphobia may in fact be a consequence of institutional discourses that frame how health care is socially organized for trans people. As Matte, Devor, and Vladicka (2009) state, "The gate keeping role which is implicit ... has remained in all versions of the SOC to date and is something to which many transpeople, and some service providers, vigorously object" (p. 48). When given the sole gatekeeping role for an extended period of time, as is the case in Ontario with the GIC at CAMH, there is less opportunity to be challenged by those who need this service and more of an opportunity to interpret the text. As Coleman (2009) informs us, "The aim of the original standards was to set minimal standards for assessment and determination of eligibility for hormonal and sex reassignment" (p. 2).

Trans activism in Ontario has concentrated on increasing the number of health care sites that could make SRS recommendations to OHIP, with the intent of reducing the gatekeeping role of CAMH. Although this is a useful recommendation for various reasons, especially as a way to create services outside of Toronto, it will not necessarily change the way trans-specific health care is discursively organized in Ontario. My research suggests that access and barriers to trans-specific health care have more to do with how the WPATH Standards of Care are manifest and mediate social relations between health care providers and trans men, and, hence, socially and institutionally organize how access to trans-specific health care unfolds in Ontario.

Perhaps it is time to move away from the WPATH Standards of Care as the basis for assessing transsexual identity and conferring access to hormones and SRS. Perhaps we need a set of guidelines that is less focused on restricting access to services and maintaining a narrow definition of what is considered to be a credible trans identity; guidelines that are also culturally and politically relevant in meeting the current needs of the trans community and the needs of health care providers who want to provide knowledgeable trans-specific care. Exploring alternatives to the SOC, such as the *Health Law Standards of Care for Transsexualism*, developed in 1993 in the US, or the *Guidelines for Health Organizations Commissioning Treatment Services for Individuals Experiencing Gender Dysphoria and Transsexualism* that came out of England in 2005, could prove valuable in lessening some barriers to accessing trans-specific health care.

NOTES

1 I am choosing to use the terms "transsexual," "transgender," and "trans" throughout this work as a reminder that these words are often used interchangeably within the community. As a member of this community, I am well aware that the identity of individuals who define as trans can be fluid and contested. Although the terms "transgender" and "transsexual" have arisen out of distinct cultural and historical times within the community and at various points have been considered antagonistic, it is near

impossible to create definitions of these terms without someone challenging the very definitions.

2 In 1998, the Clarke Institute of Psychiatry merged with the Addiction Research Foundation, the Donwood Institute, and Queen Street Mental Health to become known as the Centre for Addiction and Mental Health (CAMH). Depending on the timeline and context, both the Clarke and/or CAMH will be utilized.

REFERENCES

Bresalier, M., Gillis, L., McClure, C., McCoy, L., Mykahovskiy, E., Taylor, D., & Webber, M. (2002). *Making care visible: Antiretroviral therapy and the health work of people with HIV/AIDS.* Available at http://cbr.cbrc.net/files/1052421030/makingcarevisible.pdf

Campbell, M., & Gregor, F. (2002). *Mapping social relations: A primer in institutional ethnography.* Aurora: Garamond Press.

Coleman, E. (2009). Toward version 7 of the World Professional Association for Transgender Health's *Standards of Care. International Journal of Transgenderism, 11*(1), 1–7.

Gapka, S., & Raj, R. (2013). Trans Health Project: A position paper and resolution adopted by the Ontario Public Health Association. Available at www.opha.on.ca/ppres/2003-06_pp.pdf

JSI Research & Training Institute, Inc. (2000). *Access to health care for transgendered persons in greater Boston.* Report for GLBT Health Access Project, Boston, MA.

Kenagy, G. (2005). Transgender health: Findings from two needs assessment studies in Philadelphia. *Health & Social Work, 30*(1), 19–26.

Lombardi, E.L. (2001). Enhancing transgender health care. *American Journal of Public Health, 91*, 869–872.

Matte, N., Devor, A.H., & Vladicka, T. (2009). Nomenclature in the World Professional Association for Transgender Health's *Standards of Care*: Background and recommendations. *International Journal of Transgenderism, 11*(2), 42–52.

McCoy, L. (2006). Keeping the institution in view: Working with interview accounts of everyday experience. In D. Smith (Ed.), *Institutional ethnography as practice* (pp. 109–125). New York: Rowman & Littlefield Publishers, Inc.

Mykhalovskiy, E., & McCoy, L. (2002). Troubling ruling discourses of health: Using institutional ethnography in community-based research. *Critical Public Health, 12*(1), 17–37.

Namaste, V.K. (1995). *Access denied: A report on the experiences of transsexuals and transgenderists with health care and social services in Toronto.* Toronto: Project Affirmation and the Coalition for Lesbian and Gay Rights in Ontario. Available at www.web.ca/clgro

Namaste, V.K. (1999). HIV/AIDS and female-to-male transsexuals and transvestites: Results from a needs assessment in Quebec. *The International Journal of Transgenderism, 3*(1/2).

Namaste, V.K. (2000). *Invisible lives: The erasure of transsexual and transgendered people.* Chicago: University of Chicago Press.

Namaste, V.K. (2005). *Sex change, social change: Reflections on identity, institutions, and imperialism.* Toronto: Women's Press.

Rachlin, K., Green, J., & Lombardi, E. (2008). Utilization of health care among female-to-male transgender individuals in the United States. *Journal of Homosexuality, 54*(3), 243–258.

Shapiro, E. (2004). Transcending barriers: Transgender organizing on the Internet. *Journal of Gay and Lesbian Social Services* (Special issue on strategies for gay and lesbian rights organizing), *16*(3/4), 165–179.

Shelley, C.A. (2008). *Transpeople: Repudiation, trauma, healing.* Toronto: University of Toronto Press.

Smith, D. (1987). *The everyday world as problematic: A feminist sociology.* Toronto: University of Toronto Press.

Smith, D. (1999). *Writing the social: Critique, theory, and investigations.* Toronto: University of Toronto Press.

Ware, S. (2004). *Assessing the HIV/AIDS prevention, education, and support needs of trans people living in Toronto.* AIDS Committee of Toronto. Available at www.actoronto.org/website/research.nst/pages/transassessment

World Professional Association for Transgender Health. (n.d.). *Standards of Care for the health of transsexual, transgender, and gender nonconforming people.* Retrieved June 2009 from www.wpath.org/Documents2/socv6.pdf

Chapter 21 Agustine Only Plays with Barbies: A Psychosocial Synthesis of a Case Study

Silvia Tenenbaum[1]

INTRODUCTION

In *Thus Spoke Zarathustra*, an opus composed in several parts between 1883 and 1885 by German philosopher Friedrich Nietzsche (1844–1900), when Zarathustra is asked by a hunchback for a cure, he replies that a cure would only take away his spirit (or that which makes him distinctively him). As Phelan puts it, "Zarathustra teaches the contingency of all norms, and in so doing he teaches the value of each of our positions and knowledges. Our value does not rest in approaching 'the' norm, nor does it rest in our potential for being other than what we are; it rests in being well what we are" (Phelan, 1994, as cited in Atkins, 1998, p. 223).

In Canada, there is a paucity of ethnographic accounts of therapy with gender-divergent children and their parents.[2] Most mental health providers are neither academically nor clinically equipped to deal with this increasing population. Thus, when challenged with gender-diverse individuals of all ages, with the most vulnerable being the young, mental health providers "deal" with the issues either by referring these children to "experts" for which there are endless wait lists, or by silencing the voice of change heard in their turmoil. The emotional anguish, dissatisfaction, and discomfort that many adults and some children feel about their gender issues has been termed "gender dysphoria" (Brown & Rounsley, 1996, p. 10). Dyphoria stems from the Greek language and means "hard to bear." This is an interesting denotation given that, as I will show throughout this chapter, the significant burden of deviating from gender—a social norm—is placed on the individual and their families.

I have the honour to work with gender-divergent children, youth, and their families, which has added texture and richness to the scope of my practice. This chapter presents a case study conducted from March 2006 to July 2012 with a child and his family of origin.[3] I am an ethnically based trans positive psychotherapist, which means I work from a contextual and cultural viewpoint, always taking into consideration both the legacy of colonialism and my clients' immigration history. Within Canada, racist and colonial practices—in the sense of oppressing and silencing people who are different so that they conform to Western norms and become compliant adults—are still ongoing, and they present systemic barriers to non-conforming individuals who are at the margins of privilege. In my view, current practices in those arenas are part of my clients' context of mental health. In this chapter, I attempt to demonstrate that gender-variant children endure trauma not so much because of inner turmoil but because of external circumstances, and that, given the proper culturally sensitive intervention, they can develop into successful and functional adults.

THE CASE STUDY

One early morning in March 2006, a former patient of mine at the Barbra Schlifer Commemorative Clinic (a community-based feminist agency that deals with sexual violence against women) called to ask whether her sister and brother-in-law could bring their six-year-old child to me in my private practice for an assessment. They were artistically inclined newcomers to Canada who were seeking refugee status. They were also trying to understand their only son, Agustine (a pseudonym), whose major source of joy, according to his dad, was playing with Barbie dolls. My role consisted of providing sources of education to this family and to ensuring a sense of normalcy in this child's development, independent of their future life choices. I tried to instill a sense of freedom of choice about love, gender, sexuality, and family, and to protect their well-being while they were being questioned about the reason for their claim by immigration officials and other authority figures during their refugee case and basic settlement process.

Two years later, the family resurfaced in my clinical arena. Agustine's parents told me that after living in Quebec, and then in rural Ontario, they were considering moving to Toronto to facilitate Agustine's living with more diverse individuals in his environment. By this time, they had obtained permanent resident status, but they now needed a more subtle sense of support. Similar to Wallace Wong's discussion in Chapter 22 of this text on the part clinician's play to facilitate broader support networks for gender-divergent children, part of my role in assisting this family involved teaching them that, in figuring out who was going to be truly helpful for them and sensitive to their cultural needs, they should not make a decision based only on the person's credentials. My role also involved taking them to a welcoming community centre and putting them in touch with a non-judgmental psychiatrist for an evaluation of Agustine.

I phoned Agustine a couple of times to acquaint him with the notion of having a therapist around. I finally had the pleasure of working with him on a regular basis in individual sessions, as well as in family sessions. I also saw each of his parents in individual sessions. I made myself totally available to this family, to the point of requesting extra time at my work at the Barbra Schlifer Commemorative Clinic, which was granted. During the years I worked with Agustine and his nuclear and extended family, I saw them as part of my work at the Clinic, and then—after he was referred to Sherbourne Health Centre's Family Health Team and, subsequently for a more specific evaluation, to the Hincks-Dellcrest Institute—I saw them as part of my private practice again for a while. I have kept in contact with the family ever since.

In 2010, Agustine wished to be referred to as just "Agustine," but, if the use of a pronoun was necessary, he still opted for the male pronoun—hence my grammatical choice here. He presented as an ambiguous boy, and pictures of him reflect an artistic flair by the age of six. However, after only one year in a small-town Ontario public school, where he was increasingly bullied without any lasting support from the school administration, Agustine started to show signs of victimization. He felt he had what could be termed a handicap, which, as Brown and Rounsley suggest can result from bullying (1996, p. 10); this clouded every aspect of his life and was causing such severe emotional pain that it interfered with his day-to-day functioning. And his parents said that they felt the safety of the whole family was compromised by the lack of school support for their child. I invited the parents into the session and proposed that Augustine leave the school. I suggested he be home-schooled while his parents made the move to the more diverse Toronto, transferring the child to a setting that would be more educationally conducive and more helpful for Agustine in terms of social life in general and therapeutic possibilities in particular. Two months later, Agustine was enrolled at a school in Toronto's gay village on Church Street.

Agustine was conceived out of love and desire. His mother reported having a normal pregnancy and birth, followed by postpartum depression that lasted longer than usual due to their unstable living situation in the United States. His mother believes Agustine's early years were as normal as could be expected under the circumstances. She recalls, however, that when he started showing "girly" preferences and then a girly appearance (clothing, makeup, types of toys, gestures, and personality features), regular bouts of rejection by people in his surroundings entered this otherwise serene family life. This resulted in constant criticism from outsiders over their parenting style, as both mother and father decided to support this child's way of being in the world. Even though she is supportive, his mother is also extremely anxious, terrified that her child is not going to find happiness in a hostile world. All of Agustine's layering of performances (he was not sure whether he could really be himself in front of me when we first met) and the ambiguity of my observer's eye, combined with family dynamics and an anxious model of attachment, provided a battleground for several months. The father's paralyzed rage and the mother's long-lasting depression and heightened concern about her son's future happiness set the stage for innumerable conversations about internalized transphobia, and how to deal with rejection both from society and from caring but ignorant relatives, among other topics.

Because Agustine is his mother's only child, she provided him with oceanic amounts of attention and support from birth. However, the crystallization of core beliefs of the parents coupled with traumatic early experiences may influence their child's sense of safety within the household, especially if this takes place in the context of unresolved immigration experiences in both emotional and practical terms. This may result in what cognitive therapist Melanie Fennell (1999) termed "anxious predictions" (p. 79) or fear of the future in general, and vis-à-vis trans-gendering in particular. Issues of intergenerational trauma in Agustine's family were partly addressed in individual therapy sessions, but, given the urgency of daily events such as bullying, prior to their move to Toronto, the exploration of many deep-seated parental issues needed to be postponed until more serene times. This need for postponement poses ethical dilemmas for therapists who are painfully aware of ongoing colonial systems of oppression for those who are different (Duran, 2006, p. 26). Both parents and child were traumatized by normative practices of immigration and systemic barriers to education, employment, housing, and overall integration into society.

These normative practices and systemic barriers added another element of self-doubt for Agustine. It was therefore important that he be able to bring that to a therapist with proper training in dealing with gender-divergent children and their families. Self-doubt emerged out of the experience of being on a very personal journey. At a young age, this can be confusing, although the individuation process is never easy for anyone. A therapist's honest stance of not knowing, coupled with a collaborative model with the family (and even other supportive relatives, such as the mother's sister and her daughter, Agustine's cousin) provided a safe base for trial-and-error elements.

I struggled to be as clinically sound as possible, given the meagre scholarly support that exists in the Canadian context concerning newcomers. Even a well-intended text such as the Peterkin guide, while discussing trans people (about 2 percent of the text), uses unacceptable phrasing such as "allow young people some flexibility in questioning their gender identity" (Peterkin & Risdon, 2003, p. 290). "Some flexibility" is not enough, nor is holding a compassionate, but distant, view of those suffering. Politically aware psychotherapists and mental health providers have to engage in committed political work, here and now. As the Latin saying goes: "If you had held your tongue, you would have remained a philosopher" ("*Si tacuisses, philosophus fuisses*," cited by Jacoby, 2005, p. 6).

For the treatment plan to be genuinely client-centred, it needed to include advocacy work around immigration matters, settlement, and housing; information about ESL classes and about community resources; and allies and pertinent sympathetic people to surround the family with all possible love and support, as needed. The clinical literature about client-centred therapy defines it as that in which "the therapist understands [their] spiritual identity and has provided a space in which patients can relate to the entities causing them distress" (Duran, 1996, p. 45). To that definition we can add the aspect of client-centred therapy that is informed by the social determinants of health; namely, as basic needs to be facilitated by the clinician if needed. It is the client who is genuinely at the centre—not the ideologically driven therapist following their own (or their agency's) political agenda, or the lazy therapist applying or imposing the types of interventions they feel comfortable applying. Working with gender non-conforming kids and their parents involves accepting discomfort.

I acknowledged that the members of this family were positioning themselves within an alternative that is not of their own making. Furthermore, they were often going to be forced to endure the primal reactions of others, because repudiation is both a concept and a process (Shelley, 2008, p. 31). As explained by Christopher Shelley (2008) in his book *TransPeople: Repudiation, Trauma, Healing*: "To repudiate is to reject, refuse, condemn, repel, disown, renounce, and back away from that which engenders repulsion. Repudiation entails dynamics of denial" (p. 37). Furthermore, "repudiation of trans-subjectivity can be seen on a spectrum ranging from a conscious yet unexpressed distaste through to extreme forms of reaction that precipitate violence and destructiveness based on rage (sudden and explosive) or hatred (stable, integrated aspects of enmity towards an object)" (p. 41).

But repudiation is not normal, however common it may be. The family experienced daily incidents of harassment, and yet knew that this was not normal. These incidents were the motive behind the family's multiple relocations within Canada and the United States; unfortunately, they continued to experience the effects of racism, classism, and transphobia. After eventually finding their way to Toronto, they began to find the services they had been yearning for, leading to a feeling of triumph over despair. In the sessions following their move, I noticed the subsiding of Agustine's nervous tics.

LESSONS ABOUT THE THERAPIST'S ROLE

It is vital for any therapist seriously engaged in long-term mental health care for a gender-divergent child and his family of origin to assume that the reconstruction of the social in the new setting is going to take place. I know from direct clinical experience what the future is going to be if such a child is left isolated. We need to cultivate a trans positive atmosphere that is attuned to socialization and nationalism; trans-inclusive therapy is a political necessity. A psycho-educational element is imperative; therefore, effecting change in schools, encouraging public lectures, networking, and even adopting a political angle are, in my view, as important as the psychotherapeutic choices the therapist makes. Healing does not occur in a vacuum; it is as much an external process as it is an internal one. I treat with therapy as much as I intervene externally, with advocacy and workshops, even a radio show about mental health. Agustine as a person and as a clinical case resists simplistic notions of gender and maybe of sexuality. My role was to provide support to the patient and information to the parents, and to be a consistent advocate and mental health provider, in the long run if necessary. There is no winning role in the often-tumultuous practice of providing long-term support. As Sandra Bloom (1997) explains, we struggle to learn to resist becoming trapped in any of these roles, while continuing to safeguard the well-being of the patient. There is little to no literature about the constant ethical dilemmas therapists are facing when advocating for gender-divergent children and their families, as it may contradict the internal politics of their working organization. I personally have always felt more at ease in my private practice because I needed only to consult and ultimately respond to my chosen clinical supervisor and the family itself. I could provide ongoing and clinically sound therapy with a political angle, which might or might not have been accepted in the clinical settings I was affiliated with during those years. However, I strongly believe that it is absolutely necessary to provide as much advocacy and networking as clinical support.

One of the main issues I have to deal with is my patients' constant sense of shame, and the need to build a different sense of self-esteem. Working with a gender-divergent child brings all theories of "normative" gender development into question. Providing support for sex- and gender-variant children and youth is not for the rigid or lazy, because it brings about change in, and a constant re-articulation of, the counsellor's beliefs. I applaud children who take the "road less travelled" and who allow their incipient discomfort to fully flourish into a different gender, another reality, and a personal path without the agony of feeling ashamed. Shame is another culturally constructed concept. Its origins go back to the Bible, and the apple that gave lucidity to Eve about her nakedness in the world. Therefore, we could and have to deconstruct it, because all children need to be validated in their developmental stages.

According to the psychoanalyst Mario Jacoby (2005), shame is intricately tied to one's social context. As a Jungian, I agree with him that a science of the psyche can never sufficiently encompass the kaleidoscopic richness and complexity of the potential of the living soul in the "*mundus archetypus*" (Jung, 1977, p. 534). Thus, this chapter is merely an attempt to invite both physicians and mental health providers to consider the multi-varied set of experiences a gender-divergent child and their families can offer, if given the opportunity. Agustine uses his love for dancing, singing, and designing and creating his own clothes to express his own version of reality, however different it may appear to be.

When psychotherapist and social justice activist Larry Jin (Kwok Hung) Lee (2005) invites all of us working in the mental health field to "take off the mask," he refers to the fact that many therapists work and write under the assumption that contextual factors do not interfere directly in our patients' sense of well-being. In Agustine's case, he openly talked about contextual factors such as where he lives, school with or without support systems, and other barriers, such as not knowing if his cultural background would make him more vulnerable, or prone to ridicule, or more confident, given his dual expertise. Freddy A. Paniagua (2005) refers to some ethno-specific groups as having "healthy cultural paranoia" (p. 34). According to my own experience working with this family, as part of their emotional repertoire after complex trauma issues, now coupled with settlement issues, recovery is possible. Newcomers need to develop a healthy balance between their fear of rejection and actual rejection, especially if they do not fit preconceived notions of family. For instance, instead of talking superficially about being "part of the solution, not part of the problem," it has been much better in my experience to acknowledge actually being part of the problem, assuming that we are part of the health industry that produces illness and certainly benefits from it. Although this is a dark aspect of being a therapist, it is good to voice that we all make a living out the misery of this society. By talking about "the king being naked" we open Pandora's box for our clients' profound sense of engagement, and finally, their cultural, political and psychological safety—much-needed concepts. To summarize, I am routinely using systemic, de-colonizing, and CA/CBT (culturally adapted cognitive and behavioural therapy) approaches to increase assertiveness in a map context, to rationalize emotions (anger/frustration/confusion), and to generate healthy and realistic boundaries. Other therapeutic approaches I tend to use within this population of trans youth, in addition to a feminist (as a political stance) and anti-oppressive framework (assuming cultural critical theories) as an overarching guiding principle, are the following:

1. A Jungian exploration on the issue of shame; also a Jungian relational approach to explore attachment patterns to decrease unnecessary "drama." My operational definition of drama is "disconcerting pent-ups of anxiety."
2. Viktor Frankl (logotherapy) analysis on survivor's guilt, either in relation to one's origin, or about one's trajectory, which in trans youth is related to other's dreams—and their nightmares.
3. A non-verbal, artistic approach—in my case, done via ceramics at Sherbourne Health Centre and dramatherapy at CAMH Addiction Services—given the non-verbal repudiation many trans youth encounter on a daily basis. Processing in silence is good, but creating in silence while processing is better. This is not about talent but about creating clinical spaces for healing to take place. Professor Gary Harper (personal communication, June 2013) states that the intersectionality of contextual aspects among sexual minorities is often coupled with multiple cultural influences (ethnicity, racial characteristics, sexual orientation) to generate resilient youth.

"Trans is a rich domain," stated Oregon-based epidemiologist and glass artist Alexis Dinno (2013), with no linear answer to their many inner and outer aspects. Dinno also called trans individuals "gender elite" (personal communication, 2013).

In concrete terms, for my specific case study with Agustine and his family of origin, his mother's anger and his father's confusion over the intolerant people surrounding them—despite the fact that they had emigrated to Canada, a country whose nationalism is based on discourses of multiculturalism, tolerance, and diversity—has been a constant in the battle for the sense of normalcy that is so necessary to a basic sense of safety. Working on shifting that colonial balance meant, in clinical terms, three distinctive characteristics that I assumed and explored within this therapeutic modality:

1. Historical trauma on top of personal one(s), so that clients could access a family/community history from a dialoguing and relational framework, with an adapted systemic technique on genograms and family histories, based on Dr. Duran's approach as a de-colonizing psychologist in the US.
2. Taking responsibility and deconstructing my own sources of privilege that gave closure to clients' myriad of questions about social justice and how to manage it, within a healing encounter, based on the work of Aboriginal psychologists Dr. Jean-Paul Restoule and Dr. Suzanne Stewart at OISE, and by adapting their techniques for international ancestry issues, coupled with CAMH work in adapting CBT to specific cultural communities (CA/CBT booklet produced in 2011, when I was the Spanish-speaking clinician providing individual therapy in that pilot project).
3. Actively and routinely engaging in a commitment of writing, researching, and presenting at international conferences to open up new spaces of dialogue for different audiences. In my case I have made the commitment of travelling three times per year to different venues to increase the knowledge base of clinicians in different societies (Mexico, Japan, Sweden, and Portugal, to name a few), instead of "preaching to the choir" or hiding in the counselling room. We cannot ask our clients to open to their discomforts if we are not willing to do the same by expanding our comfort zone. Curriculum design has been another area I have been utilizing to increase counter-hegemonic knowledge from within in scholar spaces, for incoming new clinicians, both at OISE and University of Toronto Schools, and at Adler Graduate Professional School and TAPE (Training and Professional Education). Trans academics ought to increase their visibility in the international arena, open also to the general public.

Trans activism requires inner work to politicize clinical programs and to de-pathologize trans communities from within; for example, by separating older issues from the ones that new generations are presenting to trans positive psychotherapists like myself. It means being bold enough to see the valuable pioneer work vis-à-vis actualized present needs. Furthermore, some problematic mental health workers (doctors, therapists, social workers, even academics that once published with Dr. Zucker), trans or not, might not provide any more healthy a role model for the newer gender non-conforming generations. Thus, new spaces need to be generated.

Sometimes healing occurs outside the therapist's office. If and when confronted with a gender-divergent child, a mental health provider needs to address the psychosocial aspect. For instance, I was able to conduct therapy while observing Agustine in the park, filming his mother's recalling of early events, filming their move to Toronto (thanks to the professional support of Vlad Wolanyk, a client resource worker at Sherbourne Health Centre, who collaborated with this family to document Agustine's life for later potential inclusion in a work of art), and helping them to network, as needed. Indeed, therapy occurs both inside the office and outside in the community.

According to Cohen-Kettenis and Pfäfflin (2003), despite the many treatment approaches to treating gender-non-conforming children from an emotional viewpoint, controlled studies of its outcomes do not exist. In the work of some eclectic therapists, the primary focus is on any factor that may negatively influence the child's functioning, not the cross-genderness per se. A great variety of approaches exist for the treatment of children like Agustine, ranging in Toronto from the approach of the gender identity clinic at CAMH (diagnose the pathology and treat, what I call the DSM-IV deficit approach) to the Sherbourne Health Centre with their radical acceptance approach. However, I can certainly attest to the crucial role the social context plays in Agustine's life. In that sense, the course of treatment followed theoretically on David Valentine's (2007) ethnographic exploration of the concepts of gender and sexuality as distinct, if related, arenas of human experience, experiences that are neither reducible to one another nor explicable by the other. Gender and sexuality are neither self-evident experiences nor natural explanatory frameworks; rather, they are categories with complicated histories and politics.

CONCLUSION

By the end of the case study, Agustine was 11 years old. He wants to have full female breasts and is aware of both hormonal and surgical possibilities in the future, which he regularly discusses with his parents. As provocatively stated by Sally Hines and Tam Sanger (cited in WengChing, 2013), "surgery was (and still is) positioned as a route to gendered harmony." As a result of early turmoil provoked by regular social questioning of his gender, Agustine presents as a happy child at home; however, he is somewhat guarded in social situations. Family support has been crucial to Agustine's healthy development, in his own terms. The whole family is comfortable and is seeking sources of support with increasing independence and confidence.

I have had the honour to walk this family through all possible moods, but "between mania and melancholia, the affinity is evident: not the affinity of symptoms linked in experience, but the affinity—more powerful and so much more evident in the landscapes of the imagination—that unites the same fire both smoke and flame" (Foucault, 1965, p. 132).

Sometimes I feel that my work is done; at other times I fear that my work has not even begun. At times I feel confident, and on dark days, I think I have nothing to bring to such a difficult case. I have learned that this is normal, that this is all right. Indeed, this clinical engagement has provided me with the unique privilege to witness and co-facilitate the development, as healthily and strongly as possible, of the early stages of a multi-layered gender identity formation, which I consider to be a golden opportunity in my practice. As a secondary gain, I have noticed, in both my trans youth and myself, a more subtle negotiation between sanity and madness, practising a definition of sanity as a unified field, "not to be slave of blind forces" (Symington, 2006, p. 1059). As a result, I have had to increase my psychotherapeutic repertoire beyond books and theories. Indeed, Agustine has made me a better clinician and a more humane person, and I am profoundly grateful to Life for this chance encounter.

There have been more questions than answers, but Agustine himself was always included in the dialogue. General questions framed particular ones, and the conversation is never really going to end. My hope is that my clinical engagement will instill in Agustine a sense of pride, and for him to be increasingly aware of his blessing, this unique way of being in the world, and the exhilarating beauty and sense of liberation in his self-constructing of his own little persona, however difficult it feels—and is—at times.

EPILOGUE

At the time of this initial writing, Agustine was 13 years old, attending an alternative school focused on art. He is designing clothes and participating in all art-related activities at the school, where he is well liked. He is now a happy, well-adjusted youth, full of zest for life and very wise in day-to-day conversation. He is using a newly created gender-free washroom, and has just started puberty-blocking hormonal therapy under careful medical supervision. He is taking the streetcar to school without accompaniment, and feeling safe—but cautious—in his presentation to the world. His father proudly walks with Agustine when he is now dressed as a female, and his mother is dialoguing with him about the new first name he might start using soon. At the present time, I have the honour to be co-teaching a course I designed with Dr. Oren Gozlan at Adler Graduate Professional School on the matter of exploring the nuances, fantasies, and enigmas of gender transformations, and to be navigating the health system with gender non-conforming teens in Toronto.

NOTES

1 I thank Sherbourne Health Centre for their flexibility with regards to my schedule with Agustine and his family around 2009 and 2010. I appreciate the gracious comments on a first draft of this chapter by Prof. Dan Irving of Carleton University. I thank Dr. Erik Schneider for his fertile comments in Sweden in 2012, and posterior encouragements from Luxembourg. Closer to home, I thank therapist Max Carney for clinical discussions within a compassionate compass, and for complicity and laughter. Finally, I thank the three emotional pillars in my present life: my late mother, Prof. Esther Magid, who instilled a love of learning and promoted a sense of the Quixotic adventure of living one's life; my younger daughter, Laura Martínez, my best mirror, the synthesis of many arts; and my elder daughter, Ana Carla Enríquez-Johnson, with profound gratitude for the abundance she brings, together with her own children, Dylan and Daniela.

A preliminary version of this chapter was presented at the conference Trans Rights as Human Rights—The Implications for Trans Health(Care), on May 10, 2012, in Linköping, Sweden, in a round table comparing the English (educational), Dutch (legal), and Canadian (psychological) status of trans children. Some revisions occurred while pondering peace as a process in Hiroshima on November 11, 2012, and an aspect of this final version was explored at the First LGBT Psychology and Related Fields Conference in Lisbon, Portugal, on June 20, 2013, under the title "Former Supplicants of History: Neuroscience and the Healing Profession for Trans-Youth."

2 What has traditionally been available for gender-variant children is the intervention developed by Dr. Ken Zucker, known as "reparative" therapy. Dr. Zucker's ideas are summarized by Bailey (2003, p. 31) as "the Barbies have to go."

3 While all family members gave permission for the study concept and for processing it into its final written form, some details have been changed to protect the family's privacy and sense of comfort.

REFERENCES

Atkins, D. (Ed.). (1998). *Looking queer, body image, and identity in lesbian, bisexual, gay, and transgender communities*. New York: Harrington Park Press.

Bailey, J.M. (2003). *The man who would be queen: The science of gender-bending and transsexualism*. Washington, DC: Joseph Henry.

Bloom, S. (1997). *Creating sanctuary: Toward the evolution of sane societies*. New York: Routledge.

Brown, M.L., & Rounsley, C.A. (1996). *True selves: Understanding transsexualism—For families, friends, coworkers, and helping professionals*. San Francisco: Jossey Bass.

Cohen-Kettenis, P.T., & Pfäfflin, F. (2003). *Transgenderism and intersexuality in childhood and adolescence: Making choices*. Thousand Oaks, CA: Sage Publications.

Dinno, A. (2013). *On the just and accurate representation of transgender persons in research*. Paper presented at the First LGBT Psychology and Related Fields Conference in Lisbon, Portugal, June 20–22.

Duran, E. (2006). *Healing the soul wound: Counseling with American Indians and other Native Peoples*. New York: Teachers College Press.

Fennell, M. (1999). *Overcoming low self-esteem: A self-help guide using cognitive behavioural techniques*. London: Robinson.

Foucault, M. (1965). *Madness and civilization: A history of madness in the age of reason*. New York: Vintage.

Jacoby, M. (2005). *Shame and the origins of self-esteem: A Jungian approach*. New York: Routledge.

Jung, C.G. (1977). *Mysterium Coniunctionis: An inquiry into the separation and synthesis of psychic opposites in alchemy*. Collected Works, Vol. XIV. Princeton, NJ: Princeton University Press.

Lee, L.J. (2005). Taking off the mask. In M. Rastogi & E. Wieling (Eds.), *Voices of color: First-person accounts of ethnic minority therapists* (pp. 91-115). Thousand Oaks, CA: Sage Publications.

Paniagua, F.A. (2005). *Assessing and treating culturally diverse clients: A practical guide* (3rd ed.). Thousand Oaks, CA: Sage Publications.

Peterkin, A., & Risdon, C. (2003). *Caring for lesbian and gay people: A clinical guide*. Toronto: University of Toronto Press.

Phelan, S. (1994). *Getting specific: Postmodern lesbian politics*. Minneapolis: University of Minnesota Press.

Shelley, C.A. (2008). *Transpeople: Repudiation, trauma, healing*. Toronto: University of Toronto Press.

Symington, N. (2006). Sanity and madness. *International Journal of Psychoanalysis, 87*(4), 1059–1068.

Valentine, D. (2007). *Imagining transgender: An ethnography of a category*. Durham and London: Duke University Press.

WengChing, L. (2013). *Human spectrum project*. Paper presented at the First LGBT Psychology and Related Fields Conference in Lisbon, Portugal, June 20–22.

Chapter 22 Using a Family and Multi-Systems Treatment Approach: Working with Gender-Variant Children

Wallace Wong

INTRODUCTION

This chapter discusses the experiences of gender-variant children, the shortcomings of the current psychiatric diagnostic classification system (DSM-IV-TR),[1] and research related to understanding and intervening with gender-variant children, youth, and/or their families. I suggest that a working model approach to care[2] is the preferred therapeutic model because it situates the child's developmental needs as the primary focus. The working model to be discussed emphasizes that it is important to work with the family and other systems, such as school or medical, in which the child is embedded. This model focuses on educating the parents about gender-variant behaviours, and empowering them to advocate for their child, seek appropriate professional help, and organize a professional care team to support the child's developmental needs. This model is similar to other gender-affirming models used by clinicians working with gender-variant children, youth, and/or their families insofar as it focuses on psycho-education, self-empowerment, and self-advocacy when working with gender-variant children (Lev, 2004; Raj, 2007).

The family and multi-systems approach is intended to work with many different systems that affect a child's development (Boyd-Franklin, 1989; Brown, 2002; Rosenblatt, 1996). Similar to Silvia Tenenbaum's Chapter 21 in this text, I will also discuss the family and school systems, primarily because of their prominence in children's lives, but also because younger children tend to express most of their early development within these social realms. While I focus on the family and educational systems, this does not mean that other social and structural relations are less important. On the contrary, all components that support a child's healthy development should be considered within a multi-systems working model.

WORKING WITH GENDER-VARIANT CHILDREN

Working with the families of gender-variant children is essential. Normally, many older adolescents and adults with issues or concerns related to their gender identity and/or public expression of their identity are able to seek therapy on their own, while younger children must rely on their family or parents to seek help or support for them. Clients who are older adolescents and adults usually have some ideas and expectations of what they want to work on in therapy. Their expectations range from gaining more understanding of their gender concerns to seeking recommendations for sex reassignment surgery (SRS). Even individuals who are struggling with or uncertain about their gender identity can generally advocate for themselves in therapy. For instance, my adolescent or adult clients would communicate some of their expectations to me and sometimes even terminate the service if they perceived that it was not meeting their needs.

The process of therapy is very different, however, for gender-variant children. They are usually referred for therapy by someone else, such as their parents, teachers, or other counsellors. They are sent to my office because these individuals are concerned about the child's non-conforming cross-gender behaviour, such as cross-dressing or persistent cross-sex role behaviours. Adults who refer the gender-variant child to therapy are usually those who take care of the child at home or in different settings. They often have the best intentions for the child, but feel anxious or uncomfortable about the cross-gender behaviour they have observed in the child (Lev, 2004). Referring parties have clearly shared their treatment expectations with me, letting me know what they want to happen. Unfortunately, they usually expect me to "cure" the child of displaying any cross-gender behaviour, meaning that they hope the child will become more gender conforming within the social binary norm (male/female or masculine/feminine). Such desires stem from the heteronormative logics that frame Canadian society. In fact, caregivers' understandings of such non-normative behaviours as problematic issues that "ought" to be fixed are not isolated to their personal beliefs. Some clinicians also believe that using a treatment approach to reduce cross-gender behaviour is appropriate for these children (Rekers, 1995; Zucker, 1990). They develop interventions that are not based on the child's needs, but rather on the parent's expectations and society's binary gender norm.

Gender-variant children are often powerless in this process. Very often they do not have the maturity or skills to advocate for themselves. They are brought into my office and are forced to work on modifying behaviours that seem "natural" to them, and because of this, their motivation to change is low and their resistance is high. Therefore, some scholars raise concerns and believe that such interventions might actually hinder the child's future development (Burke, 1996; Scholinski, 1997; Wren, 2000).

Some gender-variant children may actually "want" to change their cross-gender behaviour, because they sense the disapproval that is coming from the adults they love and respect (Mallon, 1999). These children may think, "What would be the easiest/fastest/safest way to get their love and approval back?" They sense that the disapproval probably comes from their cross-gender presentation, which leads them to conclude that "I am the problem" and "I must change." One of my young clients once shared his experience with me of seeing his parents begin to cry when they caught him wearing a dress. He felt certain that what he did must be wrong, causing them to feel "mad" and "sad." The child learned that the only way to regain the adults' love and approval was to cease presenting any cross-gender behaviour. The child was convinced that the behaviour was the core of the problem.

Some parents may be more liberal and flexible with gender issues. They might not have any problems with their gender-variant children. Unfortunately, in our binary gender-based society, people from other contexts, such as media or peers, often remind them their gender-variant children are not "normal" by using different forms of discrimination, both overtly and covertly (Gibson, 1994; Lev, 2004).

There is no doubt that clinicians who have the privilege to work with gender-variant children should have adequate training, not only in understanding the issues related to gay, lesbian, bisexual, and transgender populations, but also in terms of family dynamics and the differing needs of children across specific developmental stages.

Even though parents are the "customers," we, as clinicians, need to know who our clients are. Caring for these children's best interests should be our first priority. Using treatment approaches that focus solely on changing the child might not be the best strategy. Instead, clinicians should educate parents and help them to understand that gender-variant children are a heterogeneous group. Clinicians need to provide education and information about the diversity of sexual behaviours and gender expressions, especially among children; "there is a greater fluidity and variability in outcomes" (Meyer et al., 2001, pp. 14–15). While some parents welcome and are receptive to this, some may prefer seeking "treatment" with other clinicians who will have a similar "treatment expectation" to theirs, which is to emphasize socially "gender-appropriate" behaviours and to eliminate behaviours that are deemed to be cross-gendered. Clinicians need to take a stand that their primary responsibility is to protect the best interests of the child. At times, this may mean that the clinician might consult child protection agencies when we see parents using treatment or behavioural approaches that can cause harm to the child's well-being.

A similar approach is suggested for school systems. They also need to know that they must be more flexible when it comes to working with gender-variant children. These children might have special needs beyond those of regular students. School systems are responsible for offering support and flexibility with rules or system modification, the same as they would for other children with special needs.

THE INFLUENCE OF THE DSM

There has been much debate concerning the use of rigid and stereotypical gender behaviours as diagnostic categories for gender identity disorder (GID) (Bartlett, Vasey, & Bukowski, 2000; Richardson, 1996). In fact, whether GID should be listed in the DSM as a disorder has evoked heavy debate. One of the criticisms of the DSM is that the diagnostic criteria for GID tend to presume universal gender-stereotyped behaviours (Lev, 2004). The DSM lists many cross-gender behaviours as diagnostic criteria, such as a preference for cross-dressing, strong preferences for cross-sex roles, an intense desire to participate in the stereotypical games and pastimes of the other sex, and a strong preference for playmates of the other sex, to name a few. Using stereotypical gender behaviours as diagnostic criteria indicates that cross-gender behaviour is a sign of pathology (Zucker & Bradley, 1995). As a result, many people, such as parents, professionals, or the children themselves, are misguided. They think that cross-gender expression or behaviours are a sign of pathology. Thus, developing "treatment" to eliminate those behaviours will be considered appropriate, and controlling those behaviours will be the measure of "success" or "being cured."

The presumption that cross-gender behaviour is a sign of pathology is especially dangerous for gender-variant children. Some parents and professionals may have uneasy feelings about the child's cross-gender behaviours to start with, but once they learn about the diagnostic criteria in the DSM, their belief that cross-gender behaviours are abnormal are confirmed and reinforced (Lev, 2004). Using these criteria to diagnose a child is not only "genderist,"[3] but actually leads parents and others to believe that cross-gender behaviour is indeed "deviant." Not only do these criteria offer little help to clinicians in distinguishing children who are struggling with gender distress (Lev, 2004; Richardson, 1999), such criteria might actually stigmatize these children to a greater extent. Some children may struggle with marked distress and discomfort with their gender and sex at an earlier age. Many gender-variant children, however, do not necessarily see their cross-gender behaviour as a "problem," at least not until they are told and reminded by others that what they are doing is "abnormal" and a sign of pathology.

These diagnostic criteria might lead these children to evaluate their "cure from the problem" based on how much they can successfully alter those behaviours and how well they can pass as the gender that matches their biological sex. In other words, these children will feel that they need to learn to suppress their authentic self and to perform a false self. This process appears to be suppressive, rather than self-actualizing for the child.

Given that the DSM diagnostic criteria are based on gender stereotypes, a gender-variant child can easily meet the diagnostic requirements and be labelled as "a child who is diagnosed with GID." From my clinical experience, whereas some parents may actually feel relief (because they finally have an explanation for their child's "unusual" gender expression), many of them feel despair because the GID diagnosis has confirmed that their child's gender-variant behaviours are signs of pathology.

When a child is labelled with this diagnosis, many parents feel that it is important to share the information that their child has GID with school authorities. They are convinced it is a necessary process because it offers teachers and school administrators an explanation for their child's gender non-conforming behaviour. Regrettably, this information is often shared among school staff and remains in the child's academic file. Such information puts the child at risk. The diagnosis of GID, which is still questioned amongst psychological and medical professionals, could affect how the child is treated at school in the future.

The criteria listed in the DSM do little to explain the diversity of the gender continuum in gender-variant children; instead, they only confirm the rigid sex and gender roles in today's society. The criteria in the DSM lack clear indication as to how to distinguish between the group of gender-variant children and the group of children who are actually struggling with marked distress due to the mismatch of their genitalia and their gender identity.

For instance, many children present some form of gender-variant behaviour during different developmental stages; this does not necessarily mean that they want to change their sex or gender entirely. This behaviour might be nothing more than part of the normative sexual and gender identity developmental process. It is not unusual for children to explore cross-gendered activities and roles throughout their developmental stages. The determination of which particular behaviours are an indication of pathology is subjective. Different people, such as parents, clinicians, and teachers, can differently interpret a child's behaviour, and such interpretations depend on their personal comfort levels, moral values, perceptions of gender roles, and so on. Moreover, our society has very different expectations as to how girls and boys should be. While it is acceptable for a girl to dress in pants and a T-shirt, it is readily considered abnormal for a boy to wear skirts and dresses. As a result, boys are more likely to be referred to treatment (Green, 1995), whereas some girls who actually struggle with gender dysphoria might be overlooked. Such gender bias delays the clinical and medical attention that these girls may require. It is important to know that if a girl struggles with a mismatch of her natal sex and her gender, delaying treatment can cause more psychological and emotional harm for her. She will have to live her life with a gender that does not fit her "authentic self." When she denies her "authentic self," she will only be able to learn the gender socialization of a female and miss the opportunity to be socialized as her authentic self.

A FAMILY AND MULTI-SYSTEMS TREATMENT APPROACH

As discussed earlier, the DSM diagnostic criteria tend to pathologize gender-variant children. Clinicians are easily misguided and often develop a working model that focuses on eliminating cross-gender behaviours (Burke, 1996; Zucker, 1990; Zucker & Bradley, 1995). When a family or, at times, a child seeks help from clinicians, instead of focusing on altering the cross-gender behaviour, we should provide a different type of assistance for this vulnerable group. Arlene Lev (2004) explains: "Families will need support to grieve their assumptions and hopes as to who their child would become, skill development to address extended family members, siblings, and school officials, and assistance in incorporating their child's needs into the daily flow of family life so that the child does not become the focal point of family 'pathology'" (p. 332).

When clinicians shift the focus away from treating cross-gender presentation as a sign of disorder, we can better assist these children and families by applying a different therapeutic working model—one that is collaborative, comprehensive, and supportive. When clinicians use the family and multi-systems approach, they have the opportunity to educate families about gender-variant children, and to help empower parents to seek appropriate help and advocate for their child.

A family and multi-systems approach for gender-variant children should include the following five components: (1) an educational component to familiarize parents with gender diversity across the continuum; (2) a learning component that informs individuals and families about resources that are available for the child; (3) a working component to enable parents to address their assumptions about gender; (4) a support component to develop a family support and professional care team for the child; and (5) a component to address the task of overseeing the team and advocating for change, as necessary.

In applying a collaborative family and multi-systems working model, I suggest dividing the approach into three phases. The first phase is to allow time for clinicians to help educate parents about gender-variant behaviours, especially those behaviours demonstrated by their children. Parents will also learn about their perceptions of gender diversity. With the knowledge gained, they will be more aware of the challenges their child might face and, at the same time, become empowered to make necessary changes for their child. Time will be devoted to helping these families access available resources for their child.

During the second phase, parents are empowered to develop a comprehensive support team (Raj, 2008) that includes different helpers and professionals, such as relatives, friends, teachers, counsellors, pastors, and so forth. A support team is critical in this process because it allows different members to contribute specific support for the child. A common challenge, however, is to maintain clear communication among team members, and this can potentially exhaust parents. This is because each support helper plays a significant role in helping the child and the parents, but very often, there is limited communication among these different systems. The parents usually have to pass on messages from one system to another to ensure that recommendations are being followed. As a result, the parents become responsible for doing all of the communicating and, thus, find themselves being stretched far too thin (below).

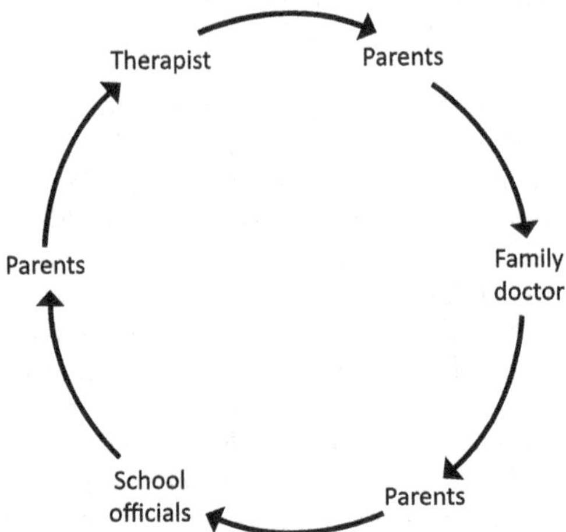

Once parents are informed, educated, and empowered, however, they will usually be able to shift from a "messenger" role to a "conductor" role, which will effectively transition them into the third phase—the "overlooking and advocating for change" process. In this "advocator" role, the parents will ensure that the different systems effectively communicate with one another, and directly oversee that the required tasks are being conveyed to, and carried out by, the various responsible systems (below).

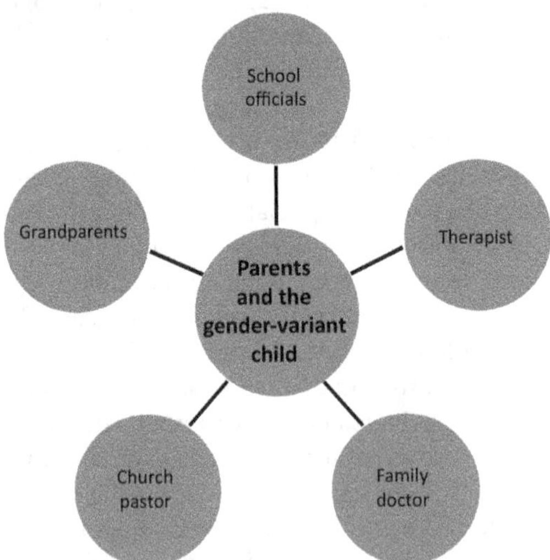

This transmission of information is especially helpful when team members have different views on ways to help the child. Parents will feel less confused because other systems are connected, thereby allowing them to communicate directly and clarify their recommendations with one another. To ensure effective communication among the various systems, parents may have to hold regular meetings with all of the members from the different systems. This helps to track the child's progress and ensures that consistency of services and support is being delivered.

Clinicians play an important role in all three phases because we can provide guidance to parents throughout the overall process. We can also facilitate the formation of a support team through helping to determine who should be included and what issues should be addressed. This might be helpful for parents, especially when they are new to this process or when they have recently learned about their child's cross-gender presentation.

Ongoing clinical guidance from therapists might be necessary for some parents. This is because each developmental stage that their gender-variant child goes through will potentially present new challenges. Once parents gain the knowledge and skills, however, they can continue to organize and orchestrate these support systems on their own. They can ensure that quality services are being delivered to their child and that these are being provided in the best interests of the child's development. This process effectively shifts these parents from a passive role (i.e., being told what to do by an "expert") to a more proactive role where they are empowered as experts in their own lives because of their intimate knowledge of the specificities of their family and lives. Thus, they become empowered and are able to advocate for changes, as needed, by their children.

WORKING WITH PARENTS AND FAMILY SYSTEMS

The primary focus in the family and multi-systems approach is usually the parents or family. This is because the family system is normally the first system with which these children come into contact. It is also the system that these children have the most interaction with throughout their lifespan. How this system views and treats gender-variant children will have a tremendous impact on their later development and self-worth (Lev, 2004).

Working with the family system will also help parents to work through their own issues, such as their perceptions of gender diversity, as well as issues around raising a gender-variant child. Parents who seek help for their child are usually in distress. Many mistakenly think that their child with cross-gender behaviours will automatically require medical transitions, such as hormonal or surgical therapies. Some are concerned about other problems, such as stigmatization, genderism, and transphobia, that their child will likely experience.

It is important for clinicians to provide information and education to parents about gender-variant children. For instance, parents will need to know that their child's gender and development are not caused by their parenting. Although their parenting skills may permit the extent of their children to express their gender, they do not contribute to the causes of their gender. Parents need to learn coping skills to deal with a social system that oppresses gender diversity.

Some children are just being who they are by being gender non-conforming. Children go through stages of identity exploration; parents need to understand that it is not unusual for children to express some desires, presentations, or even identification with the opposite gender during their developmental process. Whereas for some children, cross-gender presentation might be "a phase," others might continue with cross-gender presentation throughout their lives (Brill & Pepper, 2008). Parents need to be taught that gender roles and gender expression are on a continuum, and that society has a pre-set social boundary regarding how a boy and a girl should express masculinity or femininity, respectively. Parents might not be aware of how they are influenced by the gender binary social system. For instance, different cultural and ethnic groups also have different views on gender presentation. While some are more flexible, normalizing more cross-gender behaviours, others can be quite rigid, enforcing strict binary gender rules. Understanding their "personal" gender bias as a social construction enables parents to look at their gender-variant children from a different perspective. It helps them to realize that forcing their children to follow certain sexist gender roles may not serve the best interests of their children. In fact, these actions might actually harm these children's future development, as well as their perception of their self-worth.

With the progressive changes in today's society, not all parents are as concerned as others regarding their gender-variant child. Some parents are quite receptive to their child's cross-gender presentation. Unfortunately, many receptive parents find their accepting and "permissive" views are often challenged by others. Given our current transphobic[4] society, different members of social systems tend to stigmatize parents who support their children with cross-gender behaviours, questioning their judgment and decisions (Green, 1995; Zucker, 1990).

The pressures that a family has to deal with can be overwhelming. Supportive parents constantly find themselves in a position in which they have to defend themselves and explain to others why they support their children's cross-gender behaviours. These parents also become the target of stigmatization (Lev, 2004). Other members of society blame them for supporting their children, doubting their decision to "indulge" their child's so-called pathological behaviours. Families and parents often feel isolated and have no support systems to turn to. To avoid the pressure, parents might decide to put themselves in "the closet" by keeping their child's behaviour a secret. This can allow parents to temporarily avoid dealing with external pressures. In the long run, however, it further isolates both the parents and their child from reaching out for needed support.

Clinicians should assist parents and other family members to develop skills in addressing others regarding their child's cross-gender presentation. For example, this may include education and information that they need to be a social advocate, and ways to address the social pressure and emotional distress that they may encounter as they battle for their child's rights for gender diversity. We also need to link the family with support systems and resources, including support groups or local community trans-friendly organizations, so they do not have to rely on the clinician as the sole or primary support. Being able to connect with other social agencies and different support and advocacy groups can be a therapeutic and empowering process for these parents (Raj, 2008). It also allows parents to go beyond the medical and psychological spaces. This challenges the medicalization of gender non-normativity.

For instance, clinicians may advise parents to become an active member of some parent–school partnership programs by guiding their schools to develop policies that allow gender flexibility. This does not mean focusing only on physical facilities, such as challenging the currently rigid gender-based rules for bathroom and locker room use, but also on the general school culture, especially on ways to promote education on and acceptance of gender diversity. They will also need to know the rights that their children are entitled to. Clinicians may provide parents with referrals or a list of legal authorities in their community. Knowing which social agencies to turn to for legal advice is crucial. This allows uncertain parents to feel more empowered to fight for their children's rights.

Empowered parents can make a difference in their children's lives when they are provided with skills, training, and education (Raj, 2008). These skills prepare them to work with the different systems that their children are involved with. It is true that parents cannot protect their children completely. Parents can take an active role, however, by promoting changes and enrolling their children in systems that are more receptive to gender-variant children.

WORKING WITH THE SCHOOL SYSTEM

Some parents may be actively involved in the parent–school partnership programs mentioned above. Some, however, may know that their gender-variant child is not happy at school but feel powerless to make changes for their child. They are uncertain of the steps to take and the actions that are needed to facilitate changes. In working with the school system, clinicians can act as a mediator or a facilitator. We can help parents and the school system identify what changes are necessary to help the child function better at school.

Much of a child's social and gender development occurs in the school setting. Children will have more exposure and longer interaction with their peers than in any other earlier stage of development. They will quickly learn about the binary gender system in the school setting. While some schools are more flexible with gender-variant children, others are resistant to change. At times, this means that parents might have to move their child to a different school—one that is willing to accommodate the needs of their child in terms of bathroom usage, clothing options, and using cross-gender names and pronouns.

In working with the school system, children are often dependent on their parents to advocate for their needs. It is possible that some schools might find these accommodations cumbersome, and demand that the child accommodate to its binary gender social setting. It is interesting that almost all school systems today promote issues such as cultural sensitivity, but continue to overlook issues of gender sensitivity.

To assist these changes, it is important for clinicians to take an active role in educating the overarching school system about gender variance. It is also helpful to teach parents ways to demand changes for their child within the school system, or otherwise connect them with schools that are more receptive to their gender-variant children. The sad truth is that some parents might have to move to a different school district where their children can be safe and accepted.

It is not unusual for some schools to blame peer ostracism and other forms of bullying on gender-variant children because of their "unusual (cross-gender) presentation." Their underlying reason is that these children are being gender non-compliant, and, therefore, they "stick out like a sore thumb." A teacher once informed me about a male-born, gender-variant child who was teased and bullied in class. She reported that the child had no friends because he wore a dress to school, and this scared away his classmates. The teacher failed to see that this gender-variant child was simply expressing himself. With our current society that is still transphobic and insensitive to gender-variant children, school is one of the most important places to teach children about gender sensitivity so they can carry this valuable lesson into their adulthood. Schools, as well as other systems, need to know that gender-variant children are as emotionally healthy as other children.

It is true, however, that some gender-variant children might present with emotional issues. Instead of making an assumption that emotional issues automatically stem from their gender-variant orientation, school officials should investigate the underlying cause of the presenting issues to see if, perhaps, these issues are in fact the child's reaction to transphobic social settings (Di Ceglie, Freedman, McPherson, & Richardson, 2002). Many psychosocial issues, such as discrimination, harassment, and societal marginalization, affect a child's school performance and emotional health.

There is no overnight success in changing a school system and its policies, which are often based on rigid gender rules. At times, clinicians may have to work with the parents continuously to achieve changes that they would like to see for their gender-variant children. This process can be slow, even exhausting, at times. Despite the difficulties that some parents may face, I am amazed by how many empowered parents I have worked with in the past who have chosen to fight with the school system by taking a stand against policies that may damage their children's sexual and gender development. Indeed, the family and multi-systems approach focuses on educating and empowering parents so that they can continue to advocate for their children throughout their school years. Parents need to help the school understand that the behaviour of the gender-variant child is not necessarily "acting out," but rather a process of identity formation. By allowing them to express their authentic selves, these children do not need to force themselves to "pass" (as their designated birth sex), to deny their true identity, or to take on a false self. It can be argued that these children will actually function better at school when the environment is safe and welcomes diversity, such as in the application of flexible gender rules (Brill & Pepper, 2008).

WORKING WITH OTHER SYSTEMS

The family and multi-systems approach encourages parents to advocate for their children within other systems that might be helpful for the child's growth and development. The clinician can work with parents to collaboratively develop this support team. As a rule, many helpers are practitioners from multidisciplinary teams; however, they are not all necessarily licensed professionals. There is no limit regarding who or what other systems should be included. From my clinical experience, whoever can be part of the solution and is able to make a positive change in the child's life should be invited to join the collaborative care team.

The formation of the supportive team can be innovative and unconventional. For example, a gender-variant child whom I met was forced to move to a different school far away from his house due to severe bullying. The parents were able to find a safer school for their child; however, it was too far for a daily commute. Given that the new school was closer to the grandparent's home than the parents' home, the child was permitted to live with his grandparents during the week so that the child did not have to travel so far to school. With this transition, they invited the grandparents onto the support team so that they could ensure that the child's safety and academic growth were being addressed in this new school.

Parents and the child should have the power to determine who can be involved in the support team, and this should include the clinician as well. New issues may arise as the gender-variant child enters different developmental stages. Therefore, the support team should be modified regularly based on the child's needs at the time. It is hoped that empowered families and parents will gain the skills and knowledge that they need to initiate changes for the child and to monitor the progress made.

CONCLUSION

More resources and attention must be devoted to research that focuses on the needs and experiences of gender-variant children. As a result of the current lack of research, clinicians lack guidelines regarding how to work with families with gender-variant children. Whereas there are some standards of care with respect to treatment protocols for gender variance and transsexualism from the World Professional Association for Transgender Health (WPATH), such as the Standards of Care from the Harry Benjamin International Gender Dysphoria Association (HBIDGA) (Meyer et al., 2001), there is no detailed information regarding the best treatment approach to use with this population. Moreover, different demographic areas may require different protocols in working with gender-variant children. A rural or a conservative community will require more support and services than a city that has already established some support for gender-variant children. As a result, a specific treatment approach is often idiosyncratically determined by how the clinician views cross-gender behaviour. Varying comfort levels with gender-variant children will yield very different results. It is important for clinicians to assist parents to develop a safe and supportive environment that will allow the child to question and explore her or his identity. The primary goal is to empower the client, and to address the complexity of sex and/or gender variance as a social phenomenon to foster significant movement toward self-actualization (Raj, 2007).

NOTES

1 The Diagnostic and Statistical Manual of Mental Disorders, 4th Edition, Text Revision (DSM-IV-TR), published by the American Psychiatric Association in 2000, provides a unified set of diagnostic criteria of various mental disorders. The manual is commonly used by mental health professionals of different disciplines when diagnosing a mental disorder.

2 This is an approach that integrates family systems theory, research, and evidence-based clinical interventions, such as the wrap-around approach.

3 "Genderist" is a term derived from genderism, and is defined as a sexist belief or attitude based on gender as a whole and involves the creation of gender stereotypes, such as masculinity for men or femininity for women.

4 "Transphobic" is an adjective that refers to an irrational, persistent fear of those who are gender atypical to any degree. A transphobic person tends to have difficulties in dealing with gender ambiguity and feels discomfort with, or hostility toward, others who do not conform to stereotypical gender norms.

REFERENCES

Bartlett, N.H., Vasey, P.L., & Bukowski, W.M. (2000). Is gender identity disorder in children a mental disorder? *Sex Roles: A Journal of Research*. Available at www.finderarticles.com/cf_0/m2294/2000_Dec/75959827/print.jhtml

Boyd-Franklin, N. (1989). *Black families in therapy: A multisystems approach*. New York: Guildford Press.

Brill, S., & Pepper, R. (2008). *The transgender child: A handbook for families and professionals*. San Francisco: Cleis Press.

Brown, S.L. (2002). We are, therefore I am: A multisystems approach with families in poverty. *The Family Journal, 10*(4), 405–409.

Burke, P. (1996). *Gender shock: Exploding the myths of male and female*. New York: Anchor Books/Doubleday.

Di Ceglie, D., Freedman, D., McPherson, S., & Richardson, P. (2002). Children and adolescents referred to a specialist gender identity development service: Clinical features and demographic characteristics. *International Journal of Transgenderism, 6*(1). Retrieved from www.symposion.com/ijt/ijtvo06no01_01.htm

Gibson, P. (1994). Gay male and lesbian youth suicide. In G. Remafedi (Ed.), *Death by denial: Studies of suicide in gay and lesbian teens* (pp. 15–88). Boston: Alyson.

Green, R. (1995). Gender identity disorder in children. In G.O. Gabbard (Ed.), *Treatments of psychiatric disorders* (2nd ed., pp. 2001–2014). Washington, DC: American Psychiatric Press.

Lev, A.I. (2004). *Transgender emergence: Therapeutic guidelines for working with gender-variant people and their families.* New York: Haworth Clinical Practice Press.

Mallon, G.P. (1999). *Transgender nation.* Bowling Green, OH: Bowling Green State University Popular Press.

Meyer, W.J., III, Bockting, W.O., Cohen-Kettenis, P.T., Colemen, E., Di Ceglie, D., Devor, H., … & Wheeler, C.C. (2001). *The standards of care for gender identity disorders* (6th ed.). Minneapolis, MN: Harry Benjamin International Gender Dysphoria Association.

Raj, R. (2007). Transactivism as therapy: A client self-empowerment model linking personal and social agency. *Journal of Gay and Lesbian Psychotherapy,* (3/4), 77–98.

Raj, R. (2008). Transforming couples and families: A transformative therapeutic model for working with the loved ones of gender-divergent youth and trans-identified adults. *Journal of GLBT Family Studies, 4*(2), 133–163.

Rekers, G.A. (1995). *Handbook of child and adolescent sexual problems.* New York: Lexington Books.

Richardson, J. (1996). Setting limits on gender health. *Harvard Review of Psychiatry, 4,* 49–53.

Richardson, J. (1999). Response: Finding the disorder in gender identity disorder. *Harvard Review of Psychiatry, 7,* 43–50.

Rosenblatt, R. (1996). Bows and ribbons, tape and twine: Wrapping the wraparound process for children with multi-system needs. *Journal of Child and Family Studies, 5*(1), 101–117.

Scholinski, D., with Adams, J.M. (1997). *The last time I wore a dress: A memoir.* New York: Riverhead Books.

Wren, B. (2000). Early physical intervention for young people with atypical gender identity development. *Clinical Child Psychology and Psychiatry, 5*(2), 220–231.

Zucker, K.J. (1990). Gender identity disorders in children: Clinical descriptions and natural history. In R. Blanchard and B.W. Steiner (Eds), *Clinical management of gender identity disorder in children and adults.* Washington, DC: American Psychological Association.

Zucker, K.J., & Bradley, S. (1995). *Gender identity disorder and psychosexual problems in children and adolescents.* New York: Guildford Press.

Chapter 23 Sexual Health on Our Own Terms: The Gay, Bi, Queer Trans Men's Working Group

Ayden I. Scheim, Syrus Marcus Ware,
Nik Redman, Zack Marshall, and Broden Giambrone

> My whole life I've wanted to be a gay man and it's kind of an honour to die from the gay man's disease.... [Y]our clinic decided that I couldn't live as a gay man but I am going to die like one.
>
> —Lou Sullivan (Stryker, 1999)

HISTORY

This chapter explores how the Gay/Bi/Queer Trans Men's Working Group (part of the Ontario Gay Men's Sexual Health Alliance) has been instrumental both in the development of sexual health work with GBQ trans men in Canada and in promoting the inclusion and visibility of trans men in gay men's communities[1] more broadly. Our work emerges from historical and contemporary needs within segments of trans and gay communities. Lou Sullivan, a gay trans male activist whose provocative statement opens our piece, fought for visibility for gay, bisexual, and queer (GBQ) trans men[2] in the United States from the 1970s until his death in 1991. Sullivan lived his life as a gay man at a time when the existence of GBQ trans men was routinely denied by the medical establishment and gender clinics.

Writing prolifically about his experience at a time when few trans men were out or visible, he created *Information for the Female to Male Cross-dresser and Transsexual*, one of the first resource guides (Sullivan, n.d.) for trans men. Additionally, Sullivan provided support for many trans men throughout North America by creating FTM International, the first peer-support organization created by and for trans men. His writing made its way into Canadian trans communities largely through frequent contributions to Toronto activist Rupert Raj's FTM newsletter *Metamorphosis* from 1982 to 1986. Sullivan's written work and other activist efforts reflected a growing movement of GBQ-identified trans men emerging in gay male and trans communities across the United States and Canada. Over 20 years later, the visibility of GBQ trans men has grown considerably. Nonetheless, our unique sexual health needs were still infrequently considered or addressed in Canada until recently.

GBQ TRANS MEN AND SEXUAL HEALTH

It should not come as a surprise that some trans men are sexually attracted to other men. Historically, gatekeepers to transition-related medical care considered same-gender attraction incompatible with transition (Bockting, Benner, & Coleman, 2009), given that the perceived goal of transition was to "blend in" as a heterosexual man or woman (Stone, 1992). Although trans men generally no longer have to hide sexual attractions to men in order to transition, there is still a common misperception that trans men are largely heterosexual amongst those who conflate gender identity and sexual orientation. It is frequently assumed that trans men are exclusively attracted to women and have lesbian histories prior to transition.[3] Recent data from the Trans PULSE project (Bauer, Redman, Bradley, & Scheim, 2013) challenge this assumption, with 63 percent of female-to-male spectrum trans people in Ontario reporting non-heterosexual identities and/or past-year sex with trans or non-trans men.

Many non-trans gay men have welcomed trans men into gay communities and have increasingly recognized trans men as potential sexual and romantic partners (Cooper, 2008; Syms, 2007). Others have been baffled or even angered by our presence in (or attempts to access) gay men's social and sexual spaces. For example, in 2002, Toronto-based LGBT newspaper *Xtra* published an article by a trans man describing his experience visiting the Bijou, a gay men's porn theatre and bathhouse (Wallace, 2002). In particular, the author told of his participation in the "slurp ramp," an area designed to facilitate anonymous oral sex. The article stirred up a negative reaction from some non-trans gay men who were incensed about a perceived "infiltration" of their space by trans men. This reaction may have also represented a backlash to efforts that were underway to increase trans men's access to and inclusion in bathhouses and other gay sexual spaces, such as the Tranny Fags and Bio Boys Talk It Up discussion session hosted by The 519 Church St. Community Centre and the AIDS Committee of Toronto earlier that year. Trans men's access to gay men's sexual spaces has continued to be contested in Toronto (Noble, 2009). It is fair to say that within gay men's communities, trans men's claims to belonging often challenge rigid and phallocentric definitions of masculinity and maleness.

Such controversies related to trans men in gay male sexual spaces formed part of the impetus for the development of the GBQ Trans Men's Working Group. Another area of concern was the lack of research regarding HIV vulnerability among GBQ trans men and the lack of knowledge and resources about HIV prevention and sexual health needs for trans men and our sexual partners. A widely cited meta-analysis of HIV prevalence among trans people in the United States estimated that HIV seroprevalence among trans women was 28 percent, with self-reported HIV-positivity of 12 percent (Herbst et al., 2008). These estimates are derived from convenience samples primarily consisting of street-involved and sex-working trans women in large urban centres in the United States, so they are unlikely to represent HIV prevalence rates for all trans women in Ontario. Nonetheless, this data has been crucial for raising awareness of the HIV crisis in some trans communities. Consequently, the amount of research conducted regarding HIV in trans communities has increased, justifiably focusing on those trans people who have been identified as particularly vulnerable—low-income, street active, and sex-working MTFs who are primarily from racialized communities (Melendez, Bonem, & Sember, 2006; Operario & Nemoto, 2010). However, our search of the literature revealed no published peer-reviewed research on HIV vulnerability or prevalence among trans people in Canada between 2000 and 2011. Most recently, data from Ontario suggest that HIV prevalence and risk are high among some trans people, but lower than estimates from American convenience samples would suggest (Bauer, Travers, Scanlon, & Coleman, 2012).

Overall, trans men are under-researched. In a systematic review on transgender health and HIV (Melendez et al., 2006) a mere 12 of 354 articles focused specifically on trans men compared with 168 that focused on trans women (the others did not specify gender). In Ontario, data regarding HIV risk and prevalence among trans men who have sex with men is scarce, as HIV test site collection forms only have male and female gender options, and trans men have historically not been captured in HIV surveillance studies. In addition, recent data suggest that trans men have low rates of HIV testing uptake (Bauer et al., 2013).

This lack of data about HIV among trans men reinforces the perception of low risk relative to other populations, thus perpetuating the invisibility of trans men in HIV research. The presumption that trans men are at low risk for HIV infection is based on the assumption that they primarily have sex with non-transgender women (Kenagy & Hsieh, 2005), a scarcity of epidemiological data (Reisner, Perkovich, & Mimiaga, 2010; Sevelius, 2009), and the "erasure" of trans men in HIV prevention policy and programming (Bauer et al., 2009; Namaste, 2000). Studies of trans men have tended to report low HIV prevalence rates, from 0 to 3 percent (Adams et al., 2008; Bauer et al., 2012; Clements-Nolle, Marx, Guzman, & Katz, 2001; Sevelius, 2009; Xavier, Bobbin, Singer, & Budd, 2005). However, these estimates primarily rely on self-reports of small, non-representative samples (Sevelius, Scheim, & Giambrone, 2010).

Emerging research suggests that trans men, like trans women, may face social, interpersonal, and intrapersonal vulnerabilities to HIV infection. Furthermore, trans men may engage in high-risk activities at rates comparable to or greater than trans women (Adams et al., 2008; Clements-Nolle et al., 2001; Sevelius, 2009). There have been a number of challenges identified in qualitative research that could decrease condom efficacy and increase vulnerability to HIV infection for trans men. These include a lack of sexual health information, fear of rejection from potential sexual partners, complicated safer sex communication, low self-esteem, unequal power dynamics, transition-related sexual experimentation, increased sex drive with hormone use, desire for validation as gay/bisexual men, a perception amongst MSM (men who have sex with men) that condoms are necessary for anal but not vaginal sex, and discomfort with or dissociation from their bodies (Adams et al., 2008; Clements-Nolle et al., 2001; Kosenko, 2010; Reisner et al., 2010; Sevelius, 2009). Trans men may be particularly biologically susceptible to HIV acquisition, as testosterone use and/or hysterectomy can lead to thinning of vaginal walls and dryness, which are factors that make it easier for HIV to pass through the mucous membrane directly or through small cuts or tears (Sheth & Thorndycraft, 2009).

In Ontario, approximately one in three trans men who identified as GBQ (or as sexually active with any men) reported having sex with a non-trans man in the past year (Bauer et al., 2013). Of all GBQ-MSM trans men, about 10 percent reported high-risk receptive genital sex (fluid exposure with anyone who is not a seroconcordant monogamous partner). This high-risk sex would almost exclusively be due to those trans men having sex with non-trans men (and perhaps some having sex with trans women who ejaculate). GBQ trans men typically draw their sex partners from communities of men who have sex with men, among whom HIV prevalence was estimated to be 22 percent in Ontario as of 2008 (Remis, Swantee, & Liu, 2010). Given that trans men are reporting high-risk sex in this context, we were concerned that apparently low prevalence rates would rise without the introduction of prevention interventions relevant to GBQ trans men. In addition to facing exclusion from gay sexual life and individual-level vulnerabilities to HIV infection, GBQ trans men are, of course, situated in social contexts that place them at risk of poor health outcomes and exclusion. In the Ontario context, the Trans PULSE project, the largest study of trans health ever conducted in Canada, with 433 participants, provides evidence of the extent of social exclusion and oppression faced by trans communities in areas ranging from access to employment to experiences of physical and sexual assault (Bauer et al., 2011; Scanlon et al., 2010). In addition, specific instances of, and ongoing exposure to, transphobia may increase HIV vulnerability among trans people. For example, in a context of transphobic discrimination from potential sexual partners, trans people may be willing to trade physical for emotional well-being when a partner expresses sexual interest or validates their gender identity, but refuses to use condoms (Bockting, Robinson, & Rosser, 1998; Kosenko, 2010). Trans youth often have fewer strategies and resources for coping with transphobia, and therefore may be more vulnerable to low self-esteem and self-efficacy (Sugano, Nemoto, & Operario, 2006).

THE GAY/BI/QUEER TRANS MEN'S WORKING GROUP

In 2004, conversations about the sexual health needs of GBQ trans men, and the stigma we experience in gay men's communities, began amongst staff at the AIDS Committee of Toronto and the Ontario AIDS Bureau. In the same year, Ontario launched the Gay Men's HIV Prevention Strategy, now called the Gay Men's Sexual Health (GMSH) Alliance,[4] a provincial coalition of gay men and allies working in the community to respond to the sexual health needs of gay, bi, and other men who have sex with men. Members of the GMSH, already engaged in dialogue around the gaps in HIV prevention and sexual health work for GBQ trans men, recognized at its inception that the Alliance should be proactive in addressing the needs of trans men who have sex with men. In 2006, the GBQ Trans Men's Working Group ("the Working Group") was formed to ensure that trans men were leading efforts to address this gap. We wanted to improve the sexual health of GBQ trans men, accounting for social determinants of health including homophobia and transphobia, as well as regionalism, ableism, and racism, that impact our lives. At least 75 percent of the Working Group is composed of GBQ trans men from across Ontario, with additional representation from the Ontario AIDS Bureau and AIDS Service Organizations (ASOs). From the beginning, we strove to ensure that the Working Group was reflective of the diversity of GBQ trans men in Ontario, including representatives from smaller cities and rural areas, racialized communities, disabled trans men, and those at different stages of transition.

When we first began working together, we decided that addressing the gaps in knowledge regarding GBQ trans men's sexual health and HIV prevention needs would be one of our key priorities. We initiated a community-based needs assessment and resource development project to gather information about the HIV-related experiences, knowledge, risks, and resource needs of GBQ trans men in Ontario and incorporate what we learned into a comprehensive resource. Based on the results of the needs assessment, we also developed a series of recommendations for service providers and researchers focused on improving HIV prevention work with GBQ trans men in Ontario. Results were published in the report *Getting Primed: Informing HIV Prevention with Gay/Bi/Queer Trans Men in Ontario* (Adams et al., 2008).

Primed: The Back Pocket Guide for Trans Men and the Men Who Dig Them (Primed) (2007) is a comprehensive resource written by project staff in collaboration with Working Group members. To increase the accessibility of the information and to provide additional information about local resources, a website was also developed (www.queertransmen.org). As the first guide of its kind, *Primed*—available in print but also online as a downloadable PDF—has been an essential resource for GBQ trans men's communities and has received worldwide attention. The resource, which was officially produced in English and (Canadian) French, has been adapted into Korean, Australian English, German, French, Russian, Hebrew, and Norwegian by trans community members internationally. It has also inspired the development of other sexual health resources, including a (Parisian) French resource for trans men, *Dicklit et T Claques* (OUTrans, 2010) and *Brazen: Trans Women Safer Sex Guide* (Page, 2011). Due to its popularity, the GMSH has funded three print runs of *Primed*, and it is nationally distributed through the Canadian AIDS Treatment Information Exchange Ordering Centre.

Other significant aims of the Working Group have been to increase the capacity of those working within HIV/AIDS services to meet the prevention, support, and treatment needs of trans men. To this end, we have conducted trainings for AIDS Service Organizations (ASOs) and HIV-related service providers across Ontario that focus on recommendations from the needs assessment, and developing practical strategies for increasing the accessibility and relevance of gay men's HIV services for trans men. We have also presented at conferences of researchers, educators, service providers, and community members in Canada and internationally. These include trans-specific conferences such as Gender Odyssey (Seattle, US); the Philadelphia Trans Health Conference, and Promoting the Health of Transgender Communities through Innovative Practices (San Francisco, US); International AIDS Conferences (Mexico City and Washington, DC); Europride (Stockholm, Sweden); and the Canadian AIDS Society Skills-Building Summit (Montreal).

In our work with service providers in Ontario, we have witnessed concrete changes in service delivery and a consistent increase in knowledge and trans-specific cultural competence among our colleagues. We conduct a training session every year at the Gay Men's Sexual Health (GMSH) Summit, and in the past five years we have been able to progress far beyond Trans 101 trainings. While in the early years we would spend a lot of time answering questions about the difference between the terms "transgender" and "transsexual," we are now asked questions that push the limits of available scientific knowledge: for instance, whether genital surgeries may increase biological susceptibility to HIV. When a new ASO employee has a more basic question about trans issues, their colleagues are now able to respond with confidence. In service delivery, some ASOs have started to produce and distribute more trans-inclusive safer sex kits that include dental dams, gloves, condoms, and extra lube. When they started to distribute these kits, staff realized that many kinky non-trans men were also delighted to have more diverse kits. The latex or polyurethane gloves provided, for example, are also important for safer anal fisting. Other gay/bi men's events and support groups in Canadian ASOs now explicitly welcome trans men. Some organizations have taken a lead in challenging the exclusion of trans men from gay men's spaces to ensure that we can participate in events held in bathhouses or other sexualized venues.

Though our mandate is provincial, the HIV sector is highly networked nationally, and we frequently participate in national meetings. This has meant that our work has had a national impact as well, which supports and complements the work of GBQ trans men active in their local communities. Organizations such as the Health Initiative for Men in Vancouver have highlighted trans men's sexual health issues, in part by promoting *Primed*. While there is still much work to do in realizing the full inclusion of trans men in HIV research, we have been involved in consultations with local, provincial, and national qualitative and quantitative studies to ensure that they are able to recruit, measure, and meaningfully engage trans men as participants. For example, we were instrumental in the decision of the Ontario arm of the Public Health Agency of Canada M-Track HIV Surveillance study to add questions about assigned sex at birth and current gender identity to identify trans male participants.

Internationally, Ontario is now recognized as being one of the leading regions for sexual health work with GBQ trans men and for being at the forefront of promoting the meaningful inclusion of trans men in gay men's communities and HIV prevention work. We have been invited to participate in consultations regarding GBQ trans men's sexual health at national and global levels, and our work has been recognized and celebrated at international gatherings for trans health and HIV. *Primed* has been distributed and adapted by community organizations across Canada, the United States, and Europe. We have been involved in several collaborative projects with international colleagues, including co-authoring a fact sheet on trans men's HIV prevention needs with the Center for AIDS Prevention Studies located at the University of California, San Francisco (Sevelius et al., 2010), and preparing a case study for the Open Society Foundations' "Promoting the Health of Transgender Communities through Innovative Practices" seminar (Marshall, 2011).[5] These collaborations have been important in sharing knowledge and good practice, and we hope to continue cultivating these international connections in the coming years.

We have also supported the development of social spaces that celebrate GBQ trans men in order to reduce isolation, challenge the exclusion of trans men from gay men's spaces, and promote the creation of more trans-inclusive sexual spaces for GBQ men. We created "Stroke": A Party for Trans Guys and the Men Who Dig Them as a launch event for *Primed*. In 2007–2008, it evolved into an independently organized quarterly event for GBQ trans men and admirers of all genders, led by local DJ Nik Red. "Stroke" was a social mixer held in a sex-positive queer club that featured guest hosts (such as FTM porn star Buck Angel) and offered attendees sexual health information and resources. Since that time, new social events have been developed for trans men in Toronto, inspired by the success of "Stroke."

We feel that the most significant contribution that the Working Group has made is that GBQ trans men and non-trans men who are (or desire to be) our sexual partners now have accurate and relevant information about HIV prevention and sexual health. When we first began working on *Primed*, there was little sexual health information tailored to us. Community members had produced safer sex pamphlets independently, often with absolutely no resources or institutional support, but those pamphlets were not comprehensive, widely available, or in line with Canadian guidelines for safer sex. *Primed* provides trans men with detailed information about sexual health, HIV prevention, trans-specific safer sex concerns, and tips for seeking sex with men as a trans man. We have received emails from trans and non-trans GBQ men from around the world expressing their relief and joy in finally coming across materials that spoke to their life experiences, desires, and bodies.

Primed has been instrumental in increasing the visibility of GBQ trans men within trans communities and of trans men within gay men's communities. The intentional choice to use sexually explicit photographs of diverse local trans men really resonated with readers, who are hungry to see themselves represented in sexy and respectful ways. Our deliberate inclusion of models who are racialized, at various stages of transition, and of diverse body sizes ensured that *Primed* reflects a wide range of trans men. This fit with our goal of promoting the sexual health of trans men who are marginalized by transphobia and by racism, sizeism, ableism, and other forms of oppression that have resulted in many of us being fetishized and objectified, or rejected and desexualized. The photographs caused some controversy (most notoriously when a health centre refused to display *Primed* in common areas), but were integral to our objective to make space for and positively promote queer trans male sexuality and pleasure.

Currently, members of the Working Group are investigators in a community-based research project funded by the Canadian Institutes for Health Research. The project builds on our earlier needs assessment work through a qualitative study of safer sex decision making and HIV vulnerability among trans men who have sex with men. This collaboration between members of the Working Group and non-trans HIV prevention researchers who are committed trans allies presents an opportunity to further develop research capacities among GBQ trans men, increase the ability of gay men's sexual health researchers to address trans men's issues, and enhance our knowledge about factors that impact HIV risk among trans men who have sex with men. At the same time, we are working to support the development of a pilot social support and sexual health group for GBQ trans men in Toronto.

MOVING FORWARD

Although we have witnessed dramatic improvement in the integration of trans men in gay men's sexual health and HIV prevention work, questions remain about the capacity of gay men's work to address trans bodies and experiences that present a challenge to traditional definitions of "gay man." In particular, how can or will we respond to trans men who are not "read" as male—and to those who have no desire to be understood in such a way? How about those who do not modify their bodies through medical transition? Also, with the growing visibility of trans men choosing to parent through pregnancy, can we make space to talk about issues of pregnancy, parenting, and HIV in gay men's prevention work?

There are surely limits on the inclusiveness of our work, based on our claim to a gay/bi/queer male identity and position within a strategy that is centred around gay men. Some genderqueer-identified people within the broader FTM community have criticized us for this, but we feel strongly that specificity is important. Our sexual health concerns and sociocultural context as men who have sex with men are unique, and in the long run, we are best served by inclusion in the broader gay men's health arena. We are not looking to dismantle the categories of "gay and bi men," but rather to expand them to provide room for the recognition and inclusion of diverse trans men's experiences.

Additionally, we wonder if and how the gay men's HIV prevention field will meaningfully engage with bisexual men, trans or otherwise. The Working Group intentionally chose to name bisexual and queer-identified men in our title, mandate, and resources, in contrast to many other groups, including the GMSH that we work within. The explicit and implicit exclusion of bi men's concerns from prevention work for gay men and other men who have sex with men has been acknowledged by some researchers (Namaste et al., 2007). However, little concrete work has been done to remedy this in the Ontario context. It seems that trans men may be uniquely situated to push this issue because many of us already challenge rigid notions of sexual orientation, both on political principle and by virtue of sexual histories that defy binary categorization.

It is important to recognize that the Working Group has prioritized recruitment of racialized and First Nations/Aboriginal GBQ trans men as members and as participants in our needs assessment, but we have struggled to consistently maintain the level of meaningful participation reflective of our commitment. Unfortunately, this mirrors a broader under-representation and inadequate recruitment of racialized men who have sex with men in HIV prevention research (Husbands et al., 2008). Racialized and First Nations/Aboriginal trans men who have sex with men face additional barriers to HIV prevention and sexual health services, and may be especially vulnerable to HIV due to the consequences of historical and ongoing systemic racism and colonialism. Therefore, it is essential that not only inclusion and recruitment of racialized and Aboriginal trans men remain a priority in our work, but that our research also examines the impact of racialization and colonization on HIV vulnerability, and the importance of de-colonial and anti-racist approaches to sexual health promotion.

Finally, we must note that within the Working Group and in the needs assessment we conducted, we have not encountered any openly HIV-positive trans men who live in Ontario. Due to HIV-related stigma and the invisibility of trans men in HIV epidemiology and testing site data, we do not know whether our experience reflects a reality of low HIV rates amongst trans men. While most studies have found lower prevalence rates among trans men, relative to non-trans men who have sex with men or trans women (Sevelius et al., 2010), in many regions high levels of inconsistent condom use and low rates of HIV testing have been found (Adams et al., 2008; Bauer et al., 2012; Sevelius, 2009). We do know that researchers working in other contexts (e.g., Sevelius, 2009) have encountered HIV-positive trans men in their studies and that clinicians in some American urban centres are increasingly treating HIV-positive GBQ trans men (Radix, 2012).

As discussed earlier, HIV prevalence amongst non-trans men who have sex with men in Ontario is estimated to be 22 percent (Remis et al., 2010). Even if HIV rates are currently indeed low for GBQ trans men, and not just under-reported or undiagnosed, increasing incidence of HIV among trans men is likely if we are having condomless sex in this context. In addition, as trans men become increasingly integrated into gay men's communities, we wonder if this, paradoxically, will actually put us at greater risk. This is, in part, an epidemiological question regarding increased exposure to HIV, but also a question of whether seropositivity (or even just being at risk for HIV) may validate gay/bi identity for some trans men. This notion is reflected in the quote from Lou Sullivan that began our chapter, and was echoed by a trans man interviewed for our needs assessment:

> I worry about what it is to be a gay man. Is it to have a lot of concerns or thoughts on HIV and what it means to be poz, and all that stuff? And so, I guess part of what I worry about, as well, is if we don't feel validated and visible as gay men, I think that we are more likely to become infected? Because people see that as being gay. (Adams et al., 2008, p. 40)

CONNECTIONS TO BROADER TRANS ACTIVISM IN ONTARIO

The Working Group and our projects are part of a government-funded alliance consisting primarily of non-profit HIV/AIDS organizations. The work that we do is often considered service provision and health promotion, not activism. However, our successes are a direct result of the grassroots activism of GBQ trans men working across the country, and of our ongoing advocacy for increased attention and resources addressing the sexual health issues of trans men.

Our work and approach is embedded in a long and rich history of trans activism that makes direct links between trans inclusion, grassroots organizing, improved service access, research, and education. Sandy Leo Laframboise's chapter (Chapter 5) detailing the High Risk Project Society that operated in Vancouver's Downtown Eastside serves as one example of such a grassroots initiative. Additionally, Viviane Namaste's (1995) *Access Denied: A Report on the Experiences of Transsexuals and Transgenderists with Health Care and Social Services in Ontario* provided important data and insight. Similarly, a needs assessment conducted by Syrus Marcus Ware for the AIDS Committee of Toronto was one of the first to specifically highlight the HIV/AIDS prevention, education, and support needs of trans people living in Toronto (2004). In addition to the research contributions of Mirha-Soleil Ross (1995), Tina Strang and Monica Forrester (2005), and Kyle Scanlon and colleagues (2010), we are indebted to the labour of these activists and others who have worked tirelessly on trans inclusion and access to shelters and other social services. This has been furthered by initiatives such as the Trans Access Project at The 519 Church Street Community Centre, which has worked for the past eight years to demand access, inclusion, and attention to the unique housing and homelessness issues faced by trans people. These individuals, some of whom have contributed to the chapter entitled "Trans Access Project: Running the Gauntlet" in this text (Chapter 13), and this work created the context from which our efforts have emerged.

Many members of the GBQ Trans Men's Working Group have experience in such community initiatives that emphasize critical race, disability, and anti-oppression frameworks. This background has helped to ground us in our work and to recognize the importance of an intersectional analysis within broader social justice movements. Our organizing is concerned with ensuring that people have access to the gender- and sexuality-specific services that they consider appropriate for their needs and reflective of their lived experiences.

Twenty years after Lou Sullivan's death, there has been significant progress in visibility, community development, health care access, and sexual health work for queer trans men. This is an exciting moment in time for trans men, where we are increasingly able to live our lives as gay and bisexual men. However, we are still presented with distinct challenges in proactively addressing the sexual health and HIV prevention needs in our communities. It is our hope that gay men's HIV prevention work can continue to meaningfully address trans men and advocate for trans-inclusivity within the broader gay men's community. HIV may become a more pressing reality for many trans men who move into gay men's communities, but we have the opportunity now to enhance and build upon our prevention efforts. It is heartening to know that these interventions have a broader impact in the community outside of social service or AIDS service organizations, by raising awareness, increasing visibility, and creating an impetus for trans activism in other sectors.

ACKNOWLEDGEMENTS

Thank you to the current and former members of the GBQ Trans Men's Working Group. The Working Group consists primarily of volunteering community members and allied service providers who have so generously shared their evenings and weekends, talents, friendship, and passions to make this work possible and successful.

NOTES

1 In keeping with the language used in the Gay Men's Sexual Health Alliance, we will use the terms "gay men" or "gay men's communities" to include gay, bisexual, queer, two-spirit, and other trans or non-trans men who have sex with men.

2 We will use the term "GBQ trans men" to include gay, bisexual, queer, two-spirit, and other trans men or FTM-spectrum people who have sex with and/or are attracted to men. In research we often use the terms "trans MSM" or "TMSM" (trans men who have sex with men) to capture these experiences for the purposes of HIV prevention, but we think it is important to recognize and validate the identities and community affiliations of GBQ trans men.

3 While some trans men do identify as lesbians prior to transition, this identification is sometimes related to a desire to express "female" masculinity rather than an exclusive or predominant attraction to women (Cromwell, 1999).

4 Originally the Ontario Gay Men's HIV Prevention Strategy of the AIDS Bureau, Ontario Ministry of Health and Long-Term Care, the Alliance is now hosted by the Ontario AIDS Network. More information is available at www.gmsh.ca.

5 This case study has been published. See Z. Marshall, S. Ware, and A. Scheim (2013), "The Development, Challenges, and Successes of the Gay/Bi/Queer/Trans Men's Working Group."

REFERENCES

Adams, A., Lundie, M., Marshall, Z., Pires, R., Scanlon, K., Scheim, A., & Smith, T. (2008). *Getting primed: Informing HIV prevention with gay/bi/queer trans men in Ontario*. Ontario Gay Men's HIV Prevention Strategy, AIDS Bureau, Ontario Ministry of Health and Long-Term Care.

Bauer, G.R., Hammond, R., Travers, R., Kaay, M., Hohenadel, K.M., & Boyce, M. (2009). "I don't think this is theoretical; This is our lives": How erasure impacts health care for transgender people. *Journal of the Association of Nurses in AIDS Care, 20*(5), 348–361.

Bauer, G., Nussbaum, N., Travers, R., Munro, L., Pyne, J., & Redman, N. (2011, May 30). We've got work to do: Workplace discrimination and employment challenges for trans people in Ontario. *Trans PULSE E-Bulletin*. Retrieved from http://transpulseproject.ca/documents/E3English.pdf

Bauer, G.R., Redman, N., Bradley, K., & Scheim, A.I. (2013). Sexual health of trans men who are gay, bisexual, or who have sex with men: Results from Ontario, Canada. *International Journal of Transgenderism, 14*(2), 66–74.

Bauer, G.R., Travers, R., Scanlon, K., & Coleman, T. (2012). High heterogeneity of HIV-related sexual risk among transgender people in Ontario, Canada: A province-wide respondent-driven sampling survey. *BMC Public Health, 12*, 292.

Bockting, W.O., Robinson, B.E., & Rosser, B.R. (1998). Transgender HIV prevention: A qualitative needs assessment. *AIDS Care, 10*(4), 505–525.

Bockting, W., Benner, A., & Coleman, E. (2009). Gay and bisexual identity development among female-to-male transsexuals in North America: Emergence of a transgender sexuality. *Archives of Sex Behavior, 38*(5), 688–701.

Clements-Nolle, K., Marx, R., Guzman, R., & Katz, M. (2001). HIV prevalence, risk behaviors, health care use, and mental health status of transgender persons: Implications for public health intervention. *American Journal of Public Health, 91*(6), 915–921.

Cooper, T. (2008, March 16). The trans fags. *Out*. Retrieved from www.out.com/entertainment/2008/03/16/trans-fags

Cromwell, J. (1999). *Transmen and FTMs: Identities, bodies, genders, and sexualities*. Champaign, IL: University of Illinois Press.

Gay/Bi/Queer Trans Men's Working Group. (2007). *Primed: The back pocket guide for trans men and the men who dig them*. Retrieved from library.catie.ca/PDF/P43/24654.pdf

Herbst, J., Jacobs, E., Finlayson, T., McKleroy, V., Neumann, M., & Crepaz, N. (2008). Estimating HIV prevalence and risk behaviors of transgender persons in the United States: A systematic review. *AIDS and Behavior, 12*(1), 1–17.

Husbands, W., Makoroka, L., George, C., Adam, B., Remis, R., Rourke, S., & Beyene, J. (2008). MaBwana: Health, community and vulnerability to HIV among African, Caribbean and Black Gay and Bisexual Men in Toronto. The African and Caribbean Council on HIV/AIDS in Ontario (ACCHO) and the AIDS Committee of Toronto (ACT).

Kenagy, G.P., & Hsieh, C.M. (2005). The risk less known: Female-to-male transgender persons' vulnerability to HIV infection. *AIDS Care, 17*(2), 195–207.

Kosenko, K.A. (2010). Meanings and dilemmas of sexual safety and communication for transgender individuals. *Health Communication, 25*(2), 131–141.

Marshall, Z., for the Gay/Bi/Queer/Trans Men's Working Group. (2011). *The development, challenges, and successes of the Gay/Bi/Queer/Trans Men's Working Group*. Presented at the Promoting the Health of Transgender Communities through Innovative Practices Conference, San Francisco, CA, August 22.

Marshall, Z., Ware, S.M., & Scheim, A. (2013). The development, challenges, and successes of the Gay/Bi/Queer/Trans Men's Working Group. In K. Baker (Ed.), *Global cast study project: Rights-based approaches to health and healthcare for transgender people*. New York: Open Society Foundation.

Melendez, R., Bonem, L., & Sember, R. (2006). On bodies and research: Transgender issues in health and HIV research articles. *Sexuality Research and Social Policy, 3*(4), 21–38.

Namaste, V.K. (1995). *Access denied: A report on the experiences of transsexuals and transgenderists with health care and social services in Toronto*. Report submitted to Project Affirmation and the Coalition for Lesbian and Gay Rights in Ontario, Toronto. Retrieved from www.clgro.org/pdf/Access_Denied.pdf

Namaste, V.K. (2000). *Invisible lives: The erasure of transsexual and transgendered people*. Chicago, IL: University of Chicago Press.

Namaste, V., Vukov, T.H., Saghie, N., Jean-Gilles, J., Lafrenière, M., Leroux, M.-J., & Monette, A. (2007). HIV and STD prevention needs of bisexual women: Results from Projet Polyvalence. *Canadian Journal of Communication, 32*(3), 357–381.

Noble, B. (2009). *Trans-culture in the (white) city: Taking a pass on a queer neighbourhood*. Retrieved March 3, 2012, from http://nomorepotlucks.org/site/trans-culture-in-the-white-city-taking-a-pass-on-a-queer-neighbourhood

Operario, D., & Nemoto, T. (2010). HIV in transgender communities: Syndemic dynamics and a need for multicomponent interventions. *Journal of Acquired Immune Deficiency Syndrome, 55*(Supplement 2), S91–S93.

OUTrans, A. (2010). *Dicklit et T claques*. Paris, France. Retrieved from www.transetvih.org/dtc/

Page, M.M. (2011). *Brazen: Trans women safer sex guide*. Toronto: The 519 Church Street Community Centre. Retrieved from www.the519.org/My%20Files/Trans%20Resources/Sex%20Work/1510_519_trans-women.pdf

Radix, A. (2012). *Trans*MSM*. Panel presentation at MSM Networking Zone, 2012 International AIDS Conference, Washington, DC, July 22–27.

Reisner, S.L., Perkovich, B., & Mimiaga, M.J. (2010). A mixed methods study of the sexual health needs of New England transmen who have sex with nontransgender men. *AIDS Patient Care and STDs, 24*(8), 501–513.

Remis, R.S., Swantee, C., & Liu, J. (2010). *Report on HIV/AIDS in Ontario: 2008.* Retrieved from www.ohemu.utoronto.ca/doc/PHERO2008_report_final_rev%20June2010.pdf

Ross, M.-S. (1995). Investigating women's shelters. *Gendertrash, 3,* 7–10.

Scanlon, K., Travers, R., Coleman, T., Bauer, G., & Boyce, M. (2010, November 12). Ontario's trans communities and suicide: Transphobia is bad for our health (Vol. 1). *Trans PULSE E-Bulletin.* Retrieved from http://transpulseproject.ca/documents/E2English.pdf

Sevelius, J. (2009). "There's no pamphlet for the kind of sex I have": HIV-related risk factors and protective behaviors among transgender men who have sex with nontransgender men. *Journal of the Association of Nurses in AIDS Care, 20*(5), 398–410.

Sevelius, J., Scheim, A., & Giambrone, B. (2010). *What are transgender men's HIV prevention needs?* (Fact Sheet 67). San Francisco: Center for AIDS Prevention Studies, University of California.

Sheth, P., & Thorndycraft, B. (2009). Women and the biology of HIV transmission. *CATIE Fact Sheet.* Canadian AIDS Treatment Information Exchange. Retrieved from www.catie.ca/sites/default/files/Women-and-transmission.pdf

Stone, S. (1992). The empire strikes back: A posttranssexual manifesto. *Camera Obscura, 10*(2 29), 150–176.

Strang, C., & Forrester, D. (2005). *Creating a space where we all are welcome: Improving access to the Toronto hostel system for transsexual and transgender people.* Toronto: Fred Victor Centre.

Stryker, S. (1999). Portrait of a transfag drag hag as a young man: The activist career of Louis G. Sullivan. In K. More & S. Whittle (Eds.), *Reclaiming genders: Transsexual grammars at the fin de siècle* (pp. 62–82). London: Cassell.

Sugano, E., Nemoto, T., & Operario, D. (2006). The impact of exposure to transphobia on HIV risk behavior in a sample of transgendered women of color in San Francisco. *AIDS and Behavior, 10*(2), 217–225.

Sullivan, L. (n.d.). *Information for the female to male cross-dresser and transsexual.* Seattle, WA: Ingersoll Gender Center (1st ed., Janus Information Facility).

Syms, S. (2007, October 10). Trans men loving gay men loving trans men. *Xtra.* Toronto edition.

Wallace, J. (2002, January 24). On sacred ground: Trans men stake their place at the baths. *Xtra.* Toronto edition.

Ware, S. (2004). *Assessing the HIV/AIDS prevention, education and support needs of trans people living in Toronto.* Toronto: AIDS Committee of Toronto.

Xavier, J.M., Bobbin, M., Singer, B., & Budd, E. (2005). A needs assessment of transgendered people of color living in Washington, DC. *International Journal of Transgenderism, 8*(2/3), 31–47.

Chapter 24 Public Health Professionals, Community Researchers, and Community-Based Participatory Action Research: Process and Discovery

Kathy Chow, Jean Clipsham, Cheryl Dobinson, Susan Gapka, Elaine Hampson, Judith A. MacDonnell, and Rupert Raj[1]

The importance of creating spaces and processes to challenge the deeply embedded invisibility and exclusion of trans people and their holistic health issues is increasingly on the radar of Canadian public health nurses (PHNs) in 2013. A key factor is related to the fact that PHN practice has undergone a significant shift over the last three decades in Canada. To some extent, a traditional focus on addressing mainly biomedical concerns of disease prevention (e.g., influenza) and individual health promotion (e.g., behaviour and lifestyle changes) often continues to shape the public's understanding of what PHNs do as they work in the community setting. Yet, in fact, their practice is underpinned by an understanding that "social justice and equity are the foundations of nursing" (Canadian Public Health Association, 2010, p. 13; Falk-Rafael, 2000; Schim, Benkert, Bell, Walker, & Danford, 2007). Attention to the social determinants of health, such as income and social exclusion, that contribute to inequity, and attention to the health of populations rather than solely to individual health have enabled PHNs to more effectively promote the health and well-being of the diverse communities and populations that they serve.

Although nursing, like other health professions, has considered diversity an important dimension of health, much of the nursing literature reflects attention to visible difference related to ethnicity (see MacDonnell & Fern, Chapter 25 in this text). Despite the need for research and discussion regarding progressive and equitable public health nursing praxis, and a wealth of health promotion literature that addresses the social determinants for a range of public health practitioners (e.g., Mikkonen & Raphael, 2010; *Toronto Charter for a Healthy Canada*, 2002), there has been limited Canadian scholarship that addresses sexual and gender diversity.

Complex dynamics inform how knowledge is produced and legitimated as PHNs engage with a range of minorities and other vulnerable and/or marginalized communities. Community health nursing has a long history of advocacy. As explained in MacDonnell and Fern in this text, current Canadian PHN practice is also informed by primary health care principles and health promotion strategies in policy documents that emerged from meetings with the World Health Organization. These principles and strategies challenged health professionals to prioritize community participation and use a broader lens than conventional health services to address the roots of health inequities. Engaging in participatory processes, such as action research, that are responsive to community knowledges is certainly consistent with social justice goals (Smith & Davies, 2006). However, there has been a virtual silence about PHNs' involvement in knowledge production using such approaches and, specifically, concerning sexual and gender diverse communities in a public health context.

In this chapter, we describe how community-based participatory action research (CBPAR) provided a framework for PHNs' practice that aimed to build meaningful community capacity through research while attending to the complex power dynamics that shape public health research processes. Consistent with such ethical and political commitments to care, our goals were to understand how the communities themselves articulated issues of access to public health care in ways fostering their visibility and voice in the creation of evidence for enhancing system change. We focus on two research projects related to the health of sexually and gender diverse communities in Ontario: Improving the Access and Quality of Public Health Services for Bisexuals (Dobinson, MacDonnell, Hampson, Clipsham, & Chow, 2005)[2] and the Trans Health Project (Gapka & Raj, 2003). As community researchers and public health nurses involved in these two projects,[3] we engage in retrospective research through reflecting on some of our experiences with CBPAR.[4] We highlight benefits and challenges to carrying out the projects, identify how the process has fostered all participating researchers' continued commitment to addressing sexual and gender diversity through multiple knowledge translation initiatives in academic and community contexts,[5] and consider the continuing impact of these projects with implications for nursing that will translate into improved access and equity for trans people across the health care sector. As this reflection indicates, the potential within CBPAR to inform evidence for policy-making at multiple levels and to increase individual and community capacity-building is significant. While we understood the potential benefits on an intellectual level, it would be fair to say that we did not anticipate how each of us would be so affected personally and professionally when we began two year-long projects with three enthusiastic community researchers and a small group of PHNs a decade ago—nor did we expect that the projects would have larger impacts, sparking cohesive networks and relationships.

The Public Health Alliance (PHA) for Lesbian, Gay, Bisexual, Transsexual, Transgender, Two-spirit, Intersex, Queer and Questioning (LGBTTTIQQ[6]) [Equity] was an Access and Equity workgroup of the Ontario Public Health Association (OPHA) launched in 1997 and consisting of interdisciplinary professionals, including nurses and community members.[7] We believe that PHNs should be familiar with community-based participatory action research since "community participation is seen as a basic principle of health promotion and, by extension, of health promotion research" (Allison & Rootman, 1996, p. 336). Such health-promoting research has the potential to address the social determinants of health, foster healthy public policy, and enhance community development. CBPAR is an excellent research strategy to enable people to empower themselves to take action to transform their everyday lives and actualize their optimal health. This process includes collaboration between the researchers and the community in each stage of the research and while translating the results, attention to dynamics of power and privilege in the knowledge creation process,[8] and a combined commitment to take action on the results with goals that include more equitable outcomes and community self-determination (Public Health Alliance for LGBTTIQ Equity, 2002).

In 2002, PHA identified the need to develop position papers on equitable access to public health programs for bisexual and transsexual/transgender communities. We had created a policy resolution (MacDonnell, 2007a; Public Health Alliance for LGBTTIQ Equity, 2002), accepted by the Ontario Public Health Association (OPHA) membership, that called for CB-PAR as an ethical research approach for collaborating with sexually diverse groups to create evidence for practice. We received funding for one year from the Wellesley Central Health Corporation, OPHA, and the Canadian Institutes for Health Research to undertake two province-wide community consultations.

The principal investigators (PIs) were members of the communities being researched (Allison & Rootman, 1996; Public Health Alliance for LGBTTIQ Equity, 2002). This is consistent with CBPAR principles that value community knowledges, enhance communities' visibility and diverse voices, and build on their own expertise throughout the research process. The research team consisted of four PHNs from the PHA workgroup who brought a public health perspective to the projects. The nurses created the research proposals, obtained funding, hired the researchers, and oversaw the budget. The PHNs provided regular support and mentoring throughout every phase of the project, including sharing insights into public health theory and practice, collaborating on data analysis, writing research reports and position papers, as well as thinking through optimal implementation strategies. Additionally, they presented papers (Dobinson et al., 2005; Gapka, Raj, Chow, Clipsham, Hampson, MacDonnell et al., 2003) to the OPHA membership at their annual general meeting in 2003.

The collaboration highlighted the various skills that all co-researchers on the team brought to the project. The PHNs demonstrated skills that may often be unacknowledged and underutilized, such as strong community development experience, conflict management, group leadership and facilitation, project management, and supervisory skills. PHNs had insider knowledge gained through their professional work of how to engage in partnerships and garner support from various stakeholders, such as public health units, OPHA, and related nursing professional bodies. The principal researchers found that the collaboration not only "strengthened their voice," but also gave them additional legitimacy and the validity to be seen *as researchers* who could draw on knowledge formed from their life experiences as members of bisexual and/or transsexual/transgendered communities. In addition, an affiliation with OPHA, a public health association and provincial policy body, enhanced their credibility within a variety of health system spaces, such as research venues and professional communities, which supported them as they presented their research at national conferences, met with community groups across the province, and found employment related to the research.

Reciprocal education occurred between PHNs and the principal investigators (Hills & Mullett, 2000). These community researchers learned a broader definition of health and the role of public health in policy change and capacity building. PHNs acquired personal insight into the lives and struggles of bisexual and transsexual/transgender people. One public health member stated that she wished every public health professional could have this experience because then everyone would have the opportunity to become bi positive and trans positive. The principal researchers on the respective bi and trans projects also learned from each other, and as a result of working together, enriched each other's research projects and activism outside the project's sphere.

All members of the project committee learned more about CBPAR and its implementation. Having the opportunity to discuss research methodology and strategies to contact hard-to-reach populations enhanced the research, in addition to learning about the challenges of both communities. Finally and most importantly, the interaction between the researchers and their respective populations of study created a triangle of learning between public health professionals, researchers, and the bisexual and transsexual/transgender communities being studied. We learned that the research process itself, with both face-to-face and online opportunities to connect with the research team, created for some of the project participants a sense of community and identity, particularly for those who were hidden/invisible and/or geographically isolated. The energy and passion amongst members of these various groups, combined with our collaborative efforts and the building of trust amongst the team members, created a productive synergy. There were challenges and differing viewpoints. However, we were committed to achieving a positive outcome.

Although CBPAR produced extremely rewarding results, there were many challenges to be overcome. Researchers and public health nurses became frustrated working within a provincial public health association structure wherein particular policies impacted some members of the team negatively. For example, research costs had to be paid up front. Receipts were then submitted to OPHA following which financial reimbursement was processed and received. This policy did not take into consideration that some members of marginalized communities face economic barriers, and that these individuals were not able to pay out of pocket for transportation and/or hotel accommodation. Also, CBPAR required more time and energy than originally anticipated. Team members who worked as front-line nurses did not have dedicated or additional time for research and had to conduct it in addition to their regular work. It was also a challenge for the researchers to understand public health organizational policies and other financial or resource limitations within a seemingly large, well-to-do organization such as OPHA. Other challenges included effective communication among team members. Telephone and email systems did not consistently work, as public health nurses tend to work "on the road" and were not always available for immediate decision making. There were also barriers that limited our capacity to obtain input from potential trans and bisexual participants living in northern and rural areas given the limited resources available.

Since no single template exists for CBPAR, the public health nurses and researchers had to reflect critically on their preconceived ideas concerning power, privilege, and research to formulate equitable working relationships. For instance, we had to confront and work through our understandings concerning who "owns" the research data and who can then use the findings from the research projects, when, and for what purpose. It was decided that the research belonged to both OPHA and the researchers and could be used by the researchers as long as OPHA was credited. Such issues highlighted the need to explore and share not only the theoretical aspects of CBPAR, but also its implementation in practice (prompting this written collaboration). In terms of the financial disparities that emerged from research team members having different class locations, we encourage other CBPAR researchers to have full commitment from management at each health unit to have time to participate in the research. As well, in retrospect it would have been useful at the funding proposal stage to anticipate the need for sufficient funding to provide honoraria for research participants and to send researchers to conferences to help disseminate the findings. Similarly, at the proposal stage, it may have been useful to build in advisory group processes, although the limited time frame of one year to complete the projects presented some challenges to that process. The Trans Health Project team did seek out community research advisors, regional networkers, and volunteers from the trans communities to foster community engagement in the project. Clarifying who "owned" the research findings was important. The findings were published in open access reports on the OPHA website, and team members on the respective projects could share the data while acknowledging the funders, project team members, and communities involved.

Implementation strategies named by the researchers ranged from community and professional education to policy advocacy and further research. Knowledge translation and exchange strategies took many forms during this research process (Smith & Davies, 2006). At local and provincial levels, research participants in each project held public forums to share findings with their respective communities and to foster communities' consensus and agreement concerning strategies for action. A suggestion to "celebrate Bisexuality Day" on an annual basis emerged from one forum in 2002 and has since been promoted throughout Ontario by public health units and across Canada by other organizations such as schools. In addition, the respective community PIs and PHNs from the research team jointly facilitated numerous education and networking sessions at local health departments and community agencies across Ontario to share study findings and to create support networks for communities and providers.

Various members of the research team shared the findings at local, provincial, national and international conferences (Clipsham & Hampson, 2005; Dobinson, 2003, 2005, 2006a, 2006b; Dobinson, MacDonnell, Hampson, Clipsham, & Chow, 2004a, 2004b; Gapka & Raj, 2003, 2004a, 2004b; MacDonnell, 2002). These conference meetings addressed members of various academic disciplines and interdisciplinary fields related to sexual diversity, sexuality, health promotion, public health and education, psychology, and nursing.

Although the primary goal of this research was not publication in academic venues, publication of the projects and their findings has spanned sites with international readership. The project on bisexual access was published in *Journal of Bisexuality* (Dobinson et al., 2005). Nurses' participation in the CBPAR projects was cited in a book focused on economics and sexual orientation discrimination (MacDonnell, 2007b). The Trans Health Project (Gapka et al., 2003) was cited in Canadian clinical guidelines on mental health (Bockting, Knudson, & Goldberg, 2006) and the bisexual project in American practice guidelines, such as those on HIV/AIDS programming (Miller, André, Ebin, & Bessenova, 2007). These research projects were also listed on a variety of Web-based lists of health and social resources, such as the Canadian Women's Health Network database and EBSCOhost LGBT Full-Text Research Database, and included in other online sources of information that offer easy access to findings for community members and researchers.

Gapka and colleagues (2003) and Dobinson and colleagues (2005) reported on two of the seven Canadian research projects whose findings and methodology are described in a recent discussion paper addressing the social determinants of health (Jackson et al., 2006). This discussion paper was funded by Health Canada and the Canadian Rainbow Health Coalition. It summarized current research evidence and called for strategic planning along with the development of indicators to measure sexual and gender diversity and their integration into national surveys. It cites both projects in the discussions that address referral networks that enable children to reach their full potential, removing barriers to care to ensure dignity, targeted programs and education for health and social service professionals, involvement of communities in planning and delivery of programs, and professional curriculum and research.

The three principal investigators, Cheryl Dobinson, Susan Gapka, and Rupert Raj, have become more politically active, and the research process enhanced and supported their professional development. Cheryl Dobinson has collaborated with American partners through the Gay and Lesbian Medical Association (GLMA) on bisexual health. For instance, *Bisexual Health: An Introduction and Model Practices for HIV/STI Preventional Programming* (Miller et al., 2007), published by the National Gay and Lesbian Task Force (US), cites 2003 as the year that "North American Conference on Bisexuality hosts Bi Health Summit organized by Cheryl Dobinson, Luigi Ferrer and Ron Fox" (p. 33). Her involvement in research and education on breast health for lesbian and bisexual women has been supported by the Sherbourne Health Centre in Toronto, a centre known for generating and disseminating resources on sexual diversity. She has continued to be involved in a range of bi-related community-based participatory action and other research projects, such as those on perinatal mental health with researchers at the Centre for Addiction and Mental Health (CAMH). Publications span this decade (e.g., Li, Dobinson, Scheim, & Ross, 2013) and include those cited by the US-based National Institutes of Health (e.g., Ross, Dobinson, & Eady, 2010).

The two Trans Health Project researchers, Susan Gapka and Rupert Raj, became involved in an active campaign to reinstate public funding for sex reassignment surgery (SRS) in Ontario, and have used their research paper in their testimony at an Ontario Human Rights Tribunal regarding SRS. Rupert Raj is involved with individual and group counselling with trans communities, publishing on linkages between therapeutic outcomes for trans people and activism and clinical focus (e.g., Raj, 2007; Wassersug, Gray, Barbara, Trosztmer, Raj, & Sinding, 2007), as well as on education and advocacy with trans people across gender spectrums. Susan Gapka is founder and chair of the Trans Lobby Group, which led a lengthy campaign to persuade the Minister of Health to fund sex reassignment surgery for trans people in Ontario in 2008. The Trans Lobby Group has also been working to include explicit human rights protections for trans people in Ontario and across Canada. Toby's Act to amend the Ontario Human Rights Code to include "gender identity and gender expression" was adopted June 13, 2012. Bill C-389, an Act to Amend the Canadian Human Rights Act and Criminal Code to include "gender identity and gender expression" passed Parliament on February 10, 2011, but died when the federal election was called. Its successor, Bill C-279, received first reading in the Senate on October 17, 2013, and second on November 26, 2013, and a final vote in Parliament on March 20, 2014. The Trans Lobby Group also advocated for modernization and harmonization on the amending criteria for changing the sex designation on the record of birth via the Ontario Vital Statistics Act, which resulted in changes announced in October 2012.

The PHA workgroup received many requests for partnership and letters of support from agencies such as Rainbow Health Ontario, Rainbow Health Network, and EGALE Canada. The resolutions that resulted from the research and ensuing position papers provided an action plan to guide the workgroup for a number of years. Nurses currently affiliated with PHA created a resource manual (Public Health Alliance for LGBTTTIQQ Equity, 2006) for health units and community health centres concerning positive workplaces that incorporates and builds on the project findings. There is evidence that this research has informed best practices in the health disciplines. The Registered Nurses' Association of Ontario (RNAO) has taken a leadership role in Canadian health professions on these issues. RNAO cited the position papers in their position statement *Respecting Sexual Orientation and Gender Identity* (2007). It was disseminated widely through community, print, and Web-based media to reach communities and nurses across multiple sites of practice, and the issues were profiled in a professional publication (Scarrow, 2007). As a result of their involvement with the CBPAR projects, these nurses continue to advocate for the inclusion of sexual orientation and gender diversity across practice settings and policy venues that include program mandates, codes of ethics, and professional curriculum. Furthermore, these nurses advocate for recognition of the issues related to sexuality and gender identity at a national level through securing the support of the OPHA.

These two projects continue to have multiple impacts at the local and macro levels in Canada and beyond, both within the respective communities as well as in nursing and interdisciplinary and intersectoral contexts. For instance, the article "Improving Access and Quality of Public Health Services for Bisexuals" by Dobinson and colleagues (2005), a publication based on the bisexual project, is cited over 20 times in Google Scholar. As evidenced at international and national conferences focused on gender and/or LGBT health, Judith A. MacDonnell noted that informal dialogues and postings on listservs over the last decade have indicated that academic and trans-identified community researchers acknowledge the early contribution of the Trans Health Project to participatory approaches to trans health research. All co-researchers continue their involvement in formal implementation strategies and other knowledge translation activities that build on the knowledge and partnerships emerging from these projects, thus demonstrating increased community and professional capacity. The PHNs are now involved in a range of nursing roles that involve administration and program development, mesh clinical practice and education and/or research and education, and are engaged in LGBT nursing leadership in a variety of capacities, including through formal roles in an RNAO interest group that formed in 2006. (See MacDonnell and Fern, in Chapter 25 of this text, for recent political and policy-related activities related to bullying in schools and human rights.) The community PIs, having taken on different clinical, education, and/or political roles, are leaders in their communities.

Although CBPAR takes more time and effort, it is valuable in terms of outcomes, both for the communities and the quality of research results. The researchers gained capacity and acquired new skills to become national and international activists. All three community PIs gained employment because of participation in the projects. The PHNs became more sensitive and more understanding of bi and trans community issues and have continued to advocate on behalf of the bisexual and trans communities through OPHA and on a range of levels through RNAO, with a current focus on developing best practice guidelines for nurses (see MacDonnell and Fern in Chapter 25 of this text). In addition, Judith A. MacDonnell, for example, has been involved in LGBT-focused home care and trans-specific research, as well as nursing curriculum.

In participating in this process, we all agree that we accomplished true health promotion research that was meaningful to both the respective communities and public health nurses, and that our communities continue to build capacities to increase access and equity in health care for both bisexual and trans communities. We therefore have all been enriched by this research process, having fostered solid community–institutional relationships and respect for the potential of, and importance of, community-led creation of evidence for policy-making, as well as the possibilities of LGBT political activism through health-promoting research that can mobilize community knowledges. Recommendations from the projects included: further funding for research into bisexual and trans health concerns; increasing advocacy and ongoing alliances with trans communities; advocating for OHIP re-listing of sex reassignment surgery and electrolysis for trans people; further developing health care provider proficiency in the health needs of trans people, including surgery; advocating in sectors, such as the shelter, housing, and criminal justice sectors, to provide funding for trans positive institutions; including trans positive cultural competency in the education of health care providers and making accessible information widely available online for health care providers; developing comprehensive facilities, including community health centres and community centres in Toronto with satellite locations across Ontario; increasing community partnerships to support trans peer support groups across the province; and supporting trans-targeted hiring practices within the health care sectors.

NOTES

1 The researchers would like to thank the Ontario Public Health Association, Sophie Bart, Josée Coutu, and Marianne Clipsham for their assistance. We also very much appreciated funding from the Canadian Institutes for Health Research (CIHR), Wellesley Central Health Corporation, and the Ontario Public Health Association, which supported the community-based participatory action research studies on bisexual and trans health.

2 The bisexual project is also available online at http://opha.on.ca/Position-Papers/Improving-the-Access-and-Quality-of-Public-Health.aspx

3 We speak to our research initiative as co-researchers, initially identifying how we were situated as community members taking on a research role with public health nursing professionals.

4 This chapter is a collaborative piece about the projects that contrasts with a more theoretical piece by one of the public health nurse participants that used a feminist bioethics lens to examine the projects and larger workgroup; see MacDonnell (2007a).

5 For a discussion of the terms "knowledge transfer," "knowledge translation," and "knowledge exchange," see Smith and Davies (2006). For the purposes of this chapter, "dissemination," "knowledge translation," and "knowledge exchange" are used to signal action impacts of research processes that include, but move beyond, academic publication.

6 Sexual diversity in this paper addresses sexual orientation and gender identity. Examples of sexual orientations are: gay, lesbian, bisexual, and heterosexual. Transsexual and transgender issues relate to one's gender identity. The terms "trans" and "bi" are also used to refer to the respective communities.

7 This OPHA workgroup as it was configured for 15 years no longer exists. In 2012, OPHA's structure changed so that the LGBTTTIQQ-focused group was subsumed under a broader Equity group focus.

8 Hence, a number of conference presentations and publications cite the authors in alphabetical order rather than, more traditionally, according to "proportion" of contribution.

REFERENCES

Allison, K.R., & Rootman, I. (1996). Scientific rigor and community participation in health promotion research: Are they compatible? *Health Promotion International, 11*(4), 333–340.

Bockting, W., Knudson, G., & Goldberg, J.M. (2006). *Counselling and mental health issues of transgender adults and loved ones*. Vancouver, BC: Vancouver Coastal Health and Canadian Rainbow Health Coalition. Retrieved from www.vch.ca/transhealth/resources/library/tcpdocs/guidelines-mentalhealth.pdf

Canadian Public Health Association. (2010, March). *Public health—Community health nursing practice in Canada: Roles and activities* (4th ed.). Retrieved from www.cpha.ca/uploads/pubs/3-1bk04214.pdf

Clipsham, J., & Hampson, E. (2005). *Public health and primary care practitioners—Evaluate your services for LGBT sensitivity and inclusivity.* Paper presented at the 2nd Annual Canadian Rainbow Health Coalition Conference, "Developing Capacity to Address Our Health and Wellness," Halifax, Nova Scotia, November 3–5.

Dobinson, C. (2003). *Improving the access and quality of health and wellness services for bisexuals.* Paper presented at the 111th Annual Convention of the American Psychological Association, Toronto, August 7–10.

Dobinson, C. (2005). *Bringing bisexuality out of the closet: What health care providers need to know.* Paper presented at the 2nd Annual Canadian Rainbow Health Coalition Conference, "Developing Capacity to Address Our Health and Wellness," Halifax, Nova Scotia, November 3–5.

Dobinson, C. (2006a). *Bisexuality: The basics.* Paper presented at the 23rd International Lesbian and Gay Association Annual Conference, Geneva, Switzerland, March 27–April 3.

Dobinson, C. (2006b). *Bringing bisexuality out of the closet: What health care providers need to know.* Paper presented at the 24th Annual Conference of the Gay & Lesbian Medical Association, San Francisco, California, October 11–14.

Dobinson, C., MacDonnell, J.A., Hampson, E., Clipsham, J., & Chow, K. (2004a). *Improving access and quality of public health services for bisexuals.* Poster session presented at Working Together to Create Healthy Lives: Third National Lesbian Health Conference, Chicago, Illinois, May 19–22.

Dobinson, C., MacDonnell, J.A., Hampson, E., Clipsham, J., & Chow, K. (2004b). *Improving access and quality of public health services for bisexuals.* Poster session presented at the Community Health Nurses Initiatives Group (CHNIG) 2004 Conference, Toronto, September 24–25.

Dobinson, C., (with MacDonnell, J., Hampson, E., Clipsham, J., & Chow, K.). (2005). Improving access and quality of public health services for bisexuals. *Journal of Bisexuality, 5*(1), 39–78.

Falk-Rafael, A.R.F. (2000). Watson's philosophy, science, and theory of human caring as a conceptual framework for guiding community health nursing practice. *Advances in Nursing Science (ANS), 23*(2), pp. 34–49.

Gapka, S., & Raj, R. (2003). *Trans Health Project: Improving the access and equity of public health services for transpeople in Ontario.* EGALE Canada Conference, Montreal, Quebec, May 17–18.

Gapka, S., & Raj, R. (2004a). *Trans Health Project.* Queer Health Matters, Sherbourne Health Centre, Toronto.

Gapka, S., & Raj, R. (2004b). *Understanding trans health care.* Paper presented at the Canadian Rainbow Health Conference, "Many Faces, Diverse Voices," Gatineau, Quebec, November 4–7.

Gapka, S., Raj, R., Chow, K., Clipsham, J., Hampson, E., MacDonnell, J., et al. (2003). *The Trans Health Project* [Position paper]. Toronto: OPHA. Retrieved from http://www.opha.on.ca/ppres/2003-06_pp.pdf

Hills, M., & Mullett, J. (2000). *Community-based research: Creating evidence-based practice for health and social change.* Paper presented to the Qualitative Evidence-Based Conference, Coventry University, GB, May 15–17.

Jackson, B., (with Daley, A., Moore, D., Mulé, N., Ross, L., & Travers, A.). (2006). *Whose public health? An intersectional approach to sexual orientation, gender identity and the development of public health goals for Canada* [Discussion paper]. Ontario Rainbow Health Partnership Project. Retrieved from www.rainbowhealthnetwork.ca/files/whose_public_health.pdf

Li, T., Dobinson, C., Scheim, A.I., & Ross, L.E. (2013). Unique issues bisexual people face in intimate relationships: A descriptive exploration of lived experience. *Journal of Gay and Lesbian Mental Health, 17*(1), 21–39.

MacDonnell, J.A. (2002). *Participatory policy processes: Coalition building and research as venues for LGBTTQ health advocacy.* Poster session presented at the Conference on Social Determinants of Health: A Current Accounting & Policy Implications, York University, Toronto, November 29–December 1.

MacDonnell, J.A. (2007a). Articulating a policy resolution for sexual minorities: Nurses as moral agents. *Canadian Journal of Nursing Research, 39*(4), 74–92.

MacDonnell, J.A. (2007b). Comparative life histories of nurses who advocate for lesbian health in a Canadian context: Sexual orientation discrimination as a factor in career and workplace dynamics. In M.V.L. Badgett & J. Frank (Eds.), *Sexual orientation discrimination: An international perspective* (pp. 118–135). New York: Routledge.

Mikkonen, J., & Raphael, D. (2010). *The social determinants of health: The Canadian facts.* Toronto: York University School of Health Policy/Management.

Miller, M., André, A., Ebin, J., & Bessenova, L. (2007). *Bisexual health: An introduction and model practices for HIV/STI prevention programming.* Boston: National Gay and Lesbian Task Force. Retrieved from www.thetaskforce.org/downloads/reports/bi_health_5_07.pdf

Public Health Alliance for LGBTTIQ Equity (PHA). (2002). *Ethical research and evidence-based practice for lesbians and gay men* [Policy resolution]. Toronto: OPHA. Retrieved from http://opha.on.ca/OPHA/media/Resources/Position-Papers/2002-01_res.pdf?ext=.pdf

Public Health Alliance for LGBTTTIQQ Equity (PHA). (2006). *A positive space is a healthy place: Making your community health centre or public health unit inclusive to those of all sexual orientations and gender identities.* Toronto: OPHA. Retrieved from http://opha.on.ca/getmedia/125e32e7-f9cb-48ed-89cb-9d954d76537b/SexualHealthPaper-Mar11.pdf.aspx?ext=.pdf

Raj, R. (2007).Transactivism as therapy: A client self-empowerment model linking personal and social agency. *Journal of Gay & Lesbian Psychotherapy, 11*(3-4), 77–98.

Registered Nurses' Association of Ontario. (2007, June). *Respecting sexual orientation and gender identity* [Position statement]. Toronto: Author. Retrieved from http://rnao.ca/policy/position-statements/sexual-orientation-gender-identity

Ross, L.E., Dobinson, C., & Eady, A., (2010). Perceived determinants of mental health for bisexual people: A qualitative examination. *American Journal of Public Health, 100*(3), 496–502.

Scarrow, J. (2007, July/August). Respecting diversity and inclusivity. *Registered Nurse Journal, 24.*

Schim, S.M., Benkert, R., Bell, S.E., Walker, D.S, & Danford, C.A. (2007). Social justice: Added metaparadigm concept for urban health nursing. *Public Health Nursing, 24*(1), 73–80.

Smith, D., & Davies, B. (2006). Participatory model: Creating a new dynamic in Aboriginal health. *The Canadian Nurse, 102*(4), 36–39.

Toronto Charter for a Healthy Canada. (2002). Strengthening the Social Determinants of Health Across the Life-Span Conference, Toronto, Ontario, November 29–December 1. Retrieved from http://depts.washington.edu/ccph/pdf_files/Toronto%20Charter%20Final.pdf

Wassersug, R., Gray, R., Barbara, A., Trosztmer, C., Raj, R., & Sinding, C. (2007). Experiences of transwomen with hormone therapy. *Sexualities, 10*, 101–122.

Chapter 25 Advocacy for Gender Diversity in the Contemporary Canadian Nursing Context: A Focus on Ontario

Judith A. MacDonnell and Robin Fern

Although nurses represent the largest proportion of health providers in Canada and are ethically mandated to advocate for diverse clients and communities (Canadian Nurses Association, 2008), little has been written about their activities as advocates for trans communities. This chapter is a reflection on nursing activism in relation to trans communities from the perspective of two registered nurses who have engaged with trans health advocacy in various capacities over the last decade in Ontario.

Our purpose is to provide insight into contemporary trans activism in a Canadian context over the last decade by making visible the spectrum of ways in which nurses have advocated to foster the health and well-being of trans people. Our examples reflect mainly the Ontario context as a snapshot of nurses' activism. As we indicate, nurses' advocacy is in no way limited to clinical settings; rather, we are also advocating for the health and wellness of trans communities across all domains of practice, in fields pertaining to education, research, administration, and policy. At the same time, it is clear that many nurses lack knowledge and understanding about gender diversity and remain uncomfortable with notions of gender that transgress binary and essentialist notions of sex and gender. These dynamics also limit nurses' capacities to support trans clients and colleagues or participate in challenging organizational and professional norms that are transphobic.

We draw on our own experiences as a transgender nurse in Robin's case, and as a trans ally in Judith's case. Judith situates herself as white, middle-class, English-speaking, cisgendered heterosexual. Her critical feminist research and practice have been informed by over a decade of engagement with LGBT issues as an activist through graduate studies, public health nursing practice, education, and participatory policy research processes. Her engagement with critical scholarship, such as Krista Scott-Dixon's (2006) *Trans/forming Feminisms*, has shaped her understanding of the tensions and possibilities of nurses' roles as activists, and the value of using an integrative approach to gender that enables reflection on how it intersects with race, class, sexuality, ability, and other social relations.

Robin is a trans person who hails from Liverpool, in northern England, and now lives in Toronto, Ontario. Currently, he is not planning medical transition. The gender ambiguity that arises from living his authentic trans masculine self without hormones or surgery has made life quite interesting and sometimes very disheartening. After working very successfully as a registered midwife in London for 19 years, he struggled, during the early stages of his transition, to stay employed within the midwifery profession in Ontario. Eventually he was no longer able to find a welcoming midwifery practice within which to work and returned to nursing. Robin now works as a primary care nurse in clinical practice with subspecialities in sexual and reproductive, perinatal, and mental health nursing. He is also a trans health activist and nursing innovator in trans community health education. The Trans Fathers 2B course that he helped develop and facilitate strengthens trans community health and wellness in the field of family planning and creation. It exemplifies the value of staying true to community activist principles—keeping the focus on trans peoples' own experience and knowledge of their own needs and community capacity building.

Given the enormous everyday health and social impacts of transphobia for diversely situated trans people, the health professions such as nursing are ethically bound to foster trans communities' health and well-being with attention to their holistic health concerns (MacDonnell & Grigorovich, 2012). While guidelines for nursing ethics currently include a focus on the importance of nurses working to promote social justice for individuals, the notion of advocating for populations and communities, or working collectively to advocate, have not consistently been mandated in the same way (Canadian Nurses Association, 2008; MacDonnell, 2007a; Peter, 2008). Certainly, the historical context is relevant in terms of what health issues are deemed relevant to trans people. Trans people's health issues have often been subsumed under those related to the broader queer communities with a focus on sexuality rather than gender per se (Dean et al., 2000).

Trans communities and professional groups would both benefit from understanding how nurses have participated over time to resist trans oppression within multiple sites. The first part of this chapter touches on literature that situates nurses' roles as trans health activists in Canada, with attention to diverse contexts and sites for advocacy on individual and collective levels. The second part of the chapter examines Robin's work with trans families as politicized sites of struggle, and with community health education programming, which he has undertaken recently.

SETTING A CONTEXT

Gender diversity within nursing has historically focused on males and females, with some attention to the ways in which gender norms, for the most part, rendered same-sex orientation invisible (McPherson, 1996). Trans issues in nursing have only begun to appear in nursing literature over the last decade, with few Canadian offerings providing more than a passing reference to the trans dimensions of LGBTQ communities (Eliason, Dibble, & DeJoseph, 2010; MacDonnell & Grigorovich, 2012; Thomas, 2004).

The public face of nurses' collective activism as an explicit component of health professional advocacy with and for sexual and gender minorities has emerged over the last decade in Ontario. Individual nurses affiliated with women's studies in an academic context or community activist groups, such as the Coalition for Lesbian and Gay Rights in Ontario, whose report *Systems Failure: A Report on the Experiences of Sexual Minorities in Ontario's Health-Care and Social-Services Systems* (1997) was a watershed for LGBT professional advocacy in Ontario, were challenging institutional heterosexism, homophobia, biphobia, and transphobia. This particular form of nursing activism has been largely under the public radar. This is due in large part because the few nurses affiliated with these larger activist groups contributed in a professional context and often on a volunteer basis. Nurses have shared with us their experiences of engaging with patients, clients, students, and colleagues who represent diverse sexual and gender identities, affirming their holistic lives and exploring resources that might support them. To some extent, nurses working in community clinical contexts have been more visible. These nurses' affiliations with sexual health, HIV/AIDS, or adolescent health programs and services are seen as consistent with nurses' roles to support LGBT people who are at risk for mental health or sexual health conditions (MacDonnell, 2007a).

According to the Canadian Rainbow Health Coalition (2005), community-based activism for LGBT people in Canada emerged from the gay and lesbian social movements in the 1970s, which catalyzed the development of community-based services and support to address the fact that lesbians, gay men, bisexuals, and transgender/transsexual people were rendered invisible or marginal to health care programming, service provision, and nursing research. As Kathryn McPherson (1996) indicated in her history of the female-dominated Canadian nursing profession, nursing practice was historically constructed in relation to the assumed male physician. These dynamics established normative values related to gender, which she described in relation to the heteronormativity that shaped the profession historically, and which continue to influence nursing practice and professional education and the authority accorded their work (Giddings, 2005; Hall, 2008; MacDonnell, 2007b; McDonald, 2006). Such values are reflected in professional norms for appearance and behaviour: a dress code and a demure stance in interactions that reflect a dominant notion of femininity (MacDonnell, 2007b).

These deeply embedded social dynamics continue to contribute to a lack of knowledge and understanding and outright discomfort with trans people as clients or colleagues. These processes can be conceptualized as transphobic violence, which intersects with other types of gender-, racial-, and colonial-based violence. Such multi-dimensional forms of violence limit the possibility of creating high-quality care and work environments for diverse trans people (Mulé et al., 2009). While more attention has been given to lesbians and gay men in a Canadian nursing research context, the lack of visibility of trans issues and nurses' trans activism within Canadian nursing literature has continued. Recently, however, researchers publishing in American nursing journals have been addressing trans health in a clinical and cultural competency context more explicitly (e.g., Hanssmann, Morrison, Russian, Shiu-Thornton, & Bowen, 2010; Jenner, 2010; Polly & Nicole, 2011). The erasure of trans-specific health care issues and nursing activism constrains the opportunities for nurses to realize the potential contributions they may have to make to challenge the conditions that negate people's health and well-being.

THE MULTIPLE DOMAINS OF NURSING ADVOCACY

Dominant conceptualizations of nursing equate practice with direct clinical care at the bedside in a hospital or clinic setting. Nurses' roles in advocacy for sexually and/or gender diverse groups, then, is often taken up as *individual advocacy* to a physician on behalf of the individual patient/client in a medical context (MacDonnell, 2009). Whether they are supporting transsexual sex workers in their role as street health nurses or prescribing hormones as nurse practitioners, nurses advocate as case managers in clinical or community settings (Hilton, Thompson & Moore-Dempsey, 2000; MacDonnell, 2007b; Registered Nurses Association of British Columbia, 2009). As direct care providers in settings that include sexual health clinics or adolescent services, they are well positioned to offer supportive care that can support disclosure of identity and affirm gender expression. This is an integral part of nursing practice, especially since nurses work across all health care sectors in long-term care, hospitals, hospices, nursing homes, schools, and other community facilities and are often the consistent face of the system.

COMMUNITY SETTINGS

Primary health care philosophies in international policy documents, such as the *Declaration of Alma-Ata* (WHO & UNICEF, 1978) and the *Ottawa Charter for Health Promotion* (World Health Organization, 1986), supported health promotion practice that focused on grassroots activism and population health. This gave nurses working in public health settings in Canada opportunities to focus on vulnerable populations and move beyond primary care practice with its important, but limited, biomedical focus on treatment (Peter, Sweatman, & Carlin, 2008). Over the last decade, this has fostered some innovative initiatives in Ontario as nurses labour in ways that are consistent with ethical practice and primary health care principles. These principles and practices work toward broad goals of social justice and include intersectoral collaboration, building individual and community capacity, and fostering access and equity (Peter et al., 2008)

Public health nurses in various regions across Ontario have been involved in activities ranging from coalitions that foster trans positive services and programs, to anti-bullying programs in schools, to facilitating youth groups to create safer spaces for genderqueer youth. Nurses involved with such public health and street health teams often sit on boards of community agencies and steering committees of coalitions that challenge multiple forms of violence. Through these leadership and advisory positions, nurses work with diverse health and social services agencies to create policies in sexual health clinics that offer the possibility of trans positive care for clients seeking HIV/AIDS testing and treatment, address policies on housing and employment, as well as ensure educational curriculum that is trans positive (MacDonnell, 2007a).

The Halton Organization for Pride and Education (HOPE), formerly the Halton Anti-Homophobia Coalition (HAHC), is an example of a local community coalition. Several public health nurses who specialized in sexual health participated in the coalition, along with representatives of various sectors including community health and social services, law enforcement, education, and community members. Nurses played a key role in developing the region's local pride events and provided significant leadership in developing services for Halton Region employees and youth support services. Community nurses' support of philosophies such as harm reduction also creates spaces to serve the disenfranchised segments of trans communities who are dealing with substance use issues in a way that attends to the structural conditions underpinning their capacity to achieve good health.

EDUCATION

Given the historical invisibility of sexual diversity in nursing education, and the well-documented lack of welcoming programs and services for trans communities, nurses have also challenged the under-representation of trans health and LGB issues in curriculum. As noted by Edmonds (2004), lack of attention to sexual and gender diversity in nursing texts, as well as how issues are framed, is important. Sharing trans positive educational resources with nurse educators is crucial to ensure that there are opportunities to deconstruct stereotypical and negative views of trans people in classroom settings. In 2006, the Canadian Rainbow Health Coalition (CRHC) conducted an environmental scan of Canadian Schools of Nursing to examine the extent to which LGBT issues are addressed. As noted in their report, the inclusion of LGBT issues within and across schools varies considerably, findings that resonated with those involved with the LGTB Health Matters Project (Dunn, Wilson, & Tarko, 2007), a CRHC partnership project in British Columbia that called for attention to LGBT focus in nursing curriculum and nursing activism in this context.

The role nurses play to incorporate trans-specific health care issues and broader attentiveness to gender and/or sexuality requires much strategic thought and action. An issue with many educators, the challenge involves having nursing students develop critical thinking skills that can lead to socially just and ethical praxis. One strategy has involved arts-informed education (Macdonald & MacDonnell, 2008), which offers nursing students opportunities to address gender norms as they discuss the challenges of identity labels, medical categorizations, and the implications for their clinical practices in various locations such as within mental health settings. Such activities use an anti-oppression lens and focus on privileged social locations regarding whiteness. They also point out how racialization of trans people can occur, along with current dynamics of colonialism impacting the lives of two-spirit individuals and communities. Advocacy can involve prompting questions about who has the authority to represent diverse trans peoples' issues in the classroom or other spaces.

The use of visuals and narratives that show the humanity and importance of dignity, such as the groundbreaking documentary *Bevel Up* (Wild, 2007) created by nurses from British Columbia, is aligned with advocacy strategies to counter the stereotypical depictions of transgender often perpetuated by the media. The video shows nurses on the outreach team in Vancouver's Downtown Eastside interacting with various street-involved individuals who use substances in non-judgmental ways that show respect for their decision making at any given moment and the centrality of building relationships with them over time. The teaching materials that accompany the documentary foreground the complexity of ethics, gender, and the diversity of populations, including trans people, in a matter-of-fact way that creates much-needed space for dialogue between teachers and students about the challenges of the lives of often disenfranchised groups, such as trans people in this context, as well as illustrating the harm reduction philosophies that underpin their health promotion practice.

The Social Justice Framework for GLBTT-SQ (gay, lesbian, bisexual, transgender, two-spirit, and queer) *Wellness* (Canadian Rainbow Health Coalition, 2005) is an example of a curriculum tool used by a number of nurse educators in community nursing programs to link social justice issues existing within and extending beyond GLBTT-SQ populations. These issues include gender stereotyping, ableism, individual internalization of stigma and disenfranchisement, religious oppression, class-based determinants of health, and addiction. When not addressed appropriately, such issues can lead to a mistrust of the health care system and to disparities in the health of marginalized populations. This anti-oppression lens, along with a focus on nurses' professional responsibility and accountability to advocate for vulnerable groups, has the potential to politicize nursing students. Creating spaces for dialogue and challenging trans invisibility can foster nursing student–led advocacy groups, such as the Queer Nursing Student Alliance (Barker, Fairley, & Carey, 2003).

TRAINING

As a province-wide coalition, the Public Health Alliance for LGBTTTIQQ (lesbian, gay, bisexual, transsexual, transgender, two-spirit, intersex, queer, and questioning) Equity, the Ontario Public Health Association workgroup established in 1997, has been a key space for nursing activism. Throughout the course of this initiative, nurses were involved in intersectoral collaborations, province-wide education and networking sessions, and participatory action research, which sparked policy development at the provincial level and in nursing curriculum development (MacDonnell, 2007a). As noted by Chow and colleagues in Chapter 24 in this text, nurses were involved in creating a space for partnership, research, and community development through the Trans Health Project (Gapka, Raj, Chow, Clipsham, Hampson, & MacDonnell, 2003), which fostered community and professional education. In addition to engagement with policy and activist bodies at provincial and national levels, nurses are involved in academic research. With the advent of Rainbow Health Ontario, nurses are currently examining partnerships with interdisciplinary researchers and seeking opportunities to build research capacity that will have further impacts on trans positive approaches to health care and wellness (Daley & MacDonnell, 2011).

Nurses who openly self-identify as transgender or transsexual in a Canadian context are few and far between. While there is certainly a spirit in employment, organizational, and policy development literature that is consistent with supporting sexually and gender diverse employees, the realities of transitioning and working as a trans nurse in a Canadian context remain virtually unaddressed in the Canadian nursing literature. Recent research that examined the workplace context for nurses who self-identify as lesbian, bisexual, and questioning and/or advocate on their communities' behalf indicated that workplace and collegial support was uneven (MacDonnell, 2007b, 2009). Despite policy gains and increasing awareness of LGBT issues, nurses affiliated with these communities continue to encounter hostility and marginalization. This contributes to a lack of research on their lived experiences of nursing and on ways to challenge the barriers to healthy workplaces (MacDonnell, 2007b). Although there are certainly trans positive workplaces with explicit focus on hiring from transgender/transsexual communities (MacDonnell, 2008), findings from a study with trans providers in Canada suggests that challenges remain a reality for trans-identified health care professionals (MacDonnell & Grigorovich, 2012). In 2006, the Public Health Alliance (PHA) created a document, updated in 2011 (PHA, 2011), that offers public health units and community health centres opportunities to examine their workplace settings for heterosexism, biphobia, and transphobia with the goal of enhancing trans positive services and programs.

One of the authors completed a participatory policy study examining Ontario nurses' advocacy in relation to lesbian health (MacDonnell, 2007b, 2009). The findings of that study offered 12 policy recommendations, several of which were incorporated in a policy resolution to the provincial nursing association, the Registered Nurses' Association of Ontario (RNAO), to garner support to take action on findings relevant to nursing practice. Originally articulated as a policy resolution that focused on sexual orientation only, over the course of the year in which the RNAO policy department hammered out a position statement (RNAO, 2007b) in conjunction with stakeholder input, and the position statement emerged as one that addressed both sexual orientation and gender identity in nursing. This position statement, *Respecting Sexual Orientation and Gender Identity* (RNAO, 2007b), has been widely disseminated by the professional association itself (Mulrooney, 2009; RNAO, 2007a, 2008). The scope of advocacy through the RNAO offers a stronger voice for nurses, given the well-resourced communication and policy departments that support nursing issues. Of particular note are such initiatives as nursing leadership in implementation of the position statement in health organizations (Scarrow, 2008), and letters written to key politicians on behalf of RNAO advocating for the re-listing of OHIP funding for sex reassignment surgery (SRS) and inclusion of gender identity in the Ontario Human Rights Code. In 2010, the RNAO submitted a resolution to the Canadian Nurses Association (CNA), *Human Rights Protection for Transgender and Transsexual Canadians*, which was accepted at the annual general meeting. In its capacity as a professional body committed to structural change to health care through enhancing access to responsive health care and reducing health inequities, the RNAO garnered collective support from its members to sign an Action Alert to support Bill C-389 and advocated directly to the federal government and provincial MPPs in supporting this Bill. As the RNAO Letter to Senators (2011) indicated:

> Ontario's registered nurses urge you to support the passage of Bill C-389 to ensure explicit human rights protection for transgender and transsexual Canadians. The need to update the Canadian Human Rights Act to include gender identity and gender expression as prohibited grounds of discrimination, and amend the Criminal Code of Canada to include gender identity and gender expression in the hate crime and sentencing provisions has become even more obvious by the pejorative language associated by those who trivialize this as "the bathroom bill." Transsexual and transgender people are a highly marginalized group in our society.

Such letters, in conjunction with individual letters written by nurses belonging to RNAO, can have an important impact in framing the issues. In addition, given the Canadian Nurses Association's links to multiple stakeholder groups, this advocacy has had a broad reach in the Canadian context.

An interest group of the RNAO, the Rainbow Nursing Interest Group (RNIG), explicitly focused on LGBT issues and nursing, was formed in 2006 to offer spaces for LGBT nurses and their allies to challenge gender normativity and stereotypes in social and professional spaces. This group also supported nursing activist endeavours that included identifying and framing issues relevant to trans people, such as the recent focus on Gay-Straight Alliances (GSAs) in publicly funded school systems (RNAO, 2012). The RNAO can advocate for the establishment of such youth-based spaces through their stakeholder networks. Networking days and newsletters offer opportunities for self-reflection and the development of allies for diverse gender-variant communities (Ji, 2007; Rainbow Nursing Interest Group, 2011). Members participate in Web-based and face-to-face education of colleagues and communities alike with attention to foundational concepts regarding trans-identified experiences, as well as shifts in knowledge and terminology. Discussions addressing issues such as "cisgender," which demarcates a position of privilege for non-trans-identified subjects, often remain invisible in the nursing literature despite the emergence of this term as relevant language within some trans activist forums. RNAO support has created high visibility about nursing support for the local Pride celebrations through RNIG, as well as the National Day Against Homophobia when RNAO was a partner organization (RNAO, 2008). In July 2011, members of the RNAO interest group,

RNIG, and ONA joined forces, marching together in the Toronto Pride Parade (ONA, 2011).

Collective activism on behalf of LGBT communities through nursing unions has been part of nurses' work to advocate for trans communities, especially trans workers themselves. The Ontario Nurses Association and Canadian Union of Public Employees are two unions that have supported issues related to sexual and gender diversity for a number of years. In large part, such support comes through the equity- and human rights-focused caucus that includes a group for LGBT members.

Perinatal services represent one clinical specialty that has yet to adopt trans-affirmative policy and praxis (Adams, 2010). In the following section, Robin describes his engagement with innovative programming that sought to advance trans family creation choices and increase knowledge about assisted human reproduction services, adoption/fostering challenges and possibilities, childbirth options, early parenting experiences, and self-advocacy strategies (Ware, 2009).

PROLOGUE

Love provides the fuel for my work as a trans health activist. I carry within me a chest of tales about lost love, discovering self-love, and carving out a new way to live family. This account of the Trans Fathers 2B course is also a description of life as I live it—trans and queer. One of the stories that informs my activism is drawn from my experience of being one half of a couple hoping to have a baby. A common enough aspiration for two people in love, you may think, but when you are both trans and queer, there are subtle (and not so subtle) differences from the mainstream version of the baby-making story. Unlike straight, cisgendered couples, we're off to the fertility clinic as the first (not the last) port of call in our efforts to conceive a baby. My partner is full of hope. We pass the pre-screen counselling session required by the ethics board of the health organization with flying colours. During the history-taking session with the doctor, we identify ourselves as trans, and the doctor just keeps right on addressing us both with female pronouns. Just once I gently say, "You mean his uterus, right?" The doctor pauses but thinks better of saying anything in reply. The blood tests come next. My partner is called. The lab tech sounds and looks confused. As the door closes, my partner is chuckling at the tech guy who is confiding in a relieved voice, "I thought you were a husband in the wrong waiting room."

Fast forward to his first D&C following an early miscarriage. He's high on a "waking anesthetic." The nurse is shocked by his sex joke. I worry it will make her less compassionate as we struggle with this loss. A few months later, my partner is lying on an exam table waiting for the ultrasound tech to appear. She arrives, checking and rechecking the name-of-choice handwritten and placed in brackets on his chart in her hands. Slowly she enunciates the birth name that continues to co-exist with the bracketed name on the front of the chart as my heart sinks. Although it feels like a lost cause, we find ourselves compelled to correct, yet again, the assumption that if you're about to have a vaginal ultrasound, you must also possess a girl-name. We make every effort to transcend the institutional trans erasure (Bauer, Hammond, Travers, Kaay, Hohenadel, & Boyce, 2009) we experience during every monthly encounter at the clinic. We hold tight to our baby dreams. We steal ourselves against the additional stress caused by our invisibility as trans people. I know in my heart that I might well have prematurely abandoned our efforts to conceive a child using assisted human reproduction (AHR) services had I not already become part of a group of local trans activists and allies committed to developing community and service provider supports for trans parenting.

TRANS PARENTING

During the summer of 2004, a Toronto-based community group, the Queer Parenting Exchange, held an open forum called "Trans Parenting" for trans parents, prospective parents, and friends and allies. The forum set out to identify trans community priority needs around parenting. People's stories poured forth. Some were having legal struggles trying to maintain child custody and access after transitioning. Younger trans men voiced dreams of family creation but were unsure of their options. Still others talked about navigating day-to-day life as a trans parent with lack of family and school support. Several people identified the sense of isolation they felt and the extremely limited trans-specific parenting resources that were available. Still more mentioned the lack of awareness and familiarity amongst health and social service providers about trans parenting issues, and the virtual absence of medical, psychological, and sociological research on trans parenting. The meeting was certainly a critical juncture in the lives of many Toronto-based trans people of reproductive age, including my partner and myself. At the time, it was still not common for people to talk about, let alone embrace, the gender incongruity of trans masculine pregnancy and parenting. It was therefore incredibly affirming when forum participants discovered there were at least a handful of post-transition men and genderqueers eager to talk openly about pregnancy and birth.

THE CHALLENGES OF MASCULINE PREGNANCY

The radical heart of that first community discussion was the acknowledgement that it is not only cisgendered, straight women who desire to be pregnant and give birth; it is also envisioned and experienced by butch lesbians (Epstein, 2002), genderqueers, and trans men. Masculine pregnancy challenges gender normative assumptions in relation to child-bearing. However, extending the nature of masculinity to include conceiving, gestating, labouring, birthing, and lactation simultaneously exposes trans masculine individuals to many forms of trans oppression and repudiation (Shelley, 2008). The negative impact of censure within our own communities is also all too often mixed with the incredulity of AHR service staff, nurses, obstetricians, and midwives. For trans masculine people, this complex web of "gender policing" has in the past acted as a profound barrier to freely imagining and planning for pregnancy.

When we seek support, information, and services about conception, pregnancy, birth, newborn care, and lactation, prevailing gender-based assumptions about what men and women do are exposed at every turn. A newly delivered trans father, j wallace, described a public health nurse's "tranny-faily moment" when she entered his hospital room, looked around, and then asked, "Where's the mum?" (Wallace, 2010). Looked at another way, the societal challenge to our identities as masculine people, often living in queer community contexts and our corresponding "lack of fit" with conventional family models, offer opportunities for the conscious and politically informed development of non-traditional family structures and configurations. Trans-led families challenge gendered hierarchies and heteronormative assumptions about procreation, child-rearing, and family (Riordon, 2001).

DEVELOPING A TRANS COMMUNITY RESOURCE

The initial interest and enthusiasm that had been expressed by genderqueer and trans communities for greater support of trans parenting in 2004 continued to gain momentum in Toronto. Three multi-talented trans activists—Nik Redman, a trade union activist, DJ, and political activist; Andy Inkster, a talented academic and community activist; and Syrus Ware, a Toronto-based artist, DJ, and community activist—together with Chris Veldhoven, a trans ally and LGBT community worker working for the Queer Parenting Network at The 519 Church Street Community Centre (The 519), formed the Transparent-cy working group. Their vision was to create an education and resource initiative for trans men and genderqueer people about family creation through adoption, fostering, pregnancy, surrogacy, co-parenting, step-parenting, and other means.

Nursing, as a facilitating profession, is well positioned to counter normative assumptions about gender and raise awareness about the social construction of family. The nursing profession can improve access to and cultural safety of services by foregrounding the importance of practising using a critical social awareness. I was about to have the opportunity to put my politics into practice when I was hired by The 519 to design and coordinate delivery of the "TransFathers 2B" course during 2006–2007—the very first course of its kind to run in Canada. It was valuable to have nursing knowledge about reproductive health and hospital systems when developing the course. However, the power of this education, peer-support, and self-advocacy initiative came from the way the transparent-cy working group worked to address a community health need that had been articulated by the community itself. The working group generated their own agenda and identified their own information needs. As a result, the course focus and content were entirely community-driven. Instead of a professional expert, external to the community, "beaming in" to deliver "expert knowledge," a group of multi-skilled community activists collaborated to plan, apply for grant applications, and identify essential gaps in knowledge long before I was hired to develop the structure and content of the course.

COURSE STRUCTURE AND INFORMATION

The pilot course had nine participants. It included 12 evening workshops on a variety of topics (see Table 25.1), including self-insemination; adoption and surrogacy; how racism can operate at institutional and individual levels during adoption and surrogacy processes; legal matters relating to gamete supply, birth registration issues, and the relative value of donor and parenting contracts; pregnancy and identity; primary health care provider options; options for place of birth; postpartum adjustment; a labour ward tour; and informal community-building opportunities. Such complexity. So many issues to consider!

In terms of available information for the course, I was not surprised to find that there was next to nothing in terms of specific resources or research on transsexual and transgender pregnancy and almost no social, medical, or nursing research on trans parenting. There were simply no answers available to important questions like "Are there quantified risks from testosterone on human embryos?" "Will I get mastitis because I've had chest surgery?" There were, however, the beginnings of discussion about trans parenting within transgender and queer communities in San Francisco and Toronto, an email listserv, and an online forum for trans parents. Even images of trans pregnancy were impossible to find at the time. For this reason, Syrus Ware, a Toronto-based artist and trans activist, created a beautiful line drawing of a trans dad as the logo for our course.

TABLE 25.1: WEEKLY WORKSHOPS: TRANSFATHERS 2B CURRICULUM (2006–2007) FACILITATING A COURSE FOR A MARGINALIZED COMMUNITY

Exploring Parenthood I	**Welcome to Uncharted Territory** Introductions, group safety, questions, goals. Dreaming our families into being. Heteronormative and queer definitions of family, the effect on access and notions of entitlement.
Pregnancy I	**Getting Pregnant and Being Pregnant** Preconception workup, blood work, radiological studies, physical assessment and ultrasounds. Fertility awareness. Coping with and challenging the language of fertility and pregnancy. Speaker session on fertility signs.
Pregnancy II	**Strategies for Accessing Health Care** Resources available for self-advocacy when choosing a health care provider and during clinic visits. Fertility and pregnancy care options. Speaker session on family practice obstetrics and transgender health.
Exploring Parenthood II	**Adoption and Fostering Options for LGBT Communities** Session from adoption and social work professionals on national and international adoption options.
Pregnancy III	**Caring for Ourselves during Pregnancy and Birth** Social and personal challenge of trans masculine pregnancy. The process of birth. Speaker session on midwifery services.
Pregnancy IV	**Assisted Human Reproduction Services** Session to meet clinical staff, hear about fertility clinic protocols, ethics guidance, and pre-service counselling. Dialogue between trans and queer communities with service providers.
Exploring Parenthood III	**Legal Affairs** Q&A session with family lawyer experienced in LGBT human rights cases. Donor contracts, birth certificates, divorce and queer/trans parental rights, custody and access challenges, comparing courses and Alternative Dispute Resolution (ADR) systems.
Exploring Parenthood IV	**Anti-Racist Analysis and Action** Workshop to look at how racism influences family creation options, choices, and decisions.
Pregnancy V	**How Pregnancy Can Affect Trans Bodies and Social Identity** Anticipating effects of pregnancy and lactation on chest surgeries. The hows and whys of coming off hormones. Impact of lack of research and resources. Challenging social rules about who carries pregnancies and lactates. Trans masculine pregnancy clothing and binders.
Exploring Parenthood V	**Trans Parenting** Postpartum adjustment and the importance of self-advocacy and information sharing about comfortable places and spaces to parent. Role-playing challenging situations. Discussion about chest surgery and lactation/lactation aids/human milk donation.

Pregnancy VI	**Labour Ward Tour** The importance of becoming familiar with the hospital environment, staff, and equipment used for birth. Broadening the definition of family for staff. Q&A session on self-advocacy during labour and prior to discharge home.
Exploring Parenthood VI	**Putting It All Together** Course review. Community building for trans parents 2G and trans-led families. Course evaluation. Suggestions for trans-focused pregnancy and parenting research and resource development.

The course was designed to create opportunities to explore the many needs and issues we face as trans people seeking to parent or already parenting. Racism, classism, heterormativity, and ableism all negatively affect our ability to access services and support for parenting options. For these reasons, emphasis was placed on the development of skills necessary to self-advocate and stay strong for our children and families (Ware, 2009). Some sessions were jointly run with "Dykes Planning Tykes" and "Daddies and Papas to Be," Toronto-area reproductive groups that were already running for LGB communities.

As previously discussed in this chapter, it is folly to ignore the extent to which parenting is socially constructed as a gendered act, heavily laden with normative gender role expectations. We gingerly discussed the negative impact of gender non-conformity that repeatedly places us in the vulnerable position of being judged by professionals. Many of us cannot or choose not to conform to binary gender roles and decide to live openly as genderqueer, or choose not to/cannot afford to transition with surgical and hormonal interventions. This leaves us vulnerable in assessment situations that rarely value gender diversity, but often link gender expression, "mental instability," and "poor suitability for parenthood." As discussed by Michelle Boyce (in Chapter 7 of this text), others amongst us have former partners who are able to use gender transition or gender non-conformity as leverage in child custody disputes and win. Faced with the realities of these significant barriers to parenting, few trans people relish the thought of going through an adoption screening, a court-ordered "best interests of the child" assessment, or a fertility clinic's mandatory "counselling" process when the pregnancy option is available to them. The material reality of trans lives has a profound influence on the choices available for creating a family. Pregnancy can seem like the only realistic option for many young transsexual and transgender people hoping to have children. The options to adopt or foster are not currently felt by our communities to be accessible to people who do not conform to gender norms, particularly if they are not working in stable, high-income occupations.

The expertise at play in an education and community-building endeavour like the TransFathers 2B course has more to do with interpretation and facilitation skills than knowledge of physical mechanics and anatomy, although as shown in Table 25.1, the expertise informed by years of midwifery and reproductive nursing expertise offered key resources for curriculum material. There was a readiness in the group to try new language where there were no easy words to describe, for example, feeding a baby from your own modified sweat glands that one does not self-describe as breasts. We also sat through in-depth descriptions of different types of vaginal mucous and recommendation about milk pumps (yes, we bravely ventured over many a squishy subject). Throughout the course, we all built sufficient safety and trust to sometimes mention worries and questions about matters such as lactation possibilities and post-top surgery, and questions related to pregnancy and sexuality. A particularly powerful exercise was the practising of useful responses to intrusive questions, consternation, and social censorship that might be encountered on a family outing to a park or while a newborn is being fed. We also tried to imagine scenarios in restaurants and swimming pools where we would need to be strong for our children and advocate for ourselves.

EVALUATION OF THE PILOT COURSE

The pilot course and accompanying manual were specifically designed to focus on topics for, and specifically about, the needs and concerns of trans men and transsexual and transgender people considering pregnancy. The aim was to be responsive to the needs and interests of the group participants. Aware of the barriers to parenting through adoption, surrogacy, and AHR techniques, the pilot course focused on providing information for trans people planning pregnancies through donor insemination. This particular focus reflected my professional expertise as a midwife and reproductive health nurse, and the interests of the original working group members. There were, however, course participants who hoped to adopt, either alone or with a partner, and others who were partnered with women or other trans men who planned to be birth parents. Future courses could adapt to meet the needs and interests of trans men planning to adopt or foster, or taking on step-parenting.

The pilot course was thoroughly evaluated by the three members of the Transparent-cy working group who took the course. They also received informal feedback from other course participants. In addition, there were anonymous evaluation forms filled out at the midpoint to facilitate adaptation during the course and a further evaluation questionnaire at the end of the series. Responses and observations were analyzed during a working party debriefing session. One course participant commented: "I learned so much from this course. It gave me a space to really think about how I am going to make my dream of becoming a parent a reality, on my own terms." Another said: "I think the self-advocacy skills I learned will be very helpful as I navigate clinics and hospitals ... it's scary, but I know I can do it." One participant summed it up like this: "I still don't quite know how family and children are going to come into my life but the sessions helped me explore where I stand and what to expect. I feel better informed and more confident."

CONCLUSION

Consistent with the goals of this anthology, this chapter has illustrated the ways in which nursing professionals in Ontario participate in advocacy practices to challenge trans erasure and invisibility. We show the multiple ways in which nurses have taken on the issues, partnering and affirming community-based research and trans activist endeavours, and critically engaging with theories and strategies that can support and improve the everyday lives of diversely located trans people in Ontario.

EPILOGUE

The course feedback was intended to assist with further development of the TransFathers 2B course. Sadly, the course did not gain sufficient organizational support to make running it again possible. However, awareness of trans parents, including their support and information needs, is beginning to burgeon (see The 519 Church Street Community Centre at www.the519.org/). Health and social service professionals are also beginning to be better informed about trans families as the result of groundbreaking research and health professional educational initiatives.

ACKNOWLEDGEMENTS

We appreciate the important support for nursing advocacy for trans communities that organizations such as the Registered Nurses' Association of Ontario, Rainbow Health Ontario, and the Ontario Public Health Association have provided.

REFERENCES

Adams, E.D. (2010). If transmen can have babies, how will perinatal nursing adapt? *The American Journal of Maternal Child Nursing, 35*(1), 26–32.

Barker, A., Fairley, L., & Carey, S. (2003). *Why Q.N.S.A.? Working toward visibility in instructional environments: Queer Nursing Student Alliance.* Poster session presented at the 15th Annual McMaster University Annual Research Day, Hamilton, ON, July.

Bauer, G.R., Hammond R., Travers, R., Kaay, M., Hohenadel, K.M., & Boyce, M. (2009). "I don't think this is theoretical; this is our lives": How erasure impacts health care for transgender people. *Journal of the Association of Nurses in AIDS Care, 20*(5), 348–361.

Canadian Nurses Association (CNA). (2008). *Code of ethics.* CNA. Retrieved from www.cna-aiic.ca/en/on-the-issues/best-nursing/nursing-ethics/

Canadian Nurses Association (CNA). (2010). *Resolution 4: Human rights protection for transgender and transsexaul Canadians.* Ottawa: CNA.

Canadian Rainbow Health Coalition (CRHC). (2005). *Social justice framework for GLBTT-SQ wellness.* Retrieved from www.rainbowhealth.ca/documents/english/Actions%204%20queer%20wellness.pdf

Canadian Rainbow Health Coalition (CRHC). (2006). *Rainbow health: Improving access to care.* Ottawa, ON: CRHC.

Coalition for Lesbian and Gay Rights in Ontario. (1997). *Systems failure: A report on the experiences of sexual minorities in Ontario's health-care and social-services systems.* Health Canada, Health Promotion and Programs Branch, Ontario Region.

Daley, A.E., & MacDonnell, J.A. (2011). Gender, sexuality and the discursive representation of access and equity in health services literature: Implications for LGBT communities. *International Journal for Equity in Health.* doi:10.1186/1475-9276-10-40

Dean, L., Meyer, I.H., Robinson, K., Sell, R.L., Sember, R., Silenzio, V.M.B., … Dunn, P. (2000). Lesbian, gay, bisexual and transgender health: Findings and concerns. *Journal of the Gay and Lesbian Medical Association, 4*(3), 101–151.

Dunn, B., Wilson, S., & Tarko, M. (2007). The LGTB Health Matters Project. *Canadian Nurse, 103*(8), 8–9.

Edmonds, E. (2004). *Heterosexism in nursing.* Paper presented at the Canadian Rainbow Health Conference, "Many Faces, Diverse Voices," Gatineau, Quebec, November 4–7.

Eliason, M., Dibble, S., & DeJoseph, J. (2010). Nursing's silence on lesbian, gay, bisexual, and transgender issues: The need for emancipatory efforts. *Advances in Nursing Science, 33*(2), 1–15.

Epstein, R. (2002). Butches with babies: Reconfiguring gender and motherhood. In M. Gibson & D.T. Meem (Eds.), *Femme/Butch: New considerations of the way we want to go* (pp. 41–57). New York: Routledge.

Gapka, S., Raj, R., Chow, K., Clipsham, J., Hampson, E., & MacDonnell, J. (2003). *The Trans Health Project* [Position paper]. Toronto, ON: Ontario Public Health Association.

Giddings, L.S. (2005). Health disparities, social injustice, and the culture of nursing. *Nursing Research, 54*(5), 304–312.

Hall, J.M. (2008). Tomboys: Meanings, marginalization, and misunderstandings. *Issues in Mental Health Nursing, 29*, 555–565.

Hanssmann, C., Morrison, D., Russian, E., Shiu-Thornton, S., & Bowen, D. (2010). A community-based evaluation of cultural competency trainings. *Journal of the Association of Nurses in AIDS Care, 21*(3), 240–255.

Hilton, B.A., Thompson, R., & Moore-Dempsey, L. (2000). Evaluation of the AIDS prevention street nurse program: One step at a time. *Canadian Journal of Nursing Research, 32*(1), 17–38.

Jenner, C.O. (2010). Transsexual primary care. *Journal of the American Academy of Nurse Practitioners, 22*, 403–408.

Ji, P. (2007). Being a heterosexual ally to the lesbian, gay, bisexual, and transgendered community: Reflections and development. *Issues in Mental Health, 11*(3), 173–185.

Macdonald, G., & MacDonnell, J.A. (2008). Transforming diversity tensions: Shifting knowledge through arts-based practices. *Collected Essays on Teaching and Learning (CELT), 1*, 35–39.

MacDonnell, J.A. (2007a). Articulating a policy resolution for sexual minorities: Nurses as moral agents. *Canadian Journal of Nursing Research, 39*(4), 74–92.

MacDonnell, J.A. (2007b). Comparative life histories of nurses who advocate for lesbian health in a Canadian context: Sexual orientation as a factor in career and workplace dynamics. In M.V.L. Badgett & J. Frank (Eds.), *Sexual orientation discrimination: An international perspective* (pp. 118–135). London: Routledge.

MacDonnell, J.A. (2008). Examining career and workplace dynamics for trans-identified health professionals. Paper presented at the Trans Health Provider Day, Mazzoni Centre, Philadelphia, PA, May 29–31.

MacDonnell, J.A. (2009). Fostering nurses' political knowledges and practices: Education and political activation in relation to lesbian health. *Advances in Nursing Science, 32*(2), 158–132.

MacDonnell, J.A., & Grigorovich, A. (2012). Gender, work and health for trans health providers: A focus on transmen. *International Scholarly Research Network (ISRN)—Nursing*. Retrieved from www.hindawi.com/isrn/nursing/aip/161097/

McDonald, C. (2006). Issues of gender and power: The significance attributed to nurses' work. In M. McIntyre, E. Thomlinson, & C. McDonald (Eds.), *Realities of Canadian nursing: Professional, practice, and power issues* (2nd ed., pp. 334–347). Philadelphia: Lippincott, Williams & Wilkins.

McPherson, K. (1996). *Bedside matters: The transformation of Canadian nursing, 1900–1990*. New York: Oxford University Press.

Mulé, N.J., Ross, L.E., Deeprose, B., Jackson, B.E., Daley, A.E., & Travers, A. (2009). Promoting LGBT health and wellbeing through inclusive policy development. *International Journal for Equity in Health*. doi:10.1186/1475-9276-8-18

Mulrooney, L. (2009). Challenges and policy imperatives for sexual and gender minorities. Paper presented at the International Council of Nurses 24th Quadrennial Congress, Durban, South Africa, June 27–July 4.

Ontario Nurses' Association (ONA). (2011). ONA proudly waves the rainbow flag. *Front Lines, 11*(4), 8.

Peter, E. (2008). Seeing our way through the responsibility vs. endeavor conundrum: The code of ethics as both process and product. *Canadian Journal of Nursing Leadership, 21*(2), 28–31.

Peter, E., Sweatman, L., & Carlin, K. (2008). Ethical and legal considerations. In L.L. Stamler & L. Yiu (Eds.), *Community health nursing: A Canadian perspective* (2nd ed., pp. 39–53). Toronto: Pearson Prentice Hall.

Polly, R., & Nicole, J. (2011). Understanding the transsexual patient: Culturally sensitive care in emergency nursing practice, *Advanced Emergency Nursing Journal, 33*(1), 55–64.

Public Health Alliance for LGBTTTIQQ Equity. (2002). Ethical research and evidence-based practice for lesbians and gay men [Policy resolution]. *Ontario Public Health Association (OPHA).* Retrieved from http://opha.on.ca/Position-Papers/Ethical-Research-and-Evidence-Based-Practice-for-L.aspx

Public Health Alliance for LGBTTTIQQ Equity. (2011). A positive space is a healthy place: Making your community health centre, public health unit or community agency inclusive to those of all sexual orientations and gender identities. *Ontario Public Health Association (OPHA).* Retrieved from www.opha.on.ca/resources/docs/SexualHealthPaper-Mar11.pdf

Rainbow Nursing Interest Group. (2011, March). *SOGIRN, the RNIG [Rainbow Nursing Interest Group] Rag.* Retrieved from www.rnao.org/Storage/77/7194_SOGIRN_-_the_RNIG_Rag_March_2011.pdf

Registered Nurses' Association of British Columbia/College of Registered Nurses of British Columbia. (2009). *Registered Nurses Association scope of practice for Nurse Practitioners (family): Standards, limits and conditions (Rep. No. 424).* Vancouver, BC.

Registered Nurses' Association of Ontario (RNAO). (2007a, June 21). Nurses call for end to homophobia and heterosexism in health care [Press release]. *RNAO.* Retrieved from http://rnao.ca/news/media-releases/Nurses-call-for-end-to-homophobia-and-heterosexism-in-health-care

Registered Nurses' Association of Ontario (RNAO). (2007b). Respecting sexual orientation and gender identity [Position statement]. *RNAO.* Retrieved from http://rnao.ca/policy/position-statements/sexual-orientation-gender-identity

Registered Nurses' Association of Ontario (RNAO). (2008, June 26). Nurses celebrate diversity by marching in Toronto's Pride parade [Press release]. *RNAO.* Retrieved from http://rnao.ca/news/media-releases/Nurses-Celebrate-Diversity-by-Marching-in-Torontos-Pride-Parade

Registered Nurses' Association of Ontario (RNAO). (2011, February 15). RNAO Letter to Senators re: Bill C-389 to ensure human rights protection for transgender and transsexual Canadians. *RNAO.* Retrieved from http://rnao.ca/policy/submissions/bill-c389-ensure-human-rights-protection-transgender-and-transsexual-canadians

Registered Nurses' Association of Ontario (RNAO). (2012). Policy at work: Action against bullying. *Registered Nurse Journal, 11.* Retrieved from www.rnao.ca/sites/rnao-ca/files/7._Policy_at_Work.pdf

Riordon, M. (2001). *Eating fire.* Toronto: Between the Lines.

Scarrow, J. (2008, July). Nurses raise awareness about need to respect sexual orientation and gender identity. *Hospital News, 21*(7), 27.

Scott-Dixon, K. (Ed.). (2006). *Trans/forming feminisms: Trans-feminist voices speak out.* Toronto: Sumach Press.

Shelley, C. (2008). *Transpeople: Repudiation, trauma, healing.* Toronto: University of Toronto Press.

Thomas, S. (2004). *Competent care of the transgendered patient: Nurses as advocates.* Retrieved from http://cariebooks.com/pdf/competent-care-of-the-transgendered-patient-nurses-as-advocates.html

Wallace, I. (2010, February 2). Two trannies walk into a birthing centre in Burlington. *Livejournal.* Retrieved from http://ishai-wallace.livejournal.com/33318.html

Ware, S.M. (2009). Boldly going where few men have gone before: One trans man's experience. In R. Epstein (Ed.), *Who's your daddy? And other writings on queer parenting* (pp. 65–72). Toronto, ON: Sumach Press.

Wild, N. (2007). *Bevel up: Drugs, users and outreach nursing.* Vancouver: National Film Board of Canada, British Columbia Centre for Disease Control.

World Health Organization. (1986). *The Ottawa Charter for Health Promotion.* Retrieved from www.who.int/healthpromotion/conferences/previous/ottawa/en/

World Health Organization (WHO) and UNICEF. (1978). *Declaration of Alma-Ata.* International Conference on Primary Health Care, Alma-Ata, USSR, September 6–12. Retrieved from www.who.int/publications/almaata_declaration_en.pdf

Afterword

Viviane Namaste

This anthology breaks new ground in a number of ways, asking us to think critically about how to understand trans people and how to build a better world. The task of writing an afterword for such a book is, in one sense, impossible: no concluding words can do full justice to the diversity of perspectives in this anthology, to the complexity of the arguments presented. That said, I wish to highlight some currents at work in these chapters, and in this anthology—currents that promise to sweep us away, show us new lands, bring us to new waters altogether.

These currents are fundamentally concerned with knowledge and epistemology: how we know, what we know, what we overlook, and how and why certain realities are erased. As the editors write in their introduction, "The construction of knowledge concerning trans identities and the material lives of trans people is a political engagement." Within this framework of knowledge, and with the three major sections of this anthology (transforming oppression into social change, critical reflections on activism, transforming institutions from the inside) in mind, I wish to underline some of the currents of thought that will help us think differently and act differently.

I invite the reader to consider the currents outlined below in relation to this anthology and its texts.

RESEARCH: WHAT COUNTS AS KNOWLEDGE

This anthology opens with the bold declaration, cited above, that the production of knowledge in relation to trans lives is deeply political. And the texts herein ask us to consider, and reconsider, how knowledge itself is structured. Nick Matte brings the perspective of a historian, and reminds us that in an era prior to the Internet, simply finding knowledge about hormones, surgery, or trans-friendly businesses was a challenge for individuals. A specific focus on research and the necessity of gathering new information is evident in a number of chapters, notably in the section on history. Matte reports that Rupert Raj produced and circulated a "Confidential Research Questionnaire" in order to gather more information on female-to-male transsexuals. Similarly, j wallace discusses a group of students creating their own data with regards to violence. In her interview, "We Paved the Way," Michelle De Ville recounts her own work in gathering and ordering data—in this instance, the age and cause of death for transvestites and transsexuals in Montreal. Jamie Lee Hamilton tells us of her collaboration with other sex work activists in Vancouver in the 1990s, and the act of dumping 67 pairs of heels on the steps of Vancouver City Hall to symbolize 67 women working in the sex trade who had gone missing in recent years. Hamilton and her allies shine the light on what we do not see.

TRANS STUDIES

In the introduction to the anthology, the editors argue that this work is in dialogue with a field known as trans studies. To be sure, many of the contributors would see their work within these terms. At the level of content, the different texts herein both complement and challenge trans studies. They complement it by offering detailed empirical data from the Canadian context, adding something new to a field characterized by the study of trans culture and trans people in the United States. Yet the chapters herein also ask us to rethink the relevance of trans studies itself. Reading Sandy Leo Laframboise, for instance, one wonders if the political priority is one of naming and defining a field known as trans studies. Perhaps the political and intellectual priority is simply one of offering a hot meal to those who are poor.

Moreover, while trans studies has much to say about the idea of race, the texts herein configure questions of race in somewhat different ways. At issue is not simply a politics of naming and identity, but a thinking through of race and ethnicity laterally. This is amply evidenced in Laframboise's account of the High Risk Project Society, whose drop-in centre was housed in the basement of Vancouver Native Health in the mid-1990s, and in Grey Kimber Piitaapan Muldoon's interviews and dialogue with Dan Irving. While much of trans studies considers Aboriginal issues in relation to documenting the presence of trans and/or two-spirited people, often in dialogue with an anthropological literature, the chapters in this anthology invite us to think about Aboriginal issues in relation to community organizing. Here, then, knowledge is mobilized beyond the identity frame of reference that drives trans studies, a move that promises to incite new reflections.

COMMUNITY BUILDING

The depth and diversity of community building presented in this anthology is inspiring indeed! Whether it is Rupert Raj organizing a social night in the 1970s, a fundraiser to honour a queen who has died of complications related to HIV/AIDS, sharing a meal to build a community as part of Happy Tranny Day in Vancouver, or the solidarity of sex workers taking down licence plate numbers to protect their colleagues, the anecdotes, stories, and histories in this anthology help us imagine strategies to build community among trans people.

Yet this appeal to community is not simply a celebration. The work of community definition and community building is fraught with conflict, tensions, and even, at times, a lack of clarity. Devon MacFarlane, Lorraine Grieves, and Al Zwiers write of using a "call out" as one strategy to build community capacity, Kathy Chow and colleagues advocate for community-based research as a model of knowledge production, and Trish Salah documents the uneasy relations between some feminists and lesbian/gay union members in imagining community solidarity with trans sex workers. One reads these texts and arrives not at an easy recipe of what to do to build community, but appreciates the deep complexity of how a community defines itself as well as its relation to other communities.

REDEFINING CLINICAL KNOWLEDGE

The chapters and interviews throughout this anthology offer a damning critique of the history of psychiatric, legal, and bureaucratic knowledge on trans people. They show the way in which this knowledge effaces the complexity of trans realities. With regards to clinical knowledge in particular, this anthology offers a wealth of data. Some of this information documents limitations of traditional psychiatric paradigms, such as Silvia Tenenbaum's analysis of the limits of a framework restricted to psychological struggle, Ayden I. Scheim and colleagues' challenge of the assumed heterosexuality of trans men within clinical science, the documentation of a lack of knowledge about the North among southern psychiatry, or Will Rowe's work on the continuity of problems in psychiatric services for trans people across time.

Psychiatric knowledge on trans people has, historically, organized itself in large part in accordance with the "Real-Life Test," a moniker used to describe the evaluative criterion of psychiatrists to ensure that a trans person is "well adapted" in their chosen sex and gender. Yet ironically, this notion of a "Real-Life Test" has been something exclusively considered within the clinical context; psychiatrists did not go meet with co-workers, community agencies, or family members when considering whether or not an individual successfully passed a "Real-Life Test."

The experiences, anecdotes, and analyses presented throughout this anthology suggest that clinical knowledge needs to base itself on all the messiness and contradictions of trans lives. Collectively, then, the chapters in this anthology ought to be read in contradistinction to traditional psychiatric definitions of a "Real-Life Test." Collectively, these texts displace clinical knowledge itself.

Yet the examination of clinical knowledge moves beyond simply pointing out problems. Different texts and case studies herein offer a point of departure to imagine new clinical practices. For instance, Tenenbaum and Wallace Wong ask us to imagine what is necessary to train supportive allies, while Judith A. MacDonnell and Robin Fern think through questions of pedagogy and curriculum in the training of nurses with regards to trans people. In related ways, these texts ask us to move beyond the limitations of one of the most powerful forms of clinical knowledge that has regulated trans bodies and trans lives for decades.

ADVOCACY

The reflections put forward in this anthology encourage us to think beyond simply creating and offering services for trans people. While undoubtedly important, such an approach is limited to the extent that it can remain imprisoned within a logic that does not solve the problem of institutional exclusion at its source. More radically, then, different texts in this anthology ask us to conjoin services with advocacy, to imagine strategies that strive to understand the root cause of institutional injustice against trans people, and to fundamentally challenge the structures and logics that support such exclusion. This conjunture of services and advocacy is perhaps best illustrated in the final section of the anthology ("Transforming Institutions from the Inside"), evidenced for instance in Wong's work with gender-variant children. But this analysis is also witnessed elsewhere, as in Michelle and Jessica Boyce's consideration of a lack of understanding of custody issues for trans people and their children within legal, bureaucratic, and state institutions, and in the work on access to shelters described by Jake Pyne and colleagues. Throughout, we are challenged to think about how and why we need not only to develop services, but also to conjoin services to advocacy itself. The reflections on this nexus provide a rich point of departure for future intellectual and political work in this domain.

LISTENING

The interviews and articles that constitute this book force us to reconsider knowledge. They bring the voices of trans people to the forefront and, as the editors astutely claim, the information and analysis of this anthology force the difficult question: Who is listening?

This critical question permeates this work and its consequences. Importantly, it is a question both to refocus and redefine the limits of historical knowledge paradigms on trans people (clinical psychiatry and the law being two of the most obvious). But it is also an invitation to engage in a true dialogue within and across trans people: Who is listening when Jamie Lee Hamilton speaks of frequenting local businesses as an integral part of the community-building work done by trans women in Vancouver's West End during the 1970s and 1980s? Who is listening when people with intellectual disabilities—often considered to be legally incompetent before psychiatric and judicial institutions—name themselves as trans? Who is listening when the analyses offered in this text make connections that we might not think about a priori, for instance Calvin Neufeld's reflections on the notion of compassion and its implications for ethical trans activism?

Who is listening to the bits and pieces of trans lives that, collectively, can configure new constellations of knowledge?

*****

The strength of this anthology is its invitation to think differently. Whether in currents of research, trans studies, community building, clinical knowledge, advocacy, or the act and process of listening itself, this book challenges us to reimagine how we can know the realities of trans people, and why such knowledge matters. The editors are correct in their claim that the production of knowledge is deeply political. To extend this idea, the questions we ask are axiomatic to defining and producing knowledge itself. This anthology forces us to ask new questions, to interrogate foundational assumptions, and to query the how and why of the political work necessary. And it is in asking new questions that new possibilities can be imagined.

It is fitting that an anthology dedicated to trans realities and trans activisms closes with this invocation of the imagination. This collective work asks us to imagine new possibilities for trans people to live free of violence, discrimination, negation, and erasure. At its core, this anthology invites us to consider the relations between knowledge and imagination: a conjuncture that will surely spark further reflection and action in this domain.

Contributor Biographies

Dani Araya is a 25-year-old university student who is working toward becoming a writer and using that medium to speak out for her various communities. She is a two-spirit and trans woman of Chilean mestiza origin, who has found her place teaching people about trans experiences, knowledge, and stories. She serves both The 519, facilitating workshops with the Trans Access Project, and 2 Spirited People of the First Nations, by being part of their Trans Project storytelling workshops. Enlightening society and inspiring the youth generation is her greatest reward from doing the work she does.

Michelle Boyce has been a strong community advocate and support worker in the queer and ability/disability communities for over 20 years. Drawing on her own lived experiences and strong anti-oppression training, she employs a balanced approach of education, support, and court challenges to make a difference in the quality of life experienced by marginalized people. She is the host of Between the Margins, a show about human rights and people's pursuit of "happily ever after" on CHRW radio, as well as the executive director of Alphabet Community Centre. With Diversity Training Live, Michelle provides high-energy, dynamic workshops and keynote/speaking engagements on diversity, human rights, harassment, sexism, gender identity, sexual orientation, and ability/disability, using an entertaining and enjoyable approach to bring dignity and respect to all. At home, Michelle is the mother of two children and is happily married to her wife of five years.

Alec Butler is an award-winning playwright and filmmaker who is originally from Cape Breton Island. He has worked with the homeless population for almost 20 years and has been doing work for the Trans Access Project since 2005, where he has served as policy consultant and workshop facilitator. Alec identifies as two-spirit and intersex. He recently celebrated a half-century on this planet, and he has enjoyed spending a chunk of that time with his dog, Daisy.

Nora Butler Burke lives in Montreal, where she has spent the past decade involved in social justice movements. Most recently, she worked as coordinator of ASTT(e)Q (Action Santé Travesti(e)s et Transsexuel(le)s du Québec), a project of CACTUS Montréal, organizing front-line support for low-income, migrant, and sex-working trans people. She is currently doing research to document the impact of immigration and criminal law on the lives of migrant trans sex workers in Canada.

Kathy Chow, RN, BScN, MN, is currently working at Toronto Public Health in Communicable Disease Control as a Quality Assurance Manager. She has been working in public health for 16 years and has extensive experience in access and equity, health promotion, health education, community development, and capacity building. She has lectured at Ryerson University at the Daphne Cockwell School of Nursing and was a member of the Ontario Public Health Association's Public Health Alliance for Lesbian, Gay, Bisexual, Transsexual, Transgendered, Two-Spirit, Intersexed, Queer, and Questioning Equity.

Jean Clipsham, NP, BScN, MEd, is a nurse practitioner with the Sexual Health and Needle Exchange Program at Halton Region Health Department and has been working on developing accessible, inclusive, and equitable services for LGBTQ people for over 20 years. This work began in 1990, when several community members suggested to the Health Department that it was time to support LGBTQ youth in the community. Since then, Jean has been involved in developing local agencies such as the Positive Space Network of Halton and provincial organizations such as the Public Health Alliance for LGBTTTIQQ Equity and the Rainbow Nursing Interest Group of the Registered Nurses' Association of Ontario.

Aaron H. Devor, PhD, has been studying and teaching about transgender-related questions for 30 years. He is the author of numerous scholarly articles and the widely acclaimed books *Gender Blending: Confronting the Limits of Duality* (1989) and *FTM: Female-to-Male Transsexuals in Society* (1997). He has delivered lectures to audiences around the world, including more than 20 keynote and plenary addresses. He is a national award-winning teacher, an elected member of the International Academy of Sex Research, and a Fellow of the Society for the Scientific Study of Sexuality. He was one of the authors of Versions 6 and 7 of the WPATH Standards of Care. Dr. Devor is the founder and academic director of the world's largest transgender archives, a professor of Sociology, and was the dean of Graduate Studies from 2002 to 2012 at the University of Victoria. See http://web.uvic.ca/~ahdevor.

Cheryl Dobinson is a bisexual educator, researcher, and community activist. She holds an MA in Sociology from York University, where her studies focused on women's sexuality and queer youth. In 2003, Cheryl completed a project on bisexual health and wellness in Ontario for the Ontario Public Health Association. She has worked part-time with the Centre for Addiction and Mental Health on LGBT health research for close to a decade. Cheryl is currently the Director of Community Programming and Research at Planned Parenthood Toronto. She is passionate about the meaningful inclusion of bi and trans people in LGBT research, programming, and communities.

Tien Neo Eamas is a Singaporean-born, bi-gendered trans man of Indonesian and Chinese descent. He has lived in Canada since 1987 and has lived as male since 2003. Tien believes that trans people are the visionaries of a world where gender is no longer a construct that restricts humanity's freedom to express. He has been featured in a video about policy recommendations on how to make Vancouver a more inclusive place for transgender and gender variant folks and participated in research that fueled the book *Transforming Practice: Life Stories of Transgender Men that Change How Health Providers Work* by Marcus Greatheart. He is a professional artist and designer and divides his time between the Sunshine Coast and Vancouver.

Robin Fern lives in Toronto with his partner and three children. He practised as a community midwife for 19 years, and is now a nurse in family and community medicine. He is an advanced practice nurse (APN) in mental health in primary care, LGBT health, and perinatal care. He is currently involved in two health promotion projects that seek to provide research-based health information for trans communities. The first is focused on cancer screening, and the second on trans lactation information and support. He also sits on an advisory panel that is developing LGBT nursing best practice guidelines.

barbara findlay, QC, is a queer activist lawyer practising law in Vancouver. She has been counsel on several significant queer cases, including *Nixon v. Rape Relief*; a world-first case establishing the right of two lesbian co-mothers to be registered on their child's birth certificate when the child was born; and the gay marriage case. She is a community organizer and an anti-oppression activist. findlay has also been active inside the legal profession to make queers visible. She has written and spoken about issues of oppression at many conferences and workshops over the past 35 years. Her proudest moment was being adopted by the Wet'suwet'en people.

Susan Gapka is a community and political activist. She has degrees from both George Brown College and York University. She was co-principal investigator with Rupert Raj on the Trans Health Project completed for the Ontario Public Health Association (2003). Susan is founder and chair of the Trans Lobby Group, which led a lengthy campaign to persuade the Minister of Health to fund sex reassignment surgery in Ontario in 2008; has been working to include explicit human rights protections for trans people in Ontario and across Canada; and advocated amending criteria for changing the sex designation on the record of birth via the Ontario Vital Statistics Act. She currently advises the At Home/Chez Soi project of the Mental Health Commission of Canada.

Broden Giambrone has been involved in the Gay/Bi/Queer Trans Men's Working Group for almost two years and was the resource developer for *Primed: The Back Pocket Guide for Transmen and the Men Who Dig Them*. Broden is interested in community-based research and the development of accessible and respectful community-based health care. He is currently undertaking an MHSc in Health Promotion at the University of Toronto.

Lorraine Grieves is a cisgender, queer-identified resident of European descent, currently living in Vancouver, who was born and raised on unceded Coast Salish Territory. She has worked for over a decade in substance use services with a particular focus on supporting youth and families, both as a counsellor and in health services management. Some of her recent work has been on initiatives that build capacity across helping systems in support of LGBTQ2S youth, adults, and families/carers/supportive others. Lorraine holds a deep interest in social justice for persons of all genders and backgrounds and tries to weave this intersectional positioning through all that she does. Lorraine currently works at Vancouver Coastal Health as a manager for Youth Substance Use Services, Prism (LGBTQ2S capacity building), and the Transgender Health Program. The proud mother of a 23-year-old daughter, Lorraine enjoys spending time with loved ones, enjoying nature, and playing music with friends.

Jamie Lee Hamilton is a Canadian politician and advocate of Aboriginal people, residents of the city's poverty-stricken Downtown Eastside, and sex trade workers. Jamie is also a writer, entertainer, and guest lecturer in Women's and Gender Studies at the University of British Columbia and in Humanities at Capilano College. She currently serves on the board of directors of the Greater Vancouver Native Cultural Society, which has served the Aboriginal two-spirited community since 1978. She is the first transexual to stand for public office in Canada (Vancouver City Council, 1996). She has founded numerous businesses and initatives to improve life in the Downtown Eastside, including the Four Corners Bank, the 9 to 5 Working Society, and Rainbow's End. Jamie is a lifelong resident of the Downtown Eastside and Strathcona neighbourhoods of Vancouver.

Elaine Hampson is a Public Health Nurse and has been involved with LGBTQ issues since 1994. She started the York Region Rainbow Youth Support Group in 1994. She maintains her interest by volunteering with the Rainbow Nursing Interest Group of the Registered Nurses' Association of Ontario. She is a past chair of the Public Health Alliance for LGBTTTIQQ Equity, a workgroup of the Ontario Public Health Association, and co-authored papers on lesbian, gay, bisexual, and trans health while on that committee. She has also presented many workshops on positive space and was part of curriculum development of equity issues with the York Region Board of Education and training of staff.

Dan Irving is an assistant professor teaching in the Sexuality Studies Minor program (which he coordinates) and Human Rights Programs at Carleton University. He earned a PhD from York University in 2005. His doctoral work focused on trans identities and the cultivation of solidarity between trans activists and LGBT organizations, feminist organizations, and the labour movement in Canada. His work has been published in the *Trans Studies Reader 2*, *Temple Civil and Political Rights Law Review*, *Sexualities*, and *Upping the Anti*. His current research focuses on unemployment and underemployment amongst transsexual and two-spirit people in Ontario and British Columbia. He is also on the board of directors for EGALE Canada Human Rights Trust.

Elizabeth "Raven" James' education is less formal than most. Her strength, hope, and experience were acquired through the school of hard knocks. Born in 1972 in Toronto, she spent time in and out of the foster care system. After coming forward about her transsexualism, she ended up on the streets working as a prostitute and addicted to cocaine and heroin. She has served a five-year sentence in a men's maximum security prison for robbery. She has now conquered her addictions, learned about her two-spirit heritage, and undergone gender reassignment surgery. She has worked with the Trans Pulse Project and the Sharp Access Project to help others like her. Raven currently attends the University of British Columbia.

Sandy Leo Laframboise is a registered marriage commissioner in the Province of British Columbia, co-creator of a not-for-profit organization that is loosely based on Native American traditions, and runs spiritual ceremonies for the two-spirited people (GLBTQ) members of our community and our allies.

Judith MacDonnell is an assistant professor in the School of Nursing, York University. She has a background in public health nursing, completed a PhD in Sociology and Equity Studies in Education/Women's Studies, and has been involved in trans advocacy in education, policy, and research. As a member of the Public Health Alliance for LGBTTTIQQ Equity, she was involved with the Trans Health Project. More recently, her research has focused on work, career, and health for trans health providers and queer and trans access to home care services in Ontario. She is a member of the Rainbow Nursing Interest Group of the Registered Nurses' Association of Ontario.

Devon MacFarlane is passionate about the well-being of the full diversity of trans communities. As an active member of trans communities, and in roles within health care, Devon works from community development and organizational change perspectives, strongly informed by a commitment to social justice and intersectionality, paired with a sense of humour and playfulness. Devon is usually read as a white, middle-class, able-bodied gay man in his mid- to late thirties. The first three descriptors are accurate … the next three, though, well, you see…

Treanor Mahood-Greer first worked on farms, then in the bush of Northern Ontario as a prospector, before becoming a Native Human Services Social Worker in 1998. He obtained his MSW in 2006 with his thesis "De-constructing the Bulwark of Gender: Social Work Practices and Gender Variance in North-Eastern Ontario." Treanor's theoretical perspective is based on feminist anti-oppression methods and critical-reflexive analysis. Treanor stays connected with the bush by family camping and being an artist. He maintains intrapersonal balance with a gift from the sacred Eagle and a gift of the Anishinaabe Seventh Grandfather teaching, *debwewin* (truth is to know all these things) while walking the path of the pentacle. He strives for contentment through his relationship with his wife, Kim, and family, the music of Johnny Cash and Ferron and the work of John Wayne. Treanor once identified as a butch, then as transgender, and then as a trans man. His desire to deconstruct gender oppression is fuelled partially so he might identify as a complicated butch someday (perhaps right now).

Jazzmine Manalo joined the Trans Access Project in 2005 after leaving the fashion business to pursue a career in community services. As part of the Trans Access team, she has presented at a wide range of agencies, including the Ontario Association of Interval and Transition Houses (OAITH), the University of Toronto, York University, the Toronto Hostel Training Centre, and the HEYY Youth Line. She currently serves as the Vice-President of Administration at Asian Community AIDS Services (ACAS). She is also a volunteer member of Silayan Community Centre for new immigrants in Canada.

Zack Marshall is a community-based researcher, activist, and social worker. After working for 15 years with lesbian, bisexual, gay, and transgender (LGBT) communities in Toronto and Montreal, Zack recently returned to university to pursue a PhD in Community Health at Memorial University of Newfoundland. As someone whose identities intersect with LGBT and disability communities, Zack is particularly interested in the ways research can be leveraged as a tool for social justice. With an emphasis on critical social science perspectives, HIV, ethics, and organizational change, Zack's current work emphasizes the importance of moving beyond inclusion toward transformative community-controlled research.

Nicholas Matte is a historian of 20th-century North American social movements focusing on sex, gender, sexuality, disability, medicine, capitalism, and race in relation to trans people's emergence as a distinct minority group. His interests also include transnational activism, media history, public exhibitions, and the archiving of sex. Nick's work has been published in *Canadian Bulletin of the History of Medicine*, *GLQ: A Journal of Gay and Lesbian Studies*, *International Journal of Transgenderism*, and *Transgender Studies Reader*. He teaches at University of Toronto's Bonham Centre for Sexual Diversity Studies, where he also curates the Sexual Representation Collection, and in Women's Studies at the University of Waterloo. He has curated exhibitions for the Toronto Public Library and the University of Toronto Art Centre, and collaborated with the University of Victoria's Transgender Archives and Canadian Lesbian and Gay Archives to recover and preserve important collections in transgender history, including the Reed Erickson and Rupert Raj Collections.

Grey Kimber Piitaapan Muldoon welcomes hearing from you directly. Always an androgynous adventurer, solitary and strange, he values his lived experiences as a social girl (tomboy) and woman (free-spirit femme fairy). Currently, Grey socializes as a queer male, while travelling, making puppetry and other art, and waiting for surgery funding. He grew up anglophone in Azilda. Adopted, he was then raised by a collection of characters, chiefly a crafty, joking mom with a disability cheque, and a shy, contemplative, kind-to-everything Catholic dad with a wage-labour career. He attended two high schools for three years each, and spent nine years at the University of Toronto. For as long as he can remember, he has worked on a politic that combines a sense of place, feminism, and ecological thought. Grey sees his gender transition as, primarily, a spiritual practice, informed by an anarchic and pragmatic philosophy of the world.

Viviane Namaste is a professor at the Simone de Beauvoir Institute, Concordia University, where she holds a Research Chair in HIV/AIDS and Sexual Health. She is the author of *C'était du spectacle! L'histoire des artistes transsexuelles à Montréal, 1955–1985*; *Sex Change, Social Change: Reflections on Identity, Institutions and Imperialism*; and *Invisible Lives: The Erasure of Transsexual and Transgendered People*. Her current research examines some of the forgotten histories of the HIV/AIDS epidemic, through case studies on trans people, as well as Haitians in Montreal.

Calvin Neufeld (www.calvinneufeld.com) is a self-described speaker, writer, and thinker, "in the business of making life better for free." A vegan transsexual, Calvin is an advocate of life and quality of life for oppressed species, for sexual and gender minorities, racial minorities, the physically, mentally, and economically disadvantaged, and absolutely everybody else. He is the founder of Purposeful Publishing House and editor of the book *Suffering Eyes: A Chronicle of Awakening* (www.sufferingeyes.com).

Evana Ortigoza was born in Maracaibo, Venezuela, and is currently an outreach worker at The 519 Church Street Community Centre for trans women who are working in the sex trade in downtown Toronto. She also helps to coordinate the weekly Meal Trans Drop-In for low-income trans people. She is forever grateful for the opportunity to work with other trans people and to improve her own life. Evana is a member of the provincial Community Engagement Team that guides the Trans PULSE Project.

Julissa Penate is originally from El Salvador and has been in Canada for 20 years. For the past two years, she has worked for the Trans Access Project at The 519 Church Street Community Centre. She is also an outreach worker for the Griffin Centre. Julissa is in the process of transitioning.

Yasmeen Persad is a trans woman of Caribbean background. She has provided training workshops on trans issues, worked with trans newcomers and refugees, served as a coordinator of Supporting Our Youth's Trans_Fusion Crew at the Sherbourne Health Centre, and co-facilitated the Gender Journey's group to provide education and support to those questioning their gender identities.

Jake Pyne is a community-based researcher and PhD student at the McMaster School of Social Work. Jake has worked in a variety of research and advocacy roles in Toronto's trans community since 2001 and currently focuses his attention on building supports for gender non-conforming children and trans youth. Jake coordinated the Trans Access Project from 2002 to 2008.

Rupert Raj is a 62-year-old, Eurasian Canadian, pansexual, trans man, who's been a trailblazing trans activist throughout Canada and the United States since he transitioned in 1971. Rupert is a gender specialist and psychotherapist, and since 2000, has been counselling transsexual/transgender, genderqueer, gender non-conforming, intersex, two-spirit, and queer people and their loved ones. Operating out of his private practice (www.RRconsulting.ca), he also offers consultation services and professional training workshops to health care and social service providers, researchers, educators, human resource managers, lawyers, and policymakers.

Nik Redman is an artist, activist, and community worker. Nik is a co-investigator with the Trans PULSE Project. He is also a member of the TMSM (trans men who have sex with men) Sexual Health Study. Nik has been a member of the Gay/Bi/Queer Trans Men's Working Group of the Ontario Gay Men's Sexual Health Alliance, the MaBwana Community Advisory Committee, and the Trans Fathers 2B Parenting Course Team. Nik was an online facilitator for the Ontario HIV/AIDS stigma campaign. Nik currently works as a grievance officer with United Steelworkers Union Local 1998, representing University of Toronto staff. Nik sits on the board of the Black Coalition for AIDS Prevention. As a member of Blackness Yes! he has been instrumental in creating the Blockorama stage at Toronto Pride for the past 15 years. Nik is also a DJ and radio programmer.

Will Rowe is a trans man living in Hamilton, Ontario, with his queer femme partner and their two young kids. He has worked in social services for the past 18 years in anti-violence/anti-poverty/queer and trans movements. He currently coordinates trans outreach/advocacy and trainings for The Well, the LGBTQ Community Wellness Centre. After completing course work toward a doctorate degree in social work, Will chose to remove himself from academia, and instead focuses his time on community capacity-building projects and parenting.

Trish Salah is an assistant professor of Women's and Gender Studies at the University of Winnipeg. Her current research, funded by the Social Sciences and Humanities Research Council of Canada's Insight Grant, investigates the emergence of Transgender Minor/ity Literatures. She is widely published, most recently in the *Journal of Medical Humanities*, and the following anthologies: *Troubling the Line: Trans and Genderqueer Poetry and Poetics*; *Selling Sex: Canadian Academics; Advocates and Sex Workers in Dialogue and Trans/acting Culture*; and *Writing and Memory: Essays in Honour of Barbara Godard*. She has co-edited special issues of the *Canadian Review of American Studies* (2005) and *TSQ: Transgender Studies Quarterly* (forthcoming in 2014). Her first book of poetry, *Wanting in Arabic*, was published by TSAR in 2002 (with a second edition released in 2013); her new book, *Lyric Sexology*, is forthcoming with Roof Books in 2014.

Kyle Scanlon was a trans activist, researcher, and community worker who strived for social justice. He had been a member with the Gay/Bi/Queer Trans Men's Working Group to create the FTM sexual health resource *Primed*, sat on the Investigative Committee of the Trans PULSE Project exploring health as it relates to Ontario's trans population, and was a co-principal investigator on the FTM Safer Shelter Project, which released the report *Invisible Lives: FTMs and Homelessness in Toronto*. At the time of his passing, Kyle was the Education, Training and Research Consultant at The 519 Church Street Community Centre.

Ayden I. Scheim is a founding member of the Gay/Bi/Queer Trans Men's Working Group and a PhD student in Epidemiology at Western University in London, Ontario. His research focuses on health inequities among sexual and gender minorities and people who use drugs. He is also co-principal investigator for the Trans MSM Sexual Health Study, a qualitative study on the sexual health of trans men who have sex with men. Ayden's research is informed by a decade of activist, community development, and health promotion work in trans communities.

Silvia Tenenbaum was born in Uruguay and received her psychology doctorate from OISE, University of Toronto. Silvia is a psychotherapist in private practice and a clinical supervisor at the OISE psycho-educational clinic in the Aboriginal healing and trans-communities stream. She directs the Applied Learning Centre at Adler Graduate Professional School, co-directs its Clinical Training for master's students, and works as a senior gender specialist and clinician in the Family Health Team of the Peterborough Clinic. Silvia has earned master's degrees in Latin American literature with a collaborative program in Women's & Gender Studies (University of Toronto), and in education from the Counseling Psychology Department (OISE). She researches "border-gender children" and has presented trans-related clinical case studies in Sweden, Mexico, China, Japan, Portugal, Ghana, Cuba, and the US.

Kenji Tokawa joined the Trans Access Project in March 2008. He is also the program coordinator of the Toronto Asian Arts Freedom School, an arts-based radical Asian history and activism program for Asian youth in the Greater Toronto Area. In his spare time, he is becoming a writer and is also working hard on an undergraduate degree at the University of Toronto.

His writing has been published in *Boyoboy Alt Zine of Arts and Culture* for young queer guys and *CultureSHOCK!*, the only anti-racist literary review at Queen's University. He published his first chapbook of poetry, *Missing the Moon*, in February 2009.

j wallace is a long-time educator and activist on issues of gender and sexuality. Currently a member of the Toronto District School Board's well-known Gender Based Violence Prevention Unit, j is also an MEd candidate at OISE. His research interests focus on gender-independent children, trans youth and students, gender-related bullying, and critical intentionality. He maintains a robust and frequently updated resource list of books about LGBTQ families and children at juxtaposeconsulting.com, and blogs about gender, family, children, and gardening at ishai-wallace.livejournal.com.

Syrus Marcus Ware is a visual artist, activist, researcher, and educator. He is the Program Coordinator of Youth Programs at the Art Gallery of Ontario. In 2005, Syrus was voted "Best Queer Activist" by *NOW* Magazine, and in 2012 was awarded the Steinert and Ferreiro Award for LGBT community leadership and activism. Syrus is a co-principal investigator on the Ontario TMSM Study. Syrus is also a member of the Gay/Bi/Queer Trans Men's Working Group and one of the creators of *Primed: A Back Pocket Guide for Transmen and the Men Who Dig Them*. He helped initiate TransFathers 2B, the first course for trans men considering parenting in North America. For the past 15 years, Syrus has hosted the weekly radio segment, Resistance on the Sound Dial (CIUT 89.5FM). Syrus holds degrees in Art History and Visual Studies, and a master's in Sociology and Equity Studies, University of Toronto.

Wallace Wong is a registered psychologist and practices in the state of California and the province of British Columbia. He began working with the transgender population at the GLBT Centre in San Diego, California, in 1996. He has worked continuously with children and youth with various sexual behavioural issues. He has recently published a book for transgender children, *When Kathy Is Keith*, addressing transgender issues using a child's perspective. Wallace has made numerous presentations both locally and internationally on issues related to transgender children and youth. He is a member of CPATH and WPATH. He currently works at the Adolescent and Children Sexual Health Program for the Ministry of Children and Family Development in British Columbia, Canada, and has a private practice working mainly with gender-variant children, youth, and their families.

Al Zwiers, MSW, RSW, is a queer guy who recognizes his own cisgender privilege while living and working within the queer and trans communities. He operates from a structural social work and anti-oppression perspective, having worked in the fields of HIV/AIDS, at-risk youth, and addictions and mental health for the past 20 years. He offers clinical supervision and diversity education around queer and trans issues, and runs a counselling practice in Vancouver and online at ah-ha.ca. Al can often be found near some water with his hubby and their two pups.

Index